God
and the
Mystery of

Human Suffering

A THEOLOGICAL CONVERSATION
ACROSS THE AGES

ROBIN RYAN, CP

Paulist Press
New York/Mahwah, NJ

Cover and book design by Lynn Else

Library of Congress Cataloging-in-Publication Data

Ryan, Robin.
    God and the mystery of human suffering : a theological conversation across the ages / Robin Ryan.
        p. cm.
    Includes bibliographical references and index.
    ISBN 978-0-8091-4713-7 (alk. paper)
    1. Suffering—Religious aspects—Christianity. 2. Theology, Doctrinal—History. 3. Suffering—Biblical teaching. I. Title.
    BT732.7.R93 2011
    231'.8—dc22

                                                                2011007022

Published by Paulist Press
997 Macarthur Boulevard
Mahwah, New Jersey 07430

www.paulistpress.com

Printed and bound in the
United States of America

Contents

Discussion Questions may be accessed by selecting the Online
Resources link at www.paulistpress.com, and then selecting the book
title, *God and the Mystery of Human Suffering*.

To the members of my family,
who have lovingly supported me through the years

Acknowledgments

I wish to express my sincere gratitude to colleagues who assisted me in the writing of this book. Donald Senior and Paul Zilonka offered illuminating insights about the chapters on scripture. William Palardy provided helpful suggestions for the material on the early church. Thomas O'Meara, whose expertise on Aquinas is evident in chapter 4, carefully reviewed my drafts of this chapter. Robert Schreiter read the chapter on Schillebeeckx and contributed his insights. Carmen Nanko-Fernández offered her wisdom about the theology of Gutiérrez. Steve Bevans and Elizabeth Johnson contributed thoughtful reflections on the last two chapters of the book. I have learned much from each of these scholars through the years, and I am most grateful for their generous assistance with this book.

I also wish to extend my gratitude to Elizabeth Jennings-White, director of communications at Catholic Theological Union. Beth faithfully read all of the chapters of this book and offered her suggestions about how best to express my ideas. I sincerely appreciate her generous service.

Introduction:
Facing the Mystery

Some years ago, I gave a presentation entitled "Prayer in Times of Suffering" to a parish adult education group. About forty people gathered in the small parish hall of a New England Catholic church on a weekday evening. The presentation lasted forty-five minutes, and it was followed by a period of questions and discussion. During the discussion, a woman sitting in the back row raised her hand. I had noticed that she and her husband, a couple who appeared to be in their mid-thirties, seemed particularly attentive and engaged throughout my presentation. I will call them Mary and John. Before posing her question, Mary explained the perplexing situation in which she and John found themselves.

Mary told the group gathered that evening that about six months earlier her husband had been in a serious automobile accident. It had occurred at night on a dark, winding road. Another car, approaching in the opposite direction and traveling at high speed, had slammed into John's car. The other car had crossed over onto the wrong side of the road. The driver of the other car was injured in the collision, though he survived the accident. John's car was damaged beyond repair, but he walked away from the crash with a few minor scratches and bruises. The state trooper who arrived first on the scene expressed his astonishment that John had not been injured more severely. The trooper said that in all his years on the police force he had never seen anything like it; he called it a "miracle." In the months subsequent to the accident Mary and John, people of strong faith, told family and friends about what had happened and expressed their sincere gratitude to God

1

for God's providential care in this terrifying accident. They publicly praised God for John's escape from injury.

Mary then explained that about three months after the accident, the daughter of close friends was killed in an automobile accident. This young woman was a teenager. John and Mary had reached out to their friends to walk with them through this devastating experience. Mary explained to me and to the other parishioners that, while she and John were still very grateful to God for John's escape from injury, they no longer felt comfortable talking about his deliverance in terms of "God's protection" or "divine providence." If they continued to proclaim their gratitude for God's providential care in John's life, what would their dear friends think? Would they conclude that God had not been exercising providential care for their teenage daughter? Were they and their daughter not as worthy of God's protection as John and Mary had been? Were they undeserving of a "miracle"? Mary concluded her intervention by asking me, "What should we be saying in this situation? How should we be talking?"

Though we may never have experienced anything as tragic as the death of a child, Mary's question is one that all of us have grappled with at different moments. How should we conceive of and talk about God in the face of tragic, inexplicable human suffering? What kind of discourse is appropriate? What is God "doing" or "not doing" when a young person is killed in an automobile accident or when the life of an innocent person is snuffed out in war or by an act of terrorism? Where is God to be found in the midst of such experiences?

Those of us who exercise pastoral ministry in the church have heard questions like these on innumerable occasions. So many pastoral encounters are occasioned by experiences of suffering. It is obvious in our visits with people in hospitals, nursing homes, and funeral parlors, but it happens in countless other places too. Standing near the door of the church on a Sunday morning, a parishioner stops to ask for prayers. If you show a modicum of personal interest and concern, you soon find yourself listening to a description of a painful situation, and you are granted entrée into the sacred space of the other person's soul where he or she is grappling with the mystery of God and suffering. People come to pastoral ministers in order to try to make sense of such experiences. Or at least to find a way through them. Wise, experienced ministers are keenly aware that explanation is not the first order of business. In fact, attempts at explanation rarely accomplish much of anything and can actually do damage to the suffering person. Nevertheless, at some point in our presence to people in their suffering, we find ourselves talking about God. We engage in some kind of discourse about God—talk that is grounded in deep convictions of faith. People desire this God-talk, even if it is articulated only in the simplest of prayers.

This book is meant to be an extended reflection on such discourse about God and God's relation to suffering people.[1] I explore the ways in which significant thinkers in the Judeo-Christian tradition have spoken about God in the face of the experience of suffering. I enter into this exploration not merely to catalogue a series of theological viewpoints. While a significant amount of information is provided in this study, my intention is not simply to inform the reader about the ways in which important authors have written about this topic but rather to elicit an ongoing conversation between readers and the authors studied. It has as much to do with *formation* as with *information*. Readers are invited to reflect on the theological perspectives that are discussed as part of their own search to discover ways of talking about God and suffering that are both faithful to the tradition and responsive to people's real experience. Though this book is about theology rather than pastoral technique, the theological principles and positions discussed here have implications for pastoral care of suffering people.

Implicit Theologies

I suggest that each of us has some version of a theology of God and suffering. This theology may well be implicit. We may never have reflected on it or tried to articulate it, but it is present. The sources of this theology derive from a wide diversity of places. Our earliest education in the faith clearly has been an influence on this personal theology. Treasured scenes or stories from scripture provide images and metaphors for conceiving of God in the face of suffering. Most important, perhaps, personal experiences of acute suffering have affected the ways in which we theologize about God. Such experiences may have helped our faith in the God of Jesus Christ to mature and deepen, or they may have made it more difficult to believe in a God whom the Judeo-Christian tradition describes as "good."

Our own theology of God and suffering manifests itself when we speak to or pray with a person in the hospital or anyone grappling with illness. It is operative in our conversations with those who have lost someone or something important in their lives. This theology is expressed when one preaches at a wake or funeral or offers a reflection about the death and resurrection of Jesus Christ. It is present when we try to answer the question of children about why one of their class-mates is seriously ill or why God let their parents divorce. In an intrigu-ing way, this implicit theology is also present and operative in our most personal moments of prayer. It influences the way we talk to God and even the way we listen to God.

A variety of theological assumptions and convictions are evinced when we make certain kinds of statements. All of us have heard (and perhaps made) statements like the following: "I cannot explain why this is happening, but I am sure that God knows what he is doing." "Remember, God has a plan for us." "You just have to believe that there is a reason for everything." "God never gives us a bigger cross than we can bear." "Suffering is the path to virtue." "Our faith is tested and purified in the crucible of suffering." "I don't believe that God wants you to suffer—suffering is just part of life." "God is there with you in your suffering—God is suffering, too."

Some of these statements may have caused the reader to cringe, while others may seem more acceptable. Much to our chagrin, perhaps, every one of these statements—even those to which we have a negative reaction—can find some foundation in the Judeo-Christian tradition. In the vast majority of cases, people make such statements because they are trying to be helpful. They are striving to express compassion for others and to find meaning in a perplexing situation. Sometimes it is easier to fit an experience of suffering into a structure of meaning that involves a questionable image of God than it is simply to grapple with the mystery. I enumerate these statements not in order to endorse any of them but simply to underline the point that most of us have some operative theology of God and suffering that makes itself evident in the ways in which we speak with others. Because of our faith in Christ and in the God of Jesus Christ, there are common points of that theology that are shared among Christians. There are some "family resemblances" among our theological perspectives. But there is also real divergence in the ways we think and talk about God and the mystery of suffering, differences that reflect distinct theological presuppositions.

In his study of theological methodology, Clemens Sedmak speaks of the "dangers" of implicit theologies.[2] They are dangerous to the extent to which they remain unexamined and unrefined. Theologies can point people toward God; they can also drive people away from God. Nowhere is that more limpidly clear than in situations of suffering. We may have heard delivered in funeral homilies or at the bedside of a sick person pious nostrums that we found alienating, even oppressive. When, for example, one hears a preacher say that a child has died because "God wanted another angel in heaven," the image of God that is implied is that of a celestial kidnapper. Such an image has little to do with the God revealed in the Hebrew and Christian scriptures.

While implicit theologies can certainly be dangerous, they are, nevertheless, a fact. They exist within every person, including those who have never read a single book of theology. The critical challenge is to explore the content of one's own implicit theology, especially the way in which one characteristically thinks about God's relation to human suffering. In this journey of exploration, we allow our own theologies to enter into conversation with the tradition as it is enshrined in the scriptures, the official teachings of the church, classic works of theology, the writings of spiritual masters, the church's liturgy, and the reflections of contemporary theologians. In the course of that sustained dialogue, our personal theologies become illumined and refined. David Tracy has written extensively on his understanding of theology as a conversation between present experience and the tradition of faith. That tradition is articulated in a privileged way in texts that he calls "classics"—especially the Hebrew and Christian scriptures.[3] Authentic conversation is a dynamic and formative exercise that requires commitment to the truth as sought through the honest exploration of questions.[4] I invite readers to engage in this kind of dialogue as they explore the work of important thinkers discussed in the pages that follow.

Impact on the Theological and Spiritual Tradition

The reflective student of theology soon begins to realize that the question about God's relation to human suffering is central to the Christian tradition and has exerted a significant impact on the development of church doctrine, theology, and spirituality. I mention two examples of this influence, each of which is discussed in greater detail in subsequent chapters. The Arian crisis, which raged during the fourth century and continued thereafter, reflects theological debate about God's relation to human suffering. Richard Hanson has shown that one of the concerns that motivated the followers of Arius was the reality of the cross.[5] Arius (a priest of Alexandria in Egypt) and his followers accentuated the absolute transcendence of God to creation. This God did not traffic with the messy realities of the world of creatures. They reasoned, then, that the only begotten Son of God who became incarnate in Jesus must be subordinate to the Father. The Son could not be divine in the fullest sense of the term. The Son was a "creature," though the highest of all creatures. Hanson has shown that one of the reasons that Arius and his followers held such a position was that they wanted to construct a rational theology of the cross. If the Son really suffered on the cross, as the Arians affirmed, then the Son could not be of the same rank as the "highest God." Arians refused to admit that the transcendent God could, in Jesus, really enter into human history, especially into the reality of human suffering. Such a view would contradict the understanding of the divine that Arians shared with many of their contemporaries in the Greco-Roman world. Thus, if the Son of God suffered on the cross, the Son must be divine only in some diminished, subordinate sense.

The relation between God and human suffering has been a theme in the spiritual classics of Christianity. The symbol of the "dark night," classically expressed by John of the Cross but evident in other writers as well, is one way in which spiritual masters have articulated their understanding of the place of suffering in the path to deeper union with God. While this dark night tradition has many levels of meaning, one dimension involves the meaning ascribed to the experience of intense suffering by a person who is deeply convinced of the closeness of God. While it may seem that the mystics of our tradition would situate personal suffering into their lives with relative ease, that presumption is not always accurate. A palpable sense of the presence and providence of God in one's life can make the experience of suffering more perplexing than it might be for a person who is not as keenly aware of the nearness of God.

These two examples from the tradition show that Christians have grappled with issues related to the mystery of God and human suffering since the time of Jesus. The question posed by Mary in the New England parish hall has been asked in various ways through the centuries: "How should we talk about God in the face of suffering?" It could be argued that this question, with its attending issues, has influenced every dimension of Christian theology and spirituality.

Theology after the Shoah

The theme of this study is one that theologians have taken up with great vigor during the past fifty years. It is an exceedingly fertile and fascinating area of theological exploration that has given rise to a plethora of books and essays. In particular, it was the experience of the Shoah that impelled Jewish and Christian thinkers to address these issues in a renewed way. In describing what took place under the Nazi regime, Jewish thinkers prefer the term *Shoah*—meaning "destruction" or "devastation"—to *Holocaust*. In the Hebrew scriptures "holocaust" has a positive, spiritual meaning—a whole burnt offering to God. Jewish writers rightly argue that no term that has positive implications should be used for the murder of millions of Jews by Hitler and the Nazi regime. What happened at Auschwitz, Treblinka, Birkenau, and other death camps was truly an experience of devastation inflicted by people, many of them Christians, upon innocent Jews.

This intense experience of gratuitous evil, of the systematic effort at genocide of a people named "God's chosen people" in the biblical tradition, has forced theologians to reflect anew about how we envision God's relation to evil and suffering in the world. Elisabeth Schüssler-Fiorenza and David Tracy have called this event an "interruption" of history—a moment in which human history crashes against itself.[6] The Jewish writer Arthur Cohen has termed this event "the tremendum."[7] Jewish, Protestant, and Catholic thinkers have reread their traditions in their search for clues as to how to interpret this unspeakable tragedy and how to speak about God in the face of it. Perhaps no writer has wrestled with the questions raised by this tragedy in a more sustained and eloquent way than Elie Wiesel. Wiesel's hauntingly honest reflections on his own experience as a Jewish teenager sent to the Nazi death camps have inspired theologians and other readers to search their souls for ways to address these issues. The question that he heard in the midst of that brutality— "Where is God?"[8]—has gripped the minds and hearts of many readers: Where is God when innocent people are being tortured by others? Reading Wiesel and other voices from the Shoah has compelled theologians to ponder this question and a host of others: How could such unrelenting evil and cruelty have taken place? Why didn't God intervene to stop the Shoah? If we want to say that God did "intervene," how should we speak of that intervention? Can we speak meaningfully of God suffering with God's suffering people? From a Christian perspective, how do Jesus and the cross fit into all of this?

Since the end of World War II, our world has experienced a seemingly unending series of tragedies that have further catalyzed theological thinking about these questions. One is hesitant to enumerate these events lest some be overlooked, but we need only hear terms like *Vietnam, Cambodia, Rwanda, Bosnia, Iraq, Darfur*, and *9/11* to be reminded that the reality of evil inflicted by human beings upon one other and the horrific suffering that results from it remain very near at hand. Add to this list those events that we call "natural disasters"— the tsunami that struck

South Asia on the day after Christmas in 2004 and the earthquake that devastated Haiti in January 2010—and the mystery becomes more intractable. In a world characterized by a revolution in communications, we are present to such events with an immediacy unimagined in the past. Whether or not our world is scarred by more human suffering than in the past is impossible to ascertain. But it is undoubtedly true that our awareness of human suffering is keener than ever. This consciousness, if it does not cause us to become numb, makes the question of God's relation to human suffering inescapable for people of faith.

Theodicy

In days gone by, the enterprise in which we are engaged in this study would have been termed *theodicy*. Theodicy is a term that arose in modern philosophy and theology; it is particularly associated with the influential book *Theodicy: Essays on the Goodness of God, the Freedom of Man and the Origin of Evil*, published in 1710 by the German philosopher Gottfried Wilhelm Leibniz. The term is taken from the Greek words for God (*theos*) and for justice (*dikē*). It refers, then, to a reasoned attempt to justify the existence of a good, all-powerful God in the face of the reality of evil and suffering, particularly innocent suffering. While the term is of modern vintage, the attempt to address these issues is very ancient. In the early church, the theologian Lactantius (260–340 CE) quoted the formulation made by the Greek philosopher Epicurus (341–270 BCE) about the dilemma with which theodicy is concerned:

> God either wishes to take away evils, and is unable; or God is able and unwilling; or God is neither willing nor able; or God is both willing and able. If he is willing and unable, he is powerless, which is not in accordance with the character of God; if he is able and unwilling, he is envious, which is equally at variance with God; if he is neither willing nor able, he is both envious and feeble, and therefore not God; if he is both willing and able, which alone is suitable to

God, from what source then are evils? Why does he not remove them?[9]

In his attempt to justify the goodness of God, Leibniz developed his famous "best-of-all-possible worlds" argument. Briefly put, he asserted that God, whose infinite power, knowledge, and goodness are one, must have surveyed the entire range of possible worlds in creating this universe. Because of his infinite goodness, there is a moral necessity for God to make the best choice among all possible worlds. While Leibniz acknowledges the reality of evil and suffering in the world, he reasons that all other possible worlds that God could have chosen in the act of creation must have had a greater measure of evil and a smaller amount of goodness than that which we find in the actual world.[10]

A more recent work of theodicy is John Hick's *Evil and the God of Love*. In this well-known book, Hick formulates his "vale of soul-making" argument. Through a selective appeal to scripture and tradition, Hick argues that human beings are made in the "image" of God but are meant to develop into the "likeness" of God through a life of moral goodness. They are created to build their own moral character through the use of free will. This character building takes place "through a hazardous adventure in individual freedom."[11] A life of character building through moral striving leads us to become the mature, perfected persons God has created us to be. Hick proceeds to argue that such moral development requires a world in which there is not only pleasure, but also pain. As John Thiel aptly puts it, according to Hick, "The 'soul-making' of human persons requires a world in which evil dwells, not merely as the consequence of failed soul-making but as a necessary context in which authentic soul-making unfolds as it confronts the trials and tribulations of life."[12] We learn through suffering; it is educative. We also become more mature as moral persons through experiences of suffering. The way in which we respond to the presence of evil and the suffering it causes is an essential dimension of character building.

While it is always instructive to study attempts at theodicy like those of Leibniz and Hick, many contemporary Christian theologians object to the methods and the conclusions of theodicy.[13] They do not find such efforts to be successful and, more important, they argue that theodicies often minimize the tragedy of human suffering and domesticate evil. They fail to recognize the potency and destructive effects of evil in our world[14] and are generally inattentive to the cries of those who experience radical forms of suffering that seem to have no meaning. Theologians also argue that theodicy can instill passivity in the face of evil, which is not consonant with the message of the gospel. Contemporary theologians argue that we need to find ways to explore the mystery of God and human suffering that are different from the procedures of theodicy.

I agree with the judgments about theodicies made by contemporary theologians. While the careful student of theology recognizes that there is no hard-and-fast line between the methods of theodicy and more "theological" ways to approach this mystery, the pitfalls of theodicy are many, and they can be lethal for a life of faith. Theodicy usually tries to offer a comprehensive explanation of reality, a master narrative into which one can situate the reality of human suffering. It strives for a coherence that will leave the mind at rest—at rest in its theoretical consistency and systematic comprehensiveness. In their supposed coherence, theodicies tend to domesticate the terrible reality of evil and suffering. They leave little place for experiences of suffering that are simply scandalous.

A theological approach to the mystery of human suffering that is rooted in the Judeo-Christian tradition cannot remove the scandal of suffering. In fact, believers in the God of the Bible are precisely those people who never cease to be scandalized by the reality of suffering. A theological reflection on the mystery of suffering never leaves the mind—or the heart—at rest. At the end of our reflection, we find ourselves standing before mystery. Our best theological categories are woefully inadequate to express the inexhaustible mystery of God. Moreover, even our most enlightened theological concepts fail to "systematize" the mystery of evil and suffering. Our categories are always shattered by the mystery of God and the mystery of suffering. And we must allow them to be shattered.

Still, we must speak in faith. We must find ways to speak of God even in the face of unspeakable suffering. Searching for the most appropriate discourse about God in the face of suffering is our challenge. This discourse must be faithful to the tradition; it must also be attentive to the cries of suffering people. Perhaps the ultimate criterion for judging the appropriateness of our talk *about* God in the face of suffering is whether or not it enables people to talk *to* God in the midst of their experience of suffering. We should ask ourselves a question that is pastoral but also deeply theological: How does a particular perspective on God and suffering enhance, or detract from, healthy, vital prayer? While one might debate the meaning of the phrase "healthy, vital prayer," it seems to me that Christians instinctively know when their conversation with God is alive and dynamic. We will see that our tradition reminds us that healthy prayer can include sustained lament—a crying out to God that is filled with complaint, even anger, in the face of suffering. Some of the healthiest prayers are articulated by those who cry out to God from the depths of misery. To be appropriate, discourse about God in the face of the reality of suffering should empower suffering people to encounter God in prayer. The presentation and discussion of various theological perspectives in this book is an exercise in "faith seeking understanding"—the classic definition of theology articulated by Anselm of Canterbury. It is just as much an exercise in "prayer seeking understanding," that is, an attempt both to reflect upon how we pray when we are experiencing suffering and to illumine the invitations to prayer that are found in significant interpretations of the Judeo-Christian tradition.[15]

A Look Ahead

I take a chronological approach to this study of what the biblical and theological traditions say about God and the mystery of human suffering. We begin with an exploration of this theme in the Hebrew scriptures. There are a variety of interpretations of the meaning of personal and corporate suffering in the Old Testament. The psalms of lament eloquently express the cry of individuals and of the community during times of pain and loss. The Book of Job counters a prevailing interpretation of the reason for human suffering: the doctrine of retribution. This biblical book has become a classic for believers and unbelievers alike. Theologians from the early church (for example, Gregory the Great) to modern times (for example, Gustavo Gutiérrez) have written commentaries on Job. I survey several perspectives on suffering found in the Hebrew scriptures.

The first Christians were compelled to address the experience of suffering—the suffering that had been inflicted on the one they called "the Christ" and the persecution endured by those who had become committed followers of Jesus. They were forced to reflect upon the meaning of "the cross" for human history and for their own lives. We explore some of the directions that this reflection took in the New Testament. We look at this theme in the Gospel of Mark. Scholars conclude that this Gospel was addressed to a community of believers who had faced the reality of suffering for their faith in Jesus Christ. The evangelist presents the person and message of Jesus as the key to finding a way through suffering and shows how the sufferings of Jesus and the sufferings of the Christian community are intimately related.

Theologians of the early church were influenced by a number of factors in their reflections on God and suffering. First, they attempted to express the biblical message about God's self-revelation in Christ and the Spirit in the language and categories of Greek and Roman philosophies. Central to much of this Greco-Roman thought was the conviction about God's immutability (unchangeableness) and impassibility (immunity to suffering). Second, there was the need to specify in a more precise way what Christians believed about God and about Christ. This led to the struggles to formulate creedal and other dogmatic statements, especially in the trinitarian and christological controversies. Third, there was the experience of persecution and martyrdom, especially in the first three centuries of the church's existence. Suffering Christians were searching for meaning and hope in the midst of the ordeals they were undergoing. These theologians articulated a number of perspectives on the meaning of suffering. We investigate those points of view, paying special attention to the reflections offered by Augustine.

Thomas Aquinas gave the most comprehensive and enduring expression to what is commonly known as "classical theism." Responding to the "signs of the times" in his own day, he engaged the philosophy of Aristotle, whose works had been translated and brought to the West, in his attempt to systematize Christian revelation.[16] The way in which Aquinas envisioned the transcendent perfection of God and God's relation to the world has had lasting influence. When we look at the work of contemporary theologians like Elizabeth Johnson we see that they dialogue with Thomas, building on some dimensions within his theological system and criticizing other aspects of his thought.

The mystical tradition of Christianity includes significant reflection on the reality of human suffering and its place in the journey to God. One intriguing example of this reflection is Julian of Norwich, the fourteenth-century English anchoress and author of *Showings* (*Revelations of Divine Love*). Julian's most intense encounter with Christ took place in the context of an experience of acute personal suffering. Moreover, she lived in a time and place wherein horrific human suffering due to the bubonic plague, peasant revolts against the nobility, and the Hundred Years War ravaged the area. Julian's mystical theology, focused on the passion of Christ, evinces her profound awareness of the scourge of human suffering that was present outside the window of her anchorhold. At the same time, Julian is often cited as a mystic of profound hope; she is famous for her belief that "all shall be well and all manner of things shall be well." Many people, including this writer, find Julian's writings on the theme of God and suffering to be intriguing and instructive.

No writer has offered more compelling testimony to the reality of the Shoah than Elie Wiesel. In his classic work *Night*, as well as in his many subsequent writings, Wiesel has shared the depths of his soul with his readers. He has allowed others to witness his own grappling with the mystery of God in the face of the horrors of the twentieth century. From a perspective of Christian faith, Dietrich Bonhoeffer also opened his soul to his readers, particularly in his *Letters and Papers from Prison*. A Lutheran pastor and theologian imprisoned for his active opposition to the Nazi regime, Bonhoeffer wrestled with the question of how to conceive of God and God's presence to a world that was in complete disarray. Sitting deep within a Gestapo prison targeted by Allied bombers, Bonhoeffer concluded that "only a suffering God can help." These words, along with other dimensions of his theological reflection in these circumstances, have challenged the thinking of theologians since Bonhoeffer.

Jürgen Moltmann, who spent the years after the Second World War in a prisoner of war camp for German youth, has taken up the questions and challenges raised by Wiesel and Bonhoeffer in his efforts to construct a Christian systematic theology that keeps the stark reality of human suffering at the center. For Moltmann, the cross of Jesus is the criterion of all Christian theology. He does theology by means of dramatic narrative—telling the story, particularly the story of Jesus' cross and resurrection. He tells that story as the story of God—not only the narrative of God in relation to humanity but the story that discloses the inner life of God. We see that Moltmann's theology, particularly his account of Calvary, has elicited diverse reactions. Nevertheless, his theology has made an impact on all those concerned about the mystery of God and human suffering. Even those who disagree with Moltmann have been forced to take his work seriously and to dialogue with him.

Edward Schillebeeckx is familiar to many students of theology. Formed as a Dominican in the theology of Aquinas, Schillebeeckx developed a theology that has a Thomistic orientation. At the same time, he integrated the insights of modern philosophy and social theory into his theology and was not tied to a single philosophical school of thought. He was sympathetic to the concerns of the liberationist theology that began in Latin America, and the reality of human suffering across the globe became a starting point in his theology in the later years of his career. As with Moltmann, his theology has a christological orientation, though he narrates the story of Calvary in a way quite different than does Moltmann.

Gustavo Gutiérrez is often called the founder of Latin American liberationist theology. He developed a theological methodology that interprets the tradition and the signs of the times from the perspective of the poorest people of Latin America, those who are the most marginalized in society. Gutiérrez and his liberationist colleagues maintain that poverty is the greatest and most enduring cause of suffering within the world. In his theology, Gutiérrez has consistently spoken of the God revealed in the ministry and the person of Jesus as the "God of life"—the God whose deepest desire is that people experience the fullness of life.[17] The theme of God and suffering is found throughout Gutierrez's theological works, though it is present in a particularly focused way in his book *On Job: God-Talk and the Suffering of the Innocent*. Gutiérrez engages in a rereading of this classic biblical text in an effort to interpret it for contemporary women and men, especially the poor and marginalized of the world.

Elizabeth Johnson has become a leading voice in feminist theology in the United States. She reads the Christian tradition with a critical eye, conscious of the history of suffering and oppression that women have experienced in the church and society. She engages in this reading, however, with the intention of offering a constructive theology that will be life giving for women and for men and, as such, will be authentically faithful to the tradition. Much of her research has focused on discourse about God—the ways in which we speak of God and how such language functions. The experience of suffering is for Johnson a critical test case for Christian discourse about God. Based on her extensive knowledge of the conversation among theologians concerning God and suffering, as well as her sensitivity to the concerns of suffering women, Johnson offers her own proposals about the most appropriate ways to talk about God in the face of suffering.

Eavesdropping on a Conversation

Theology involves a "conversation" between present experience (which is always culturally situated) and the tradition of faith. This conversation, however, is not engaged in merely by theologians sitting alone in their offices. The conversation takes place among all of us who are serious about gaining a better understanding of our faith. That ongoing conversation creates a milieu in which deeper insight into the truth of the revelation of God in Jesus Christ can emerge. Sometimes the conversation is a literal one that takes place between thinkers discussing important questions in a seminar room or conference hall. It is a synchronic conversation. At other times, the conversation is a diachronic one, that is, it involves theologians dialoguing with important thinkers who wrote in the past. This is clear, for example, as one reads Aquinas's *Summa Theologiae* and sees him "conversing" in very subtle ways with the ideas of Augustine. It is evident, too, as you read Schillebeeckx or Johnson and notice the ways in which they dialogue with Aquinas and classical theism.

Readers of this book are invited to "listen in" on a conversation that has been taking place for many centuries. This conversation is about how to conceive of and talk about God in the face of the stark reality of human suffering. As readers proceed through the subsequent chapters, they might think of themselves as eavesdropping on a round-table discussion among important thinkers about this critical topic. In listening to this conversation, I suggest that readers keep in mind some key questions. These questions will facilitate understanding of the positions adopted by these thinkers, as well as interpretation of these positions for contemporary application.

- How does this author conceive of the nature of God from the standpoint of the experience of human suffering? What kind of God does this author present?
- According to this author, where is God to be found within the experience of human suffering?
- What is God doing with regard to the suffering? What is God not doing?
- Is God affected by human suffering? If so, in what way?
- If the author is a Christian, how does he or she integrate the ministry, death, and resurrection of Jesus into his or her treatment of the issues?
- According to this author, what should believers do in the face of suffering? What should they not do?
- What are the possibilities for prayer offered in this author's theology?
- What do I have to learn from this author with reference to pastoral ministry to suffering people?

In the course of eavesdropping on this rich theological conversation, readers should not remain passive listeners. We must be actively engaged in this conversation, ready to enter into vigorous dialogue with the authors being studied. We should bring our own personal and pastoral experience to the table and relate what is being said to that experience. We need to pose critical questions to these authors—enter into debate with them. It is by means of that "conversation within a conversation" that our own theology of God and suffering will be deepened and refined.

Discussion Questions: www.paulistpress.com, Online Resources.

1

The Hebrew Scriptures: Suffering and the God of the Covenant

The Hebrew scriptures are a diverse collection of documents written over a span of almost a millennium. Some of the oral traditions that lie at the basis of these written texts reach back to the earliest history of Israel. The books of the Hebrew Bible represent a number of literary genres: poetry, narrative, theological history, wisdom sayings, prophetic oracles, apocalyptic visions, and more. Sometimes people ask, "What does the Bible say about God and the mystery of human suffering?" There is no simple answer to that question. The Bible as a whole, and the Hebrew scriptures in particular, do not offer a single, uniform perspective on the reality of suffering and God's relation to suffering people. These texts offer a number of key insights that were articulated in light of the experience of Israel through history. An awareness of this rich diversity of views is important in order to contextualize individual passages that we read or hear proclaimed in liturgical settings.

Israel interpreted its entire life in light of its covenant with the God who had liberated a people from slavery and formed them into a nation. This covenantal relationship, depicted in great detail in the Pentateuch, celebrated in the psalms and other hymns of the Hebrew Bible, and recalled by the prophets in their compelling proclamations of the word of God, was the lens through which the biblical authors interpreted the significant events of Jewish history. The people of Israel were convinced that they belonged to the God of Abraham and Sarah. The famous "eagles' wings" passage in Exodus celebrates this sense of belonging that was at the heart of Israel's identity: "You have seen what I did to the Egyptians, and how I bore you on eagles' wings and brought you to myself. Now therefore, if you obey my voice and keep my covenant, you shall be my treasured possession out of all the peoples. Indeed, the whole earth is mine, but you shall be for me a priestly kingdom and a holy nation" (Exod 19:4–6a). Israel interpreted times of prosperity and of hardship in light of its covenant relationship with God: "Yahweh has entered into a relationship of patronage with Israel (Exod 3:6 ff; 24:11); it is counted among his possessions. He saves and blesses his people. And any disruption of the relationship of trust, any turning away of Yahweh from his people, is equivalent in meaning to suffering and decline."[1]

Daniel Simundson and Daniel Harrington have catalogued the major views on suffering present in the scriptures of Israel.[2] Their work is helpful in displaying the development of diverse perspectives within Israel, particularly as it experienced political defeats, exile, and arduous attempts to regroup and rebuild. Harrington enumerates five key themes within the Hebrew scriptures that represent different ways of interpreting and engaging the experience of suffering: (1) lament; (2) the law of retribution; (3) suffering as mystery, articulated in classic form in the Book of Job; (4) suffering and sacrifice; (5) the apocalyptic solution. In my summary of Hebrew perspectives on suffering, I make use of Harrington's categories, though in a slightly different order. I also add a sixth theme: the suffering of God.[3] An exploration of these themes will help us to see the ways in which the people of Israel grappled with the mystery of suffering.

The Theory of Retribution

Many believers exhibit a visceral reaction to the idea of a punishing God or a God who exacts retribution in God's relationship with people. It is true, however, that the "law of retribution"[4] is a significant theme in the Hebrew scriptures. Righteous people are rewarded with blessings, and evil people are cursed with misfortune. The fate of Israel is directly related to its fidelity to the covenant. Since belief in life after death is a late development present in only a few traditions in the Hebrew Bible, this notion of reward and curse was usually limited to earthly existence. While this biblical theme may seem repugnant to many people of faith, we often encounter it in the scriptures, and we need to wrestle with it as we explore ways to talk about God in the face of human suffering.

The law of retribution plays a prominent role in the Book of Deuteronomy and in the theological history of Israel composed by the Deuteronomistic authors and found in the Books of Joshua through Second Kings. Scholars conclude that this Deuteronomistic history was not completed until the time of the exile in the sixth century BCE.[5] As these authors look back on the roller coaster of Israel's history, they interpret the fortunes of the people as a direct result of their faithfulness or infidelity to the God of the covenant. The sermons attributed to Moses in Deuteronomy display a style of exhortation that accentuates this theme. A list of blessings and curses in chapters 27 and 28 depicts the consequences of obedience and disobedience to the covenant. In Deuteronomy 30, Moses places before the people a choice between two "ways" related to faithful worship of the God of the covenant. One path leads to life; the other to death:

> See, I have set before you today life and prosperity, death and adversity. If you obey the commandments of the LORD your God that I am commanding you today, by loving the LORD your God, walking in his ways, and observing his commandments, decrees, and ordinances, then you shall live and become numerous, and the LORD your God will bless you in the land that you are entering to possess. But if your heart turns away and you do not hear, but are led astray to bow down to other gods and serve them, I declare today that you shall perish; you shall not live long in the land that you are crossing the Jordan to enter and possess. (Deut 30:15–18)

This same perspective is articulated with reference to Israel's fate during the period of the judges in Judges 2:6–23. In reflecting on the history of the people after the death of Joshua, the biblical author presents a recurrent pattern. The Israelites repeatedly turned away from the God of the covenant to worship of the gods of their neighbors (Judg 2:13). This infidelity provoked the anger of God, who delivered them into the hands of enemies who plundered them. Oppressed by their enemies, the people cried out to God, who raised up a judge to deliver them from the power of their oppressors. After the death of the judge, however, the people would inevitably fall away again "and behave worse than their ancestors, following other gods, worshiping them and bowing down to them" (Judg 2:19). The Deuteronomistic author interprets Israel's political fortunes as a direct result of its behavior in relation to the covenant. This view of human history perceives an inbuilt order to reality. It is also a way of making sense of the sufferings of God's people.

The "interpretation of ancient Israel's history in terms of the law of retribution had its roots in the warnings of the great prophets."[6] In both the northern and the southern kingdoms, those called to the prophetic vocation warned the people of impending disaster because of pervasive idolatry and injustice. The prophet Amos uses particularly harsh language in denouncing the social injustice that he perceives in the northern kingdom in the middle of the eighth century BCE:

> Thus says the LORD:
> for three transgressions of Israel,
>   and for four, I will not revoke the punishment;
> because they sell the righteous for silver,
>   and the needy for a pair of sandals—
> they who trample the head of the poor in the dust of the earth,
>   and push the afflicted out of the way. (Amos 2:6–7)

In the tumultuous years before the conquest of Judah by Babylon, Jeremiah argues that by their infidelity the people have brought evil upon themselves. Their own actions will punish them: "Your wickedness will punish you, / and your apostasies will convict you" (Jer 2:19). Many other prophetic texts could be cited to illustrate this theme. The preexilic prophets "made a connection between the sins of the people, especially of the political, religious and business leaders, and the national disaster which was coming."[7]

The Hebrew prophets, however, do not focus only on punishment. Most of them preserve a profound hope for the salvation of the people that will come with repentance. These prophets "refuse to give sin and suffering the last word."[8] They are not fixated on a God of retribution; rather, they are grounded in their faith in a God whose justice is salvific. After the horrific destruction of Jerusalem, Jeremiah utters his famous promise of a new covenant between God and the people (Jer 31:31–34). This sacred bond will result in an inner transformation by which all will have personal knowledge of God. It will be a covenant rooted in divine mercy. While the prophets attribute the misfortunes of the people of Israel to sin, they also express their strong conviction that the God of the covenant deeply desires the well-being of the people.

The view that suffering is the result of immoral behavior is also found in some of the wisdom literature of Israel. These postexilic writings bear similarities to a genre of literature that was also important to Israel's Near Eastern neighbors. The righteous person, the one who attunes his or her life to the wisdom of God inherent in creation, will find prosperity in this life. The fool, the one who forsakes the ways of God, will end in misery. This perspective is especially clear in the Book of Proverbs. In chapter 11, the sage instructs his students through a repetitious series of two-line proverbs that elucidate this point of view:

> The integrity of the upright guides them,
>   but the crookedness of the treacherous destroys them....
> The righteousness of the blameless keeps their ways straight,
>   but the wicked fall by their own wickedness. (Prov 11:3, 5)

The wisdom authors drew their teachings from reflection on the experience of life in the world. This experience taught them that a way of life characterized by wisdom usually leads to happiness and that foolishness is, in the end, disastrous. Still, the wisdom literature of the Bible is not of one mind in this viewpoint. The author of Ecclesiastes is not so sure about the equation between righteousness and prosperity. He observes that "there are righteous people who perish in their righteousness, and there are wicked people who prolong their life in their evildoing" (Eccl 7:15). We will see that the Book of Job, which is also an expression of wisdom literature, presents a serious challenge to the theory of retribution.

The notion of retribution also seems to be present in the Yahwist creation account in Genesis 2—3. Christians are quite familiar with this biblical account of "the fall" and its use in the doctrine of original sin. Genesis 2 and 3 paint a portrait of primeval beginnings consisting of two contrasting panels. In Genesis 2, the author depicts the utter goodness of God in creating an environment of life within which human beings can flourish. God plants a lush garden with four rivers flowing through it wherein there is communion between God and the human being. God crowns the creation of the man with the creation of the woman. The woman is to be the man's partner; there is meant to be a mutual sharing between them in every sphere of life. Having blessed them with this rich environment for life, however, God commands them not to eat of the fruit of the tree of the knowledge of good and evil. If they do so, they will die. This command introduces Adam to freedom.[9] Freedom belongs to the essence of what it means to be human. The man and woman must trust that God has their well-being at heart in giving this command. When they follow the promptings of the serpent and eat the forbidden fruit, they disrupt the proper relationship between God and humanity. The consequences of their action are devastating, as the man and woman are expelled from this primeval place of goodness and life. Their new existence will be characterized by hardship, suffering, and distance from God. In the succeeding chapters of Genesis, this biblical author chronicles the rapid spread of evil throughout creation that leads up to the flood.

According to this biblical account, to which Paul alludes in his Letter to the Romans (Rom 5:12–21), what God intends for creation is goodness and life. Suffering follows from human rebellion against the commandments of God. "The human beings—the man and woman—are the ones who must bear the responsibility for the pain and suffering of the world. This is the story of the whole human race."[10] The evil

24

introduced into God's good creation by sinful human beings increases exponentially throughout the world. In this ancient story, the expulsion from the garden leads to an existence in which all human beings are vulnerable to suffering.

There is, however, one dimension of this Yahwist creation account that remains mysterious and is incongruous with the logic of the law of retribution: the presence of the serpent in the garden. How does this creature that provokes human beings to sin fit in with the unalloyed goodness of the garden? It is important, as Simundson observes, to note that the presence of the snake adds mystery and complexity to the story.[11] While this motif of the serpent does not represent a conception of Satan or the devil that will be developed later in Christian theology, it does suggest that "there is a mysterious force for evil that seems to push humans into action that will be detrimental to themselves and to others."[12]

In the Hebrew scriptures there is a corporate and cross-generational dimension to this theory of retribution. The sins of one person affect the entire community, and the sins of ancestors can wreak havoc on the lives of their descendants. One of the classic texts to this effect is Exodus 34:6–7:

The LORD passed before him [Moses], and proclaimed,

"The LORD, the LORD,
a God merciful and gracious, slow to anger,
and abounding in steadfast love and faithfulness,
keeping steadfast love for the thousandth generation,
forgiving iniquity and transgression and sin,
yet by no means clearing the guilty, but visiting the iniquity
    of the parents
upon the children
and the children's children,
to the third and the fourth generation."

Here the biblical writer affirms that the fidelity and steadfast love of God (extending to the thousandth generation) is much more expansive than divine punishment (extending to the third and fourth genera-tions). Nevertheless, the message is conveyed that subsequent genera-tions suffer from the effects of the evil deeds of their ancestors.

There is an attenuation of this stress on the corporate and cross-generational aspects of sin and suffering in prophetic literature closer to the exile. The two classic passages are Ezekiel 18 and Jeremiah 31:29–30. The catastrophe of the destruction of Jerusalem and the widespread suffering caused by the exile seem to have elicited further reflection about responsibility for sin. Thus Ezekiel quotes a favorite saying about the consequences for children of the deeds of their par-ents: "The parents have eaten sour grapes, and the children's teeth are set on edge" (Ezek 18:2). Speaking in God's name, the prophet rejects this view, teaching that God will reward or punish the individual according to his or her behavior. "Know that all lives are mine; the life of the parent as well as the life of the child is mine: it is only the person who sins that shall die" (Ezek 18:4). Jeremiah quotes the same proverb and proclaims a similar notion of individual responsibility (Jer 31:30). Bernhard Anderson argues that in this teaching the prophets were attempting to correct an attitude of fatalism, in which exiled people felt that they were simply victims of the sins of their ancestors.[13] The exiles are summoned to move from a stance of victimization to one of personal responsibility. While this perspective represents an advance on an absolute collectivism, problems will arise when the notion of individual responsibility is taken to mean that personal suffering is nec-essarily the consequence of personal sin. Such an understanding will be challenged in the Book of Job and in the Johannine account of Jesus' encounter with the man born blind (John 9).

Contemporary believers usually resist the theory of retribution because of the stark reality of innocent suffering and the apparently unequal distribution of suffering among humanity. What would have inspired such a perspective among the people of the Bible? Are there important truths to be found in this perspective? This viewpoint proves true to human experience in many instances.[14] There is a grain of truth to the adage that a person reaps what he or she sows. Those who are sincere and faithful in their love for others usually discover fulfillment in their lives through the relationships they form and the satisfaction that comes from these relationships. Those who are selfish or even hateful usually end up isolated and miserable. And we know that the conduct of one generation affects later generations, as is evident in the painful legacy of racism and in the ecological crisis that we face today. Moreover, there are several essential biblical affirmations implicit in the law of retribution: God is personal and active in the arena of human history; God is just; human beings have freedom; there is an order in the world, implying that cause-and-effect relationships do exist; human beings need evidence of God's justice in the world; our actions do affect one another.[15]

The difficulty with this perspective, of course, is that it does not always illumine specific situations of suffering. Indeed, I propose that, if applied rigorously, it does not apply to the vast majority of instances of human suffering. Most experiences of pain and tragedy are much too complex for such a simplistic explanation. If one reverses the sequence of this theory and argues that suffering must be an indication of personal wrongdoing (or foolishness), then the harmful effects of this perspective become manifest. Anyone who has engaged in pastoral care to the sick and dying has experienced the damage that is done when people simplistically conclude that their illness or injury is the result of their past wrongdoing.

The Cry of Lament

The interpretation of suffering as the result of the sin of the community or the individual manifests prolonged reflection after the fact. When the people of Israel were more immediate to the situation of suffering, they cried out to God in their pain. They believed that the God of the covenant was accessible in both individual and communal prayer. The Hebrew scriptures bear direct and compelling testimony to the crying out of the sufferer. The plaintive cries of the people of Israel gave rise to the rich biblical tradition of the lament. Of all the categories of psalms within the Bible, the largest by far is the lament.[16]

The psalms of lament, Harrington observes, are "full of activity."[17] The speaker, whether the individual or the community, addresses God

directly and boldly. Though the lament psalms vary somewhat in structure, they generally follow a pattern that is not dissimilar to lament
prayers in the religious traditions of Israel's neighbors. The usual
"script" of the lament consists of an opening address of God; the articulation of the complaint; a confession of trust in God, often based on
the great deeds of God in the past; a petition for deliverance from the
present suffering; and a concluding thanksgiving.[18] The complaint is
stated in terms generic enough to allow for use of the psalm in a variety
of circumstances of suffering. In Psalm 3, for example, the individual
exclaims:

> O LORD, how many are my foes!
>   Many are rising against me;
> many are saying to me,
> "There is no help for you in God." (vv. 1–2)

The confession of trust entails an acknowledgment that God has
demonstrated his fidelity in protecting and delivering his people: "But
you, O LORD, are a shield around me, / my glory, and the one who lifts
up my head" (v. 3). The petition for deliverance is forthright and
includes harsh words against the perceived enemy:

> Rise up, O LORD!
> Deliver me, O my God!
> For you strike all my enemies on the cheek;
> you break the teeth of the wicked. (v. 7)

The concluding thanksgiving is an expression of gratitude and praise
to the faithful God: "Deliverance belongs to the LORD; / may your
blessing be on your people!" (v. 8). This final verse may indicate that
the psalmist has already experienced relief from suffering and is now
offering a thanksgiving sacrifice.[19]

Lament psalms are usually emphatic in their confession of trust
that God will hear the petitioner and respond with aid.[20] Perhaps the
most famous lament is Psalm 22, the opening words of which are presented as spoken by Jesus from the cross in the Gospels of Matthew

and Mark (Matt 27:46; Mark 15:34). We consider the Gospel use of this psalm, as well as the interpretation of its significance by modern authors, in later chapters. This psalm, which is so bold and graphic in its description of trouble ("My God, my God, why have you forsaken me? Why are you so far from helping me, from the words of my groaning?"), concludes with exuberant words of praise and thanksgiving ("I will tell of your name to my brothers and sisters; in the midst of the congregation I will praise you").[21] The words of thanksgiving may have been preceded by an "oracle of salvation" that was uttered in a liturgical setting.

While these psalms express trust in the power and fidelity of God, their realistic descriptions of the experience of suffering are striking. They show that the Hebrew ideal was not that of suffering alone or suffering in silence. "The Old Testament exhibits a surprising tendency to bring the calamity of individuals, as well as of entire groups, out into the open."[22] Walter Brueggemann has reflected deeply on the significance of the lament tradition for Israel's view of God and God's relation to human suffering. He says, "The world of lament speech thus is based on the premise that the speech of Israel draws God into the trouble. God will act and life will be restored."[23] He calls the laments "psalms of disorientation."[24] The honest acknowledgment of negativity in these psalms represents an act of bold faith, a faith that is also transformed. It is *bold* faith because it insists that the world must be experienced as it really is and not in some pretended way. It is a faith that makes the claim that experiences of disorder are a proper subject for discourse with God.

> There is nothing out of bounds, nothing precluded or inappropriate. Everything properly belongs in this conversation of the heart. To withhold parts of life from that conversation is to withhold part of life from the sovereignty of God. Thus these psalms make the important connection: everything must be *brought to speech,* and everything brought to speech must be *addressed to God,* who is the final reference for all of life.[25]

The courageous faith manifested in the lament psalms is also a *transformed* faith. It reflects belief in a God who is present to and participates in the darkness, weakness, and displacement of life. This is a God of sorrows who is characterized more by fidelity than by immutability. The laments also reveal that life is transformed through these prayers. Life comes to be understood as a pilgrimage through the darkness that is intrinsic to being human. The psalms of lament presuppose "that precisely in such deathly places as presented in these psalms new life is given by God."[26]

The psalms of lament endure as a treasured part of the prayer of Jews and Christians. While the psalms do not provide answers to the mystery of suffering, they offer eloquent testimony to the fact that for the Hebrew people the God of the covenant was so real, so close at hand and directly involved in their lives, that they knew they could, and even should, cry out to God. They were convinced that they should complain—they should bring their plight directly to God. And that was precisely the way in which God remained real to them, even through experiences of suffering that defied explanation. "The lament does not solve all of the sufferer's intellectual questions about the origin and meaning of the suffering but does provide a structured way for the faithful to bring their suffering to God's attention and to cope with it."[27] The lament psalms, notes Harrington, "can help sufferers develop a vocabulary about their condition, raise the theological issues at stake in their suffering, and recognize that as human beings and religious people we belong to a community of fellow sufferers."[28]

These psalms help initiate people into an experience of God in the midst of suffering. It is almost as if these prayers can take a suffering person by the hand and lead him or her to personal encounter with the living God. The encounter may well be one that is shrouded in darkness. It may be a pilgrimage through the darkness into deathly places. This journey may involve the paradoxical experience of the presence of God in absence described by many mystics. Nonetheless, it is a real encounter that reveals God walking through the deathly places.

The Sacrificial Understanding of Suffering

The two perspectives on suffering presented earlier focus on the negativity of the experience of suffering. Sometimes, however, people attempt to discover positive meaning in suffering. They profess that the experience of suffering by an individual or a group has accomplished something, has effected some good. There is a minority tradition within the Hebrew scriptures that assigns a sacrificial meaning to the suffering of the people of Israel and of certain chosen individuals among the people.[29]

Sacrifice was an essential part of the covenant tradition of Israel, as it was a feature of the religious practice of Israel's neighbors. The first seven chapters of Leviticus provide a description of the various kinds of sacrifices that are prescribed by God. The classic description of the offering to be made on the Day of Atonement is found in Leviticus 16 (see also Num 29:7–11). Different meanings were assigned to the offering of sacrifice to God.[30] A sacrifice could be offered as a gift to God—the gift of a prized possession like a young animal or the first fruits of the harvest. The famous story of Abraham and Isaac in Genesis 22, while complex in meaning, features Abraham's willingness to offer his only son to God as an act of obedient faith. Sacrifice was also made in order to establish communion with God. And a variety of kinds of sacrifice were prescribed in order to atone for voluntary or involuntary breaches of the covenant.

The most notable instance of interpreting the suffering of Israel in sacrificial terms is found in Second Isaiah (Isa 40—55). As the exile was coming to an end with the victory of Cyrus of Persia over the Babylonians, an anonymous author or authors spoke a profound word of hope to a people exiled in Babylon.[31] In language that evoked the saving action of God in the exodus, the prophet assured the suffering people of Israel that God was about to act in a new way to liberate God's people and lead them home. In his message of salvation, this prophet was in continuity with Isaiah of Jerusalem (who wrote in the eighth century BCE) in interpreting the devastation of the nation as a consequence of its infidelity to God. The prophet asks and answers the question about the reason for the exile:

> Who gave up Jacob to the spoiler,
> and Israel to the robbers?
> Was it not the LORD, against whom we have sinned,
>   in whose ways they would not walk,
>   and whose law they would not obey? (Isa 42:24)

But the author moves on from the traditional retributive understanding of Israel's suffering in his presentation of the figure of the servant. In the well-known "servant songs" found in Isaiah 42:1–9; 49:1–6, 50:4–11, and 52:13—53:12, we meet a figure whose experience and destiny are emblematic of Israel. In the last two of these four poems, the suffering and vindication of this servant are set forth in compelling imagery. The third song presents a graphic description of the servant's ordeals: "I gave my back to those who struck me.... / I did not hide my face from insult and spitting" (Isa 50:6).

The identity of this famous servant has long been a matter of dispute among biblical scholars. In certain places, the servant seems to be the nation of Israel itself. The close identification with Israel is made in the second song, when the servant receives his call from God and discerns the words: "You are my servant, / Israel, in whom I will be glorified" (Isa 49:3). Two verses later, however, it appears that the servant has a special mission to bring Israel back to God. Harrington notes that there are both collective and individual interpretations of the identity of the servant.[32] Collective interpretations include the entire nation or a specific group within Israel, such as the exiled community. Individual interpretations "include the legitimate claimant to the high priesthood or the kingship of Judah, some leader of the exiled community, a prophet, the author himself or Moses."[33]

In the fourth song we find the clearest and most influential interpretation of the servant's suffering in the category of sacrifice. This poem contains a variety of voices, including that of God at its beginning: "See, my servant shall prosper; / he shall be exalted and lifted up, / and shall be very high" (Isa 52:13). Further along, human speakers (the nations,

32

the exiled community, or the servant's followers) profess astonishment at what God has done in and through the servant: "Who has believed what we have heard? / And to whom has the arm of the LORD been revealed?" (Isa 53:1). This servant, who had no exalted status, performs a singular service on behalf of the people and is granted "a portion with the great" (Isa 53:12). The theme of the vicarious and expiatory character of the servant's sufferings is expressed in 53:4–6 and 12:

> Surely he has borne our infirmities
> > and carried our diseases;
> yet we accounted him stricken,
> > struck down by God and afflicted.
> But he was wounded for our transgressions,
> > crushed for our iniquities....
> Therefore I will allot him a portion with the great,
> > and he shall divide the spoil with the strong;
> because he poured out himself to death,
> > and was numbered with the transgressors;
> yet he bore the sin of many,
> > and made intercession for the transgressors.

As Harrington explains:

> It is as if all the punishments due to all the sins of God's people have been visited upon the figure of God's Servant....And the result of the Servant's suffering is the healing and the wholeness of God's people. In the background is the logic of sacrifice as a means of atoning for sin and renewing the relationship with God. With the Jerusalem temple destroyed, it was not possible for Jews to offer material sacrifices, and so the suffering of God's Servant does what material sacrifices could not do. It brings about right relationship with God and makes it possible for the exiled community to return to its Holy City.[34]

Richard Clifford highlights the influence of the fourth servant song in particular.[35] It is evident in the later Book of Daniel, especially

33

Daniel 11:33–35. The influence of this poem is also manifest in the portrayal of Jesus in the New Testament. The important saying found in Mark 10:45 borrows from the fourth servant song: "For the Son of Man came not to be served but to serve, and to give his life a ransom for many." This poem is also the focal point of the scene in Acts 8 in which the deacon Philip encounters the Ethiopian eunuch, who is puzzled by the meaning of Isaiah 53:7–8. Philip proclaims that this passage has found its fulfillment in Jesus; having heard this "good news," the eunuch asks to be baptized. "One can infer from the eunuch's request for baptism that the text was very important in early Christian instruction, providing a way of understanding the death and resurrection of Jesus."[36] Whether Jesus interpreted his own mission and destiny in terms of the suffering servant of Second Isaiah is a matter of debate among New Testament scholars, but it is difficult to imagine that, as a faithful Jew immersed in the scriptures, reflection on this key text did not influence his self-understanding.

The sacrificial interpretation of suffering is deeply embedded in the Christian imagination. The interpretation of the saving work of Jesus in terms of sacrifice suffuses the tradition of Christian soteriology, including that of Anselm of Canterbury and Thomas Aquinas. Many Christians have been exhorted to offer their own sufferings to God for the benefit of others or themselves. This perspective insists that suffering should not be envisioned as a purely negative reality. It highlights the opportunity for good inherent in suffering, an opportunity that should not be wasted. Suffering freely offered to God can effect good beyond what is immediately evident. While it represents a minority tradition within the Hebrew scriptures, this viewpoint has exerted great influence on Christian theology, spirituality, and piety.

The Book of Job

The most famous and sustained biblical treatment of the reality of innocent suffering is found in the Book of Job. This biblical text has consistently been commented on by great thinkers within the church, from Augustine and Gregory the Great in the early church, to Thomas

Aquinas in the Middle Ages, to Gustavo Gutiérrez in modern times, as well as Jewish Shoah survivor Elie Wiesel. Commentaries on Job give evidence of the many textual difficulties in this book and the wide diversity of interpretations of its meaning. As John McKenzie observed, while Job clearly challenges the doctrine of retribution, the book's precise message always seems to elude its interpreters: "[The doctrine of retribution] was not enough for an anonymous writer who possessed the most profound mind and the most eloquent gift of language" in the Old Testament. Inevitably every Old Testament scholar claims to have figured out the meaning of this book, "and always, when the book is read again, we find that it says more than its critics can tell us."[37]

There is no consensus about the provenance of the Book of Job. The text contains no reference to historical persons or events that would suggest a precise date of origin. The literary setting is simply long ago and far away. The story does not take place within Israel, though the majority of scholars argue that the book was composed by an Israelite. Most scholars conclude that the book was written in the early postexilic period. The time of composition is usually placed between the sixth and fourth centuries BCE.[38] Some experts detect the influence of Jeremiah and Second Isaiah in the book. Job is usually classified as part of the Hebrew wisdom literature, that genre of Hebrew writing that is relatively late in the Old Testament and that is reflected in works like Ecclesiastes, Sirach, Wisdom, and Proverbs. Wisdom literature included practical reflection on human existence aimed at deriving the basis of a good and happy life. "Wisdom literature is centrally concerned with the nature of the proper moral and religious conduct of an individual and with the relation of such conduct to personal and communal well-being."[39]

Most scholars argue that the author of this book took an ancient folktale and reshaped it.[40] The folktale was a familiar story about a legendary wise man who was tested, found to be faithful, and subsequently rewarded for his faithfulness. This folktale is found in the prose prologue in 1:1—2:10, with an appendix (2:11–13) joining this prologue to the longer poetic section, as well as in the prose epilogue found in 42:10–17, which also has a connecting passage (42:7–10). The figure of

Job is mentioned in the Book of Ezekiel, along with Noah and Daniel, as a man of paradigmatic righteousness (Ezek 14:14, 20). The author of the Book of Job adopted this folktale and inserted into it the lengthy poetic section, which consists of a series of dialogues between Job and his friends and concludes with two long speeches by God.

This biblical author presents a direct challenge to a worldview based on the principle of strict retributive justice. The prologue assures the reader that Job is a righteous man, that he has been faithful to the demands of God. "That man was blameless and upright, one who feared God and turned away from evil" (1:1). In his dialogue with the satan, God is depicted as confirming the righteousness of Job (1:8). God will testify to the righteousness of Job again in the epilogue, when he rebukes the friends of Job and makes his mercy toward them dependent on Job's intercession on their behalf (42:8). The satan questions the real motives of Job's fidelity and is given permission to test Job. Job's world is turned completely upside down, as he loses everything and everyone important in his life and is himself afflicted with loathsome sores. The order of his life is entirely disrupted. His suffering is so severe that he utters a lengthy, heartfelt lament in which he curses the day of his birth (chap. 3).

In their long and repetitive speeches, Job's friends become ever more implacable and unflinching supporters of the doctrine of retribution. There is little flexibility in their worldview, and they grow increasingly impatient with Job's refusal to acquiesce to the traditional teaching. Job's misfortunes must be the consequence of some sin, even if it is one of which he is unaware. Eliphaz speaks of suffering as a discipline, a correction through which God wounds but then heals us (5:17–27). Bildad offers a straightforward expression of the theory of retribution:

> If you will seek God
>   and make supplication to the Almighty,
> if you are pure and upright,
>   surely then he will rouse himself for you
>   and restore to you your rightful place. (8:5–6).

Zophar reinforces this perspective by enunciating the doctrine of the two ways (11:13–20).

Job, however, stands his ground. He remains true to his own experience in spite of the authority of the traditional doctrine. He insists that his troubles are not the result of his guilt but represent some kind of disruption of cosmic order. "Since Job does not question the omnipotence of God, he argues that God is being unjust in his case."[41] Job is convinced that in some mysterious way the order of divine justice has been perverted. With this in mind, he expresses his desire to present his legal case before the divine tribunal. He wants to take God to court: "I have indeed prepared my case; / I know that I shall be vindicated" (13:18). The great difficulty, of course, is that in the divine tribunal Job's adversary is also his judge. Still, Job does not completely lose hope. In a stirring passage he proclaims his trust in a divine redeemer:

> For I know that my Redeemer lives,
>   and that at the last he will stand upon the earth;
> and after my skin has been thus destroyed,
>   then in my flesh I shall see God,
> whom I shall see on my side,
>   and my eyes shall behold, and not another. (19:25–27)

This famous passage, replete with textual uncertainties,[42] expresses Job's hope in a redeemer, a *go'el*. In ancient Israel a *go'el* was one who acted on behalf of a relative to buy back family property (Lev 25:25), to avenge a wrong inflicted on kin (Num 35:19–21), or to marry a widow (the Book of Ruth).[43] Job desperately clings to the hope that God will be this vindicator in his life. As the book progresses, Job's yearning for vindication of his innocence takes precedence over his desire for relief from the misfortunes he is enduring.

After what seems like an eternity, God finally speaks to Job "out of the whirlwind" (38:1). Job is reduced to reverent silence while God acts as a wisdom teacher in directing Job's attention to the wonders of creation. In two long speeches, God instructs Job to contemplate the marvels of nature. Rhetorical questions are addressed to Job that compel him to acknowledge his limitations, beginning with the query: "Where were you when I laid the foundations of the earth?" (38:4). These divine speeches elucidate the wonder and the purposefulness of creation. Animals like the wild ass and regions of the earth like the desert, which seem to have no purpose for the lives of human beings, are shown to be dimensions of God's good creation and objects of God's watchful care. In the second speech, God directs Job's gaze toward the wild beasts Behemoth and Leviathan. These animals have characteristics that resemble the hippopotamus and crocodile, respectively, but they also seem to possess primordial features. They are "liminal creatures, betwixt and between the categories of ordinary animal and mythic being."[44] These creatures represent chaos, but they are chaotic forces that are subject to the creative and providential activity of God. Nowhere in these speeches does God answer the questions that Job posed in his laments. In particular, God does not provide an answer to the question of the *why* of Job's suffering. Nor does God countenance Job's request to enter into a legal disputation that would settle the issue of divine justice. Job is simply overwhelmed by his experience of God and by the questions God puts to him.

At the end of the second speech, Job "repents":

I had heard of you by the hearing of the ear,
    but now my eye sees you;
therefore I despise myself
    and repent in dust and ashes. (42:5–6)

The interpretation of these verses is much disputed. The Hebrew word in this text is *niham* ("be sorry, relent, be comforted"), rather than the usual word for "repent," *shub*.[45] It seems clear that Job is *not* repenting of any sin that would have been the cause of his suffering. God never accuses Job of having sinned, and the reader knows from God's statements in the prologue and the epilogue that Job is a righteous man. It does appear, however, that his experience of God's word has compelled Job to alter his perspective on the world and his own life. Job now possesses new insight into the divine through his encounter with God. He has experienced God with an intimacy that he has never before known.

This experience of communion with God has made it possible for Job to discover a sense of peace even in the midst of his suffering.

In the prose epilogue of the book, God restores Job's fortunes: "And the LORD gave Job twice as much as he had before" (42:10b). This ending creates "dissonance and disruption" in the text, since it seems to reinforce the very doctrine of retribution that was put into question in the poetic dialogues.[46] After the reader has worked through the dialogues and contemplated the speeches of God, it seems that the book should conclude simply with Job's experience of God in the midst of suffering. Some commentators note, however, that for the Hebrew author it was important not to leave the final word to suffering. Belief in an afterlife in which divine justice might be manifested was not in the purview of this biblical author. The restoration of Job's earthly fortunes, then, represents the manifestation of God's saving justice.

As McKenzie noted, interpretations of the Book of Job are quite diverse. I will summarize the conclusions of three biblical scholars.

Dianne Bergant observes that through the divine speeches Job's anthropocentric view of the universe is challenged. He is forced to look beyond himself to the mystery of creation and there to recognize the power of God present and at work. The author of the book does not want to humiliate Job but to manifest the dominion of God and to show that, despite the harsh reality of innocent suffering, chaos does not reign. Job is able to move to a renewed confidence in the power of God and deepened trust in God's care for him and for all of creation. He is brought to a deeper level of faith. As Bergant puts it, "There can indeed be innocent suffering and, while he may never be able to comprehend it, he knows that he will be able to endure it with an unshakeable faith in God's universal providence and personal solicitude."[47]

Carol Newsom highlights the ambiguities in the message of the Book of Job. She thinks that the text is intentionally enigmatic because the author wants readers to assume an active role in construing the meaning of the divine speeches and of Job's response.[48] As she puts it, "The ambiguities inherent in the divine speeches and Job's reply resist every attempt to reduce them to a single, definitive interpretation."[49] Nevertheless, she does highlight the change in perspective that Job experiences through his encounter with God. Job recognizes that the legal framework of his thinking is too narrow to encompass the ways of God in creation. Newsom also attends to the motif of order and chaos in creation. The descriptions of Behemoth and Leviathan, in particular, reveal to Job that in creation chaos is restrained but not fully eliminated.[50] Though no explanation for the presence of the chaotic is offered, Job comes to realize that it is indeed a dimension of reality. Nevertheless, the chaotic element in the world "is contained within the secure boundaries of a created order that is also rich with goodness."[51] In a further comment, Newsom points out that his encounter with God also challenges Job's view of where the presence of God may be experienced.[52] In his mournful recollections of his past relationship with God (found especially in chapter 29), Job recalls his experience of God's presence in his family life and in the good deeds performed for the community. The divine speeches demonstrate to Job that God can also be experienced as present in the midst of darkness and desolation.

In her literary analysis of Job, Susan Mathews takes a different approach to deciphering the message of the book.[53] She tries to demonstrate the way in which key words and phrases, as well as certain literary techniques, point us to the meaning of the book. Mathews places special emphasis on the Hebrew word *hinnam*, meaning "for nought" or "gratuitously." In the prologue, the satan challenges God with the question: "Does Job fear God for nothing (*hinnam*)?" (1:9). Mathews argues that the book is not directly about the mystery of suffering; rather, it is primarily about the relationship of Job to God and the role of Job's affliction in that context.[54] It is not as much about Job's suffering as it is about his piety. The challenge that the satan puts to God involves a test of Job's piety: Does Job truly fear God for nought? In other words, is Job faithful to his covenant relationship with God for God's sake, or because of what he can gain from the relationship? In his laments Job's one desire is to speak *with* God, not *about* God. Job's wish is to have his relationship with God intact in the midst of his suffering, and this wish is granted. "Job is not so much about the meaning of suffering but rather what the person of integrity does in the face of it. Job's integrity enables him to find the Lord in the midst of suffering, because he clings to God with a faith that is built on serving God for nought."[55] If God were to offer an explanation for Job's suffering it could be construed as a reason for Job to serve God. Job simply needs to cling to God in complete faith. Job's repentance at the conclusion of the theophany is another expression of his acceptance of his relationship with God as it is. The satan is proven wrong: Job is, in fact, willing to serve God for nought. "The point of Job is not to solve the problem of suffering but to illustrate what a person of integrity does in the face of it: cling to God in faith and continue to serve God for nothing save that relationship." [56]

These interpretations attest to the complexity and ambiguity of the book. Nevertheless, in this classic biblical text several key ideas emerge with relative clarity. First, the book shows that a strict doctrine of retribution is inadequate to the human experience of suffering. There is such a thing as innocent suffering. The prologue and epilogue make this clear for the reader. Second, the book is a compelling expression of the place of lament in the Hebrew faith tradition. While it may be that Job becomes overly assertive and accusatory in his speech, his honest crying out in the face of intense suffering is an expression of his faith in the God of the covenant. Even in his darkest moments, he trusts that God will hear and respond. Third, the experience of God's presence in the midst of suffering is transformative for Job. While he does not receive an explanation for his predicament or an answer to his questions about divine justice, he is given another perspective on the situation and, most important, he is assured of God's presence and God's care for all creatures. Job, the suffering one, is granted an experience of communion with God.

A related theme in the Book of Job is the experience of the silence of God in the midst of suffering. If readers know the end of the book, they are aware that God eventually speaks. But throughout the lengthy cycles of speeches, Job experiences and complains about the disturbing reality of God's silence. God seems to be hidden, to have turned his face away from the innocent suffering person. God appears to have become inaccessible. In a famous passage, Job says:

Oh, that I knew where I might find him,
   that I might come even to his dwelling....
If I go forward, he is not there;
   or backward, I cannot perceive him;
on the left he hides, and I cannot behold him;
   I turn to the right, but I cannot see him. (23:3, 8–9)

This is a classic text about Job's search for God in the midst of feeling abandoned, a passage quoted in the writings of the mystics and applied to the experience of the dark night of the soul. This biblical theme of God's accessibility and inaccessibility and of his apparent silence is one that contemporary theologians comment upon as they reflect on the mystery of suffering. Some authors have asked whether God was silent throughout the tragedy of the Shoah.

The Apocalyptic Perspective

In times of severe distress, some Hebrew authors addressed the situation of Israel's suffering in the language and worldview of apocalyptic. These writings are among the latest in the Old Testament, though they are related to earlier expressions of eschatology in exilic and postexilic prophecies found in Isaiah (especially chapters 24—27, 56—66), Ezekiel, and Zechariah. As Harrington notes, "Apocalyptic is the literature of a dispossessed and oppressed people."[57] The authors of this literature attempt to keep hope alive in situations of conflict and persecution by announcing a climactic intervention by God that will put an end to the suffering and vindicate the righteous. They exhort the people of Israel to trust in God and to await God's decisive action on their behalf.

John Collins describes apocalyptic as "a genre of revelatory literature with a narrative framework, in which a revelation is mediated by an otherworldly being to a human recipient."[58] Apocalyptic thinking envisions eschatological salvation and engages a world that is transcendent to earthly experience. While looking toward the future and the heavenly realm for hope, the intention of apocalyptic is to strengthen suffering people in the present. Apocalyptic "is intended to interpret present, earthly circumstances in light of the supernatural world and of the future, and to influence both the understanding and the behavior of the audience by means of divine authority."[59]

Jewish apocalyptic writings arose during the period of the domination of the Mediterranean world by the successors of Alexander the Great (d. 323 BCE). The clearest example of apocalyptic in the Hebrew Bible is the Book of Daniel, written about 165 BCE. This book reflects the situation of the people of Israel under the reign of the Syrian (Seleucid) ruler Antiochus IV Epiphanes (ruled 175–164 BCE). While previous Egyptian and Syrian Hellenistic emperors had been tolerant of Jewish religious practice, Antiochus altered the policy and tried to compel Jews to accept his own version of worship. He prohibited observance of the Torah and introduced his own cult "of the Most High God" into the Jerusalem Temple (1 Macc 1:41–61).[60] Though some Jews acceded to this new policy, others viewed it as a desecration and resisted the commands of the king. Punishment for such disobedience included martyrdom. The military victory of Judas Maccabeus and his supporters in 164 resulted in the liberation of the temple area and greater freedom for Jews. It appears that the Book of Daniel was composed during the period of persecution by Antiochus but before the Maccabean victory.[61] The tradition in Daniel counsels a response to persecution that is different from the Maccabean military solution.

The first six chapters of the Book of Daniel consist of tales about contest and conflict in which Daniel emerges victorious. The final six chapters include apocalyptic visions given to the wise Daniel so that he will be able to interpret past events of history as well as God's plans for the people of Israel and for the nations. The literary setting of the tales and the apocalyptic visions is the era of the Babylonian exile and immediately thereafter—the time of the hegemony of the Babylonians, Medes, and Persians. This tragic experience of suffering and disruption for the people of Israel is chosen as the context for instruction about the current experience of oppression under Antiochus.

The unifying theme of the book is the sovereignty of God over human history. This conviction is evident in chapters 8 and 12 of the book. In chapter 8, Daniel receives a vision of a ram and a goat. The ram represents the Medes and Persians, whom the redactor of Daniel merged into one kingdom for the purposes of his interpretation of history. This charging ram is met by a male goat coming from the west that has a great horn between its eyes. This horn represents Alexander the Great, founder of the Hellenistic empire. The goat tramples the ram and grows "exceedingly great," only to have its horn broken at the height of its power. The breaking of the goat's horn refers to the death of Alexander the Great. In place of this horn four other horns arise, representing the four generals among whom Alexander's empire was divided. Out of one of these horns emerges a little horn, that is, Antiochus Epiphanes. Antiochus is presented as posing a direct challenge even to the powers of heaven: "It [the horn that is Antiochus] threw down to the earth some of the host and some of the stars, and trampled on them" (8:10). The text clearly alludes to the desecration of the Temple and the repression of Jewish religious practice by speaking of the arrogance of Antiochus against even "the prince of the host" (God). Gabriel helps Daniel interpret this vision, indicating that the vision is "for the time of the end" (8:17). After the transgressions against God have reached their full measure through the wicked actions of Antiochus, the latter "shall be broken, and not by human hands" (8:25). It is God who will defeat Antiochus and reign victoriously.

Chapter 12 gives another vision of end-time events. The scene again moves beyond the bounds of earth with its reference to Michael, "the protector of your people" (12:1). It will be a time of anguish, but the "wise" shall be delivered through the definitive action of God in history. The author affirms that "many" of those who sleep in the dust of the earth shall awake—an apparent reference to resurrection of the dead. Some of these shall arise to everlasting shame, but the faithful will awake to everlasting life. This reference to resurrection and an implied judgment of the dead is characteristic of apocalyptic, in which divine justice is granted to the faithful who have been victimized by the powers of evil. Daniel is told to await the fulfillment of this vision, though he is given three different timetables for that fulfillment: "A time, two times, and half a time" (12:7, probably three and a half years), 1,290 days (12:11), and 1,335 days (12:12). Though the timetable is imprecise, the underlying conviction is that the tyranny of evil is only temporary; before long the sovereign God will intervene in human history to vindicate the faithful and punish the wicked.

In Daniel and other apocalyptic works, the theory of retribution is articulated again, though retribution is delayed to a future time, an end-time of definitive divine action. "The principle of retribution remains in force—but its execution is not in the present time. When God's kingdom comes, then the righteous will be vindicated and the wicked will be punished or annihilated. This approach preserves the justice of God by deferring rewards and punishments to the last judgment or some other divine intervention."[62] The literature of apocalyptic exhorts believers to cling to their faith in the justice of God, which, though it may seem to be obscured in the present, will eventually be manifest to everyone.

In apocalyptic literature, the forces of evil that inflict suffering on God's people are presented in a superhuman way. The kingdoms referred to in the Book of Daniel, though ultimately under the sovereignty of God, are symbolized by beasts that embody evil as a powerful, almost cosmic, force. Harrington calls this perspective "modified apocalyptic dualism."[63] In this vision of human history, the world that was created by God is now under the direction of two lesser powers, one good and the other evil. At the end, God will destroy the evil power and the suffering it inflicts. This perspective is a dualism in that it depicts two opposing powers; it is modified in that it upholds the ultimate sovereignty of the good God; and it is apocalyptic in that it presents revelations about the future course of history, especially about the end-time intervention of God.[64] This modified apocalyptic dualism suggests the possibility that evil in the world is not caused solely by human beings; the forces of evil that inflict human suffering transcend the intentions and actions of human agents alone.

Apocalyptic, then, is imbued with the language of hope articulated for believers who are experiencing the effects of egregious injustice with no apparent way to rectify the situation. It exhorts people of faith to "hold on" amidst the present suffering with the trust that God will ultimately establish justice and put an end to suffering. This message is presented through a code language replete with symbolism meant to be interpreted for the righteous. Apocalyptic does not offer an explanation as to why the sovereign God allows the forces of evil to wreak havoc in the world; it does offer a way through the suffering by counseling steadfast trust in the fidelity and justice of God. It sometimes suggests that people's faith is purified and strengthened by endurance in the face of oppression. The final victory of God that is envisioned in apocalyptic will mean the end of suffering for the righteous and new life in the reign of God.

The Suffering of God

A critical issue in the theological conversation about God and suffering is the image of God that informs one's theology. We will see that some theologians think there is a tension, even a certain degree of contrast, between the biblical portrait of God and the concept of God that was developed in classical Christian theology. They argue that the image of God found in the Bible is dynamic, passionate, involved. This image became obscured when, with the help of Greek philosophy, the biblical narrative was translated into theological concepts that accentuated the transcendence, eternity, and immutability of God. Some contemporary theologians insist that the God of the Bible suffers with his people.

In their respective studies, Erhard Gerstenberger and Terence Fretheim conclude that the Hebrew scriptures portray a God who suffers.[65] Gerstenberger points out that the nearness of God is the real concern of the Hebrew scriptures. God's transcendence, which is also a concern of the biblical authors, is actualized in God's nearness to humankind. God shares in the pain and suffering of the human family. God's pain for the world "is never the wailing sympathy of an uninvolved onlooker, but the genuine pain of one who is directly affected, the suffering of a comrade, who takes upon himself a part of the burden."[66] This divine suffering is not presented as the result of some deficiency or intrinsic unhappiness in the divine life. Rather, the pain felt by God is the result of human misconduct. The lengthy oracular poem found in Jeremiah 2:1–37 begins by depicting God as a husband who has lost the devotion of his bride. God is offended and hurt by the infidelity of Israel:

> What wrong did your ancestors find in me
>> that they went far from me,
> and went after worthless things,
>> and became worthless themselves? (Jer 2:5)

The prophecy of First Isaiah commences with an oracle that likens God to a parent who is pained by the rebellion of his children:

> Hear, O heavens, and listen, O earth;
>> for the LORD has spoken:
> I reared children and brought them up,
>> but they have rebelled against me. (Isa 1:2)

In his exploration of this biblical theme, Fretheim categorizes passages about divine suffering according to a threefold schema based on the reasons for God's suffering.[67] God suffers *because* of the people's rejection; God empathizes *with* the people who are suffering; and God suffers *for* the people. Isaiah 63:7–10 is an important text that speaks of a God who grieves over the rebellion of the people. Even though God has redeemed and carried this people, they have rebelled and "grieved his holy spirit" (63:10). "It is not considered in the least incongruous to juxtapose grieving and holiness; it is God in all his Godness who grieves."[68] The biblical authors are careful to show that this vulnerable God is not overwhelmed or embittered in his grieving; God remains God. Still, God mourns *because* of the rebellion of God's people. "God is like a person who has been rejected not only by his spouse but by his children as well. God suffers the effects of the broken relationship at multiple levels of intimacy. The wounds of God are manifold."[69] Given this rejection and the destructive consequences for Israel that follow, God must continually devise new ways to rescue and redeem the people. "God has absorbed the people's rejection, has reflected upon what it means, and through statements and questions seeks to find a way into the future that will transcend the breach."[70]

Other passages witness to the suffering of God *with* the people. "The God who tearfully allows the judgment to fall does not leave those in the lurch who suffer as a result. God is immediately back on the scene, sharing in the suffering of the people...."[71] Isaiah 54:7–8 is a classic text that articulates God's tender compassion for a people who have suffered the consequences of divine judgment because of their infidelity:

> For a brief moment I abandoned you,
>   but with great compassion I will gather you.
> In overflowing wrath for a moment
>   I hid my face from you,
> but with everlasting love I will have compassion on you,
> says the LORD, your Redeemer.

The Hebrew words used in these texts indicate that God experiences this suffering from the inside. Nevertheless, God's suffering with his people does not mean that God is powerless to transform the situation. God remains on the move to redeem and offer relief to the suffering.[72] Certain passages, such as Jeremiah 48:36, extend this compassion of God to other nations. We read in this text that God "moans for Moab like a flute." Fretheim observes, "That God is represented as mourning over the fate of non-Israelite peoples as well as Israelites demonstrates the breadth of God's care and concern for the sufferers of the world, whoever they might be. Israel has no monopoly on God's empathy."[73]

Fretheim argues that while there is no specific doctrine of atonement in the Hebrew scriptures there are texts that describe God as suffering *for* the people. They depict a God who is "burdened" by the sins of the people. Second Isaiah presents God as speaking this way: "But you have burdened me with your sins; / you have wearied me with your iniquities" (Isa 43:24). Still, God is the One who will blot out Israel's transgressions and forget the sins of the people (43:25). "By bearing the sins of the people over a period of time, God suffers in some sense on their behalf. By holding back on the judgment they deserve, and carrying their sins on his own shoulders, God chooses the road of suffer-ing-for."[74] This divine bearing of the burden of sin makes possible the redemption and new life of the people. "God so gives of self for the sake of the relationship with the people that in some sense God's life can be said to be expended so that Israel's could be continued."[75]

Later theology distinguishes between analogical and metaphori-cal speech about God. It usually assigns biblical statements about God's grief, personal injury, jealousy, and the like to the category of metaphor. Such language is akin to calling God a "rock" or a "mighty fortress." God is not, of course, really a rock, though God is strong and dependable like a rock. In a similar way, classical theism maintains that God does not really grieve, though God cares about God's people. Analogical language about God, on the other hand, predicates something about God that exists in the real order. Naming God as "good" is true, even though God's way of being good infinitely transcends our finite expe-rience of goodness.[76] As biblical scholars, neither Gerstenberger nor Fretheim addresses these later theological distinctions. It appears, how-ever, that they wish to argue that for the Hebrew authors God's suffer-ing with God's people was predicated as belonging to the real order, even though the biblical writers knew that God's way of suffering is distinct from that of creatures. Some of the contemporary authors whom we explore argue that theology should take this biblical witness more seriously and speak of a God who *really* suffers, who is *really* affected by the suffering of people.

Conclusion

This summary of themes in the Hebrew scriptures shows that the various ways of interpreting the causes and meaning of suffering are based upon the fundamental reality of Israel's covenant relationship with God. The people of Israel were convinced that God was directly related to them in kinship or covenant. Thus individual and corporate experiences of suffering were reflected upon in the light of faith in this God who had promised to redeem and to guide his people. The people of Israel viewed God as the transcendent Creator; even more, they were convinced that God had drawn close to them and was involved in every sphere of their lives. There was no aspect of life that was disconnected from their covenant relationship with God.

In the light of this covenant faith, the people of ancient Israel grappled with the meaning of their suffering. They attempted to make sense of suffering. The theory of retribution was a prominent way of interpreting this experience, and it is present in many of the literary genres of the Hebrew Bible. It was based on an awareness of God as sovereign judge and on an honest acknowledgment of the ways in which the people had been unfaithful to their covenant responsibilities. The cry of lament was a profound expression of faith in God's nearness to his people and of trust that their bond with God enabled them to call out to God with complete honesty. In a culture in which sacrifice was a standard part of religious ritual, it was natural for believers to interpret certain instances of suffering as an offering to God that had beneficial effects for the people. The author of the Book of Job knew the traditional interpretations of suffering, especially the theory of retribution, but he was convinced that they were inadequate to explain every form of suffering. This author crafted a text that is complex and ambiguous but that also depicts a God who draws close in the midst of intense suffering. The Job story suggests that communion with God is transformative. Hebrew authors who employed the genre of apocalyptic envisioned the suffering of the people as caused by the enemies of God—both earthly and cosmic agents of evil. They counseled hope in the God who would eventually triumph and, in the meantime, unyielding fidelity to the covenant. Finally, some authors, especially those in the prophetic tradition, spoke of a God who was so closely bonded to the people that God suffered from their rejection and felt their pain. The awesome God is also the vulnerable God.

Discussion Questions: www.paulistpress.com, Online Resources.

2

New Testament
Perspectives on Suffering

Christian perspectives on the mystery of human suffering assume the revelation of God proclaimed in the Hebrew scriptures. The scriptures of the first Christians consisted of the Hebrew Bible, and it was in light of this word that they interpreted the meaning of the sufferings and death of Jesus and their own suffering. Nevertheless, believers in Jesus Christ profess that something entirely new has taken place in his life and ministry, his death and resurrection. The ministry and the destiny of Jesus shine new light on the relationship of God to the human family. This revelation illumines the way Christians think about the presence of God in the midst of suffering and death.

In his treatment of the mystery of suffering, Daniel Harrington discusses the perspectives found in the New Testament under three major headings: Jesus and the kingdom of God; death and resurrection; and suffering for the gospel.[1] I employ these same headings in my overview of New Testament approaches to suffering, supplementing Harrington's discussion with the insights of other scholars. I then examine the Gospel of Mark in greater detail. New Testament scholars conclude that Mark's Gospel was addressed to a community of believers who were grappling with the experience of suffering in light of their faith in Jesus Christ. This Gospel represents only one of several New Testament perspectives on suffering, but it plays a significant role in the theological conversation about God and suffering.

Jesus' Proclamation of the Kingdom of God

Most scholars agree that the major focus of Jesus' public ministry was his proclamation of the kingdom, or reign, of God. While the notion of the kingdom of God was not the only way in which first-century Jews envisioned God's definitive, salvific action, it did hearken back to earlier ideas of God as sovereign ruler, hymned in the psalms and some of the prophets. N. T. Wright observes that by using the language of the reign of God Jesus evoked an entire story line for the Jewish people of his day. His announcement of the kingdom pointed to the longing of Israel for the God of the covenant to come in power and rule the world in the way that God had always intended.[2] In a similar vein, John Meier suggests that the kingdom of God "is meant to conjure up the dynamic notion of God powerfully ruling over his creation, over his people, and over the history of both."[3] The primary meaning of this concept, then, is dynamic rather than spatial. It refers to an activity, that is, God drawing near to establish his rule over creation.

This proclamation of the reign of God assumes that all is not right in God's beloved creation. It presupposes that there are powers active in creation that are distinct from God and opposed to the divine purposes. Jesus' announcement of the kingdom suggests that God's rebellious creation has fallen away from God's righteous rule and come under the domination of evil. "Faithful to his promises and prophecies in the covenant, God is now beginning to assert his rightful claim over his rebellious creatures and will soon establish his rule fully and openly by gathering a scattered Israel back into one holy people."[4] This fall from God's righteous rule has resulted in a creation that is wounded by evil and the intense suffering that results from the presence of evil.

There is an irresolvable tension between the future and present dimensions of Jesus' proclamation of the reign of God. Jesus' message "was focused on a future coming of God to rule as king, a time when he would manifest himself in all his transcendent glory and power to regather and save his sinful but repentant people Israel."[5] This future dimension is evident in the petition "Your kingdom come," found in the prayer that Jesus taught his disciples. The future coming of God would mean the reversal of all unjust oppression and suffering.[6]

At the same time, there is an inescapably present dimension to Jesus' message about the kingdom. A number of sayings and actions of Jesus show that at times he spoke of the reign of God as already present in his ministry.[7] A key verse in this regard is Luke 11:20: "But if it is by the finger of God that I cast out the demons, then the kingdom of God has come to you." When some of the opponents of Jesus suspect that his power to expel demons derives from Beelzebul, the prince of demons, Jesus responds by assuring them that his actions manifest instead the presence of God's rule. "Effectively, Jesus declares his exorcisms to be both manifestations and at least partial realizations of God's coming in power to rule his people in the end time."[8] The famous saying in Luke 17:21 also suggests that the reign of God is already present through the person and ministry of Jesus: "For, in fact, the kingdom of God is among you." Raymond Brown asserts that the careful reader of the New Testament must include both the future and the present dimensions in interpreting the meaning of Jesus' proclamation: "The kingly rule of God was already making itself present in Jesus' person, proclamation, and actions, but the complete and visible manifestation of the kingdom lay in the future and would also be brought about through Jesus, the Son of Man."[9]

Jesus proclaims the reign of God in word and deed. Through his teachings about the Law and his provocative parables, he compels his hearers to reconsider their conception of the ways in which God relates to creation. The hated Samaritan turns out to be the person who acts as neighbor to the Jew left half-dead on the road; workers hired late in the day receive a full day's wage from an uncommonly generous employer; the prayer of the despised tax collector is more acceptable to God than that of the righteous Pharisee; the spurned father runs out of the house and embraces his prodigal son when he spies him from a distance. There was a performative, efficacious quality about the telling of these stories:

> The parables are not simply *information about* the kingdom, but are part of the *means of* bringing it to birth.... They invite

people into the new world that is being created, and warn of dire consequences if the invitation is refused. Jesus' telling of these stories is one of the key ways in which the kingdom breaks in upon Israel, redefining itself as it does so.[10]

Jesus' table fellowship, as well as his acts of healing and exorcism, were intrinsically related to his proclamation of the reign of God. Part of the eschatological imagery of Israel was a great banquet that would be celebrated by the just with God. Jesus made use of this imagery in his parable of the wedding banquet given by the king for his son (Matt 22:1–14; Luke 14:16–24). A vivid memory associated with Jesus' ministry was his meals with those considered to be outside the circle of Jewish orthodoxy, including tax collectors and others known as "sinners" (for example, Mark 2:15–17). The evangelists recount the religious leaders' harsh criticism of Jesus for his behavior in sharing meals with such people. His claim to have authority to forgive sins is sometimes associated with this experience of table fellowship. Jesus' fellowship with tax collectors and sinners was an anticipation of the eschatological banquet in which the gracious mercy of God was already being extended.[11] This sharing of table with the unrighteous, then, has a meaning that is more profound than mere social benevolence. It was an expression of the forgiving and redeeming love of God. Through his welcome of the outcast, Jesus brought them into fellowship with God.

After recounting Jesus' initial proclamation that the kingdom of God has come near, Mark introduces the ministry of Jesus with a breathless account of his healing activity: the cure of a demoniac in the Capernaum synagogue, the healing of Simon's mother-in-law, the cleansing of a leper, and the cure and forgiveness of the paralytic brought to Jesus by his friends (Mark 1:16—2:12). In the midst of this flurry of activity, the evangelist writes, "That evening, at sundown, they brought to him all who were sick or possessed with demons. And the whole city was gathered around the door. And he cured many who were sick with various diseases, and cast out many demons; and he would not permit the demons to speak, because they knew him" (1:32–34). The reader immediately receives the impression that the announcement of the kingdom and what is taking place in these life-giving actions of Jesus are inextricably linked.

Most scholars who sift through the layers of the New Testament to construct a portrait of the historical Jesus conclude that Jesus' actions as a healer and an exorcist are among the most ancient recollections of his ministry. Wolfgang Schrage comments, "Even when one allows for a critical stance and for methodological caution toward the miracle-tradition, which in its style appropriates typical characteristics of form from ancient miracle-stories, there can be no doubt that Jesus healed sick people and drove out demons."[12] John Meier concludes that "various criteria of historicity suggest that the historical Jesus performed certain actions during his public ministry that both he and some of his contemporaries thought were miraculous healings of the sick or infirm."[13]

Jesus' healings and exorcisms did cause people to wonder, to marvel at the power that was displayed in them. When the restored Gerasene demoniac begins to proclaim "how much Jesus had done for him," Mark tells us that "everyone was amazed" (Mark 5:20). But the Gospels make it clear that the dimension of the marvelous was secondary to Jesus' real intent. These deeds are often described in the Gospels as "acts of power" (*dynameis*). They are not intended as external proofs of the coming of the kingdom; rather they are "one of the means by which the kingdom came."[14] When God's reign became present in Jesus, people found life. These acts of power represented Jesus' personal warfare against the forces of evil that drain the life out of people. "The acts of power were weapons Jesus used to reclaim people and the world from the domination of evil. When Jesus healed the sick or resuscitated the dead, he was breaking the Satanic power that manifested itself in illness and death."[15]

What would have been seen in Jesus' mighty works according to the first-century Jewish worldview was the restoration of creation that Israel expected with the advent of God's rule.[16] With respect to the human predicament, this means that the presence of the reign of God in Jesus affects the whole person. It means more than just the salvation of the "spiritual dimension" of the human person. The blind beggar,

Bartimaeus, receives *insight* into who Jesus is and follows him on the road of discipleship, but he is also granted physical *sight* and, presumably, no longer has to beg for a living (Mark 10:46–52). The woman with the hemorrhage experiences salvation in her encounter with Jesus, which includes healing of the malady from which she had suffered for twelve years (Mark 5:25–34). The paralytic receives forgiveness of his sins, but Jesus also empowers him to rise from his mat and walk (Mark 2:1–12). Schrage accentuates this wholeness of body and spirit that the presence of God's reign brings to people: "Jesus cannot be charged with the interiorizing and assignment of a transcendent character to salvation, as is often the one-sided representation of Christianity; on the contrary, he is strongly committed to the view that the liberating power of the rule of God concerns the body as well as the soul."[17]

This brief exploration of Jesus' proclamation of the reign of God shows that the rule of God as disclosed and made present in his public ministry has the effect of alleviating human suffering. It is true that Jesus did not heal everyone in first-century Israel. In his reflection on the question about why Jesus did not cure everyone in need, Harrington says, "His healings were signs pointing toward the fullness of God's kingdom, where there will be no more suffering. But for now, suffering remains part of human existence."[18] Nevertheless, the Gospels suggest that Jesus engages in a kind of mortal combat against all the forces that take life away from people. Schrage puts it succinctly when he states that "Jesus himself was less engaged in interpreting suffering than he was in actively working to overcome it."[19] He proceeds to argue that "Jesus himself not only pointed those who suffered to God's future, but in a comprehensive way stood up to the affliction and misery of this world and in accordance with the holistic view of suffering also brought to man [sic] holistic help and salvation."[20] We will see that contemporary authors like Edward Schillebeeckx, Gustavo Gutiérrez, and Elizabeth Johnson place great emphasis on Jesus' proclamation of the reign of God in their reflections on the mystery of human suffering.

The Death and Resurrection of Jesus

The Death of Jesus

Christians make the scandalous claim that one who entered into the uttermost depths of human suffering, who was brutally executed as a criminal, is the savior of humanity. They even confess him to be the Son of God. When believers search for the meaning of human suffering and the presence of God in the midst of the experience of suffering, they inevitably turn to the destiny of this one they call the Christ. In his study of the theme of suffering in the New Testament, Schrage says that "it is above all *his* suffering and dying that is the theme of the New Testament. The very one who is appointed by God to put an end to all suffering is involved in the deepest distress and becomes the sufferer in a unique sense."[21] At the same time, the early Christian community reflected on the sufferings of Jesus from the vantage point of their faith in Christ as risen, as brought to new life with God and to victory over death.

New Testament scholars reflect carefully on what we can say about Jesus' approach to his own death. Opposition to the teaching and actions of Jesus arose relatively early in his ministry. Mark places this mounting hostility near the beginning of Jesus' public ministry in Galilee, suggesting that the religious leaders were already conspiring to find a way to get rid of him (Mark 3:6). It is notoriously difficult to reconstruct the precise charges that were brought against Jesus and the exact sequence of events that led to his condemnation and death. But it is apparent that Jesus' words and deeds provoked a negative reaction from some devout Jews and that he proved to be a threat to the religious establishment. Jesus' final journey to Jerusalem brought this opposition to a head. If there are genuine historical events that lie behind the Gospel stories of Jesus' entry into Jerusalem and his action in the Temple, such actions would have elicited further opposition at the time of the Passover. The entry into the ancient Davidic capital, even if much more modest in form than the way it is presented in the Gospels, would have meant that Jesus was making a symbolic claim to messianic status. The "cleansing of the Temple" may have been "an ominous prophetic sign that the present Temple was about to be destroyed to make way for a new and perfect one."[22] Such actions would have been particularly provocative to the priestly aristocracy of Jesus' day.

While some New Testament scholars have argued that we can know very little about Jesus' approach to his death because the Gospels reflect later interpretations of this death by the Christian community, most mainline exegetes claim that we can draw at least some general conclusions about his attitude.[23] Such conclusions do not assume that Jesus had a detailed foreknowledge of future events in his life. The affirmation of a unique human consciousness in Jesus, a consciousness of his unique relationship with the Father and of his own mission, does not necessarily imply that for Jesus life was like seeing a movie for the second time. Limitations to Jesus' knowledge and foreknowledge were precisely a part of his being human and not an imperfection from which he should have been preserved.[24] The Jesus who was human as well as divine had a real human history. This means that he, too, had to journey into the future of his own life with trust in the God he called "Abba."

Apart from the question of special knowledge, Jesus must have realized the danger that was mounting in his life. The death of John the Baptist would have caused him to reflect upon the lethal rejection of one who spoke God's word and with whom Jesus had been associated. Near the end of Jesus' life the prospect of a violent death must have become even clearer. Meier notes that Jesus must have foreseen the real possibility of violent death when visiting the capital city at Passover.[25] "Despite his efforts, whole cities had rejected his message (Matt 11:20–24 par). Herod Antipas, Pontius Pilate, the high priest and the Sadduccean party, the scribes and the pious lay movement of Pharisees all had their varied reasons for being opposed to Jesus....."[26] Moreover, there is evidence that first-century Jewish piety increasingly viewed the prophets of Israel as rejected figures who were often martyred. Raymond Brown concludes that we should not undervalue the general agreement of the Gospel tradition that Jesus was convinced beforehand that, although his life would be taken from him violently, God would ultimately vindicate him. In addition to Jesus' consideration of the death of John the Baptist, his reflection on figures such as Jeremiah and the suffering servant of Deutero-Isaiah would have inspired such a conviction.[27]

In discussing Jesus' approach to his death, Gerald O'Collins appeals to the conduct of his public ministry. The Gospel descriptions of Jesus' ministry suggest that "he consistently behaved as one utterly subject to his Father's will and completely available for the service of all those who needed mercy and healing."[28] This same commitment to service characterized Jesus' attitude about his death. "A straight line led from his serving ministry to his suffering death."[29] Meier argues along similar lines, pointing out that "as a person lives, so that person dies."[30] Jesus' message and behavior consisted of radical love for God and neighbor. His life was marked by humble service to and sacrifice for others. And this message and praxis were grounded in profound confidence in and surrender to the God he called "Abba." "Jesus was indeed the 'man for others' whose whole life interprets his death—and vice versa."[31] Thus, we can safely presume that he approached his death in the same way in which he approached his life and ministry—in a spirit of generous, faithful service to others and of reverent trust in his Father.

While affirming the theological significance of the passion predictions found in the Gospels (Mark 8:31–32; 9:30–32; 10:32–34 and par), New Testament scholars are cautious about attributing to the historical Jesus these statements about the impending suffering and resurrection of the Son of Man, at least in their detailed form. For one thing, such detailed predictions would make the utter confusion of the disciples during and after Jesus' passion difficult to understand. Nevertheless, as Brown points out, this pattern of three predictions is present quite early in the Jesus tradition, antedating the Gospels.[32] There is also a distinct pattern of three predictions found in the Gospel of John, with a more general reference to the "lifting up" of the Son of Man (John 3:14; 8:28; 12:32–34). At least at the early level of the Jesus tradition there was a pattern of three prophecies about the suffering and victory of the Son of Man that were phrased in the language of the Hebrew scriptures.[33]

Other Gospel texts may offer more direct insight into Jesus' attitude toward his death. Meier mentions Matthew 23:37–39, where Jesus excoriates the Jerusalem that has rejected him, rebuking the city with the reminder that it has a history of killing the prophets who were sent to it. In the famous Markan passage about the ambition of James and John, Jesus refers to the "cup" that he will drink and the "baptism" with which he will be baptized (Mark 10:35–40). Meier asserts that "the vague reference to Jesus' sufferings, the affirmation of Jesus' impotence to grant places in the kingdom, and the bad light in which James the protomartyr among the Twelve is placed argue in favor of historicity."[34] Matthew and Mark also recount Jesus' stinging rebuke of Peter after Peter rebels against the idea of Jesus' suffering (Mark 8:32–33). Even if the passion prediction itself bears the marks of later reflection by the church, it is not likely that the later church would have created this strong reprimand of Peter by Jesus.

In a study of the Last Supper narratives, Meier also finds evidence of Jesus' approach to his death.[35] After examining 1 Corinthians 11:23–26, the three Synoptic narratives, and John 6:51–58, Meier concludes that the historical Jesus probably did not pronounce any of the exact formulas over the bread and cup that we find in the New Testament. His words at the Last Supper were most likely a simpler form that was later expanded upon by New Testament writers, expansions that reflected the liturgical traditions of different Christian communities. At the same time, Meier thinks that Jesus did speak of the bread as his body (or his flesh) and the cup as the covenant in his blood. The designation of the bread as Jesus' body refers to "the whole person, in all that person's vulnerability and mortality."[36] This sharing of the bread indicated that Jesus went to his death "giving his flesh, his whole self, his very life, even unto suffering and death, to bring about the restoration of Israel in the end time."[37] The one cup that is shared mediates the covenant that Moses sealed at Sinai with the blood of bulls, but which Jesus is about to renew and bring to consummation with his own blood. "In the face of death, Jesus celebrates this unique ritual at his farewell meal to proclaim his own faith that God his Father would not let Jesus' work be destroyed, that somehow God would integrate even Jesus' death into his life's work, yes, that God would vindicate Jesus beyond death and bring him to the eschatological banquet."[38]

The Resurrection

The early Christian community reflected on the meaning of Jesus' suffering and death in light of its faith in the risen Christ. The tradition about Jesus' resurrection is expressed in three main forms in the New Testament: confessional or creedal statements (for example, 1 Thess 4:14; Rom 10:9; 1 Cor 15:3–8), stories about the empty tomb, and narratives about appearances of the risen Christ.[39] The traditions about the finding of the empty tomb and the appearances of the risen Jesus vary considerably and cannot be blended into a single, uniform account. These narratives are more divergent than the accounts of Jesus' passion. The Gospel stories of the empty tomb are unanimous in reporting that women found Jesus' grave empty two days after his crucifixion. But they vary in many other details, including the message they receive and their reaction to it. Traditions about the appearances of the risen Jesus are attached to two distinct locales: Jerusalem and Galilee. Neither of these two traditions shows any awareness of a tradition of appearances in the other location.[40] There are other differences as well. Raymond Brown argues that each tradition in the Gospels centers on an all-important appearance to the Twelve in which they are commissioned for their mission. What was essential for the early Christian community was the testimony that a well-known apostolic witness had seen the risen Jesus.[41]

New Testament scholars highlight the enduring significance of the tradition about the resurrection cited by Paul in his First Letter to the Corinthians (1 Cor 15:3–8).[42] Paul uses the technical terminology of "received" and "handed on" in this passage, signifying a critical message of salvation. Whether this tradition was originally formulated in Aramaic or in Greek is a disputed question among biblical scholars, but its antiquity is acknowledged.[43] It is somewhat fixed in its language and has a definite structure. Moreover, it is the direct expression of one who claims to have been an eyewitness of an appearance of the risen Lord.

> For I handed on to you as of first importance what I in turn had received: that Christ died for our sins in accordance with the scriptures, and that he was buried, and that he was

61

> raised on the third day in accordance with the scriptures,
> and that he appeared to Cephas, then to the twelve. Then
> he appeared to more than five hundred brothers and sisters
> at one time, most of whom are still alive, though some have
> died. Then he appeared to James, then to all the apostles.
> Last of all, as to one untimely born, he appeared also to me.

In this formula the title *Christ* is used almost as a proper name. The death of the Messiah is understood to be "for our sins." His death is not simply a brute fact but is confessed as having salvific significance. Jesus' death and resurrection are understood to be "according to the scriptures." This is a general reference that views scripture as a unity[44] and envisions the destiny of Jesus as integral to the revelation of God's saving will. Explicit mention of Jesus' burial confirms the reality of Jesus' death. Reference to the resurrection is stated in the passive voice: "he was raised" (*egēgertai*). This is a respectful divine passive; it signifies that the resurrection of the Christ is an act of God. "On the third day" is applied to the resurrection itself. This phrase may have a temporal reference, or it may have a theological meaning that denotes the moment of decisive divine action, as in Hosea 6:1–2.[45] The term translated as "appeared" (*ōphthē*) is used in the Greek translation of the Old Testament to speak of theophanies: manifestations of God (for example, Gen 12:7, 26:24; Exod 6:3; 1 Kgs 3:5, 9:2). Raymond Collins observes that "the use of this verb form in the creedal formula indicates that the appearance of Jesus inaugurates a new era of salvation."[46] This word connotes an initiative from outside: the risen Christ lets himself be seen by chosen witnesses. This experience establishes faith in Jesus' resurrection while also confirming the ecclesial status of the recipients.

Christian theologians offer diverse interpretations of the confession "Jesus is risen."[47] There are, however, certain affirmations that are foundational for Christian belief in the resurrection. First, this confession refers to an event that affected Jesus personally. Jesus himself has been raised up by the Father; he lives on in a transformed state. "His human life or total embodied history rose with him and was transfigured into a final mode of existence."[48] Second, the New Testament, through a variety of literary genres, speaks of something definite taking place after Jesus' death in and through which the presence of the risen Jesus was revealed to certain followers. There are elements of continuity and discontinuity in these accounts: it is truly Jesus of Nazareth who has been raised up, but now he exists in a transformed state. Third, the disciples' experience of the risen Christ is spoken of using the language of sight, though this experience involves a distinctive kind of seeing. It is different from ordinary empirical seeing. This is a perception that involves faith and is not objectively available to a neutral bystander. Walter Kasper calls it a "believing seeing."[49] At the same time, it is an experience that leads to faith and generates a whole new perspective on reality. Fourth, as John Galvin points out, the experience of the risen Christ should be related to Jesus' entire life and message.[50] Just as one cannot understand the meaning and significance of Jesus' death apart from his life and message, neither can the meaning and significance of his resurrection be understood apart from his public life. Through his abiding trust in the Father, Jesus gave grounds for hope that he and his mission would be vindicated.

Gerald O'Collins elucidates the revelatory significance of Jesus' resurrection.[51] The experience of Christ risen from the dead provided new insight into the person of Jesus, especially the uniqueness of his relationship with God. If Jesus has been raised up and exalted, then God is ultimately revealed in Jesus.[52] The resurrection revealed that in Jesus the kingdom of God had been inaugurated, even though its fullness was still to come. It also showed that Jesus' death as an act of loving service had been accepted by the Father. The raising of Jesus from the dead in anticipation of the universal resurrection manifested the universal significance of Jesus' person, message, and saving work. This conviction soon led to the Gentile mission. "In short, the resurrection fully and finally revealed the meaning and truth of Christ's life, person, work and death. It set a divine seal on Jesus and his ministry."[53]

The resurrection of the crucified Jesus also led believers to "a fresh understanding of God."[54] First, the vindication of Jesus in the resurrection discloses that God can be found in the suffering one, even in one undergoing a shameful and horrific death by crucifixion. "But with the resurrection the disclosive power of the cross comes into play, and shows that the weak, the despised, and the suffering—those who become fools for God's sake—can serve as special mediators of revelation (and salvation)."[55] Second, the experience of the risen Christ suggests that the God of life proclaimed by Jesus in his ministry is the One who brings life out of death. This is God's signature activity. As Paul would argue in his letters, God is the Resurrector, the one who raised Jesus and who will raise all the dead.[56] Finally, this experience proved to be the decisive manifestation of the character of God's love.

> In the story of Jesus' crucifixion and resurrection, Christians perceived the initiative of self-giving love which led God to be personally involved in our sinful history (Rom. 8:3)— even to the extent of an appalling death on the cross: "God shows his love for us in that while we were yet sinners Christ died for us" (Rom. 5:8).[57]

The crucified-and-risen Jesus became for Christians the love of God made flesh.

Suffering for the Gospel

One major New Testament motif related to the experience of suffering highlights the cost of following Jesus. The one who summoned his disciples to take up their crosses and follow him to Jerusalem is a messiah who invites believers to share in his suffering. In Luke's version of this summons, this bearing of the cross is a daily experience (9:23), including not only extraordinary moments of persecution but also the ordinary hardships that accompany faithful discipleship. Those who strive to bear witness to Jesus and the kingdom he proclaimed can expect to experience misunderstanding and direct opposition in this world. They will suffer for the gospel. This theme emerges in virtually every New Testament text. Here we explore its presence in the writings of Paul, the Letter to the Hebrews, and the First Letter of Peter.

Paul

Paul speaks directly and boldly about the sufferings that he has endured as an apostle. He usually thinks of his trials as an opportunity for closer union with Christ and as a source of benefit for the church. For Paul, Jesus' suffering and dying have an inclusive, prototypical significance.[58] The sufferings of the apostle, as well as those of other believers, participate in and are modeled on those of the Lord. At the beginning of his Letter to the Philippians, Paul reflects on the experience of being imprisoned for his apostolic work. He wants the community at Philippi to know that what has happened to him "has actually helped to spread the gospel, so that it has become known throughout the whole imperial guard and to everyone else" that his imprisonment is "for Christ" (1:12). This apparent setback has had the effect of strengthening other Christians who have been given confidence "to speak the word with greater boldness and without fear" (1:14). Paul does not explore the reasons for the presence of suffering in his life; rather, he focuses on the blessings that God has brought about as a result of it.

The theme of suffering for the gospel is central to Paul's correspondence with the Christians at Corinth. In response to those in the community who trumpet their own spiritual gifts and lay claim to special knowledge, Paul develops his theology of the cross. The divine wisdom revealed in the crucified and risen Christ is foolishness and a stumbling block to both Jews and Gentiles. Paul is convinced, however, that "God's foolishness is wiser than human wisdom, and God's weakness is stronger than human strength" (1 Cor 1:25). In his Second Letter to the Corinthians, Paul applies this wisdom of the cross to his own ministry and to the experiences of the Christians to whom he writes.[59] In the introductory blessing found in this letter he testifies to his participation in both the sufferings and the consolation of Christ: "For just as the sufferings of Christ are abundant for us, so also our consolation is abundant through Christ" (1:5). He reminds the Corinthians that they experience the same consolation when they patiently endure their own sufferings. Commenting on this passage, Jan Lambrecht remarks, "Paul understands what happened to him in a thoroughly apostolic way. He accepts his suffering as well as his consolation in view of their efficacy for other Christians."[60] The theme of participation is sounded again when Paul speaks of the power of God at work through his weakness. He likens himself to a "clay jar" that bears a treasure: the treasure of the gospel of Christ (4:7–12). Of himself and his coworkers Paul observes, "We are afflicted in every way, but not crushed; perplexed, but not driven to despair; persecuted, but not forsaken; struck down but not destroyed" (4:9). The dying of Jesus continues to be made visible in him as he experiences these afflictions. But his participation in the death of Jesus has the effect of making the life of Jesus visible as well. "A kind of ontological oneness with Christ is postulated by Paul" as he reflects on the suffering he has experienced as an apostle.[61]

These reflections reach a climax in Paul's famous "fool's speech" (2 Cor 11:16–33). In response to other missionaries who have questioned Paul's apostolic credentials, Paul enumerates a long list of hardships he has undergone in the service of the gospel. These experiences of apparent "weakness" have actually become opportunities for the power of God to be revealed. These are Paul's apostolic credentials. He refers to an extraordinary vision of God that he received where he "was caught up into Paradise and heard things that are not to be told, that no mortal is permitted to repeat" (12:4). He prefers, however, to focus on his weaknesses, mentioning even the "thorn in the flesh" that God has not sought fit to remove. This mysterious affliction, whatever it was, is a weakness through which the power of God is revealed. Paul concludes this extraordinary personal testimony by extolling the power of God made evident in weakness: "Therefore I am content with weaknesses, insults, hardships, persecutions, and calamities for the sake of Christ; for whenever I am weak, then I am strong" (12:10). In reflecting on the sufferings he has endured, Paul has applied his theology of the cross to his own life. As it happened with the cross of Jesus, God's power and wisdom continue to be revealed through weakness and foolishness.

Hebrews

The Letter to the Hebrews, the author of which is unknown, is an extended sermon addressed to a community of Christians who were experiencing suffering for their faith. Harrington suggests that it may have been written for Jewish Christians in Rome during the 60s of the first century.[62] The author of this letter writes to encourage believers to remain steadfast in their faith in Christ despite the reality of opposition from forces outside the community. This experience of hostility may well have pertained especially to increasing tension with the Jewish community.[63] It appears that the resolve of these believers was weakening and that they may have been tempted to return to their previous religious practice. Harold Attridge explains that amid the threat of persecution the author "responds with stern warnings and his exhortations to faithful discipleship." With regard to the problem of waning commitment to faith in Jesus, the writer "proposes a deepened understanding of the community's confession that will inspire covenant fidelity."[64] In order to respond to the situation of this community, this biblical author must address the experience of suffering that the community has undergone as a result of their faith in Jesus. He does this by relating their suffering to that of Jesus, to whom he refers as the great High Priest.

In imagery that resembles the hymn in Philippians 2:6–11, the author of Hebrews refers to the abasement and exaltation of Jesus. Commenting on Psalm 8, he says that "we do see Jesus, who for a little while was made lower than the angels, now crowned with glory and honor because of the suffering of death, so that by the grace of God he might taste death for everyone" (2:9). Jesus is the high priest who made "a sacrifice of atonement for the sins of the people" (2:17). "The central theological message of Hebrews is that Jesus Christ is both the perfect sacrifice for sins and the great high priest who willingly offered himself for sins."[65] The death of Jesus is an offering for others and an offering for sins, that is, it is a vicarious and expiatory sacrifice.

In the course of this description of Jesus' humiliation and exaltation, the author makes an extraordinary claim: "It was fitting that God, for whom and through whom all things exist, in bringing many children to glory, should make the pioneer of their salvation perfect through sufferings" (2:10). First of all, Jesus is envisioned as the pioneer (*archēgos*) in salvation. This description evokes the notion of one who leads others on the journey toward a new land.[66] Second, Jesus is depicted as being brought to perfection through the experience of suffering. Attridge explains that the language of perfection employed here does not refer to moral or cultic perfecting. Rather, it is a vocational process by which Jesus is made complete or fit for his office as high priest. "Through his suffering, Christ becomes the perfect model, who has learned obedience (5:8), and the perfect intercessor, merciful and faithful."[67] The author of Hebrews wants his addressees to know that in their suffering they are following a "pioneer" who was brought to fulfillment by experiencing death and is able to help them in the trials they are undergoing. "The word of encouragement that the first readers of Hebrews needed to hear was that they belonged to a community of suffering people and that in suffering Jesus was their pioneer and leader."[68]

Further along in this letter, the author refers to Jesus as "the pioneer and perfecter of our faith, who for the sake of joy that was set before him endured the cross, disregarding its shame, and has taken his seat at the right hand of God" (12:2). Employing an athletic metaphor, he exhorts believers to keep their eyes on this pioneer as they run the race of faith. The biblical writer expounds on this call to perseverance in faith by conceiving of suffering as God's discipline of his beloved sons and daughters. The notion of suffering as divine discipline is found in the wisdom literature and in 2 Maccabees.[69] The author of Hebrews adduces Proverbs 3:11–12 to support this interpretation:

> My child, do not regard lightly the discipline of the LORD,
>   or lose heart when you are punished by him;
> for the LORD disciplines those whom he loves,
>   and chastises every child whom he accepts. (12:5–6)

The members of this community have not yet resisted to the point of shedding their blood (12:4). They are exhorted to understand their suffering as the discipline of God, who like a caring parent "disciplines us for our good, in order that we may share his holiness" (12:10). The author then challenges these believers to continue on the journey of faith with strength and determination.

The interpretation of suffering as divine discipline is, of course, an ambiguous one. It is simply one interpretation among many others.

If all suffering were understood in this way, one could ascribe to God the worst forms of evil that human beings inflict upon one another. It appears that the author of Hebrews is appealing to this biblical theme out of a sense of the urgency he feels to strengthen these believers in their commitment to Christ. Juliana Casey observes that the author "is attempting to make sense out of suffering and to give a positive meaning to something which is experienced as decidedly negative." He tells a community possibly threatened with persecution and tempted to give up that Jesus has been there before them; "it hurts now but will benefit us in the end." Although his arguments are somewhat weak and unconvincing, his anxiety "on behalf of the community pervades this section and witnesses to his own urgent need to encourage one another as the Day draws near (10:25)."[70]

First Peter

The author of the First Letter of Peter also writes to Christians who are undergoing hardship for the gospel and facing the challenge of integrating their experience of suffering into their faith in Jesus Christ. While this letter may be the New Testament's most exuberant book, pulsating with joy, hope, and optimism, it also dwells on the question of suffering, that of Jesus and the Christian, "with unparalleled single-mindedness."[71]

The Christians to whom this author wrote lived in a broad area of northern Asia Minor (1:1–2). They are addressed as "exiles" (1:1) and "aliens" (2:11). It seems that the suffering these believers were undergoing involved, not systematic persecution by the Roman state, but the social ostracism and alienation inflicted upon adherents of this new and suspect religion, perhaps the ridicule and oppression that a dominant culture can inflict on a minority.[72]

The author begins his letter by recalling the good news of the resurrection of Jesus and the experience of new life given to those baptized in Christ. He reminds the community that God in his mercy "has given us a new birth into a living hope through the resurrection of Jesus Christ from the dead" (1:3–4). They can find meaning in the sufferings of Christ and in their own sufferings because of their faith in the resurrection. He exhorts these Christians to keep their eyes focused on the future, to look toward "a salvation ready to be revealed in the last time" (1:5). The author clearly believes that the end of history is imminent and thus that suffering and injustice will soon be overcome.

The theme of suffering as a purifying force is prominent in First Peter. The writer tells his audience, "For a little while you have had to suffer various trials, so that the genuineness of your faith—being more precious than gold that, though perishable, is tested by fire—may be found to result in praise and glory and honor when Jesus Christ is revealed" (1:6–7). The notion of suffering as a trial was part of the wisdom tradition of the Hebrew scriptures (for example, Wis 3:5–6). The purifying effect of suffering is one of the reasons that Christians can maintain a spirit of joy throughout their endurance of hardship. Their faith is becoming more authentic—more radiant—by means of this experience.

In addressing the reality of suffering, the author of First Peter also articulates a spirituality of Christian witness. He applies this in a particular way to the afflictions endured by slaves and by the wives of non-Christian husbands, the two groups of believers who were the most vulnerable to abuse. He exhorts them to endure their suffering in a way that will give testimony to their faith in Christ. The believer must witness to his or her faith by doing good, knowing that such conduct may lead to unjust suffering, as it did for Jesus. Indeed Jesus is presented as the true exemplar of faith in adversity: "When he was abused, he did not return abuse; when he suffered, he did not threaten; but he entrusted himself to the one who judges justly" (2:23). In extolling the conduct of Jesus in his passion, the writer appeals to the Suffering Servant of Isaiah: "He committed no sin, / and no deceit was found in his mouth" (1 Pet 2:22; Isa 53:9).

In the final section of First Peter, the author reminds these Christians that, in following Jesus, it should be no surprise to them that they would be involved in suffering. As he does throughout the letter, he emphasizes that it is not just any suffering that is worthwhile, but the suffering that results from doing good as believers in Christ. He reprises the theme of the joy and hope that arises from looking forward to the eschaton: "But rejoice insofar as you are sharing Christ's sufferings, so that you may also be glad and shout for joy when his glory is revealed" (4:13). The language of "sharing Christ's sufferings" represents an intensification of association with Christ that goes beyond that of imitation.[73] Through their suffering, believers participate in the reality of Christ and share in his redemptive work of bringing the world to glorify God.

The concentration on the passion of Jesus is the key to the message of First Peter: "The author lingers over Jesus' agonizing struggle from death to life because this is the decisive pattern of all Christian existence, indeed of all human existence."[74] This biblical writer does not command flight from the hostile world in which these believers are living but exhorts them to remain active in the world, offering credible witness to the faith and hope that is in them (3:15–16). The author does not speculate as to why such righteous conduct should lead to suffering in the world. He accepts the stark reality of the world as it is, which includes the hostility of many to the gospel and to the kind of good deeds exemplified by Christ. He simply encourages these Christians to persevere in their trust in God and to link their own experience of suffering with that of Christ.

The Gospel of Mark

The three themes discussed in this chapter—Jesus' proclamation of the reign of God, the death and resurrection of Jesus, and suffering for the gospel—are integrated in a compelling manner in the Gospel of Mark. This evangelist, apparently the first to produce a Gospel, grapples with the mystery of suffering and death in his proclamation of the good news. He faces the reality of suffering head-on: the suffering of Jesus and that of his disciples.

Setting of the Gospel

There are differing views among New Testament scholars concerning the setting of this Gospel. It has traditionally been associated with the Christian community living in Rome after the persecution under Nero. There is substantial evidence that this Roman community faced persecution, brutal executions, and intracommunity betrayals after the great fire of 64 CE, which Nero blamed on the Christians.[75] Other scholars argue that the Gospel was written for a community that was located farther to the east, in Syria or Palestine. They speculate that the Christians for whom Mark wrote were adversely affected by the Jewish revolt against the Romans in 66–70 CE.[76]

The common denominator among these divergent theories is the conviction that Mark addressed his Gospel to a community that had been exposed to the pain and tragedy of human history. Whether it involved the violent oppression of Christians in Rome under Nero or the hardships imposed on believers who lived in closer proximity to the Jewish revolt, Mark's community knew suffering and upheaval first-hand. They had experienced the difficulties of discipleship and the reality of betrayal (see Mark 13:9–13) as well as the terrible divisions that are caused by such failure. In the face of this suffering, Mark skillfully interweaves his description of Christology and discipleship throughout the Gospel. For Mark, coming to know who Jesus really is and coming to know what it means to follow him go hand in hand. In fact, it is only in and through the following of Jesus that one understands what kind of messiah he is.

Jesus and the Reign of God

In the first half of the Gospel, Mark depicts Jesus as the herald of the kingdom of God.[77] The initial words of Jesus form the overarching context for the public ministry recounted by the evangelist: "The time is fulfilled, and the kingdom of God has come near; repent and believe in the good news" (1:14–15). Mark then describes the flurry of activity that comprises the first "day" of Jesus' public ministry. On the second day of his ministry, Jesus encounters a leper. This is a scene filled with divine power and raw human emotion. This man is an outcast with a ravaged body and no future. The depth of his need is evident in the way he approaches Jesus: he comes to him begging for help, kneels at his feet, and utters a request filled with trust. Mark tells us that Jesus was "moved with pity" (1:41). This phrase translates a Greek participle (*splanchnistheis*) the root of which "designates the seat of affective feeling and emotion (our 'guts'), and is often translated 'heart.'"[78] Jesus experiences a visceral reaction in this encounter; the plight of this suffering man moves him at the deepest part of his being. He then does the unthinkable in reaching out to touch this leper, thereby incurring ritual defilement. Despite the fact that he has violated Jewish laws of purity, Jesus orders the leper to obey the prescriptions of the Law by showing himself to the priests and offering for his cleansing what Moses had prescribed. In this story "the humanity and compassion of Jesus and the experience of freedom that the healed man enjoys are the main centers of attention."[79]

Mark wants his readers to know that the kingdom of God announced by Jesus is beginning to be present now.[80] God is acting in a decisive way, drawing close to his people. In this divine action the powers of evil that drain people of life are directly confronted.

> Through Jesus' mighty deeds, then, the kingdom of God invades Galilee and displaces Satan's rule. By recounting Jesus' powerful deeds, the Markan narrator enhances his initial christological portrait of Jesus. He portrays Jesus as someone who teaches with authority (*exousia*; 1:21–22, 27), for not only does Jesus proclaim that the kingdom of God is at hand but he effects its presence by casting out demons and healing the sick.[81]

People in need—those who have been deprived of life—experience restoration to life when they encounter this Jesus who makes the gracious rule of God present.

A Crucified Messiah

It is against the backdrop of Jesus' proclamation of the kingdom that Mark portrays the mystery of death and resurrection. While this evangelist clearly affirms the vindication of Jesus in the resurrection (16:1–8), the shadow of the cross dominates the Gospel. "Perhaps the special feature of Mark's account is his emphasis on the *passion* side of the death-resurrection schema."[82] This emphasis becomes clear in the gripping conflict stories found in 2:1—3:6, depicting incidents that take place early in Jesus' ministry. These controversies arise from actions taken by Jesus and his disciples: his healing and forgiveness of the paralytic, with the ensuing controversy over the authority to forgive sins; his dining with Levi and "many tax collectors and sinners" (2:15); disputes about fasting and about the disciples plucking grain on the sabbath; and Jesus' cure of a man with a withered hand in the synagogue on the sabbath. Indeed, the account of the cure of the man with the withered hand has the effect of underscoring Jesus' intent and authority. Only at this moment does Jesus show anger toward his opponents, and only here do they conspire to destroy him. Calling this disabled man to the front of the synagogue, Jesus poses a critical question: "Is it lawful to do good or to do harm on the sabbath, to save life or to kill?" (3:4). Grieved at the silence of the congregation, Jesus cures the man simply by telling him to stretch out his hand. Jesus reveals that the God of the sabbath is One who offers healing to people in need; God is the One who saves life. This revelation, however, arouses the hostility of those who are unwilling to accept the proclamation of the kingdom.

Situated within the context of Jesus' ministry, Mark presents the cross not as a passive fate that Jesus simply endures, but as an active symbol. Jesus takes up his cross. His death becomes the ultimate expression of his commitment to give life to others. "The Jesus of Mark's Gospel is no mere victim, passively accepting an unjust death. He 'takes up his cross,' not by morbidly choosing death, but by choosing a way of life that would ultimately clash with those who could not see Jesus' way as God's way."[83] This insight is of critical importance for any evaluation of the theme of suffering in the Gospel. It places the emphasis on Jesus as the one who came to offer salvation from God. If the passion of Jesus is disconnected from his life-giving ministry, one can end with a distorted notion of the meaning of the cross. Edward Schillebeeckx, along with other contemporary theologians, emphasizes this point. Such distortions are sometimes implicit in accounts of Jesus' death as a redemptive sacrifice. The Abba-God to whom Jesus entrusts himself in Gethsemane (14:36) is the same God who in the ministry and person of Jesus was granting freedom and life to people in need of it.

The turning point of the Gospel is Peter's confession of Jesus as Messiah (8:27–31) and the subsequent journey to Jerusalem. The second half of the Gospel narrative is dominated by the mystery of the cross, beginning with a central section that features Jesus predicting his imminent rejection and suffering three times (8:31–32; 9:30–32; 10:32–34). It is by design that Mark frames the center of his Gospel with two stories of healing from blindness (8:22–26; 10:45–52). These stories are about physical healings, but they are also symbolic of that spiritual sight that is necessary to grasp the true identity of Jesus. Peter's response to the question about who Jesus is—"You are the Messiah"—exhibits an initial burst of insight into the identity of Jesus. But his understanding proves to be inadequate, because as soon as Jesus begins to speak about his rejection Peter objects. The narrative immediately moves from the identification of Jesus as Messiah to his self-designation as Son of Man. The response of Jesus to the ambition of James and John expresses the meaning of this shift in identification most forcefully: "For the Son of Man came not to be served but to serve, and to give his life in ransom for many" (10:45). "In effect, the Gospel of Mark redefines messiahship in terms of suffering, death and resurrection. It replaces the royal Davidic messiah who defeats Israel's enemies in this age with a messiah who must fulfill his destiny as the Son of Man."[84]

Mark's account of the passion of Jesus has an uncompromising and even stark quality to it. Though the evangelist does not linger over the physical aspects of Jesus' sufferings, he does portray Jesus as one who is plunged into the very depths of human suffering. Jesus exemplifies the prayer of lament in Gethsemane (14:32–42). "The evangelist presents Jesus as an example of biblical faith, a tormented child of God in love with life and fearful of death, without support except for the bedrock of God's fidelity."[85] The Jesus who had asked James and John, "Are you able to drink the cup that I drink?" now asks his Abba-God that the cup be removed from him. "The raw honesty and stunning humanness of such a prayer is totally within the great tradition of the Jewish lament."[86] In the end, however, Jesus' "Not what I want but what you want" becomes an expression of the commitment to the will of the Father that has suffused his ministry. Donald Senior captures this dynamic well:

> Mark leaves no doubt about the fierce commitment of Jesus, the beloved Son, to the will of God. The Gethsemane prayer is a lament but through the choked voice of the prayer is expressed the tenacious dedication of Jesus to his mission of compassion and service to the point of death (10:45). The Son of Man would drink the cup because in the baffling paradox of God's will, this was the way.[87]

Mark's depiction of Jesus' death (15:33–41) is also sobering in its realism. Jesus is entirely alone. At his betrayal in the garden, Mark tells us that all the disciples left him and fled (14:50). The last spoken words of Peter before the death of Jesus are, "I do not know this man you are talking about" (14:71). On the cross, Jesus is taunted by passersby, the religious leaders, and the criminals who have been crucified alongside him. Mark depicts Jesus as uttering the prayer of lament found in Psalm 22: "My God, my God why have you forsaken me?" (15:34). He dies with "a loud cry" (15:37). Senior highlights the boldness of this Markan description of the crucifixion:

> Mark's description of the instant of death is raw and stunning....Although various attempts have been made to find in these expressions some direct theological significance such as the "cry" of the Just One in Psalm 22, or a victory shout or even an act of exorcism, it seems preferable to allow the words to have their unadorned brutality. The other evangelists all soften this moment, giving Jesus in death a greater sense of control....But for Mark Jesus dies without such control: he screams and expires. The torments of the Just One have crossed the final boundary....No New Testament text more boldly expresses the reality of Jesus' humanity or the manner of his dying.[88]

Contemporary theologians disagree in their interpretation of the cry of abandonment in Mark's description of the crucifixion. Some speak of Jesus as experiencing real abandonment by the Father. Others argue that the articulation of the first line of this psalm (Psalm 22) implies the praying of the entire psalm, which concludes with an expression of trust and thanksgiving. While it is impossible to determine whether these were the actual words of the dying Jesus, it is clear that an ancient Christian tradition associated Jesus' death with Psalm 22.[89] Through this depiction of Jesus on the cross, Mark portrays Jesus as the embodiment of the suffering Just One of the Hebrew scriptures (for example, Wis 3:1–13). Within the Jewish theology of the Just One and in the overall context of Mark's Gospel, these words represent a prayer of trust, not of despair or bitterness. But this prayer of trust is expressed through a lament. "In Mark's account, Jesus dies in agony, a wordless scream on his lips. Jesus' trust in God will not be broken, but Mark allows the fierce assault of death to be felt."[90]

At the moment of Jesus' death, however, the vindication of which he had spoken (14:25) begins to be manifested. The curtain of the Temple sanctuary is torn in two, "indicating that in Jesus' death God has opened definitively the way between heaven and earth through Jesus' death on the cross."[91] And the centurion, the captain of the execution team, confesses, "Truly this man was God's Son!" (15:39). The centurion's affirmation is the one most correct human confession of Jesus in Mark's Gospel. He can make this confession because he saw the way that Jesus died. The most unlikely candidate makes the supreme profession of faith from the vantage point of the cross. "In this moment the evangelist has pushed his Christology to its most eloquent and radical expression."[92]

Mark includes the motif of the divine "must" (*dei*) when he speaks of the suffering of Jesus. In the first passion prediction, the evangelist tells the reader that Jesus "began to teach them that the Son of Man must undergo great suffering" (8:31). This same idea is evident in Mark's frequent use of the verb *paradidōmi*. In most cases the verb is used in the passive voice, meaning "handed over."[93] In the third prediction of the passion Jesus tells the disciples that "the Son of Man will be handed over to the chief priests and the scribes" (10:33). This use of the passive voice implies that God's design is mysteriously at work in these events. In an article entitled "What and Why Did Jesus Suffer According to Mark?" Daniel Harrington says that one of the reasons for Jesus' suffering adduced in the Gospel is that the cross is God's will. This theme is also evident in the many allusions in the passion narrative to Old Testament texts, especially to Psalm 22, the psalm of the righteous sufferer.[94] This motif of the divine will is also found, of course, in the prayer of Jesus in Gethsemane.

Given Mark's account of Jesus' proclamation of the kingdom, which depicts a God of life, scholars offer nuanced interpretations of this theme of the divine will in the Gospel. It is clear that the evangelist is reflecting on these events from the vantage point of the resurrection and, from that angle, he sees them as encompassed within God's salvific plan. Harrington suggests that Mark regarded Jesus' suffering as the paradoxical wisdom of God, as did Paul in First Corinthians 1–4.[95] Commenting on this theme, Senior says, "In the mystery of God's sovereignty the death of Jesus is no tragic accident or triumph of evil. The life that would flow from the death and resurrection of Jesus guaranteed that even the dark moment of crucifixion was somehow according to God's unfathomable plan of salvation."[96] Similarly, W. Schrage notes that this divine "must" represents an a posteriori interpretation of an event. It is utilized in Mark and in other places "when sufferings have already appeared and there is no escape, but a person still maintains God's purpose and saving intention, in spite of all the enigmas."[97]

Mark makes it clear that those who wish to become disciples of Jesus must be willing to journey with him to the cross and to share in the "cup" of suffering that he drinks. The Markan ideal of discipleship is summarized in 3:14–15: "And he appointed twelve, whom he also named apostles, to be with him, and to be sent out to proclaim the message, and to have authority to cast out demons." Following Jesus, then, means being with him on the journey and participating in his mission of proclaiming the reign of God. Though the disciples start off well, their tendency to failure soon becomes clear to the reader of the Gospel. After the first multiplication of the loaves and the encounter with Jesus in the storm, the evangelist tells us that the disciples "did not understand about the loaves, but their hearts were hardened" (6:52). In the Gospel's central section (8:22–10:52), the misunderstanding of the disciples is accentuated by Mark. Each of the three passion predictions leads to misunderstanding on the part of the disciples. This failure to understand the true identity and destiny of Jesus reaches the level of the absurd in the request of James and John (10:35–45), leading to Jesus' pivotal declaration, "For the Son of Man came not to be served but to serve, and to give his life in ransom for many." Jerusalem becomes the place where the weakness of the disciples is most vividly exposed. The disciples scatter at the arrest of Jesus, leaving him alone.

The exception to this negative portrayal of the disciples is found in the women of the Gospel. At Bethany, an unnamed woman anoints the body of Jesus "beforehand for its burial" (14:8). "The woman's recognition of Jesus' approaching death and her graceful and lavishly generous response define authentic discipleship for Mark."[98] The women who are present at the death of Jesus are introduced as having followed Jesus and provided for him during his ministry in Galilee. The verb *diakonein* is used to describe the service they have rendered to Jesus, a word that is "a quasi-technical word for Christian ministry in the world."[99] These same women discover the tomb empty on the first day of the week and are recipients of the good news of Easter: "He has been raised; he is not here" (16:6). "The women are the great principle of continuity and fidelity in the passion narrative."[100]

Mark's depiction of the disciples' weakness and misunderstanding is striking. Jesus' closest followers seem to move through a negative progression from lack of perception of the true identity of Jesus through rejection of the way of suffering that he predicts to flight and outright denial of him.[101] This dark picture of the disciples suggests that the Gospel was written with memories of persecution vivid in the minds of its readers. Many scholars think that this involved the persecution of Christians under Nero, during which some Christians failed under pressure and even betrayed fellow believers.[102] The figure of failing disciples, especially that of Peter, would have been a symbol of hope for members of Mark's community who had failed in some way. Since it is likely that Peter died as a martyr during this very persecution, his rehabilitation as a disciple would have been a source of consolation and strength for disheartened Christians. This Gospel portrait would also inspire those in the community who had remained faithful to be reconciled with believers who had failed. "The failure of the disciples thus paradoxically becomes good news for a community struggling with failure and apostasy while called to repentance, forgiveness and reconciliation."[103]

Conclusion

Even this incomplete treatment of the New Testament shows that one can find a number of interpretations of suffering in the Christian scriptures. Suffering can be understood as a trial through which the faith of believers is purified and matures. In such trials believers can identify with Jesus himself, whose fidelity to the Father was tested in the desert and through the ordeal of his passion. We have also seen that the sufferings of Jesus and of his disciples are associated with the will of God in the Gospel of Mark. However, the New Testament authors do not speculate about the precise way in which suffering fits into God's will, focusing instead on the benefits and new life that result from suffering endured faithfully. The Letter to the Hebrews draws on the wisdom tradition of the Hebrew scriptures in speaking of suffering as divine "discipline," though once again it does not develop this explanation in any detail. Suffering is also viewed as a temporary reality that will be overcome when the reign of God comes in its fullness. Believers, then, are exhorted to keep their eyes fixed on the future and to hold on with courage. Suffering is understood as the effect of powers in the world that are opposed to the intentions of God. This view is evident in the Gospel presentation of Jesus' ministry of healing and exorcism.

The authors of the New Testament sought to inculcate in believers an attitude of identification with the crucified and risen Christ. They reflected on the destiny of Jesus when they searched for the meaning of suffering and the presence of God in suffering. The risen Lord is the Lamb who was slain. He is the one who approached his death in freedom and faithfulness, as an act of loving service and sacrifice for others. To suffer, particularly as a result of fidelity to Christ, represents an opportunity for close association with Jesus, whose passion was in some mysterious way salvific. For Paul, suffering for the gospel is a mark of the authentic apostle who has imbibed the wisdom of the cross. The faithful Christian experiences union with Christ in and through suffering. The spirituality of witness that is evident in First Peter maintains that experiences of suffering are occasions for believers to offer credible testimony to their belief in Christ in a world that is hostile to the ways of God. This witness in and through suffering is beneficial for others, as was Jesus' faithful witness in his own suffering.

In reflecting on these New Testament interpretations of suffering it seems particularly important for contemporary believers to situate the experience of suffering in the context of Jesus' proclamation of the reign of God and the vindication of his person and message in the resurrection. New Testament authors do not speculate about the ultimate reason for the presence of evil and suffering in the world. Rather, they face its reality and testify to God's will to overcome it. Jesus' suffering and death, then, must be contextualized within his ministry of proclaiming the reign of God and making that reign present in the lives of people. When God's reign became present through the words and deeds of Jesus, people found life. They experienced wholeness of body and spirit. The coming of the reign of God meant the restoration of God's good creation. Moreover, as Gerald O'Collins put it, Christian confession of the resurrection of Jesus disclosed a fresh understanding of God. It revealed that God is indeed present in the midst of suffering and that God is active, on the move, to bring life out of death. The God of Jesus Christ is the Resurrector. The resurrection of the crucified Jesus was the decisive manifestation of the love of God.

Discussion Questions: www.paulistpress.com, Online Resources.

3

Early Christian Sources

The Experience of Suffering

In examining the themes of the suffering of Jesus and the suffering of believers in the New Testament, we recognized the importance of context. Biblical scholars conclude that the Christian communities addressed by Mark the evangelist, the author of Hebrews, and the author of First Peter were experiencing suffering that included persecution for their faith in Christ. In the case of the audience addressed by Mark, this hostility had most likely led to betrayal and division within the community. The questions we are exploring about the meaning of suffering, the relation between God and the suffering person, and the experience of God within suffering, were existentially real for these communities. They were not a matter of theological abstraction. Just as much of the recent literature on this topic has emerged from the devastating experience of the Shoah, so the treatment of suffering in Mark and other New Testament texts emerged from the events of real life.

When we consider theological sources from the period of the early church, we must also acknowledge the context of suffering. The period before the official toleration of Christianity in the early fourth century was a time in which Christians were often marginalized as a minority and sometimes persecuted with severity. The suffering that resulted from such marginalization and persecution demanded a theological interpretation. For example, Cyprian, the famous bishop of Carthage in the middle of the third century, wrote to Christians who had suffered from the savage persecution initiated by the Roman emperor Decius in 250–251. Christians were obliged to offer sacrifice to the imperial gods under the penalty of imprisonment, torture, or

82

even death. A number of believers succumbed to the pressure of perse-cution and either offered sacrifice or bribed officials in order to secure a certificate attesting that they had done so. In his treatise *The Lapsed*, Cyprian addresses believers who had renounced their faith under the pressure of this persecution. He interprets the suffering that North African believers had experienced as a test or even a punishment by God due to the fact that many Christians had grown lax in the practice of their faith.[1]

When Augustine wrote his famous work *The City of God* in the early fifth century, he did so in light of the tumultuous experience of the sack of Rome in 410 by Alaric, leader of the Visigoths. The fall of Rome was an experience of suffering for the people of Rome, of course, but it also had symbolic significance for all of the citizens of the Roman Empire. The fall of the "eternal city" provoked a discussion of divine providence in history by Christians and non-Christians alike.[2] Augustine wrote his great work in part to defend Christians against charges of being a major cause of this catastrophe. Many non-Christians thought that this disaster had been inflicted by the gods of the Roman pantheon who were angry because of the refusal of Christians to ven-erate them. "The pagans blamed Christian neglect of the old gods, and asked why in Christian times disasters were more numerous."[3] Augustine attempts to refute these charges and to articulate a Christian view of providence. Throughout *The City of God*, he displays a keen awareness of the reality of suffering, not only that inflicted by Alaric but also the suffering that permeates all of the dimensions of human life.

Cyprian and Augustine exemplify the fact that much of what early Christian authors say about suffering emerges from concrete experience. Prior to Constantine, the experience of persecution was a major catalyst for reflection on suffering. By the time of Augustine and later, disruption caused by the migration of northern European peoples was another catalyst. Throughout the period of the early church, writ-ers also addressed suffering that is encountered in the ordinary course of life, such as the death of a loved one. Their theological reflection on the mystery of suffering, then, was written out of pastoral concern.

Philosophical Influences

In the early church, Christian theologians attempted to forge a synthesis between the biblical message of revelation and the great philosophical currents of the day. They sought to articulate the meaning and intelligibility of Christianity in categories that their contemporaries could understand. The philosophical currents prevalent during the first centuries of the church were diverse and complex. They included Stoicism, various forms of dualist philosophy, and a developing Platonism that, in its Neoplatonist expression, incorporated elements of Aristotelian thought. In the past, some accounts of early Christian theology presented its development in a simplistic manner, as if the message of Christian revelation was co-opted by the principles of Hellenistic philosophy. Recent studies of early Christian thought emphasize the diversity of philosophical influence in the Greco-Roman world. Hellenistic philosophy was far from a single, uniform strain of thought. Moreover, while Christian thinkers appealed to and employed Greek philosophical categories, they did so critically, in light of the revelation of God in Christ.

Evil as a Privation of the Good

The interpretation of Plato that was developed by Plotinus in the third century (Neoplatonism) asserted that evil is not a substance in itself but a privation. Reacting against forms of Gnosticism, Plotinus teaches that evil is the lack of a good that should be present for the integrity of something. Christian thinkers adopt this principle as a way of expressing their belief that the created world is the essentially good gift of a good Creator. This idea becomes integral to the Christian tradition, and it is reasserted at various times through the centuries when other forms of dualistic thought arise. These dualistic strains of thought usually present evil as a metaphysical principle in conflict with the good God, and they invariably depict the material world as evil.

In his work *Against the Pagans*, Athanasius of Alexandria rejects dualism, affirming the unity and goodness of the Creator. He writes, "Now if God is one, and he is Lord of heaven and earth, how could there be another god beside him? And where will this god be, since the one true God fills everything comprehended in heaven and earth?"[4] He argues that evil did not exist from the beginning but was introduced into God's good creation through the misdeeds of human beings. From Athanasius's perspective, this human failure fundamentally consisted of a turning away from contemplation of God to become fixated on created things. He concludes that "evil is not from God nor in God; it did not originally exist and it has no substance."[5] Later in the fourth century, Basil of Caesarea wrote a treatise entitled *God Is Not the Author of Evils*. He strongly admonishes his readers against regarding God as the cause of evil. He asserts, "Do not imagine that evil has a substance peculiar to it. Wickedness does not exist like some living thing. We cannot set it before our eyes as something existing. Evil is a privation of the good."[6]

Augustine grappled with the problem of evil throughout his life. His temporary association with the Manichaeans as an auditor in their sect reflects his search for an answer to the dilemma of evil. Manichaeism provided a straightforward solution to this dilemma, positing two absolute principles, a source of goodness and a source of evil. Augustine's wrestling with the mystery of evil is evident in the seventh book of his *Confessions*. In this passage, Augustine reflects honestly on his personal struggle:

> But a problem remained to trouble me. Although I affirmed and firmly held divine immunity from pollution and change and the complete immutability of our God, the true God who made not only our souls but also our bodies, and not only our souls and bodies but all rational beings and everything, yet I had no clear explicit grasp of the cause of evil. Whatever it might be, I saw it had to be investigated, if I were to avoid being forced by the problem to believe the immutable God to be mutable.[7]

Augustine reflects further in this passage on the Christian teaching that free will is the cause of our sinning, though he continues to grapple with the question of how free will came to be influenced by evil in the first place. He then turns to the scriptures to focus on the way of salvation that God has provided in Christ. He ponders the mystery of the incarnation, a truth that he did not find in the books of the Neoplatonists. In the context of this reflection, Augustine proceeds to affirm that creatures, even though they are liable to corruption, are essentially good:

> Therefore as long as they exist, they are good. Accordingly, whatever things exist are good, and the evil into whose origins I was inquiring is not a substance, for if it were a substance, it would be good....Hence I saw and it was made clear to me that you [O God] have made all things good, and there are absolutely no substances which you did not make. As you did not make all things equal, all things are good in the sense that taken individually they are good, and all things taken together are very good. For our God has made "all things very good" (Gen 1:31).[8]

In his later handbook on the faith, *The Enchiridion on Faith, Hope and Love*, Augustine reaffirms this teaching in a more straightforward way. Writing in a rhetorical fashion, he asks, "For what is that which we call evil but the absence of the good?"[9] Evil is like a sickness or a wound; it represents the absence of a good that should be present. Evil is the corruption of something that is essentially good: "All things that exist, therefore, seeing that the Creator of all is supremely good, are themselves good. But because they are not, like their Creator, supremely and unchangeably good, their good may be diminished and increased."[10] In the context of this discussion, Augustine makes an important affirmation of faith that will be quoted by later Christian theologians, including Thomas Aquinas: "For the Almighty God, who, as even the heathen acknowledge, has supreme power over all things, being himself supremely good, would never permit the existence of anything evil among his works, if he were not so omnipotent and good that he can bring good even out of evil."[11]

This teaching on evil as a privation of the good represents a fundamentally positive, optimistic view of creation that, in a sense, "keeps evil in its place." Goodness is primary, since existence comes from the hands of a God who is absolute goodness. This affirmation became essential to Christian teaching and remains so today. Christian belief in the goodness of creation (and belief in the incarnation) poses the challenge of dealing with the mystery of evil. Augustine grapples with this dilemma in his *Confessions*. From one perspective, forms of metaphysical dualism provide an easier solution to the mystery of evil. There is something, or someone, to which or to whom the origin of evil can be attributed. To hold a fundamentally positive view of creation as the good gift of a good Creator, and still to recognize the reality of evil, presents a greater theological challenge.

John Hick is one modern thinker who has raised a question about this traditional view of evil as a privation of the good.[12] He asks whether the notion of evil as a privation is sufficient when we face the dynamic malevolence behind a terrible event like the Shoah. Hick suggests that we may need to speak of something more positive with respect to such malevolence. It is easy to resonate with Hick's suggestion from an experiential perspective. Nevertheless, when one begins to speak of evil as a positive reality, one encounters a host of philosophical and religious problems, including the risk of denying the essential goodness of creation. Hick's observation does, however, raise an important question for Christians who wish to face the reality of evil and suffering: How do we remain faithful to the Christian affirmation of the essential goodness of creation and also acknowledge evil as a powerful force present in the world?

Divine Immutability and Impassibility

Christian theologians in the early church were also influenced by the Greek philosophical principle that the divine is immutable and impassible, that is, not subject to alteration or to suffering. Though Plato's teaching about the nature of the divine is not entirely clear, he does assert divine immutability. In his *Symposium*, he speaks of the discovery of the beautiful in a vision of eternal being, neither becoming nor perishing, neither increasing nor diminishing. The beautiful becomes neither greater nor less and is not affected by anything.[13] This is the final object of love. In the *Republic*, Plato argues that the best things are least liable to change or alteration: "Anything then which is in good condition, either by nature or as the product of a craft, or both, is least changed by anything else."[14] Since "the god"—whom Plato identifies as the Good—is in every way the best thing, he would be least likely to change. For Plato change entails decay and thus should not be predicated of the divine.

For Aristotle, the divine is absolutely perfect, and thus unchanging, since the divine need not change for the better and cannot change for the worse.[15] In his *Metaphysics*, he speaks of the Unmoved Mover who acts as the final cause of the world. "The final cause, then, produces motion as being loved, but all other things move by being moved."[16] For Aristotle "God is the Unmoved Mover in that he sets in motion all else, not by an action on his part, but by his mere perfect and unchangeable presence as the Final Cause, the perfect attraction which draws all else to become as he is."[17] In this section of the *Metaphysics*, Aristotle argues that since this final cause is fully actualized, it can in no way be otherwise than it is.[18] As the highest instance of being, God is Self-Thinking Thought, since for Aristotle thinking is the highest expression of being.[19] Aristotle can conclude, then, that God "is a substance which is eternal and unmovable and separate from sensible things." Moreover, God "is impassive and unalterable."[20]

The Neoplatonism of Plotinus, which influenced Augustine, also posits the immutability of the divine. Plotinus posits a triad of three divine hypostases: the One, Intellect, and Soul. Intellect and Soul (the World Soul, which is distinct from the souls of individual human beings) emanate from the One and are subordinate to it. Plotinus's teaching encompasses a path of contemplation whereby the human soul ascends from this world of sense toward union with the divine. The soul makes this ascent by entering into itself. This is a journey toward a vision of the beautiful described by Plotinus in his first *Ennead*. The divine that the soul seeks in contemplation is not capable of being changed or affected by another.[21] For Plotinus, "Being is not impassible because it is isolated, but because it is being. It is completely sufficient unto itself."[22]

Theologians of the early church generally affirm the immutability and impassibility of the God of Christian revelation. Several of the second-century apologists place strong emphasis on these principles. Justin Martyr asserts that God is incomprehensible, inexpressible, immutable, impassible, and noncorporeal. In his First Apology, Justin says that because God is unchanging God is superior to changeable things.[23] Unlike the pagan deities, God is impassible and unbegotten. Aristides places particular stress on the transcendence of God, which entails divine immutability and impassiblity; God is superior to passions and infirmities.[24] God is unlike a human being, who is "subject to anger and jealousy and desire and change of purpose and many infirmities."[25] In his writings against the Gnostics, Irenaeus of Lyons also affirms the immutability and impassibility of God. He asserts that God is "truly and forever the same, and always remaining the same unchangeable Being."[26] He argues that "the Father of all is at a vast distance from those affections and passions which operate among men."[27]

As the passage from Augustine's *Confessions* on the mystery of evil suggests, the bishop of Hippo vigorously affirms the immutability of God. This is true even though he is convinced that God continues to work within human history. Through this teaching on divine immutability, Augustine would have a significant influence on later Christian thinkers, including Aquinas. Joseph Hallman suggests that for Augustine "immutability may have been God's most important attribute."[28] Augustine accentuates the immutability of God because for him it is this characteristic that distinguishes the Creator from creatures and grounds the immutability of truth. It is a principle that governs Augustine's treatment of the incarnation, God's will and providence, and the various emotions that are attributed to God in the scriptures.

Augustine stresses that the incarnation did not entail any alteration in the Son (Word) of God: "For He, abiding unchangeable, took upon Him our nature, that there He might take us to Himself; and holding fast to His divinity, He became partaker of our infirmity...."[29] In his exposition of Psalm 74, he writes:

> And as he took to himself the form of a slave, so did he also take time to himself. Was he changed thereby? Was he

diminished? Was he left the poorer? Did he fall or decline by accepting it? Far be it from us to think so....He is said to have emptied himself because he took to himself what was lower, not because he degenerated from his equality with God.[30]

Because God dwells in eternity, not in time (time is a created reality for Augustine), God's will is also eternal and unchangeable. Near the end of *The City of God*, Augustine reflects on the eternal and unchangeable will of God. He says that when God is said to change his will—when God becomes angry with God's people, for example—"it is rather they than He who are changed, and they find Him changed in so far as their experience of suffering at His hand is new, as the sun is changed to injured eyes, and becomes as it were fierce from being mild, and hurtful from being delightful, though in itself it remains the same as it was."[31] Later in the same section of this work, he states, "But if we speak of that will of His which is eternal as His foreknowledge, certainly He has already done all things in heaven and on earth that He has willed—not only past and present things, but even things still future."[32] All events have been prepared and even accomplished from eternity in God's unchangeable will.

Augustine deals with emotions ascribed to God in the Bible—such as anger, repentance, jealousy, love, and mercy—in such a way as not to compromise divine immutability.[33] In *The City of God*, he discusses the anger attributed to God in the scriptures, and he argues that this anger "is not a disturbing emotion of His mind, but a judgment by which punishment is inflicted upon sin."[34] In the same text he says that, despite biblical passages that refer to God's regretting or repenting of past divine actions (for example, Gen 6:5–6), God does not repent of anything God has done "because in all matters His decision is as inflexible as His prescience is certain."[35] When scripture describes God as "jealous" for God's people, Augustine interprets this jealousy as either God's unchanging eternal providence or God's justice as applied to certain situations.[36] With regard to divine love and mercy, Augustine denies that God can begin to love anyone; God's love for and predestination of God's saints are eternal. We can speak of God as merciful toward us because God helps us and frees us from misery. This does not mean, however, that God feels our misery. Augustine writes, "With regard to pity, if you take away the compassion which involved a sharing of misery with him whom you pity, so that there remains the peaceful goodness of helping and freeing from misery, some kind of knowledge of the divine pity is suggested."[37]

There are texts in the literature of the early church, however, that stand in tension with this standard teaching on divine immutability and impassibility. Hallman has catalogued these passages. For example, on his way to martyrdom, Ignatius of Antioch writes a letter to the members of the Christian community in Rome urging them not to intervene on his behalf. Envisioning martyrdom as the culmination of Christian discipleship, Ignatius writes, "Let me imitate the passion of my God."[38] Here he directly ascribes passion to the divine. A section of Origen's *Homilies on Ezekiel* is another text that attributes suffering to God:

> Something of this sort I would have you suppose concerning the Savior. He came down to earth in pity for humankind, he endured our passions and sufferings before he suffered the cross, and he deigned to assume our flesh. For if he had not suffered he would not have entered into full participation in human life. He first suffered, then he came down and was manifested. What is that passion which he suffered for us? It is the passion of love. The Father himself and the God of the whole universe is "long-suffering, full of mercy and pity" (Ps 86:15). Must he not, then, in some sense, be exposed to suffering? So you must realize that in his dealing with men he suffers human passions. "For the Lord thy God bore thy ways, even as a man bears his own son" (Deut 1:31). Thus God bears our ways, just as the Son of God bears our "passions." The Father himself is not impassible. If he is besought he shows pity and compassion; he feels, in some sort, the passion of love, and is exposed to what he cannot be exposed to in respect of his greatness, and for us men he endures the passion of mankind.[39]

This remarkable text ascribes suffering to the Savior (the Logos) even before the incarnation, and it attributes pity and compassion to the Father. Origen calls this the "passion of love" and argues that it is a passion in which the divine endures human suffering. Hallman cites a comment on this passage made by the distinguished scholar of the early church, Robert Grant, who asserted that "something of great theological significance has happened here."[40] There are other passages in Origen's writings in which he also speaks of God's feeling compassion for those God loves.[41] But the evidence in Origen is complex and ambiguous, because in other writings he denies emotions to God and asserts the impassibility of the divine. Sometimes he says that biblical passages that speak of God's lamenting or rejoicing are simply figurative.[42] In one place he writes, "God's anger is not to be considered a passion. How can an impassible being have a passion? God does not suffer, he is immutable."[43] In *On First Principles*, he attributes the sufferings of Jesus to his humanity, not his divinity: "The Word remains Word in essence. He suffers nothing of the experience of body or soul."[44] Thus, Origen is not altogether consistent concerning divine immutability and impassibility, and scholars offer varying interpretations of this evidence.

Tertullian is also quite complex in his approach to this issue. On the one hand, in writing against Marcion, Tertullian insists that one can attribute anger to God on the basis of God's goodness. God's essential goodness means that God must be angry over sin and must judge evil.[45] Emotions like wrath, jealousy, and severity also flow from God's goodness. God responds to the changing circumstances of human history, and therefore God is affected by the actions and attitudes of people.[46] Tertullian insists that God has these emotions in a divine manner, not in a human way. This distinction is due to the fact that the divine essence is incorruptible, while human beings are corruptible. On the other hand, in his *Treatise against Hermogenes* Tertullian insists that because God is eternal, God is immutable. God cannot change for the worse because eternity cannot involve loss. Because God is the highest good, neither can God change for the better or become something greater.[47] Thus, the evidence in Tertullian, like that in Origen, is ambiguous regarding divine immutability and impassibility.

There are other texts from early Christian writers that attribute change and suffering to God. One example is a treatise addressed to

Theopompus, purportedly written in the third century by Gregory the Wonderworker, a student of Origen.[48] The author of this work argues that a dimension of divine perfection is the capacity to choose to suffer freely for the good of the human family. God enters into suffering in order to conquer suffering. There is also a commentary on the psalms that was written in the late fourth century, the authorship of which is unknown. In its discussion of the divine kenosis (self-emptying) in the incarnation, this work ascribes change (*alloiōsis*) not simply to the humanity of Jesus but to the divine Word as well.[49] The author distinguishes various types of change, and he describes the alteration of the Word in the incarnation as a change in quality, not in quantity. Hallman concludes that the author of this commentary "tries to do justice to the fact that the Incarnation of God's Word makes a real difference to God."[50]

This ambiguity in early Christian literature is assessed in differing ways by modern scholars. For example, Joseph Hallman argues that the tension that is evident in some of these writings reflects the tension between Greek thought and the biblical testimony. He thinks that the biblical portrait of a dynamic and involved God, responsive to human history, became obscured when early Christian theologians utilized the categories of Greek philosophy, which insisted on divine immutability and impassibility. Commenting on Tertullian's writings, Hallman asserts, "Because the philosophical heritage was so negative about it, the incarnational mutability of God became difficult to conceptualize."[51] Thomas Weinandy, on the other hand, deals with this material quite differently. While he acknowledges the ambiguity of the evidence in the works of some of these authors, he finds a basic line of consistency grounded in two principles. First, while clearly influenced by Greek philosophical ideas, these authors were guided more fundamentally by the biblical teaching on creation. When they distinguish divine and human characteristics, they are making distinctions between the Creator and creatures. "It cannot be overemphasized that it is the act of creation that scripturally and philosophically grounded the early Christian understanding of God and distinguished its doctrine of God from that of the Greek philosophical tradition."[52] The

Christian belief in creation (*creatio ex nihilo*) "established the inherent ontological otherness of God, in a manner far more radical than that of the Greek philosophical and Gnostic traditions" and, at the same time, affirmed God's involvement in and care for creation.[53] Second, in describing God as immutable and impassible these theologians are primarily saying what God is not rather than what God is. Thus, to say that God is impassible is to affirm that God "does not undergo successive and fluctuating emotional states" and to deny that God can be altered by anything in the created order in such a way that the divine would suffer any modification or loss.[54] "For the Fathers, to deny that God is passible is to deny of him all human passions and the effects of such passions which would in any way debilitate or cripple him as God."[55]

The differing interpretations offered by Hallman and Weinandy are emblematic of the debate about divine immutability and impassibility that we will encounter when we examine the positions of other contemporary theologians. While Hallman thinks that change is essential to divine involvement in a changing world, Weinandy argues that God can be involved with and totally loving of creatures precisely because divine mercy and love are not predicated of a changeable being. When we examine the contemporary discussion of these questions, we will see that a salient issue is that of the nature of love and what is entailed in loving. Is there an inherent reciprocity in the human experience of mature love that should be ascribed, analogically, to divine love?[56] Is a perfectly loving God affected by creation? Does the world make a difference to God? These are questions that are part of the theological conversation about God and suffering that continues today.

The Scandal of the Cross and the Christological Debates

The question of the relationship between God and suffering and the conviction about divine immutability and impassibility were important in the patristic debates about the person and saving work of

Christ.[57] Christians worshiped a person who suffered a most ignomin-ious death by crucifixion, and they confessed this crucified one to be divine. Paul Gavrilyuk observes, "In her worship of the Crucified the church wanted to make one thing clear: God is faithful to his redemp-tive purposes in history even if that entails assuming fragile humanity and dying the death of slave on the cross."[58] How could Christians wor-ship one who had been crucified? What did this say about God's rela-tionship to human suffering? These questions were debated vigorously in the early church in a number of controversies: conflicts that arose over docetic interpretations of Christ; the quarrels between Arian and pro-Nicene Christians; and the debates between Cyril of Alexandria and the followers of Nestorius.

Docetism

Docetism, a term deriving from a Greek word meaning "to seem" or "to appear," was a tendency that permeated a number of strains of early Christianity. Many (though not all) Gnostic Christians were docetic in their thinking about Christ. The most extreme version of docetism held that the humanity of Jesus, and thus his suffering, was only an appearance. It was not real. Other forms of docetism tended to divide Jesus into two subjects, one divine and the other human. They attrib-uted the title Christ to the divine subject and Jesus to the human. Jesus was the subject of human experiences in the Gospels, including suffer-ing, while Christ was not implicated in such experiences.[59] In whatever form it took, docetism involved a denial of a true incarnation.

Those who espoused docetism affirmed the divinity of Christ and held strongly to the impassibility of the divine. A Christ who truly suf-fered the pains of the crucifixion, therefore, was viewed as theologi-cally problematic. Some docetists were attempting to respond to popular critiques directed at Christianity by adherents of Greek and Roman religion.[60] "The pagans were disgusted with the appalling inno-vations that the atheistic Galileans introduced into the traditional ways of imaging the divine realm....To claim that the Omnipotent God was crucified seemed both impious and inconsistent with the nature of God."[61] Docetists "broadly agreed that certain human experiences of

Jesus Christ were not God-befitting and that a thorough reinterpretation of the gospel narratives was in order."[62] An example of a docetic interpretation of the death of Jesus is found in the apocryphal *Acts of John*, a Gnostic work that may have been written in the middle of the second century. It depicts the apostle John fleeing to the Mount of Olives and hiding in a cave at the time of Jesus' crucifixion. While John is weeping, he hears the voice of Jesus, who has come to inform him about what is really happening. In fact, according to this work, Jesus has suffered none of the pains of the crucifixion; it only seems that way to those who do not know the real truth. Jesus reveals a cosmic cross of light to John, and he explains that this cross is different from the cross of wood:

> But this [the cross of light] is not the cross of wood which you will see when you go down here, neither am I he who is upon the cross, whom now you do not see, but only hear a voice. I was reckoned to be what I am not, not being what I was to many others; but they [orthodox Christians] will call me something else, which is vile and not worthy of me....Therefore I have suffered none of the things which they will say of me.[63]

Orthodox Christians rejected docetism, affirming that the suffering of Christ was historically undeniable and soteriologically significant for salvation. Christian theologians appealed to the biblical vision of creation, which presented the material world as the good work of an all-powerful and all-good Creator. The material world, then, was the place where God's saving purposes were effected, and it was a fitting realm for the Son of God to embrace in the incarnation. This conviction was foundational for early Christian understanding of the sacraments, particularly the Eucharist. In his letter to the church at Smyrna, Ignatius of Antioch reports that some docetists "hold aloof from the Eucharist and from services of prayer, because they refuse to admit that the Eucharist is the flesh of our Savior Jesus Christ" who suffered for the sins of people and was raised from the dead.[64] Christian affirmation of the reality of Christ's humanity was directly related to belief in the presence of Christ in the Eucharist.

Christian authors also adduced a theology of martyrdom in their arguments defending the true humanity and real suffering of Christ. They affirmed that Christ must have truly experienced the pains of persecution and death if he called followers to take up their crosses and follow him. On the way to his own martyrdom, Ignatius of Antioch presses this conviction in his Letter to the Trallians: "And if, as some atheists (I mean unbelievers) say, his suffering was a sham (it's really *they* who are a sham!), why, then, am I a prisoner? Why do I want to fight with wild beasts? In that case I shall die to no purpose. Yes, and I am maligning the Lord too!"[65] Gavrilyuk points out that the Christian theology of martyrdom progressed from a notion of imitating Christ to one of participation in his sufferings. This participation was viewed as mutual: the martyr partakes of the sufferings of Christ, and Christ shares in the pains of the martyr, giving him or her the strength needed to endure terrible afflictions. For example, in the third-century North African work *The Passion of Perpetua and Felicitas*, Perpetua responds to her jailer, who in seeing the young woman writhe in pain while giving birth in prison doubts her ability to withstand the suffering of martyrdom. She says, "I suffer now myself that which is natural. But then, another will be in me who will suffer for me, because I am about to suffer for him."[66] Thus, the reality of the sufferings of Christ was a belief that was pivotal for Christian witness in a hostile world.

The Arian Controversy

The controversy that arose in the early fourth century about the divinity of Christ dominated the doctrinal history of that century and significantly affected the life of the church in subsequent centuries. Arius, an older, respected priest in Alexandria, taught that there was a radical difference between the unbegotten Father and the only begotten Son. The Father—the "highest God" in the Arian schema—is absolutely unique and transcendent. The Father's being cannot be shared. The Son is a creature (*ktisma*) who is created by the will of God. According to the Arians, the Son did exist before the creation of everything else and is a higher, perfect creature who should not be compared with other creatures. The Son is created directly by God and is the creator of time and of everything else belonging to the world of contingency. The Son, who is not coeternal with the Father, can be called a "second God."[67] A famous Arian slogan expressed this belief that the Son is not coeternal with the Father: "There was when he [the Son] was not." Thus, the Son, the One who became incarnate, is a kind of demigod— superior to creatures but not fully divine. For the Arians, the transcendent God remains at a distance from human history and human salvation.[68] In this theological framework the Son occupies a subordinate, mediatorial position in the divine hierarchy.

Arian Christology depicted a Savior who was not fully human, either. The Word became united to a human body that lacked a rational soul. The Word took the place of the human soul and thus was the subject of all of Jesus' experiences. The Arians opposed the idea of Christ having a human soul because they thought that the Word (Logos) must be the source of all of Christ's saving actions.[69] The author of a fifth-century Arian work in Latin articulated this conviction: "For if a mere man suffered, I give up, because the death of a man, not of God, does not save us."[70] Thus, for the Arians, the Son or Word must be the subject of all of the redemptive actions of Christ, though the status of the Son is not equal to that of the Father.[71]

One of the motivating forces behind Arian theology was the desire to take the scandal of the cross seriously. "The Arians saw that the New Testament demanded a suffering God, as their opponents failed to see."[72] But if it was God in Christ who had suffered and died on the cross, this God must be lower than the transcendent God, who is impassible. In his *Orations against the Arians*, Athanasius, patriarch of Alexandria, quotes an accusatory question posed by the Arians: "How dare you assert that someone who has a body and so can suffer these things is the Logos who belongs to the essence of the Father?"[73] Gavrilyuk summarizes this pivotal Arian principle: "In the Arian scheme, the Logos had to be both more than a mere man, in order for his suffering to have universal significance attested by the gospels and less than the High God, in order to be capable of change and suffering."[74]

The position of Arius and his supporters was, of course, rejected at the Council of Nicaea. The council taught that the Son is "one in being with" (*homoousios*) the Father. While the exact meaning of this term was not clarified at the council and remained a source of contention in the decades after Nicaea, the Nicene bishops used it to affirm the equality and coeternity of the Son with the Father and the unity of God. The council taught that the Son is God in the very sense that the Father is God. Athanasius, the staunch defender of Nicaea, stressed that what was at stake in this controversy was the understanding of the reality of salvation in Christ. Athanasius envisioned salvation as a transforming participation in the life of God, a profound communion with God that makes us "godlike." He writes, "We partaking of the Son himself are said to partake of God. This is what Peter said: 'That you might become partners of a divine nature' (2 Peter 1:4)."[75] Athanasius steadfastly argued that, if this is what salvation is, the Son must be fully divine; otherwise Christ, the incarnate Son of God, could not impart this gift of divine life to human beings.

In his Christology, Athanasius was compelled to attend to the real sufferings of Christ while also affirming his true divinity. Though he did not deny the presence of a human soul in Christ, he did not usually appeal to the soul as a way of dealing with the sufferings and other human limitations that the New Testament attributes to Jesus. He distinguishes between the Word as such and the Word made flesh, attributing human weaknesses and sufferings to his fleshly nature.[76] Athanasius argues that scripture gives us a double account of the Savior: "It says that he has always been God and is the Son, because he is the Logos and radiance and Wisdom of the Father. Furthermore, it says that in the end he became a human being, took flesh for our sakes from the Virgin Mary, the God-bearer."[77]

Richard Norris concludes that the Christology of Athanasius becomes strained when he has to deal with human weakness and suffering, particularly ignorance. Athanasius usually argues that when ignorance is ascribed to Christ in the scriptures it is feigned ignorance.[78] It seems that the Christology of Athanasius, particularly because it does not pay adequate attention to a human soul in Christ, does have difficulty dealing with suffering and other forms of human limitation. Both sides of the Arian debate had to grapple with the scandal of the cross in their attempts to give a cogent account of the person and saving work of Christ. For believers who trusted in and worshiped a crucified Christ, a salient issue was how to speak of the relationship between God and human suffering.

The Nestorian Conflict

In the fifth century another doctrinal dispute arose that included concerns about divine impassibility and the relationship between the divine and the sufferings of Jesus. This was the controversy between Nestorius, patriarch of Constantinople, and Cyril, patriarch of Alexandria, leading up to the teaching of the Council of Ephesus (431). This dispute is typically depicted as a conflict between the diverse christological perspectives of Alexandria and Antioch, with Alexandria focusing on the divinity and the unity of Christ, and Antioch emphasizing the integrity of Jesus' humanity and the real distinction between his divine and human natures. Divergence in methods of biblical interpretation is also adduced as a leading factor in these debates, with Alexandria favoring typological exegesis and Antioch employing a more literal approach. These points of divergence were clearly significant influences in this controversy. At the same time, the issue of God's relation to suffering was also a central focus in the arguments between the two sides—one that has not always received adequate attention in standard interpretations of this debate.

Soon after he became patriarch of Constantinople, Nestorius was drawn into a dispute about attributing to Mary the title of *Theotokos* ("God-bearer" or, more commonly, "Mother of God"). This title, already used in popular devotion, assumes the unity of Christ. One can call Mary the Mother of God because she gave birth to Jesus, who is the incarnate Son of God. Use of this title assumes that there is one subject in Christ. It is a way of speaking based on the principle of the "communication of idioms"—a principle that had influenced the Christologies of fourth-century theologians and is implied in the creed of Nicaea-Constantinople. This principle entails predicating of Christ attributes of one nature even when he is being named with reference to his other nature, for example, "The Son of God died on the cross" and "The Son of Mary created the world."[79] This way of speaking is based on the conviction that the divine and human natures were united in the one person of the Son of God.

Nestorius objected to the use of the title *Theotokos* for Mary.[80] While there is scholarly debate about the precise position of Nestorius, it seems that he exaggerated the Antiochene tendency to distinguish the divine and human natures in Jesus. He sometimes spoke of two subjects in Christ, the man assumed by the Logos and the Logos indwelling the man. Emphasizing that redemption needed to be effected by a second Adam who was truly human, he wrote:

> Our nature, having been put on by Christ like a garment, intervenes on our behalf, being entirely free from all sin and contending by appeal to its blameless origin, just as the Adam who was formed earlier brought punishment upon his race by reason of his sin. This was the opportunity which belonged to the assumed man, as a human being to dissolve, by means of the flesh, that corruption which arose by means of the flesh.[81]

In describing the relationship between the humanity and divinity of Christ, Nestorius preferred the term *conjunction* (*synapheia*) to the language of "union" (*henōsis*). With his emphasis on the distinction between the natures in Christ, Nestorius had difficulty with the principle of the communication of idioms. Gerald O'Collins points out that his opponents "accused Nestorius of turning the distinction between Christ's two natures into a separation and proposing a merely moral unity between the eternal Son of God and Jesus as adopted Son."[82] Nestorius attempted to defend himself against such charges, but in the end his christological teaching was rejected.

Cyril argued that Christ is one subject and, therefore, that the communication of idioms is completely legitimate. Thus, Mary should be called Theotokos, since the humanity conceived in Mary's womb was the humanity of the Son of God. He disliked the terminology of "conjunction," preferring to speak of a "hypostatic union." In his description of the mystery of the incarnation, he said, "God the Logos did not come into a man, but he 'truly' became man, while remaining God."[83] In his Second Letter to Nestorius, Cyril affirms the reality of two natures in Christ, and he speaks of Christ's human nature as "flesh enlivened by a rational soul."[84] For Cyril, then, Christ has an integral human nature. He emphasizes, however, that "while the natures which were brought together into a true unity were different, there is nevertheless, because of the unspeakable and unutterable convergence into unity, one Christ and one Son out of two."[85] John O'Keefe argues that what was of utmost importance for Cyril was the conviction that in Christ is found the fullness of God's presence in the world. He was convinced that the Jesus whom we encounter in the Gospels "is none other than the incarnate presence of the second person of the Trinity."[86]

A prominent feature of the debates between Nestorius and Cyril was the question of divine impassibility. Nestorius accused Cyril of jeopardizing God's immutability and impassibility by employing the terminology of hypostatic union. For Nestorius, it was not appropriate for the impassible Logos to be associated in any way with change and suffering. In his Second Letter to Cyril, Nestorius argues that to attribute to the Logos "the characteristics of the flesh that has been conjoined with him—I mean birth and suffering and death" is the work of an erring mind.[87] "The central preoccupation of Nestorian piety and theology was to purify theological discourse of any suggestion of divine suffering."[88]

Cyril's Christology, which grew out of his study of the scriptures, was grounded in the notion of the self-emptying of God, as expressed most poignantly in the famous hymn found in Paul's Letter to the Philippians (2:6–11). In Christ, God emptied Godself and accepted the limitations of human existence. Like Nestorius, Cyril affirmed divine impassibility. In a letter addressed to monks, he says, "For he was the Word in his own body born from a woman, and he gave it to death in due season, but he suffered nothing at all in his own nature for as such he is life and life-giver." In the next sentence, however, Cyril asserts, "Nonetheless he made the things of the flesh his own so that the suffering could be said to be his."[89] Employing paradoxical, or dialectical, language Cyril could speak of the "impassible suffering of the Son."[90] In the famous twelfth anathema found in his Third Letter to Nestorius, Cyril declared, "Whoever does not acknowledge God's Word as having suffered in the flesh, being crucified in the flesh, tasted death in the flesh and been made first-born from the dead because as God he is Life and life-giving shall be anathema."[91] This kind of talk sounded scandalous to Nestorius and his followers because, in their minds, it attributed suffering to the divine. For Cyril, however, the incarnation meant God's "descent to the limits of humanity" and God's allowing of "the limitations of manhood to have dominion over himself."[92] The thrust of Cyril's teaching stressed the fullness of God's presence with us in Christ, "even when such an affirmation strained the limits of language and forced him into paradoxical and awkward formulations."[93]

The scandal of the cross and allied questions about God's relation to human suffering played a central role in the conflicts surrounding docetism, Arianism, and Nestorianism. In his study of these questions, Paul Gavrilyuk argues that the early church opted for a tension-filled position that preserved "an account of divine involvement worthy of God."[94] The church came to reject "the three inadequate strategies that aimed at eliminating the tension between Christ's divine status and the human experiences of his earthly ministry."[95] Theologians who would come to be affirmed as orthodox espoused a "qualified divine impassibility" that was "compatible with certain God-befitting emotions and with the incarnate Word's suffering in and through the human nature."[96] Early Christian theologians were convinced that something entirely unprecedented had taken place in the Christ-event. In Christ, God had become flesh and, in so doing, had united Godself with humanity and with human experience. In this event God had drawn so close to the "nondivine" experience of suffering that these theologians were compelled to speak in paradoxical phrases like "impassible suffering." In so doing they were stretching human language to the breaking point while trying to find an appropriate way to speak about this mystery. These early Christian theologians testify to the Christian belief that the God who is revealed in Jesus Christ has freely and graciously embraced the suffering endured by the human family.

Patristic Reflections on Human Suffering

Biblical authors offered a number of different interpretations of the meaning of suffering. In a similar way, theologians in the early church expounded a variety of interpretations of the experience of suffering in their theological and pastoral writings. Since patristic writers often practiced theology as commentary on scripture, most of these themes were drawn directly from the Bible. Without presuming to provide an exhaustive list of these interpretations, I enumerate some of the major themes that emerge in early Christian theology.

Punishment

In chapter 1, we saw that the theory of retribution plays a significant role in the Hebrew scriptures. Inherent in this view is the conviction that misfortune is sent by God to those who do evil or to those who are unfaithful to the covenant. While the Christian belief in the resurrection of the dead and eternal life changed the this-worldly limitations of this theory, early Christian theologians do sometimes speak of suffering as the result of divine punishment or penalty. Cyprian of Carthage spoke of the suffering that resulted from the persecution under the emperor Decius in terms of God's punishment for the worldliness of Christians. Cyprian was particularly critical of bishops who had forsaken their pastoral responsibilities, concentrating instead on enriching themselves. In pressing this point, Cyprian quotes the words of Psalm 89:31–33: "If they violate my statutes and do not keep my commandments, then I will punish their transgression with the rod and their iniquity with scourges."[97]

The notion of suffering as the result of divine punishment is also found in the writings of Augustine of Hippo. Augustine occasionally speaks of God's punishment for the personal sins of individuals. At the beginning of *The City of God*, referring to the experience of the sack of Rome in 410, Augustine argues that divine providence "is wont to reform the depraved manners of men [sic] by chastisement."[98] Further along in the same work, Augustine speaks of punishments, whether temporal or eternal, that are inflicted by divine providence "either on account of past sins, or of sins presently allowed in the life, or to exercise and reveal a man's graces."[99] Most often, however, when Augustine invokes the idea of divine punishment for sin he has in mind original sin, which in his view has vitiated human nature and turned human history into a welter of suffering. Augustine expresses this conviction in very striking terms in the last book of *The City of God*: "That the whole human race has been condemned in its first origin, this life itself, if life it is to be called, bears witness by the host of cruel ills with which it is filled."[100] Augustine envisioned the miseries endured in this life as the result of the introduction of evil into God's good creation through the sin of the first human beings. And in some places he speaks of these miseries in terms of divine wrath or punishment.

Testing

The idea that human suffering is a means by which God tests and purifies a person's faith and virtue is also found among early Christian theologians. These theologians generally interpreted the suffering of Job as a test of his virtue, and this view colors their discussion of human suffering in general.[101] In his treatise addressed to lapsed Christians, Cyprian speaks of the experience of persecution in terms of trial: "The Lord wanted his household to be tested."[102] Augustine also incorporates this theme into his reflections on the meaning of human suffering. In a sermon for Easter week he tells his congregation that each one of them is like a piece of pottery that is shaped by instruction and fired by tribulation. He insists, however, quoting Paul in First Corinthians 10:13, that God is faithful and does not let us be tested beyond our strength.[103] Lauding the ways of divine providence, John Damascene says, "The just man is often permitted to meet with disasters, so that he may show to other men the virtue hidden within him; this happened in the case of Job."[104] This biblical theme is one way in which early Christian theologians find positive meaning in suffering; they identify it as an opportunity for growth in Christian perfection.

Education

Closely allied to the theme of trial or testing is the interpretation of suffering as divine education—God's way of instructing human beings in divine wisdom. Some early Christian theologians hold that there is such a thing as a "school of suffering." Titus of Bostra, a fourth-century bishop who wrote in opposition to Manichaean dualism, argues that "evil will seem to school us better than good towards virtue, for often the assault of grief and misfortune converts those whom prosperity failed to attract to better ways." This author is convinced that human beings "need reminders such as these at vital moments to awaken their minds, and to rid themselves of the soft living which is excessive."[105] Augustine also seemed to adduce this theme when he spoke of the suffering that ensued from the sack of Rome in terms of God reforming the depraved manners of human beings through chastisement.[106]

Medicine and Healing

Patristic writers also employ medicinal metaphors in their efforts to discover meaning in human suffering. These allusions reflect their conviction that human nature and human history have been severely wounded by sin and are in need of divine healing. Sometimes, they argue, God heals us by sending hardship and suffering. In his defense of the goodness of the Creator, Basil of Caesarea teaches that deprivations like loss of wealth, illness, and even death are imposed on us by God for our benefit. He writes, "Just as a beneficent physician may inflict sufferings and pain on the body as he grapples with the sickness and not the patient, so the good God dispenses salvation for the whole by punishment of the parts."[107] A lengthy poem that has traditionally been attributed to Prosper of Aquitaine, a fifth-century admirer of Augustine, also contains this theme.[108] The author of this poem asserts that the experience of suffering can be the result of God correcting our faults, and he interprets this corrective action of God in medicinal terms: "When God deigns to send down from heaven his healing cure and utterly to excise diseased fibres, we feebly rebuke his aid, and prefer to waste away with disease rather than to steel ourselves to endure the force of the enemy."[109] He proceeds to observe, "So what we consider evils are not evils. When the right hand of the healing Physician does not spare the foul tumors, we should embrace that salvation rather than sharpen our complaints."[110] Thus, certain patristic theologians teach that suffering can have a salvific quality because it heals and strengthens a soul that has become enfeebled by the effects of sin.

Harmony

The belief that the universe is an ordered whole, a harmonious totality that is the product of a wise and all-good Creator, is sometimes brought to bear on the reality of evil and suffering. John Hick calls this the "aesthetic theme," and he traces its development in the writings of Augustine.[111] Augustine was influenced by the thought of Plotinus, who envisioned the universe as emanating from the One and including a great chain of being comprised of a rich diversity of gradations. Augustine draws on this principle of plenitude, though he insists that the universe is not the product of unconscious emanation from the divine but of a conscious choice by God to form a world comprised of a multiplicity of kinds of being. In his *Confessions*, Augustine articulates his vision of the natural world as deriving from the hands of the Creator and thus as essentially good. Nothing outside the universe can break in and destroy the order God has imposed on it. Inferior beings, and even those creatures that humans consider as antithetical to their well-being—"deeps, fire, hail, snow, ice, the hurricane and tempest"—all contribute to the complex perfection of the whole. "I no longer wished individual things to be better, because I considered the totality." While "superior things are self-evidently better than inferior,…all things taken together are better than superior things by themselves."[112]

Augustine sometimes appeals to this aesthetic motif when he deals with evil and suffering in the world. The aesthetic theme in Augustine can include even moral evil because of his conviction that God deals with sin justly and, therefore, the balance of the moral order is preserved.[113] In *On Free Will*, Augustine says, "There is no interval of time between failure to do what ought to be done and suffering what ought to be suffered, lest for a single moment the beauty of the universe should be defiled by having the uncomeliness of sin without the comeliness of penalty."[114] This theme is also found in *The City of God*. In God's infinite wisdom, God knows how to accomplish his good purposes even in the face of human malice. "For God would never have created any, I do not say angel, but even man, whose future wickedness he foreknew, unless he had equally known to what uses in behalf of the good he could turn him, thus embellishing the course of the ages, as it were an exquisite poem set off with antitheses."[115] He develops this theme of antithesis, or contrast, further and quotes Sirach (Ecclesiasticus) to support his argument:

> As, then, these oppositions of contraries lend beauty to the language, so the beauty of the course of this world is achieved by the opposition of contraries, arranged, as it were, by an eloquence not of words but of things. This is quite plainly stated in the Book of Ecclesiasticus, in this way: "Good is set against evil, and life against death: so is the sinner against the godly. So look upon the works of the Most High, and these are two and two, one against another."[116]

Though life would look vastly different if human beings had not rebelled against God out of pride, the sins of angels and human beings are incorporated by God into the overall order and beauty of the universe:

> Was it not obviously meant to be understood that there was no other cause of the world's creation than that good creatures should be made by a good God? In this creation, had no one sinned, the world would have been filled and beautified with natures good without exception; and though there is sin, all things are not therefore full of sin, for the great majority of heavenly inhabitants preserve their nature's integrity. And the sinful will, though it violated the order of its own nature, did not on that account escape the laws of God, who justly orders all things for good. For as the beauty of a picture is increased by well-managed shadows, so to the eye that has skill to discern it, the universe is beautified even

by sinners, though considered by themselves, their defor-
mity is a sad blemish.[117]

Contemporary theologians find this aesthetic theme problematic
when applied to individual instances of suffering, as well as when faced
with radical evil like the Shoah. It seems inappropriate to compare
the suffering caused by sinful actions to a shadow in a beautiful paint-
ing. This is, however, just one aspect of Augustine's approach to evil
and suffering. It appears that the aesthetic motif was ultimately an
expression of his belief in divine providence over human history and a
development of the more fundamental, and theologically significant,
principle expressed in *The Enchiridion on Faith, Hope and Love*: "For he
[God] judged it better to bring good out of evil, than not to permit any
evil to exist."[118]

Witness

In our exploration of the New Testament, we encountered the
theme of suffering as an opportunity for Christians to offer credible
witness to Christ. This is evident, for example, in the First Letter of
Peter. This same theme is found in the writings of early Christian theologians. In one of his letters, Cyprian of Carthage extols the example
of Christians who have suffered persecution, affirming that these
believers are the pride of the church. "She makes her boast especially
in the steadfast witness given by Christ's confessors and the punishment recently embraced which has made them exiles. Your present witness is more splendid and brings you greater honor because it became
more assured in suffering. For when the battle grew fiercer, so the feats
of the warriors increased in glory."[119] In the poem on divine providence
attributed to Prosper of Aquitaine, the author extends this theme to
experiences beyond that of direct persecution for the faith. He
acknowledges that acts of God's justice that punish the guilty—which
he associates with wars, the destruction of cities, disease, and so
forth—sometimes also bring suffering to the innocent. But, he stresses,
the suffering of the innocent can be turned to good purpose.

In this world many shared experiences await worthy and unworthy alike. The sun shines on all alike; cold and heat are endured equally. And just as water, light, air are shared by all, so the just must endure the evils of the unjust, so that whilst the innocent suffer many things in company with the wicked, there may be those whose merit ensures that wicked people are spared, and who by the witness of their virtue guide the others to conversion.[120]

This conviction about the opportunity for witness found in experiences of suffering—grounded in the scriptures and enduring long after the patristic period—is another way in which early Christian theologians discover meaning and positive benefit in human suffering.

Mystery

James and P. G. Walsh point out that in spite of sustained efforts to demonstrate God's loving care for people amidst great suffering, "many of the Fathers inevitably fall back on Paul's statement that God's judgments are incomprehensible and his ways unsearchable to men; our limited intellects cannot penetrate the mysterious motives of Providence, and we must rest content with the impaired vision which is ours."[121] In a work on divine providence, John Chrysostom puts it simply: "If you do not have recourse to the inscrutability of God's plans, and if you have always made it a practice to question everything, there will be many things to trouble you in your course."[122] Augustine often refers to the Pauline statement in the Letter to the Romans: "O the depth of the riches and wisdom and knowledge of God! How unsearchable are his judgments and how inscrutable his ways!" (11:33). In *The City of God* Augustine confesses, "For we do not know by what judgment of God this good man is poor and that bad man rich; why he who, in our opinion ought to suffer acutely for his abandoned life enjoys himself, while sorrow pursues him whose praiseworthy life leads us to suppose he should be happy...."[123] He proceeds in this text to expose the limitations of human judgment about the fortunes of people, while affirming that on the last day everyone will recognize the justice of God's judgments. While Augustine offered a variety of interpretations of the experience of suffering in his many writings, he was acutely aware of the limitations of these interpretations in the face of the mystery of God and the mystery of human suffering.

Two Additional Augustinian Themes

William Palardy, an Augustinian scholar, argues that study of Augustine's corpus reveals a theologian and church leader who took the reality of human suffering very seriously.[124] As the bishop of a busy seaport city—a pastor closely in touch with his own society— Augustine was keenly aware of the stark reality of human suffering and he grappled with it. He never tried to explain suffering away by means of facile theological formulas. As we have seen, he sometimes speaks of suffering as divine punishment for sin, though he is usually referring to original sin, which affects the whole human race. He can also speak of suffering as a test of Christian faith and virtue and as a correction for faults. The passages cited above also demonstrate that he could be "agnostic" about the reasons for suffering, appealing to the inscrutability of God's judgments and citing biblical passages like Romans 11:33. Underneath these diverse statements was Augustine's firm belief in the providence of God and his conviction that God would make every-thing—even experiences that seem blatantly contrary to the will of God—work together for the realization of God's wise purposes.

In her work *The Origenist Controversy*, Elizabeth Clark demonstrates the way in which the development of Augustine's doctrine of original sin was related to his experience of evil and suffering in the world.[125] Augustine developed his theology of original sin in large part in response to the teaching of Pelagius and his followers. Pelagius, a lay monk from the British Isles, came to Rome in the latter part of the fourth century and gained fame for his learning and devotion. He was part of an ascetical movement that placed great stress on growth toward perfection through the wise and disciplined use of one's natural powers. Shocked by the moral laxity of Christians of the Roman Empire, he urged a stricter asceticism and a deeper loyalty to the gospel. While Pelagius speaks of the sin of Adam in his commentary on the letters of Paul, he generally identifies the harmful effects of this "first" sin with the bad example of the first human being.[126] Augustine's reading of Pelagius convinced him that Pelagius failed to give an adequate account of human solidarity in sin and of the need for grace to heal our affections and our will. The conflict between Augustine and the followers of Pelagius intensified as the years went on, particularly with the acrimonious debate between Augustine and Julian of Eclanum.

Augustine's writings cover a span of more than forty years, and there is development in his thought on grace, freedom, and sin. As the years went on, Augustine became less optimistic about the powers of human nature unaided by grace. He read Romans 5:12 to mean that all people sinned in Adam: "Therefore, just as sin came into the world through one man, and death came through sin, and so death spread to all because all have sinned...."[127] Augustine had an exalted understanding of the state of the first human beings in paradise. They were immune from physical ills and had extraordinary intellectual gifts; they lived in enjoyment of God, with surpassing natural powers and the gifts of grace necessary for obeying the will of God. They not only had free will (liberum arbitrium) but also true freedom (libertas), which for Augustine means free will oriented toward goodness. Adam's only weakness was that he was a creature and could fall away, which, of course, he did through pride. In Augustine's mind, this first sin was a grievous fault, a heinous crime that adversely affected the entire human race and all of human history. Augustine thought that the ancient ecclesial practice of baptizing infants and including exorcisms in the baptismal rite was proof that all people are born infected with sin. He was convinced that because of original sin human nature has been wounded; it is like the man left half-dead on the road in the parable of the Good Samaritan. All people are in desperate need of Christ the Good Samaritan, who alone can heal our nature, orient us to the good, and empower us to live as disciples of Jesus.

There were many influences that drove the development of Augustine's thought on original sin and humanity's absolute dependence on the saving grace of God. One of these factors was his grappling with the mystery of evil and suffering in light of his belief in a just and good God. The suffering that marked the lives of so many with whom he was in contact was one factor that led Augustine to believe that something had gone terribly awry in God's good creation. In *The City of God*, for example, he reflects on the travails of this life, which begin in infancy and last until death. Even baptized babies, the most innocent of God's creatures in Augustine's mind, "suffer many ills, and in some instances are even exposed to the assaults of evil spirits."[128] Babies are born with terrible disabilities that cannot be understood as a penalty for personal sin. The process of learning for children is an ordeal that usually necessitates severe discipline. For Augustine, the harsh conditions of this world can be understood only as the consequence of the disorder in creation that resulted from the misuse of human freedom at the origin of human history and the ensuing penalty that was imposed on sinful humanity as a whole. "From Augustine's standpoint, God's justice is under attack by anyone who thinks that human misery, from infancy on, is *not* the consequence of sin."[129] While the merits of Augustine's theology of original sin can be debated (and are vigorously debated today), what is important for us to notice is that the strength of this Augustinian teaching manifests his wrestling with the reality of evil and human suffering as he encountered them in his own experience of pastoral ministry. His theology of original sin is directly related to his sober reflections upon the mystery of human suffering.

The final aspect of Augustine's thought that needs to be considered here is his notion of the "whole Christ" (*totus Christus*). For Augustine the church is first and foremost the Body of Christ. Bernard McGinn observes, "It would be hard to exaggerate the emphasis that Augustine placed on the Body of Christ."[130] Augustine's understanding of deification (divinization)—our sharing in the very life of God through the grace of Christ—is worked out in the context of his theology of the Body of Christ. Christians are divinized by being united with Christ through his Body, the church. "The unity between Christ and his Body means that by our membership in the church we share in all the *magnalia Christi*, the great mysteries by which the God-man wrought our redemption. This is an ontological bond, a real participation in his life, and not just some form of moral imitation of Christ's good example."[131] For Augustine, our sharing in the life of the triune God, and thus our re-creation in the image of the Trinity, occurs not by means of an individualistic mystical journey to God but through our active participation in the life of the church.

Augustine frequently draws upon this theme of the "whole Christ" in his *Expositions of the Psalms*. When the church prays the psalms it is the "whole Christ," head and body, who utters these prayers. Commenting on Psalm 62 (63), he says, "This psalm is spoken in the person of our Lord Jesus Christ, and that means head and members.... If he is the head, we are the limbs. The whole Church spread everywhere is his body, and of that body he is the head."[132] Because of Christ's self-emptying in the incarnation and his union with his church, even those expressions of the psalms that seem unbefitting to the Lord are prayed by the "whole Christ." In his exposition of Psalm 85 (86), Augustine lays out this theme at the start:

> God could have granted no greater gift to human beings than to cause his Word, through whom he created all things, to be their head, and to fit them to him as his members. He was thus to be both Son of God and Son of Man, one God with the Father, one human being with us. The consequence is that when we speak to God in prayer we do not separate the Son from God, and when the body of the Son prays it does not separate its head from itself. The one sole savior of his body is our Lord Jesus Christ, the Son of God, who prays for us, prays in us, and is prayed to by us. He prays for us as our priest, he prays in us as our head, and he is prayed to by us as our God.[133]

Augustine appeals to this principle when he comments on various psalms that articulate experiences of human suffering. In so doing he accentuates the closeness of Christ to the suffering members of his body. Just as Jesus prayed the psalms when he suffered on earth, so the risen Christ prays in those believers who cry out in lament to God:

> Accordingly, when we hear his voice, we must hearken to it as coming from both head and body; for whatever he suf-

fered, we too suffered in him, and whatever we suffer, he too suffers in us....This solidarity meant that when Christ suffered, we suffered in him; and it follows that now that he has ascended into heaven and is seated at the Father's right hand, he still undergoes in the person of his Church whatever it may suffer amid the troubles of this world, whether temptations, or hardship or oppression....[134]

Augustine's conviction about the profound union between Christ and the church led to his exquisite reflections on the intimacy between the risen Christ and all suffering members of his body. This belief appears to be more foundational and perhaps far more significant than Augustine's other interpretations of suffering as testing, punishment for original sin, and so forth. The fact that God caused the Word to be the head of the body means that for Augustine God is in the closest possible solidarity with the suffering members of the body.

Discussion Questions: www.paulistpress.com, Online Resources.

4

Thomas Aquinas:
God Acting to Dispel Misery

Thomas Aquinas (1225–74) developed a theology that became a highly influential expression of classical theism. Aquinas drew heavily upon the insights of Augustine, whom he cites hundreds of times in his *Summa Theologiae*, and he took Aristotle as his philosophical conversation partner in his exposition of the faith. Although written more than seven centuries ago, the theological synthesis that Aquinas constructed forms an important part of the backdrop for the contemporary discussion about God and the mystery of human suffering. His conception of God and of God's relation to the world has influenced Christian thinking for centuries, though it has been subjected to critique by some modern theologians. In this chapter, I focus on what Aquinas has to say about God, God's relation to the created world, the reality of evil, and the incarnation. I pay special attention to his teaching in the *Summa Contra Gentiles* (*SCG;* written between 1258 and 1264) and the *Summa Theologiae* (*ST;* begun in 1269 and left unfinished at the time of Aquinas's death), with preference given to his mature thought as articulated in the *Summa Theologiae*.

Two themes in the thought of Aquinas underlie much of what is discussed in this chapter: (1) truth is one; and (2) the universe is an orderly place.[1] Aquinas is convinced of the unity of truth because he is certain that there is one God, who is the First Truth (*Veritas Prima*). This God is the source of all truth discovered by human beings. This means that, for Aquinas, there can be no ultimate contradiction between faith and reason. While there are limits to what we can know by reason, Aquinas has a fundamental confidence in the use of reason and, thus, in the employment of philosophy to assist us in gaining insight into the truth revealed by God. For Aquinas, the light of faith does not destroy the light of reason. The truth discerned through philosophical reasoning cannot be contrary to what belongs to faith, even though it does fall short of it.

Aquinas also thinks that the world is an orderly place. The order of creatures on Earth and in the skies has a goodness and glory, and it points to the wise plan of God. He perceives a fundamental harmony in the universe, and this lends a certain serenity to his thought. In his discussion of Aquinas's five arguments for the existence of God (*ST* I, 2, 3), Thomas O'Meara observes, "Aquinas noticed the omnipresent order in all of creation and asked: Who planned this?"[2] The first word about creation for Aquinas is existence and its goodness. It is a very good thing just "to be," and the world in which we live is the good gift of the One who is the source of all existence.

God as Incomprehensible Mystery

Aquinas wrote primarily about God's relationship to creation. He was aware that we cannot know much about the God who is so different from us. He had a profound and enduring appreciation for the mysteriousness of God, whose nature and ways can never be comprehended by the human mind. This conviction is expressed in the prologue to the third question of the *Summa Theologiae*, which immediately follows the five arguments adduced by Aquinas through which a person might be led to affirm an Uncaused Cause. Aquinas writes, "Having recognized that a certain thing exists, we have still to investigate the way in which it exists, that we may come to understand what it is that exists. Now we cannot know what God is, but only what he is not; we must therefore consider the ways in which God does not exist, rather than the ways in which he does."[3] He argues in similar fashion in the *Summa Contra Gentiles*, where he writes:

> For, by its immensity, the divine substance surpasses every form that our intellect reaches. Thus we are unable to apprehend it by knowing what it is. Yet we are able to have

some knowledge of it by knowing what it is not. Furthermore, we approach nearer to a knowledge of God according
as through our intellect we are able to remove more and
more things from Him. (*SCG* I, 14, 2)[4]

Scholars underline the significance of Aquinas's respect for the
mystery of God. In his study of the spirituality of Aquinas, Jean-Pierre
Torrell observes, "Far from thinking it possible to appropriate the mystery of God by way of mastery through his concepts and reasonings,
Thomas never ceases to be aware that the mystery escapes our every
grasp and he invites his disciple to prostrate himself alongside him in
adoration of the Ineffable."[5] Aquinas's language is strong when he says
that we do not know much about God. Herbert McCabe comments,
"Readers of Aquinas, however, including some of those who see themselves as his disciples, have the utmost difficulty in taking him seriously
when he says that we simply know nothing of the nature of God."[6] In
arguing that we cannot know the nature of God, Aquinas is saying that
we cannot define God. We can know about God by projecting what
we know about creation and saying that it has a high intensity when it
is applied to God. In his commentary on the Gospel of John, Aquinas
concludes that not even the human soul of Christ had comprehensive
knowledge of the divine. He writes, "No one comprehends the divine
essence except God alone, Father, Son and Holy Spirit."[7]

Aquinas suggests that we should begin by denying to God characteristics that apply to creatures. This method of negation can lead,
ultimately, to meaningful affirmations about God. For Aquinas, "negative theology is by no means a theology of negation."[8] Through our
experience of the world, which always begins in the senses, we can be
led to make statements about God that are true, even though they are
always inadequate to the transcendent mystery of God. Even the
knowledge given by God's self-revelation does not remove the mystery
of God. He acknowledges that revelation offers us a more perfect
knowledge of God than that attained by natural reason. Still, God's
self-revelation "joins us to him as to an unknown" (*ST* Ia., 12, 13, ad 1).

Aquinas asserts that our speech about God arises from our experience of the perfections we discover in creatures. Such speech is not

univocal—having the same meaning when applied to creatures as when attributed to God—because the Creator is utterly transcendent to creation. Neither is this talk equivocal—having an entirely different meaning when applied to creatures as when attributed to God— because creatures are related to their Creator as effects to their cause. In our talk about God, words are used analogically, since "whatever is said both of God and creatures is said in virtue of the order that creatures have to God as to their source and cause in which all the perfections of things pre-exist transcendentally" (*ST* Ia. 13, 5). Because Aquinas is convinced that effects resemble their causes, he can argue that our experience of the created can lead us to some insight into the Creator. "Analogy is a juxtaposition of linguistic terms and mental ideas with the claim that the divine and human realms have a slight similarity: in the way the artist is in the art work, the creator is present in creation."[9] For example, our experience of the love of a fellow human being leads us to affirm that God is loving. We make the judgment that the reality of love must exist in God; we affirm that it is indeed true that God is loving. Not to make this affirmation would be to miss out on something of utmost importance about the divine. But our experience of love and our way of understanding and speaking about love are limited; they are marked by all of the limits and imperfections of finite, fallible human beings. Thus, while we affirm the reality of love in God, we also must negate the creaturely limitations that are intrinsic to our understanding of and speaking about love.

> When we say that God is loving, we affirm a love in God setting forth a world of beauty and light, but we do not have much information about what God's love is like. Ultimately we must find human ideas, images and languages for the divine. Aquinas' theory of speaking about God permits and encourages discussing God while at the same time affirming mystery and transcendence.[10]

For Aquinas, this dynamic of analogical predication applies not only to the work of theology but also to the ways we speak about God in preaching, prayer, and everyday parlance.

God Is Pure Activity

In the third of his "five ways" of reasoning to the affirmation of God's existence, Aquinas adduces the experience of contingency (*ST* I, 2 ,3). As he puts it, "Some of the things we come across can be but need not be, for we find them springing up and dying away, thus sometimes in being and sometimes not." Aquinas is drawing on our experience of the fragility of creatures—indeed, the fragility of our own lives. If everything need not be, there was a time when there was nothing. But, Aquinas insists, if that were true there would be nothing now, because what does exist can only be brought into existence by something that already exists. He concludes that there has to be something that must be—a necessary being. Otherwise, there would be nothing in existence. "One is forced therefore to suppose something which must be, and owes this to no other thing than itself; indeed it itself is the cause that other things must be." This necessary being, this first cause, is the reality to which we give the name "God."

Employing the Aristotelian categories of potency and act, Aquinas teaches that God, as necessary being and first cause, must be completely actualized. There can be no unrealized potentialities in God. In his treatment of the simplicity of God, he writes, "For what is able to exist is brought into existence only by what already exists. Now we have seen that the first existent is God. In God then there can be no potentiality" (*ST* I, 3, 1). He speaks of God as "Pure Activity" (*Actus Purus*). He makes this same point in another way when he argues that God's essence is God's existence (*ST* I, 3, 4; *SCG*, I, 22). The essence of something is that which it is—the "whatness" of something. The existence of something is that by which a thing is—that which makes the essence real and actual.[11] Every creature is a composite of essence and existence. No creature has to be. Existence (*esse*) is something that creatures *have* as gift. But the Creator—the first cause and the giver of all existence—is the One whose essence is his existence. For Aquinas "God is not something with the potentiality of not being."[12] God is God's own existence and is the reason why other beings have existence. Creatures have existence through participation in the fullness of

God's existence. As fully actualized, as the One whose essence is to be, God is perfect: "Thus the first origin of all activity will be the most actual, and therefore the most perfect, of all things. For things are called perfect when they have achieved actuality, the perfect thing being that in which nothing required by the thing's particular mode of perfection fails to exist" (*ST* I, 4, 1). Pure activity means that God is not subject to another being but is fully in act all of the time.

Aquinas wants us to think of God as dynamic, as full of life. When he speaks of "existence" he does not use the noun form of the word (*existentia*); instead, he employs the infinitive form of the verb "to be" (*esse*).[13] William Hill observes that "existence or actuality for Aquinas is not mere facticity nor givenness but the exercise of existential act."[14] For Aquinas the essence of God is simply to-be.[15] O'Meara remarks, "Thus God's reality is not an activity but activity, and God is not just living but is life (I-II, 55, 2, 3; I, 18, 3)."[16] The way in which Aquinas speaks about God is exactly the opposite of a static deity. This leads Elizabeth Johnson to translate Aquinas's understanding of God as "sheer liveliness."[17]

Aquinas argues that the transcendent perfection of God is the ground of God's immanence. As the giver of all existence, God exists in everything, not just at the beginning of something's coming to be but as long as it exists. Thomas employs the images of fire and the sun in speaking of God as the perduring cause of existence:

> Now since it is God's nature to exist, he it must be who properly causes existence in creatures, just as it is fire itself sets other things on fire. And God is causing this effect in things not just when they begin to exist, but all the time they are maintained in existence, just as the sun is lighting up the atmosphere all the time the atmosphere remains lit. During the whole period of a thing's existence, therefore, God must be present to it, and present in a way in keeping with the way in which the thing possesses its existence. (*ST* I, 8, 1)

McCabe comments on Aquinas's teaching about the immanence of God: "If the creator is the reason for everything that is, there can be no actual being which does not have the creator at its centre and holding it in being."[18] The God about whom Aquinas writes is indescribably close to creation and to each creature. "Aquinas insisted that God be sovereignly free from creation, infinitely different, and yet also be intimately directive of and present to each being."[19]

Divine Immutability and Impassibility

Aquinas maintains that if God is pure activity then God must be unchangeable. If God changed it would mean that there were unrealized potentialities in God. This would make God less than pure activity. He asserts that God "is sheerly actual and unalloyed with potentiality" while "any changing thing is somehow potential" (*ST* I, 9, 1). Moreover, if we were to say that God changes it would mean that God acquired something. Aquinas argues, "God, being limitless and embracing within himself the whole fullness of perfection of all existence, cannot acquire anything, nor can he move out towards something previously not attained" (*ST* I, 9, 1). In his reflections on the incarnation, Aquinas insists that the incarnation did not involve any sort of change in God's eternal existence. It entailed something created (the human nature of Jesus) becoming united to God. The change (the becoming) took place on the side of the created reality (*ST* III, 1, 1, ad 1). For Aquinas, affirming the immutability of God entails denying to God the change we experience as creatures: "Immutability remains a negative concept, denying to God all forms of creaturely alteration; though it does intend to designate a positive divine attribute, this is something we can neither know nor represent in itself."[20]

For Aquinas, divine immutability implies divine impassibility. Because to suffer means to be acted upon and changed, suffering cannot touch the divine nature. To suggest that God suffers would mean that one had detracted from the transcendent perfection of God. It would entail reducing God to the level of the creaturely. Contemporary Thomistic scholars argue that by denying suffering to God, Aquinas was convinced that he was affirming divine transcendence. Torrell asserts, "And if we really wish to implicate God in his creation (to make him share our sufferings, for example, as many theologians try to do today), we would only be making an unnecessary idol, nothing more. That god would not be God."[21] O'Meara takes note of Aquinas's analogical thinking in the latter's attempts to depict the transcendence of God:

> Indecision and illness do not best characterize human beings, and so too God is not passive or searching for an identity, not paralyzed by sorrow over the casualties of history deformed by human coldness, nor a heavenly watcher or repair-person, always judging and always disappointed. A purely becoming god is a freak in a world out of control, a suffering god is a momentarily consoling myth for the sick but not a credible cause of the universe. God is not to be limited by human psychology and earthly history.[22]

Thus, for Aquinas, the transcendence of God entails that the suffering of the world does not impinge upon the divine nature.

God's Relation to the World

In a famous and much-discussed article of the *Summa Theologiae*, Aquinas argues that when we speak of God as related to the world (as the Bible often does) we do so only within our limited understanding. Such a relation is not real in God. Aquinas says, "Now since God is altogether outside the order of creatures, since they are ordered to him but not he to them, it is clear that being related to God is a reality in creatures, but being related to creatures is not a reality in God, we say it about him because of the real relations in creatures" (*ST* I, 13, 7). To illustrate this point Aquinas uses the example of the person standing on the right side of a pillar and then moving to the left of the pillar. The change in relation is not because of any alteration in the pillar but simply because the person has changed places. The relation is real in the person but not in the pillar. Just so, Aquinas concludes, "God's temporal relations to creatures are in him only because of our way of thinking about him, but the opposite relations of creatures to him are realities in creatures" (ST I, 13, 7, ad 4). This teaching, which was not unique to Aquinas in the thirteenth century, has evoked a reaction of puzzlement from many readers. Among other things, it seems to be foreign to the covenantal language of the scriptures. What does Aquinas mean when he argues that a relation to creatures is not real in God?

First of all, since relation is one of Aristotle's nine accidents, Aquinas cannot attribute it to God, since there are no accidents in God. An accident is a way of being that is not attributed to a subject necessarily but contingently or incidentally.[23] Divine simplicity excludes the attribution of anything contingent or incidental to God. More important, Aquinas thinks that if you posited a real relation to creatures in God it would mean that you had made God dependent upon creatures and had reduced God to the ontological order of creatures. This principle should not be understood in a psychological sense, but in its metaphysical meaning. It simply means that God is outside of the whole order of created things. "He [God] gives creation its constancy, but the opposite is not true. The relation is necessarily asymmetrical."[24] Fergus Kerr connects this teaching on real relation with a concern that he thinks is central to the thinking of Aquinas, that is, his determination not to depict God as ontologically dependent on creatures for God's fulfillment and happiness. Aquinas was passionately concerned "to stop Christians from thinking of God as being under some compulsion or obligation to create the world in order to complete his life."[25]

Despite this teaching about God having no real relation to creatures, Aquinas insists that God knows and loves the world. We have already seen that in his teaching about divine immanence Aquinas asserts that God is intimately present to every creature. "At the heart of every creature is the source of *esse*, making it to be and to act."[26] He also maintains that God has complete knowledge of the world in that God knows other things through knowing Godself (ST I, 14, 5). And God knows creatures not just in a general manner but in all of their particularity. "We must therefore say that he knows things other than himself in what is proper to each; not only in what they have in common as beings, but in the ways in which they are different from one another" (ST I, 14, 6).

God's love for creatures, according to Aquinas, is also complete. Because God has will, and will for Aquinas means being drawn to the good that is perceived, God loves the creatures God has made. Aquinas calls love a "binding force" and attributes this even to God. Love joins the lover to the beloved (*ST* I, 20, 2, ad 3). Aquinas distinguishes between love of desire and love of friendship. In love of desire one is drawn to the other for the fulfillment of one's own needs. Love of friendship, however, is a benevolent love in which the lover is focused on the good of the beloved (*ST* I, 20, 2). It is this second kind of love that is superior and that is characteristic of God's love for creatures. "To act from need is the mark only of an agent which is unfulfilled and made to be both acting on and acted upon. But this is not the case with God. He alone is supremely generous, because he does not act for his own benefit but simply to give of his goodness" (*ST* I, 44, 4, ad 1).

Aquinas emphasizes that God loves all existing things, each of which, insofar as it is real, is good. "God therefore wills some good to each existing thing, and since loving is no other than willing good to someone, it is clear that God loves everything" (*ST* I, 20, 2). It is not just that God loves creatures because they are good. For Aquinas, God's love creates the goodness in things. Torrell observes, "Like a sun that could make a flower bloom even without seed or water, so God's love makes being arise from nothingness—at every instant."[27] Herbert McCabe draws the connection between Aquinas's account of God's love for creation and his teaching that God does not have a real relation to creatures:

> The point about the lack of real relation on God's part is simply that being creator adds nothing to God, all the difference it makes is *all* the difference to the creature....But it makes no difference to God...because he gains nothing by creating. We could call it sheerly altruistic, except that the goodness God wills for his creatures is not a separate and distinct goodness from his own goodness. The essential point that Aquinas, surely rightly, wants to make is that creation fulfills no need of God's. God has no needs.[28]

This view of God and God's relation to creatures influences Aquinas's discussion of divine compassion. He maintains that mercy (*misericordia*) belongs properly to God and is the source of all God's works.[29] For Aquinas God does not have "compassion" in the literal sense of "suffering with" another because God cannot suffer in Godself.[30] In his discussion of divine mercy he writes, "Above all mercy is to be attributed to God, nevertheless in its effect, not in the affect of feeling" (*ST* I, 21, 4). Convinced of divine immutability and impassibility, Aquinas does not want to attribute passion to God. Thus God's mercy does not entail a feeling of sadness about the misery of another because sadness, as a form of passion, does not befit God. God is merciful in that God acts out of love to dispel the misery that afflicts creatures. Aquinas argues that mercy "involves giving from one's abundance to others, and, what is more, relieving their needs" (*ST* II-II, 30, 4). This is exactly what God does in being merciful toward us—giving from the fullness of God's being in order to relieve the misery of beloved creatures, not out of any need of God's own, but purely for our benefit.

Some thinkers argue that this view of divine mercy is deficient. They wish to ascribe compassion, in the sense of suffering with another, to God. They view this attribute as a perfection, not a deficiency, in God. Several modern scholars of Aquinas have defended his treatment of divine compassion and mercy. They argue that to speak of God as suffering with us would be to detract from the divine transcendence and to introduce need into God. This would make God's love less than purely benevolent and, thus, less than perfect. They maintain that compassion is a form of finite love on the part of human beings who are limited in their efforts to dispel the affliction of others. Michael Dodds asserts that a suffering God "will inevitably seek his own perfection and try to overcome his own deficiency. Only an entirely perfect being, subject to no defect and lacking in nothing, is able to love with a fully gratuitous love."[31] William Hill, summarizing this topic, points out that "genuine compassion...characterizes love as finite, not love as such. The core reality of love as such is the affective union with another or others, [shown as] a willing of good to that person...for the other's own sake." God in his omnipotent divine love ranges himself against all forms of evil and suffering on behalf of humanity. Because "God does not and cannot suffer in himself," God can love unfathomably and altruistically—love that the New Testament calls *agape*.[32]

Evil in the Universe

Aquinas addresses the topic of evil in the First Part of the *Summa Theologiae*, immediately after treating the doctrine of creation. Here Aquinas gives only "a preliminary assessment of the problem as it stands for a Christian view of the universe" or "a grammar of thought to aid an approach to the mystery of sin and its resolution in the Passion of Christ, to be meditated on later at length."[33] The fuller extent of Aquinas's view of evil and the divine remedy for evil is found in his treatment of sin and grace.

Aquinas rejects the notion of an absolute principle of evil in the universe. He insists that "the sovereign good is the cause of the whole of being." Being as such is the good gift of the Creator. There is no contrasting principle that is the source of evil (*ST* I, 49, 3). He adopts the Neoplatonic and Augustinian view that evil has no nature or essence. It is, rather, the privation of being; it is the absence of something that ought to be present for the integrity of a thing. "Like night from day you learn one opposite from the other. So you take good in order to grasp what evil means....Consequently we are left to infer that it signifies a certain absence of a good" (*ST* I, 48, 1). The first and last word about the universe is goodness, since everything that exists has its source in the Creator who is supreme goodness. He asserts that "evil belongs neither to the integrity of the universe nor serves its development, except incidentally because of an accompanying good" (*ST* I, 48, 1, ad 5).

In this general discussion, Aquinas distinguishes between two kinds of evil: *malum poenae* and *malum culpae*. These terms can be translated as "pain" and "fault" or as "evil suffered" and "evil done."[34] Each of these kinds of evil is the result of a privation of the good. *Malum poenae* is evil consisting of the loss of a form or part required for a thing's integrity. It is what is sometimes called "natural evil" or "physical evil," such as illness or the death of a creature. Aquinas views this loss of form in a creature as the result of something else achieving its good. One can say that God wills this kind of evil indirectly for the sake of the overall good of the universe:

> God's principal purpose in created things is clearly that form of good which consists in the order of the universe. This requires, as we have noticed, that there should be some things that can, and sometimes do fall away. So then, in causing the common good of the ordered universe, he causes loss in particular things as a consequence and, as it were, indirectly, according to the words, "The Lord kills and brings to life." But we read also, "God has not made death," and the meaning is that he does not will death for its own sake. (ST I, 49, 2)

Aquinas assigns God an indirect role in the origin of natural evil. In creating a dynamic universe in which things flourish and then decay, God is willing the good of the universe as a whole. This is a universe that includes a rich diversity in grades of being. God creates "a world in which natural evil is always a matter of there being nothing but good derived from God."[35] Aquinas speaks of God causing evil suffered in the lives of human beings for the sake either of correction or of justice. Thus, he likens God to a surgeon who amputates a limb in order to save a person's body. Just so, "divine wisdom inflicts pain to prevent fault" (ST I, 48, 6). And he argues that God's punishment of sinners contributes to the justice that characterizes the order of creation: "The course of justice, which belongs to the universal order, requires that punishment be visited on sinners. On this count God is the author of the evil which is called penalty, but not of that which is fault" (ST I, 49, 2).

Evil done is equivalent to what is usually called "moral evil" or "fault." It refers to people acting in a way that is wrong or failing to do what is right. Aquinas describes it as "the evil of withdrawal in activity that is due, either by its omission or by its malfunctioning according to manner and measure" (ST I, 48, 5). Moral evil results from a person not acting in accord with right reason. "With voluntary causes, the deficient action proceeds from an actually deficient will, that is a will not submitted to its rule or measure" (*ST* I, 49, 1, ad 3). In distinction from evil suffered, with evil done there is no concomitant good.[36] It is nothing but a case of privation or defect. Davies explains, "For him, moral evil is even more a privation than 'evil suffered,' for unlike 'evil suffered' it is not the obverse of some good."[37] In committing moral evil, it is not only that I inflict harm on others; for Aquinas, I also harm myself. He argues that the quality of evil is stronger in evil done than in evil suffered since "a person becomes bad because of fault" (*ST* I, 48, 6). When I act in a way that is morally wrong, I become diminished as a human being. I become less human.

Aquinas stresses that evil done arises completely from the human side. Its origin is not to be traced to God in any sense. "Hence the evil which lies in defective activity or which is caused by a defective agent does not flow from God as its cause" (*ST* I, 49, 2). God can be termed the cause of moral evil only to the extent that God creates people, preserves them in being, and empowers them to act. But the failure in such action—the defect—derives solely from the creature, not the Creator. God permits such evil but does not directly cause it. O'Meara observes, "Nothing is clearer than that before the principles of Aquinas's theology God could not be directly involved in evil, for whatever is bad is the opposite of the supreme Good, the wisest Plan, the most loving Source." Sin, an evil act that flows from a free, intelligent creature, is a deliberate bad action. Having bestowed individual freedom, "God permits men and women to commit their own personal sins." Grace may try to dissuade from evil, but human will prevails. God has chosen not to interfere with this freedom: "Human responsibility perdures."[38]

While recognizing the presence and power of evil, Aquinas argues that evil can never destroy the good entirely. Likening goodness to the light from the sun, he compares evil to a series of screens set up between the sun and the atmosphere. Though the light would be indefinitely diminished, it would never be completely lost. He proceeds to state that, even if sin were piled on sin, weakening the soul's capacity to receive grace, the readiness (*habilitas*) for grace would still be present because it follows from the very nature of the soul (*ST* I, 48,

5). Once again, for Aquinas the foundation of reality is goodness since existence is the good gift of a good Creator. He is convinced that "the first source of good things is the supreme and perfect good anticipating all goodness within itself" (*ST* I, 49, 3). Therefore, "even though evil may indefinitely diminish good it can never entirely consume it, and so, while good remains, there cannot be anything wholly and completely evil" (*ST* I, 49, 3).

Original Sin

The metaphysical discussion of evil needs to be supplemented by what Aquinas says about original sin. In chapter 3 we saw that Augustine developed his teaching about original sin, in part, to account for the reality of evil and innocent suffering that he saw all around him. Aquinas inherited the church's teaching about original sin and was aware of developments in the theological tradition that had taken place between the time of Augustine and his own day. The notion of human solidarity in the sin of Adam had been explained in various ways by theologians who wrote before Aquinas. There had also been discussion about the essence of original sin. For example, Anselm of Canterbury had proposed that the essence of original sin consists of the privation of original justice—the loss of the justice possessed by Adam in paradise, due to his disobedience.[39]

Aquinas draws on this idea of original sin as a privation of original justice. For him the state in which Adam and Eve (whom he takes as historical individuals) were created was that of original justice. This condition was not simply a state of natural happiness; it was a way of being made possible by the gift of God's grace. As Aquinas puts it, "That he [Adam] was actually set up in grace seems to be required by the very rightness (*rectitudo*) in which God made man for his first state…" (*ST* 95, 1). Thus the gift of grace, which for Aquinas refers to the action of God leading us to union with God, was present before the "fall" of the human race.[40] The state of "rightness" in which the first human beings were created included a harmony between the various powers of the human person. Aquinas describes it as a condition in which human reason was submissive to God, the lower powers of the human soul were submissive to reason, and the body was submissive to the soul (ST, I, 95, 1). In this graced condition, the first humans possessed all of the virtues. Their entire being was completely oriented to God and to obedience to the divine will.

This state of original justice was for Aquinas a gift divinely bestowed upon human nature in the parents of the human race. It was not something owed to Adam and Eve by reason of nature. It did, however, entail the perfection of human nature, including freedom from suffering and death, the integration of human desires (appetites), and the gift of charity in the will. Aquinas argues that Adam was created immortal because "his soul was equipped by God with a supernatural force capable of preserving the body from all decay, as long as it remained submissive to God itself" (ST I, 97, 2). Original justice also entailed immunity from suffering. Adam "was immune from it [suffering] both in body and in soul, just as he was immortal, for he could have kept suffering away just as much as death, if he had persisted without sin" (ST, I, 97, 2). Moreover, the condition of original justice, while not entailing the beatific vision, included a higher knowledge of God than that possessed by human beings after the fall. Aquinas argues that those who enjoy the vision of God (the knowledge of God possessed by the blessed in heaven) "are so solidly established in the love of God that never can they sin" (ST I, 94, 1). Since Adam sinned, he could not have had this gift. Nevertheless, "he did know God with a loftier knowledge than we do now; and thus his knowledge was somehow or other half way between knowledge in our present state and knowledge in the home-country, where God is seen in his essence" (ST, I, 94, 1). If there had been no sin, human beings would not have died but would have been transferred into the state of beatitude—the condition of beholding the essence of God.

Given this account of the creation of the first human beings in a state of original justice, Aquinas then views the essence of original sin as the loss, or privation, of original justice. Through the sin of Adam, humanity lost the gift of original justice, and human nature was modified as a result of this privation. Employing Aristotelian terminology, Aquinas speaks of original sin as a "habit," that is, a disposition according to which a subject is well disposed or ill disposed toward something. Original sin is "a disordered disposition growing from the dissolution of that harmony in which original justice consisted" (*ST* I-II, 82, 1). He likens this disordered disposition to a bodily illness. Human nature has become sick because of the effects of the sin that occurred at the very origins of human history. In this condition, the powers of the human soul have become disturbed. Drawing on the classic image of "wounds," Aquinas speaks of the wounds of ignorance, malice, weakness, and concupiscence. Ignorance damages human reason, malice wounds the will, weakness affects the irascible appetite (the capacity to face situations that are difficult), and concupiscence wounds the concupiscible appetite (the attraction to things that are desirable). Death and other forms of human suffering are also the results of original sin (*ST* I-II, 85, 5). He writes:

> In this way the sin of the first parents is the cause of death and of all like defects in human nature. For the sin of the first parents removed original justice; through this not only were the lower powers of the soul held harmoniously under the control of reason but the whole body was subordinated to the soul without any defect....Once, therefore, original justice was lost through the sin of the first parents, just as human nature was injured in soul by the disordering of the powers, so also it became corruptible by reason of the disturbance of the body's order. (*ST* I-II, 85, 5)

A complete treatment of Aquinas's approach to sin would include an account of his rich and textured theology of grace. In his discussion of grace Aquinas asserts that we need the gift of God's action within us both as elevating and as healing. First, in order to experience communion with God, we need grace to move us beyond the capacities of human nature. He describes grace as "a certain participation in the divine nature." By communicating a share in the divine nature God makes us "godlike" (*ST* I, 112, 1). While this gift is something that exceeds the capacities of human nature, it is not foreign to our humanity because human nature has its finality in God.[41] Second, because of the debilitating effects of original sin as well as personal sin, we need God's grace to heal our sick nature. And Aquinas is convinced that when God graciously acts within us, this divine action makes a real difference. In Aristotelian terms, he speaks of grace as a "habitual gift" that modifies the human spirit, making a person exist differently (*ST* I-II, 111, 3). As original sin leaves us with a disordered disposition, grace renews us with a disposition oriented to God. Aquinas conceives of grace "as something which makes a definite, historical difference in people." It is not just that we are loved by God; we become lovable because of the healing, life-giving action of God within us.[42] In a kind of summary statement, Aquinas offers a deep and expansive account of the effects of grace: "Now there are five effects of grace in us: firstly, the healing of the soul; secondly, willing the good; thirdly, the efficacious performance of the good willed; fourthly, perseverance in the good; fifthly, the attainment of glory" (*ST* I-II, 111, 3). Aquinas, then, underlines the primacy of grace in the Christian life; like Augustine, he is convinced that grace is needed at every step along the path of salvation. And he depicts a God who is generous in offering this grace, bestowing his presence in our lives in a way that is transformative.

Aquinas's treatment of the effects of original sin in the *Summa Theologiae* includes an intriguing objection—an argument with which he will not be in full agreement. In addressing the question of whether death and other bodily ills are the effects of sin, he cites an opposing position that claims that if this were the case then baptism and penance, by which sin is removed through sacramental grace, should also remove death and bodily ills. People living in the state of grace, then, should no longer experience suffering and death. In his response to this argument, Aquinas affirms that the grace of these sacraments does in fact remove both sin and the effects of sin. He quotes the Letter to the Romans, in which Paul speaks of the indwelling Spirit that brings life to our mortal bodies (Rom 8:11). But, Aquinas explains, each of these benefits of the sacraments "takes place according to the order of divine wisdom at a fitting time." He asserts:

> For it is right that we pass to the freedom from death and suffering proper to the glory begun in Christ and acquired

by Christ for us only after being made conformed to him in his suffering. Thus it must be that subjection to suffering remain for a time in our bodies that in conformity with Christ we may merit the freedom from suffering proper to the state of glory. (*ST* I-II, 85, 5, ad 2)

Thus, for Aquinas, the Christian is meant to configure his or her life to the crucified and risen Lord and, through union with Christ, be delivered from suffering in eternal life. The postponement of this freedom from suffering is in some mysterious way in keeping with the wisdom of God. This reference to conformity to Christ leads us to consider Aquinas's theology of the incarnation.

The Incarnation and God's Relation to Human Suffering

How does Aquinas's theology of Jesus touch upon suffering? We examine three relevant aspects of his thinking about the person and saving work of Jesus: his discussion of the unity of Christ and the communication of idioms; his reflection on the grace of Christ as head of the church; and his treatment of the saving work of Jesus.

First, in his christological reflection, Aquinas presumes the teaching of the early councils of the church, especially Ephesus and Chalcedon. The very first question in his treatment of Christ in the *Summa Theologiae* concerns the fittingness of the incarnation. As such, Aquinas integrates the traditional principle of the communication of idioms into his description of the person of Jesus. Following the teaching of Ephesus, he argues that because Christ is one person in two natures, we may predicate of God that which is attributed to the human nature of Christ (*ST* III, 16, 4). Aquinas affirms that "the passion is to be attributed to the divine person, not by reason of Christ's divine nature which is impassible, but by reason of his human nature" (*ST* III, 46, 12). He immediately quotes the Third Letter of Cyril to Nestorius, in which Cyril asserts that "the Word of God suffered in the flesh and was crucified in the flesh." In his exposition of Paul's First Letter to the

Corinthians, he numbers as one of the articles of faith "that the impassible God suffers and dies" (*quod impassibilis Deus patiatur et moriatur*).[43] Because of the unity of Christ, the suffering that he undergoes in his human nature can be attributed to the one divine person.

In an essay on Aquinas and human suffering, Michael Dodds highlights the role that the communication of idioms plays in his Christology. For Aquinas, we can truly confess that Jesus' suffering is the very suffering of God, that the human suffering of Jesus is itself the suffering of the Logos. "And what we say is not a mere matter of words but of fact and reality."[44] Appealing to this Thomistic teaching as an alternative to the idea that suffering touches the divine nature, Dodds maintains that if we "recognize that...Jesus of Nazareth *is* God, we will not be inclined to postulate some suffering of the divine nature as belonging more really to God, or being more really God's own, than is the human suffering of Jesus." No suffering is "more really God's own than the suffering of the man, Jesus of Nazareth." We are predicating of God not some sort of "divine suffering," but "rather a human suffering like our own." He who is like us "in all things but sin" "suffers *as we do*, as human; and yet that human suffering is the suffering of God."[45]

Second, like Augustine, Aquinas pays particular attention to the Pauline theme of the Body of Christ and to Christ's role as the head of the body. This is evident in the question in his *Summa Theologiae* in which he treats the grace of Christ as the head of the church (*ST* III, 8). Aquinas thinks that all grace derives from Christ as the Son of God—as one who is truly divine. But he also thinks that the humanity of Christ, which possesses the fullness of grace, has an instrumental role in the bestowal of grace upon humanity:

> In his view it is not the case that the eternal God remains apart from his creation, handing out grace in the role of a distant divinity with a soft spot for human beings. He holds that God is also a man, and that grace derives from him on that basis and since Christ is the founder of the Church, he puts this by saying that there is such a thing as the grace of Christ as head of the Church.[46]

Thus, appealing to Paul's statements in Romans 12 and First Corinthians 12, Aquinas affirms that "the whole Church is called one mystical body by analogy with the physical body of man." The risen Christ has the power to infuse grace into every member of the church (*ST* III, 8, 1). This influence of Christ in bestowing grace is realized principally through participation in the sacraments.

Aquinas's reflection on the grace of Christ as head of the church has the effect of illuminating the organic connection between Christ and every member of his body. In his exposition of the Letter to the Ephesians, he says that Christ loves the church "as something of himself" because believers are members of his body.[47] When he discusses the famous passage in Colossians about the suffering of the apostle making up for what is lacking in the suffering of Christ (Col 1:24), he refers to the suffering of the whole church whose head is Christ. Aquinas comments, "For this was lacking, that as Christ suffered in his own body, so he would suffer in Paul, his member, and similarly in others."[48] For Aquinas, "the sufferings of Paul were the sufferings of Christ, since Paul was a member of Christ. Our sufferings are also Christ's own, since we are members of Christ."[49] Aquinas's profound reflections on the intimate connection between Christ and the members of the church remind readers of Augustine's meditations on the "whole Christ." They manifest his deep conviction about the closeness of Christ to every believer and Christ's participation in the sufferings of all the members of his body.

Third, Aquinas's exploration of the saving work of Christ (soteriology) also provides insight into his approach to God and the mystery of suffering. In his soteriology, Aquinas draws upon the theory of satisfaction worked out by Anselm of Canterbury in the latter's *Cur Deus Homo*. He thinks that one way to express the meaning of the saving work of Christ is to speak of Christ as making satisfaction for the debt owed to God by the human race because of sin. For Aquinas, however, this was not the only way that God could have saved us. He argues that neither the incarnation nor the passion of Jesus was absolutely necessary for the salvation of the human race. God could have saved us in other ways. If God had wished to free people from sin without any satisfaction, God would not have been acting against justice because God is not answerable to any order outside of Godself. Thomas does think, though, that the incarnation and the passion of Christ represented the most fitting way for God to enact God's saving power. The incarnation was the best way to evoke faith in us, to build up hope in us, and to enkindle charity in us (*ST* III, 1, 2). And the passion of Jesus was the most excellent way to liberate humankind from sin because it showed us how much God loves us, provided an example of humility and obedience, and restored human dignity (*ST* III, 46, 3).

Aquinas expands the range of metaphors used to describe Christ's saving work beyond that of satisfaction to include merit, sacrifice, and redemption. He does not think that we should focus on just one image in our reflection on salvation. Throughout the discussion in his two *Summas*, he consistently highlights the *obedience and charity* of Christ as the true source of salvation. In the *Summa Contra Gentiles*, he says about the death of Christ "that it had its satisfying power from His charity in which He bore death voluntarily, and not from the iniquity of His killers who sinned in killing Him" (*SCG* IV, 55, 25). In his discussion in the *Summa Theologiae*, when he asks whether God the Father gave Christ over to his passion, he admits that the Father did not shield the Son from suffering. But what is most significant is that the Father filled Christ with charity, inspiring him to will to suffer for us. "It was from love that the Father delivered Christ, and that Christ gave himself up to death" (*ST* III, 47, 3). Aquinas adds, "To show the abundance of the love which led him to suffer, Christ on the cross sought pardon for his persecutors," and "Christ's passion was the offering of a sacrifice inasmuch as Christ, by his own will, suffered death out of love" (*ST* III, 47, 4, ad 1 and ad 2). He asserts that "the love of the suffering Christ outweighed the wickedness of those who slew him" (*ST* III, 49, 4, ad 3). Thus, for Aquinas it is the divine and human charity in Christ expressed in and through his suffering that saves, not his suffering as such. There is no glorification of human suffering in Aquinas's reflections on Christ. Mary Ann Fatula highlights this salient theme in Aquinas, commenting, "Thomas saw that Jesus' death saves us not because it was full of pain, but because it was full of love."[50] Fatula proceeds to observe, "In Christ's passion, therefore, Thomas contemplates his most intimate act of *friendship* for us; the salvation that Jesus brings is not only our healing but also the deepest intimacy with him."[51] Jesus' free act in taking up his cross is for Aquinas the ultimate act of friendship-love. Commenting on Aquinas's discussion of the passion, O'Meara remarks, "In the last analysis it is God's countering moves of love which save humanity, for Calvary is an example and climax of divine activity struggling with evil in history."[52]

Conclusion

Thomas Aquinas wrote about the Christian faith to try to make understandable to his own culture and to us God's plans for us. A complete understanding of the divine being, human life, and evil escapes us. Nonetheless, Aquinas thought that God's self-revelation in nature and especially in Jesus Christ offers us some insights. He emphasized that God is utterly transcendent to created beings, existing in an ontological order that is entirely distinct from that of creatures. God is fully actualized—dynamic and full of life. Aquinas concludes that this transcendent divine perfection entails divine immutability and impassibility, though we do not know exactly what these characteristics mean in God. God is not dependent upon creatures for divine fulfillment; rather, God freely decided to create for the sole purpose of communicating God's own goodness. At the same time, as the source of all existence, God is indescribably close to every creature, holding it in being. The God whom Aquinas darkly surmises is just the opposite of a static, remote deity.

God knows and loves creatures in all of their particularity, and God's love is completely benevolent, not seeking any gain for itself but simply willing the good of the other. This love of God is marked by enduring mercy and compassion, not in the sense that the divine nature is affected by the plight of others, but insofar as God is faithfully at work to dispel the afflictions experienced by beloved creatures. God's love for human beings takes the reality of evil into account: both "evil suffered" and "evil done." Human beings share an existence that has been modified for the worse because of the evil committed at the very origins of human history. Human nature has become infirm, and we suffer the consequences of sin, which include death as we know it and all of the other debilities that affect us. God, however, is at work to overcome the effects of sin through the gift of grace, which heals our sick nature and enables us to share in God's very life. This grace empowers us to live in charity, in friendship with God.[53]

This healing and transformative grace of God is mediated through Jesus Christ, the incarnate Word. In Jesus the divine has drawn incomparably close to humanity. Because of his enduring love for us, the Son of God incarnate effects redemption for us through his death and resurrection. Ultimately we are saved by the boundless divine and human charity of Christ that led him to take up his cross. Because of the unity of Christ's person, we confess that the sufferings of Jesus are the sufferings of the Son of God. Through the incarnation God has become involved in the sufferings of the human family. God has become united not only with the human nature of Jesus but in some sense with every human being throughout history. This miracle of grace means that there is an intimate connection between God and every suffering person. As risen and head of the mystical body, Christ has an intimate connection with each member of his body. He loves the church as something of himself. Therefore, the sufferings of the members of the body of Christ are also the sufferings of Christ.

Building on the work of Augustine and other theological fore-bears, Aquinas constructed a synthesis of the Christian faith that has influenced thinkers through the centuries. It is a carefully nuanced account of God and God's relation to the world that is intended to reflect the God of the Bible, on whom Aquinas regularly lectured and wrote commentaries. We will see that modern authors like Jürgen Moltmann, Edward Schillebeeckx, and Elizabeth Johnson engage in critical dialogue with Aquinas in their efforts to address the mystery of human suffering from the vantage point of Christian faith. Before exploring these more recent efforts, we turn to the writings of a four-teenth-century mystic whose spirituality was influenced by medieval scholasticism but who reflected on her faith from the perspective of her intense encounter with Christ in prayer.

Discussion Questions: www.paulistpress.com, Online Resources.

5
Julian of Norwich:
All Shall Be Well

Julian of Norwich is one of the most intriguing and mysterious figures in the history of Christian spirituality. She lived in England in the fourteenth century as an anchoress, an enclosed solitary dedicated to a life of prayer. Julian wrote in the vernacular and is the author of the work *Showings*.[1] Her spirituality is notoriously difficult to interpret; Edmund Colledge and James Walsh, editors of the critical edition of *Showings*, remark simply, "Julian is hard going."[2] Nevertheless, Julian has enjoyed widespread popularity among readers of Christian spirituality in recent years. The appeal of her work is due, at least in part, to the fact that she integrates two contrasting experiences of human life and the search for God: a profound immersion in the mystery of sin and suffering on the one hand, and compelling insight into the joy and hope that God's love offers us on the other.

Life and Times

We know very few of the facts of Julian's life. Her given name was probably not Julian, as it was the custom of anchoresses to assume the name of the church to which their anchorhold was attached; in this case it was the church of Saint Julian in Norwich.[3] Margery Kempe, another English spiritual writer, reports on a visit to Julian to seek her advice in either 1412 or 1413, noting that Julian was an expert in spiritual guidance.[4] Julian herself tells us that she was thirty-and-a-half years old when she had her seminal mystical experience, in May 1373.[5] Thus she must have been born near the end of 1342. Historians conclude that records indicating bequests made to a person named Julian that date from 1413 to 1416 most likely refer to her, so she probably lived until at least the age of seventy-four. As Grace Jantzen observes, "When she died and where she was buried nobody knows. No doubt she would have preferred it that way."[6] Colledge and Walsh remark, "Had it not been that she was convinced that she was divinely commanded to write down her record of her visions, she might have been no more today than one among the thousands of names of those who in mediaeval England lived as solitaries for the love of God, but of whom nothing else is known."[7]

Julian's work exists in two forms: a short text and a long text. Scholars conclude that the short text was written not long after the mystical experience on which it is based. The long text manifests sustained reflection and theological elaboration on this experience. In her reflection on one of her visions—that of a lord and his servant—Julian tells her readers, "For twenty years after the time of the revelation except for three months, I received inward instruction, and it was this: You ought to take heed to all the attributes, divine and human, which were revealed in the example, though this may seem to you mysterious and ambiguous."[8] Thus it appears that she wrote the longer version of her *Showings* in about 1393. Scholars debate about other details of Julian's life, especially at which stage of her life she undertook her vocation as an enclosed solitary and what she did before her enclosure.

Norwich was a dynamic center of religious life in the fourteenth century, with houses of many of the major religious orders. A Benedictine convent just outside of Norwich held the benefice for St. Julian's Church and also conducted a school for girls.[9] Some scholars conclude that Julian must have been a nun before she became an anchoress.[10] They suggest that her writing manifests a person with a substantial education in theology, and she would have had the opportunity for such training only if she was a member of a religious community. The long text of *Showings* discloses a familiarity with the ideas of prominent spiritual writers such as the Cistercian William of St. Thierry, as well as knowledge of theological themes found in Augustine and Thomas Aquinas. Whether Julian read these authors is impossible to ascertain;

their ideas were widely disseminated throughout Europe at the time. But her work shows that she must have received an education in some setting. Colledge and Walsh speculate that Julian was educated as a nun in a religious community and entered the anchorhold after she completed the long text.[11] Grace Jantzen, on the other hand, argues that Julian's work betrays no evidence of having been written in a convent or of her ever having been a nun. Julian herself tells us that she writes for her fellow Christians, not specifically for religious. Jantzen suggests the possibility that she was already an anchoress at the time of her severe illness and mystical experience of Christ.[12] In the end, we do not know when Julian became an anchoress or where she received her education. In fact, we are left with scholarly guesses about most of the facts of her life.

We do know that the time in which Julian lived was a period of great tumult and profound human suffering. The Hundred Years War (1337–1453) between France and England dragged on in various phases, draining both countries of manpower and other resources and resulting in heavy taxation of the people.[13] Because it was a secure inland port (on the river Wensum) that was connected to London, Norwich became an important center during this conflict and a crossroads of commerce. In England, peasants felt more and more disenfranchised until they finally revolted against the nobility in 1381, only to be brutally repressed. One of the leaders of this suppression was Julian's warlike and ostentatious bishop, Henry Despenser. In the life of the church, the papacy was exiled in Avignon (1309–77), and, after its return to Rome, there was the scandalous period of the Great Western Schism (1378–1417), during which there were two and then three rival claimants to the papacy. Most significant, the Black Death ravaged Europe in intermittent waves, crossing over to London in the fall of 1348 and infecting the population of Norwich in January 1349.[14] There were additional outbreaks of this epidemic in 1361 and 1369. This astoundingly virulent disease killed people within days or even hours of infection. A large number of priests who tended to the sick and dying became victims of this epidemic. While scholarly accounts of the death toll vary, most estimate that more than a third of the population of Europe perished in the Black Death. The impact on survivors was traumatic. Jane Maynard observes, "It is indeed clear from reading the chroniclers' accounts of the plague's devastation that those remaining alive survived a situation of unspeakable horror."[15]

Julian's writing gives evidence of her acute awareness of the turmoil and suffering that must have been taking place outside the window of her anchorhold. With her eyes focused on the suffering Christ, she engages in profound exploration of the mystery of sin and suffering. Her spirituality is the product of someone who spent much of her life alone with God. But it is not the thought of one who was unfamiliar with the outside world—with the realities of society, politics, and the church and with the suffering that ordinary people were facing. "It is clear from her book that Julian identified deeply with the suffering and brokenness of humanity, refusing to accept even the experience of God himself as a substitute for an answer to her urgent questioning about why all of this should be necessary."[16]

Julian's Experience of God

Julian's spirituality is rooted in an extraordinary experience of God that she had at a time of severe illness when she was thirty years old. She relates this experience in both versions of her *Showings*. A person of ardent devotion from her youth, Julian tells us of three graces that she specifically sought from God.[17] First, she desired a profound recollection of the passion of Jesus. She wanted to enter into the mystery of Christ's passion as if she had been present at the crucifixion, even to the extent of having a vision of this event: "Therefore I desired a bodily sight, in which I might have more knowledge of our saviour's bodily pains, and of the compassion of our Lady and of all his true lovers who were living at that time and saw his pains, for I would have been one of them and have suffered with them."[18] Second, she wanted to experience a bodily illness of such severity that she would be convinced she was going to die. She explains that she wished for such an illness because she "wanted to be purged by God's mercy, and afterwards live more to his glory because of that sickness."[19] She realized that these two desires were extraordinary, so she prayed that they would be given to her only if they were in accordance with God's will. Third, she prayed for three "wounds": the wounds of true contrition, loving compassion, and longing with her will for God. She asked for the gift of these wounds without condition, trusting that this prayer was in accord with the teaching of the church.

Julian relates the experience of illness that occasioned her sixteen revelations ("showings") from God, though she focuses more on the revelations than on the details of her sickness. She reports that she became so ill that after three days a priest came to give her the last rites. She lingered for two more days and nights after receiving the sacraments. This priest set a crucifix before her eyes and instructed her to gaze on it, saying to her, "I have brought the image of your savior; look at it and take comfort from it."[20] While gazing on the crucifix she began to feel relief from her illness. Then she entered into a series of unusual spiritual experiences, beginning with the sight of blood running down the face of Jesus. Her descriptions of some of these visions are quite vivid, as when she depicts the way in which the flesh of Christ became dry in the midst of his suffering, causing him severe pain. Julian tells her readers that some of these showings were visual in form, others involved spiritual understanding, and others consisted of words from God (locutions) that were imprinted on her intellect. She outlines her sixteen revelations in the first chapter of the long text. Though they vary in content, all of these showings are connected with her immersion in the mystery of the passion and her gradually deepening insight into the love of God revealed in the suffering Christ.

Scholars of medieval mysticism point out that Julian's desire to contemplate the passion of Jesus was consonant with the spirituality of her time. Grace Jantzen takes note of the focus on the humanity of Jesus that emerged in Christian theology and spirituality after the time of Anselm of Canterbury (1033–1109).[21] This development represented a shift from emphasis on the victorious Christ who conquered humanity's foes, as found in earlier works like the *Dream of the Rood*. Fascination with the suffering Christ was also reflected in developments in art, for example, in the motif of the *Pietà*. It was evident in the monastic spirituality of Anselm, Bernard of Clairvaux, and William of St. Thierry. Focus on the passion was also found in the English spirituality of Julian's day, such as the *Meditations on the Passion* of Richard Rolle (ca. 1300–1349).[22] Contemplation of the sufferings of Christ was characteristic of anchorite spirituality, as manifested in the *Ancrene Riwle*, a thirteenth-century instruction written for three young women who were aspiring to be anchoresses. The author of this work "holds up as extremely profitable both the cultivation of an awareness of Christ's physical sufferings and the healing effects of illness sent by God."[23]

Julian manifests a deep yearning for complete identification with Jesus in his suffering, for authentic compassion in the sense of "suffering with" the crucified Christ. Reflecting on her experience in the midst of illness, Julian writes, "For I wished that his pains might be my pains, with compassion which would lead to longing for God."[24] She perceives Mary as the exemplar for her own engagement with the suffering Christ. In commenting on the eighth revelation, she says, "Here I saw part of the compassion of our Lady, St. Mary; for Christ and she were so united in love that the greatness of her love was the cause of the greatness of her pain."[25] Because Mary had a greater love for her son than has any human being, she suffered the most intense pains during his passion. Julian's desire to identify with the suffering Jesus was "a request to develop the sympathetic entry into his death which would increase her love for him and awareness of his goodness, and would facilitate her salvation and the transformation of her life."[26] Julian became convinced that contemplation of the suffering Christ was the most effective means of personal transformation, resulting in a more profound love of Christ. It was also the pathway to deepened insight into the mystery of God.

Julian writes not just for religious or for other anchoresses but for all of her fellow Christians. She claims no special spiritual status because of her revelations, acknowledging that there are many in the church who have not had such experiences but who have more love for God than she does. As her work progresses, it becomes evident that her entry into the mystery of Christ's passion also entails an abiding concern for the suffering of humanity that was so palpable in her day.

She asserts that in his passion Christ "saw and he sorrowed for every man's sorrow, desolation and anguish, in his compassion and love."[27] She proceeds to affirm of the risen Jesus, "And now he has risen again and is no longer capable of suffering; and yet he suffers with us...."[28] Her conviction about Christ's solidarity with all suffering people intensifies Julian's consciousness of the suffering of her fellow men and women. This awareness becomes more evident in *Showings* as she ponders the meaning of sin and suffering in God's good creation. The intimate relationship between the suffering Christ and suffering humanity becomes clearer to her as she considers the meaning of the allegory of the lord and the servant. In her desire for recollection of the passion, Julian "is surely also seeking greater solidarity with suffering humanity, identifying simultaneously with the suffering of Christ and of humankind, and thus able to mediate his compassion."[29]

The fact that Julian's teachings are grounded in an experience of visions raises the question of the authenticity of her spirituality. Might such an extraordinary experience derive from purely psychosomatic causes, putting into question the validity of her teaching? Both Jantzen and Joan Nuth emphasize that these experiences need to be situated within the overall context of her life and historical situation.[30] Nuth notes the predominance of visionary experiences among Christian mystics in the thirteenth and fourteenth centuries, especially in continental Europe. She asserts that "visions gave validity to women's religious autonomy and authority in a day when these were not respected."[31] Moreover, she emphasizes that Julian's focus is not on the visions themselves but on her growth in understanding of their meaning. Jantzen underlines Julian's own disclaimer about any special prerogatives that might derive from her experience: "I am not good because of the revelations, but only if I love God better; and inasmuch as you love God better, it is more to you than to me."[32] For Julian, "what is truly important is not the fact of the experiences themselves but the deepened love of God which results from them and the insights communicated with them."[33] Her progress in contrition, loving compassion, and longing for God is the true measure of the validity of these experiences. Such mystical experiences "take place in the context of a lifestyle of belief and devotion, and serve in turn to deepen that lifestyle."[34] While it is impossible for contemporary readers to arrive at a definitive judgment about the authenticity of Julian's mystical experience, it is possible to critically engage her understanding of the meaning of these experiences as conveyed in her teaching.

The Meaning of Christ's Passion

Julian's experience of the crucified Christ leads to her to ponder the significance of the passion of Jesus. She articulates various dimensions of the meaning of Jesus' suffering and death, informing her readers that she learned three ways of contemplating the passion.[35] The first "is to contemplate with contrition and compassion the cruel pain he suffered."[36] Julian echoes the common opinion of her day that in his passion Jesus suffered more than anyone else in human history. She thinks that because of the union of divinity and humanity in Jesus, he was given the strength to undergo the greatest possible suffering. To this she adds, "I mean not only more pain than any other one man could suffer, but also that he suffered more pain than all men who are to be saved, from the first beginning to the last day, may tell or fully think, if we have regard to the honour of the highest, most majestic king and to his shameful, grievous and painful death."[37] Thus, Julian takes very seriously the physical dimensions of the passion of Jesus. The second way of meditating on Christ's passion is to move beyond consideration of his suffering to contemplation of the love that motivated it. The third is to consider prayerfully "the joy and the bliss which make him take delight in it."[38] While consideration of the physical sufferings of Jesus is important to Julian, it becomes clear that the second and third ways of contemplating his passion offer the deepest insight into its meaning. Contemplation of the love of God and even of the delight of God revealed in the crucified Christ is where Julian places her emphasis.

Julian speaks of the passion of Jesus as the ultimate source of healing for a wounded humanity. The symbol of the blood of Jesus assumes a prominence here. Julian observes that God has created bountiful waters on the earth for our physical needs and comfort. But, she asserts, "It is more pleasing to him that we accept for our total cure his blessed blood to wash us of our sins, for there is no drink that is made which it pleases him so well to give us."[39] She also appeals to the pierced side of the crucified Jesus, from which flowed blood and water. She perceives the wound in Jesus' side to be "large enough for all mankind that will be saved and will rest in peace and in love."[40] The wounds that human beings suffer because of the effects of sin in the world are healed by the wounds that Jesus suffered in his passion. There is in Julian a "fine counterpoint" among the wounds of sin, the wounds of Christ, and her own prayer for the three wounds of contrition, compassion, and longing with her will for God.[41] Jantzen relates this complex theme to the vocabulary of woundedness that was prevalent among medieval writers, having as one of its prime sources the *Confessions* of Augustine, who often speaks of the wounds of sinful humanity. Julian's consistent focus is God's redemptive action in Jesus to heal our wounds, a healing that is effected through the wounds of the crucified and risen Christ.

Julian also meditates on the passion of Christ as the means of God's triumph over the powers of evil that oppress humanity and the world. The reader hears echoes of the patristic theme of *Christus Victor*, though Julian focuses more on the suffering of Christ than on his resurrection and exaltation. In her account of the fifth revelation, Julian reports that she was given insight into the malice of "the fiend"—the devil. But in this perception she also came to see the impotence of the devil. She says that God formed in her soul the saying, "With this the fiend is overcome."[42] While the devil still possesses unrelenting malice toward God and humanity and always opposes the will of God, his power has ultimately been negated through the suffering of Christ. In fact, Julian asserts, God turns everything that he permits the devil to accomplish into joy for us and pain and shame for him. Further on in the long text, as she is reflecting on the sixteenth and final revelation, this theme of the defeat of the powers of evil is reprised. The message is personalized for her in the words, "You will not be overcome." Julian is assured that in spite of the difficulties of life, and despite her own sinfulness, the victory of God effected through the passion of Jesus means that for her and for her "fellow Christians" the saving love of God will have the final word. She writes, "He did not say: You shall not be troubled, you will not be belaboured, you will not be disquieted; but he said: You will not be overcome. God wants us to pay attention to these words, and always to be strong in faithful trust...."[43] Julian wants her fellow Christians to concentrate not on the powers of evil but on the triumph of God over these powers through the crucified Christ. It is this conviction of faith that provides hope to fearful, suffering people.

The salient feature of Julian's reflection on the meaning of Jesus' passion is her consistent emphasis that in the suffering Christ is revealed the depth of God's love for the human family. This theme is the leitmotif of her work and is repeated with many variations. Reflecting on her intense experience of the crucified Jesus, she is moved to ponder the motivation behind Jesus' taking up the cross. For Julian, Jesus is no passive victim in his suffering and death; rather he freely engages his destiny out of love for a human race that is in desperate need. Julian writes, "The love which made him suffer it [the passion] surpasses all his sufferings, as much as heaven is above earth; for the suffering was a noble, precious and honourable deed, performed once in time by the operation of love. And love was without beginning, it is and shall be without end."[44] This is the governing principle in Julian's interpretation of the passion: "Every detail of the passion deepened her understanding of the intimacy, depth and intensity of Christ's love for humanity."[45]

This insight into the love of God in Christ is underlined in a remarkable passage in the *Showings*. Julian writes about a "dialogue" with Christ that was part of her mystical experience. In this exchange she perceives Christ asking her an astonishing question:

> Then our good Lord put a question to me: Are you well satisfied that I suffered for you? I said: Yes, good Lord, all my thanks to you; yes, good Lord, blessed may you be. Then Jesus our good Lord said: If you are satisfied, I am satisfied. It is a joy, a bliss, and endless delight to me that I ever suf-

fered my Passion for you; and if I could suffer more, I should suffer more.[46]

She goes on to affirm about Jesus, "I saw truly that as often as he could die, so often should he die, and love would never let him rest till he had done it."[47] Her experience of Christ leads Julian to the conviction that his love for her and for all humanity is so great that he would suffer more if only he could. The love that impelled him to take up his cross "would never let him rest" until he had done everything possible to effect salvation and win over the hearts of believers.

This same theme is evident in Julian's reflections on the "spiritual thirst" of Jesus. Glossing the familiar verse in the Johannine passion narrative, "I thirst" (John 19:28), Julian relates it to God's intense desire for us. While the God about whom Julian writes is indeed transcendent, her experience of the divine impels her to speak of "longing" in God as well as longing in Christ. She speaks of Christ's spiritual thirst, "which persists and always will until we see him on the day of judgment, for we who shall be saved and shall be Christ's joy and bliss are still here....Therefore this is his thirst and his longing for us, to gather us all here into him, to our endless joy, as I see it."[48] She becomes convinced that Christ "still has that same thirst and longing which he had upon the Cross, which desire, longing and thirst, as I see it, were in him from without beginning, and he will have this until the time that the last soul which will be saved has come up into his bliss."[49] This thirst or longing is not only a characteristic of the human Jesus; Julian suggests that there is in God this same quality of thirst and longing, which comes from God's everlasting goodness. Reflecting the Christian (especially the Augustinian) teaching about the primacy of grace in the path of salvation, Julian argues that it is the longing of God in Christ that enables us to respond to God's longing. God's intense desire for us empowers us to accept the divine love poured out in Christ.

Julian's conviction that the passion of Jesus is ultimately the revelation of divine love is echoed in her use of maternal images for God and Christ. She likens the suffering of Christ in his passion to the travail of a woman in childbirth, though she declares that the life brought about by Christ's suffering is enduring in a way that earthly life is not.

Julian says that our earthly mothers bear us for pain and death, while "our true Mother Jesus, he alone bears us for joy and for endless life."[50] She develops this birthing motif further: "So he carries us within him in love and travail, until the full time when he wanted to suffer the sharpest thorns and cruel pains that ever were or will be, and at the last he died."[51] Though Jesus cannot suffer any more than he did, and he cannot die again, the love that he has for us impels him to continue his saving work by nourishing us with his very self. Here Julian compares the nourishment Christ offers in the sacraments to the milk with which a mother feeds her child. Julian employs this maternal imagery for Jesus in her attempt to convey the strong and tender love which Christ has for every person—the same love that motivated him to endure the cross. Julian even argues that the word applies to Christ in a preeminent way: "This fair lovely word 'mother' is so sweet and kind in itself that it cannot truly be said of anyone or to anyone except of him and to him who is the true Mother of life and of all things."[52]

In the end, Julian's sustained contemplation of the passion of Jesus deepened her experience and conviction of the saving, life-giving love of God. Through her meditation on Jesus' suffering, "Julian is able to communicate to us that God's love for the world, the proof of which is the sacrificial death of his Son, is as sure and active and manifest now as it was at the time of the Passion."[53] Observing that "all of her theology ultimately finds its focus in the passion of Christ,"[54] Jantzen argues that while Julian speaks of sixteen revelations, "there was in the basic sense only one revelation, and that was the revelation of love."[55] Julian's perception of divine love revealed in Christ's suffering entails a redefinition of love:

> The passion itself is understood as love, as the supreme manifestation of the love of God. But this in turn brings with it a revision of the common understanding of what love means. It is true that love is the measure; but this is not just any sentimental idea of love. The passion of Christ offers a principle for understanding what love really is: it is the standard by which love itself must be measured.[56]

As with Aquinas, for Julian what is most significant about the passion is the supreme charity that was made manifest and efficacious in the suffering and death of Jesus.

Sin and Suffering

It is in the context of Julian's experience of God's love revealed in the suffering Jesus that we must situate her approach to sin and suffering, which are very closely related in her theology. The reader encounters a paradox here. On the one hand, Julian ponders the gravity of sin and its effects at great length. On the other hand, her experience of God convinces her that she and all Christians should concentrate more on God's salvific grace than on sin. This becomes evident in her reflection on the parable of the lord and servant in chapter 51—a passage of critical importance in the long text. In many ways this parable, and Julian's entire treatment of sin, suffering, and salvation, echo Paul's teaching in Romans 5:12–21. In that famous passage Paul associates the universality of sin with the universality of death. But the main point that he wants to convey to the Christians at Rome is not the abundance of sin but the superabundance of God's grace in Jesus Christ: "But where sin increased, grace abounded all the more" (5:20). In this respect Julian's theology is very Pauline.

Living during a period of protracted war, devastating plague, ecclesiastical scandal, and social unrest, Julian takes sin very seriously. Reflecting the traditional view of evil as a privation of the good, she claims that sin is not a substantial reality: "But I did not see sin, for I believe that it has no kind of substance, no share in being, nor can it be recognized except by the pain caused by it."[57] This assertion rests on her positive view of creation: creation as such is the good gift of a good Creator. In the same passage, however, Julian proceeds to say that "sin is the cause of all this pain."[58] Julian does not distinguish between moral evil and natural or physical evil; she simply professes that sin is the cause of all that is disfigured in God's good creation. Sin is the cause of all woundedness and, thus, of all suffering. She says that the only obstacle to her union with Christ is sin. In the thirteenth showing she perceives that "Adam's sin was the greatest harm ever done or ever to be done until the end of the world."[59] Sin is "the sharpest scourge with which any chosen soul can be struck,"[60] causing grief that can even lead a person to the brink of despair. God wants us to recognize our sin so that we will not continue to fall and will seek forgiveness in a spirit of sincere contrition. In heaven each of us will see the extent and the gravity of the sins we have committed. In this life, however, God permits us to see only a certain measure of our own sinfulness because "our sin is so foul and horrible that we should not endure to see it as it is."[61]

Julian's intense awareness of the overwhelming goodness of God and the destructive power of sin leads her to question why God did not prevent sin at the beginning of human history. She ponders this mystery for many years in light of her experience of God during her illness. She is convinced that "if there had been no sin, we should all have been pure and as like our Lord as he created us."[62] Thus, she says that she "often wondered why, through the great prescient wisdom of God, the beginning of sin was not prevented."[63] She never discovers the answer to this mystery, instead experiencing God assuring her that in spite of the scourge of sin "all shall be well." The reader recognizes in Julian's intense questioning her profound sensitivity to the effects of evil—especially the toll of human suffering—in the world around her.

Julian's mystical experience leads her to conclude that "sin is necessary."[64] She writes, "Though our Lord revealed to me that I should sin, by me is understood everyone."[65] By this startling statement she does not mean that God is the cause of sin. She speaks of God's "toleration" of sin and evil: "For our Lord does everything which is good, and our Lord tolerates what is evil."[66] God allows but does not cause us to fall into sin in order that we may know "how feeble and how wretched we are in ourselves...."[67] For Julian the necessity of sin is not an ontological necessity. Human beings are not predetermined or "programmed" to sin. Rather, Julian comes to the recognition that "sin is a fact of human temporal existence, universally affecting the whole human race, that must be accepted and endured."[68] At the same time, Julian's experience of God leads her to conclude that God protects us even in our sin and raises us to a fulfillment that is more glorious than we would have enjoyed if there had been no sin. The traditional theme of the *felix culpa* resounds throughout her work. This is clear from her discussion of the parable of the lord and the servant, which is Julian's gloss on the biblical story of the fall.

Joan Nuth likens the story of the lord and servant to a medieval *exemplum*—a brief illustrative story used by preachers to emphasize a point.[69] Such stories had grown in popularity by Julian's time, and there were even collections of these "examples." Julian experiences this story as a vision that is set before her as part of the revelation given in her illness. After the vision "vanishes," Julian is led to reflect on it for twenty years. The vision is of a lord sitting in state whose beloved servant stands before him, eager to do his lord's bidding. In his haste to please his master the servant dashes off, but he falls into a ditch and is injured. His greatest hurt is that he can no longer turn his face to look at his lord, "who was very close to him, in whom is all consolation."[70] Immersed in grief, the servant also loses touch with himself, with his own identity as a beloved servant. The lord imputes no fault to his servant, since the cause of his falling was his good will and great desire to please his lord. Rather, the lord looks on his fallen servant with tenderness and pity. Seeing the harm and injuries that the servant has suffered in his efforts, the lord promises to reward the servant. As Julian explains it, the lord's "great goodness and his own honour require that his beloved servant, whom he loved so much, should be highly and blessedly rewarded forever, above what he would have been if he had not fallen, yes, and so much that his falling and all the woe that he received from it will be turned into high, surpassing honour and endless bliss."[71] The wounds suffered by the servant in his fall will be turned into honors by his lord.

Julian realizes that aspects of this vision are not congruent with what she had been taught about the biblical story of the fall, especially the attitude of the lord toward the fallen servant. As she puts it, "For in the servant, who was shown for Adam, as I shall say, I saw many different characteristics which could in no way be attributed to Adam, that one man. ..."[72] Initially perplexed by this example, she continues to meditate on it and to seek deeper understanding. Eventually she comes to recognize that the servant represents both Adam, that is, humanity, and Christ. Echoing the Pauline (and Irenaean) motif of Christ as the New Adam, Julian says that simultaneous with the fall of Adam was "the falling of [God's] dearly beloved Son," who "went down with Adam into hell, and by this continuing pity Adam was kept from endless death."[73] In a seminal passage Julian declares, "In the servant is comprehended the second person of the Trinity, and in the servant is comprehended Adam, that is to say all men....When Adam fell, God's Son fell; because of the true union which was made in heaven, God's Son could not be separated from Adam, for by Adam I understand all mankind."[74] Thus, for Julian an inseparable union exists between the Son of God and humanity from the very beginning of human history. The Son takes upon himself all the blame that belongs to fallen humanity. When God looks at sinful human beings he sees Christ, the Son incarnate. God does not, then, assign blame to us for our sinfulness; God is not angry with human beings for their failures any more than God is angry with Christ. The Father "does not wish to assign more blame to us than to his beloved Son Jesus Christ."[75] Drawing upon the theme of the church as the body of Christ, Julian concludes that all humanity that will be saved through the incarnation and passion "is Christ's humanity, for he is the head, and we are his members, to which members the day and the time are unknown when every passing woe and sorrow will have an end, and everlasting joy and bliss will be fulfilled, which day and time all the company of heaven longs and desires to see."[76] One hears in this passage as well reflections of the Augustinian theme of "the whole Christ" and Aquinas's discussion of the grace of Christ as head of the church.

This account of the fall of humanity is markedly distinct from most classical versions, for example, from Augustine's view of Adam's sin as a heinous crime of rebellion rooted in human pride. Julian's mystical experience leads her to the conclusion that, despite the gravity of sin and its consequences, there is no wrath in God. Though we deserve "pain, blame and wrath" because of our sin, "God is that goodness which cannot be angry, for God is nothing but goodness."[77] God is ultimately the one who invites us into friendship; thus "it is the most impossible thing which could be that God might be angry, for anger and friendship are two contraries...."[78] Julian thinks that if God were ever angry with us we would simply cease to be, since our existence is completely dependent on the goodness and favor of the Creator. While we are often angry with ourselves and feel that God is angry with us, we are actually enveloped in the mercy of God. According to Julian we are clothed in the love of God.

With this interpretation of God's attitude toward the sinner, it is understandable that Julian experiences God instructing her to focus on the atonement whenever she is tempted to become preoccupied with sin. Though the showings convince her that Adam's sin was the greatest harm ever done, she immediately reports that she was taught to "contemplate the glorious atonement, for this atoning is more pleasing to the blessed divinity and more honourable for man's salvation, without comparison, than ever Adam's sin was harmful."[79] Julian tells her readers that if they are inclined to contemplate the condition of the damned they should instead focus on Christ and rejoice in their savior and the salvation he has gained for them.[80] She is also assured that God does not demand that we live completely free of sin. "He loves us endlessly, and we sin customarily, and he reveals it to us most gently."[81] Even in our sin God protects us in the divine love. The reader soon realizes that Julian was a person of very sensitive conscience whose love for God impelled her to strive for perfection. Perfectionism can lead to despair when one realizes just how far from perfection he or she is. Julian was protected from such a tendency to despair by her experience of God as one who continually urged her to focus on the abundance of grace and the power of divine love.

Julian accepts the fact that life in a world wounded by sin entails suffering. Though she wonders why God ever allowed the entrance of sin into God's good creation in the first place, she knows that once this has taken place suffering is the result. While she does not suggest that specific instances of human suffering are directly attributable to specific sins, she accepts the church's teaching that all of creation, including human life, is fractured as a result of sin. She asserts that Christians are meant to accept suffering in this life with meekness and with abiding trust in the God who saves. This stance involves a suffering with Christ: "So was our Lord Jesus afflicted for us; and we all stand in this way of suffering with him, and shall till we come to his bliss...."[82] In a few places she suggests that suffering is given to us by God for a purpose. For example, she writes that God "imposes on every person whom he loves, to bring him to his bliss, something that is no defect in his sight, through which souls are humiliated and despised in this world, scorned and mocked and rejected."[83] Such suffering breaks down human pride and fosters closer union with God. Julian exhorts her readers to bear and suffer the penance God gives them, with recollection of the passion of Jesus. Articulating what must have been the experience of many people of her day, she proceeds to say, "This place is prison, this life is penance, and he wants us to rejoice in the remedy."[84] Rejoicing in the remedy means entrusting oneself to the presence and protection of a loving God and keeping ever in mind the atonement accomplished through the passion of Jesus.

Joy and Hope in Salvation

It should be clear from what has already been said that in Julian's spirituality salvation occupies the central place. She is most famous for her statement, "All shall be well." Julian is deeply conscious that sin has wounded God's good creation—and yet her strongest conviction is that God is at work in Christ to heal these wounds. Thus her spirituality and theology are suffused with hope. She consistently experiences God inviting her to trust in the divine presence and power, which is the source of healing for her and for all of creation. Christians must keep their eyes focused on God's redemptive action in Christ; otherwise "we fall back upon ourselves, and then we find that we feel nothing at all but the opposition that is in ourselves, and that comes from the old root of our first sin...."[85]

Julian repeatedly professes her adherence to the church's teaching about the possibility of final loss, of eternal separation from God. The reader receives the impression she was afraid that her emphasis on God's faithful and redemptive love would lead to suspicion that she was espousing universalism—the doctrine that all people will definitely experience eternal salvation. She observes, "And one article of our faith is that many creatures will be damned, such as the angels who fell out of heaven, who now are devils, and many men upon earth who die out of the faith of Holy Church, that is to say those who are pagans and many who have received baptism and who live unchristian lives and so die out of God's love."[86] She even desires a vision of hell and purgatory, asserting that she "believed steadfastly that hell and purgatory exist for the same ends as Holy Church teaches."[87] She is not given such a revelation, though an insight she gains through the fifth revelation about God's repudiation of the devil leads her to conclude that "every creature who is of the devil's condition in this life is no more mentioned before God and all his saints than is the devil...."[88]

While Julian offers these professions of her agreement with church teaching, it is evident to the reader that she struggles with this doctrine. As she admits, it is not clear to her how all can be well if there are people who will be eternally condemned.[89] In her showings she experiences God revealing a "great deed" that will be done on the last day that will make all things well. She writes, "This is the great deed ordained by our Lord God from without beginning, treasured and hidden in his blessed breast, known only to himself, through which deed he will make all things well. For just as the blessed Trinity created all things from nothing, just so will the same blessed Trinity make everything well which is not well."[90] She searches for insight into what this deed will be and how God will accomplish it, but she is told that it is a mystery not knowable to human beings in this life. She must simply trust in God's promise that it will take place, that what is impossible for human beings to conceive is not impossible for God to effect. Thus, Julian becomes convinced that she must hold both ends of the rope: her adherence to church teaching about the possibility of eternal loss and her trust in the great deed by which God will make all things well:

> And in this I was taught by the grace of God that I ought to keep myself steadfastly in the faith, as I had understood before, and that at the same time I should stand firm and believe firmly that every kind of thing will be well, as our

Lord revealed at the same time. For this is the great deed which our Lord will do, and in this deed he will preserve his word in everything. And he will make well all which is not well. But what the deed will be and how it will be done, there is no creature who is inferior to Christ who knows it, or will know it until it has been done, according to the understanding which I received of our Lord's meaning at this time.[91]

For Julian, the salvation won by Christ that will be definitively established by God on the last day is a more abundant salvation in the wake of sin and the suffering that sin has caused. There is a level of fulfillment that human beings will experience that we would not have known if sin had never entered into creation. Therefore sin and suffering have a mysterious role to play in God's salvific plan. This conviction is found throughout her work, and it undergirds the hope that permeates it. In a key text, Julian affirms that "grace transforms our dreadful failing into plentiful and endless solace; and grace transforms our shameful falling into high and honourable rising; and grace transforms our sorrowful dying into holy, blessed life." This transformation through grace is "so superabundant" that when we receive our eternal reward "there we shall thank and bless our Lord, endlessly rejoicing that we ever suffered woe; and that will be because of a property of the blessed love which we shall know in God, which we might never have known without woe preceding it."[92] Julian develops this idea near the end of her work when she reflects on the vision we will be given at the time of judgment. At that time the mysteries now hidden in God will be revealed and no one shall say, "Lord, if it had been so, it would have been well." Rather, Julian thinks, everyone will be moved to say that "because it is so, it is well; and now we see truly that everything is done as it was ordained by you before anything was made."[93]

What should one make of such a statement? Is this a simplistic answer to the questions about why God allowed sin and suffering to enter into creation in the first place and about the meaning of suffering in a creation loved so deeply by God? The terrible toll of human suffering in Julian's own day would seem to contradict such an answer. And

Julian's honest grappling with the mystery of suffering throughout her work seems inconsistent with a position that suggests that the reward of salvation will be so great that human beings will no longer lament the tragedies of history. Jantzen raises similar questions in her study, noting that "it seems wicked even to contemplate giving thanks for such tragic events as the Black Death and all the suffering this caused."[94] She contends that Julian can make such assertions only because she believes that there is an intrinsic link between the suffering caused by the presence of sin in the world and the experience of salvation in Christ. This intrinsic connection is the development of the "wounds" of contrition, compassion, and longing for God that comes about in and through suffering.[95] Julian thinks that these qualities are essential for our reception of the gift of God's love and that they begin to take root in us when we experience sin and suffering in our lives. These are the wounds for which Julian prayed, and she considers them to be medicines for the soul by which we are healed and granted a deeper experience of the love of God.[96] This is why she can teach that our sins will "be rewarded with various joys in heaven to reward the victories over them."[97] We will come to a more profound and integral fulfillment in God because we have passed through the experience of sin and suffering than we would have if there had been no sin and suffering. There is no pain or suffering that will be wasted; rather all of it will in some mysterious way contribute to and enrich our experience of salvation.

Jantzen raises critical questions about these conclusions offered by Julian, though she observes that "her [Julian's] assurance that all sin and pain will be rewarded and will bring about a good out of comparison to the pain itself is of great significance."[98] Nuth summarizes Julian's teaching on salvation in the following way: "Her whole effort is to present to her troubled times the picture of a God who loves absolutely the whole creation which is itself an expression of divine love. Eschatological hope is not misplaced when it trusts that this love can bring all into eternal fulfillment."[99] For Julian this fulfillment consists ultimately in seeing "the blessed face" of God. We are destined in Christ to see God clearly, "face to his blessed face," and in that vision "no woe can remain, no well-being can be lacking."[100]

Images of the Divine

Julian's view of God is one that is explicitly affective and filled with life. Her speech about God is consistently trinitarian, though the trinitarian language she employs is distinctive. Near the beginning of her work, as she is reflecting on her vision of the crucified Jesus, she reports that "suddenly the Trinity filled my heart full of the greatest joy."[101] She professes her belief that the Christian form of monotheism is trinitarian: "For the Trinity is God, God is the Trinity. The Trinity is our maker, the Trinity is our protector, the Trinity is our everlasting lover, the Trinity is our endless joy and our bliss, by our Lord Jesus Christ and in our Lord Jesus Christ."[102] Julian follows the theological tradition in speaking of the first person of the Trinity as the Father. She attributes the properties of power (might) and protection to the Father. As she uses maternal language to describe the person and saving work of Jesus, so she often speaks of the second person of the Trinity as our Mother. The attributes of knowledge, wisdom, and mercy are associated with the Mother. She says about the second person, who became incarnate for our salvation:

> And furthermore I saw that the second person, who is our Mother, substantially the same beloved person, has now become our mother sensually...and so our Mother is working on us in various ways, in whom our parts are kept undivided; for in our Mother Christ we profit and increase, and in mercy he reforms and restores us, and by the power of his death and his Resurrection he unites us to our substance.[103]

Julian often attributes love, lordship, and grace to the Holy Spirit, and she associates the Spirit with our fulfillment in God: "He [the Holy Spirit] works, rewarding and giving. Rewarding is a gift for our confidence which the Lord makes to those who have labored; and giving is a courteous act which he does freely, by grace, fulfilling and surpassing all that creatures deserve."[104] In a passage that celebrates the nearness of the triune God to believers, Julian exclaims, "And so I saw that God rejoices that he is our Father, and God rejoices that he is our Mother, and God rejoices that he is our true spouse, and that our soul is his beloved wife."[105] Thus, while Julian is traditional in rooting her vision of God in the trinitarian confession, she is distinctive in language she employs for the Trinity, particularly in her use of maternal images for the second person.

The sense of reverence and awe that permeates Julian's *Showings* reflects her keen awareness of the transcendence of God. While she communicates a profound understanding of the goodness of creation, she also recognizes that the Creator transcends everything that has been made. In commenting on the first showing she says, "For I know well that heaven and earth and all creation are great, generous, beautiful and good. But the reason why it seemed to my eyes so little was because I saw it in the presence of him who is the Creator."[106] At the same time, what is most important for Julian is to assure her readers of the indescribable nearness of God to us. Her experience convinces her that we dwell in God/Christ and God/Christ dwells in us. Sometimes she uses the imagery of clothing to express this conviction. In reflecting on her vision of the bleeding head of the crucified Christ she receives insight into his love for us; this leads Julian to say, "He is our clothing, who wraps and enfolds us for love, embraces and shelters us, surrounds us for his love, which is so tender that he may never desert us."[107] Further along she says that "as the body is clad in the cloth, and the flesh in the skin, and the bones in the flesh, and the heart in the trunk, so are we, soul and body, clad and enclosed in the goodness of God."[108] Julian is absolutely convinced of the classical mystical teaching that God is closer to us than we are to ourselves. Her descriptions of the divine nearness and indwelling have a noticeably tender quality, evincing her experience of the gracious mercy and faithful protection that God offers to us. Julian's God is accessible, filled with compassion and tenaciously faithful.

Julian's spirituality is sufficiently influenced by classical Christian theology to prevent her from asserting that the Creator is in any way dependent upon creatures. Nevertheless, the language that she uses manifests her conviction that we do make a difference to God. She speaks of God's delight in us and God's intense desire (longing) for us.

For Julian, human happiness brings joy to God: "For it is God's will that we have true delight with him in our salvation, and in it he wants us to be greatly comforted and strengthened, and so joyfully he wishes our souls to be occupied with his grace. For we are his bliss, because he endlessly delights in us; and so with his grace shall we delight in him."[109] Employing another metaphor, she asserts that we are God's crown: "For it was revealed that we are his crown, which crown is the Father's joy, the Son's honour, the Holy Spirit's delight, and endless marvelous bliss to all who are in heaven."[110] She makes her strongest statement in this regard when she claims that God "will never have his full joy in us until we have our full joy in him, truly seeing his fair, blessed face."[111] Julian's understanding of God's relationship with us is marked by a profound sense of reciprocity, or mutuality. While God is God and we are creatures, utterly dependent upon God for our very existence, God has freely entered into such a deep and enduring relationship with us that our destiny makes a difference to God. Drawing on the societal relationships of her own day, Julian often speaks of God's "courteous" or "familiar" love. Like a person of royal status who humbles himself or herself to associate with a mere servant, treating the servant as a friend, so God has lowered Godself to enter into a relationship of familiar friendship with us. This is a free action of God that has its source in divine love. "There is no requirement laid upon God to treat us so generously; indeed it is the humility of God which places self-imposed restraints on the exercise of his power so that he can be, in Julian's words, 'familiar' with us, just as the lord would have to impose restraints on his own right to command if he were to treat his servant as a friend."[112] As one who has become utterly "familiar" with us God has a stake in our fulfillment.

Conclusion

Julian never succeeds in finding an answer to her question about the "why" of sin and suffering. Her inquiry into the reason that God allowed sin to enter into creation is left unanswered. And Julian assumes that all suffering is somehow the result of sin. Her suggestion that in the vision afforded us in heaven ("when the judgment is given") we will no longer lament the evils of human history seems simplistic and even superficial. It is virtually impossible to imagine that those in heaven will look back on the horrors of the Black Death (or the Shoah) and "say with one voice: Lord, blessed may you be, because it is so, it is well."[113] Believers may imagine, rather, that fulfillment in God will leave appropriate "space" for lament over the tragedies in history and the suffering of countless victims. If one looks at Julian's spirituality as a whole, especially her emphasis on God's profound compassion in Christ, it seems that she would eschew any simplistic reconciliation with the pain and sorrow suffered by so many through the centuries.

What makes Julian's thought compelling for many people today is her sustained emphasis on the superabundance of God's love, which she consistently affirms even in the context of the intense suffering that was taking place all around her. In the final chapter of the long text, she says that she had wondered about the meaning of the showings, and she articulates the "answer" that was given her in this way: "What, do you wish to know your Lord's meaning in this thing? Know it well, love was his meaning."[114] Julian's is not a sentimental understanding of God's love; the light of divine charity is revealed to her through the prism of the suffering Christ. And she relates the passion of Jesus to the passion of humanity that was so evident in her world. Julian recognizes that the redemptive love of God that was revealed and made effective in Christ was a costly love, even for God. But Julian's experience of God, and her prolonged reflection on her experience, convinced her that this divine love is more powerful and more real than the evil and suffering that plague the world.

In the end, perhaps it is the image of God conveyed by Julian that is most inviting for people grappling with the mystery of suffering in their lives. The God about whom Julian writes is an affective, life-giving, faithful God whose transcendence is actualized in God's drawing near to beloved creatures. This is the trinitarian God who in the Son (Mother) has united Godself with humanity. For Julian, God passionately longs for us and intensely desires human wholeness. God has freely determined that our happiness will be God's happiness. Julian's contention that there is no wrath in God may neglect an important biblical theme derived from belief in divine justice and opposition to evil. Her emphasis on God's boundless compassion for human frailty may underestimate the malice that often resides in the human heart. Nevertheless, her experience of God's indomitable love for a wounded humanity becomes the foundation of a spirituality that is suffused with hope. While her mantra "All shall be well" may sound shrill in the ears of people who are enduring inexplicable suffering, her vision is not a Pollyanna optimism. Rather it is a genuine expression of the theological virtue of hope, since it is grounded in her firm belief in the power and the intense desire of God to heal a fractured world. And for Julian God does not just promise relief at the end of life but draws near in the present to embrace the suffering person with a depth of compassion that gives new life.

Discussion Questions: www.paulistpress.com, Online Resources.

6

Two Voices from the Shoah

The theological conversation about God and suffering that has taken place during the past sixty years was stimulated in a special way by the Shoah, or Nazi Holocaust. The systematic effort to exterminate the Jewish people in Europe has forced Jewish, Protestant, and Catholic thinkers to grapple with the mystery of suffering in a sustained way. Between 1933 and 1945 the Nazi regime murdered about six million Jews as well as several million non-Jewish persons. Approximately two-thirds of the Jewish population of Europe was destroyed simply because of their Jewish identity. The Nazis initially tried forced emigration as a means to rid Nazi-occupied lands of Jews and then employed strike forces to execute Jews. When these means proved to be too cumbersome, the government resorted to extermination camps where Jews and other prisoners were gassed and their bodies incinerated in crematories.

In any discussion of this horrific event, it is imperative to listen to the voices of those who were victimized by it, men and women who experienced it from the inside. In this chapter we listen to two such voices, those of Elie Wiesel and Dietrich Bonhoeffer. Wiesel, well known for his autobiographical work *Night*, was a fifteen-year-old Jewish boy from Transylvania whose entire family was deported to Auschwitz in the spring of 1944.[1] He survived to tell his story and has dedicated his life to serving as a witness to the Shoah. Awarded the Nobel Peace Prize in 1986 for his work, Wiesel has become a spiritual mentor for people from diverse religious backgrounds. Dietrich Bonhoeffer was a Lutheran pastor and theologian who opposed the Nazi regime from the beginning of Hitler's rule. He was imprisoned and eventually executed in April 1945. Bonhoeffer's writings from prison have made a direct impact on the conversation about the mystery of human suffering. His sustained and courageous opposition to Nazism has won him the respect of people of all faiths and even of those with no religious affiliation.

Elie Wiesel

Early Years

Wiesel was born in Sighet, a small valley town in Transylvania, which at the time was part of Romania. It was later annexed by Hungary, one of the Axis powers. Wiesel was an intense, introspective boy with a strong love for his Jewish faith and a penchant for asking deep questions. He expressed an early interest in Hasidic Judaism, a mystical renewal movement that originated in the eighteenth century in Poland and the Ukraine and spread to other parts of eastern Europe. This early interest in Hasidism made a deep impact on him and has influenced his later writings, in which he has turned to the Hasidic masters and their style of storytelling to communicate his own ideas, including his understanding of the relationship between God and humanity.[2]

The Nazis marched into Sighet in the spring of 1944, rounded up the Jewish population of the town, and placed them in a ghetto. The Jews were soon loaded onto sealed trains and taken to Auschwitz. One of the most troubling aspects of this experience for Wiesel was the silence of the town's Christian population. Christians simply watched from the windows of their homes as the Jews were forcibly seized and then led through the streets to the trains. In Wiesel's later book, *The Town beyond the Wall*, he draws from this deeply troubling experience. He incorporates a story of a concentration camp survivor who returns to his home town and confronts a former neighbor whose face he had seen staring out the window as the Nazis were brutalizing the Jews.[3] Michael, the character in the novel, says that the face of this man was more haunting than those of the German officers or the cruel Hungarian police. He asks, "How can anyone remain a spectator indefinitely?"[4] In a 1988 interview, Wiesel was asked about the nature of evil. His response reflects his early experience of the passivity of the Christians in Sighet: "I think that evil has many faces, but I would say that all of these faces have masks, and beneath the mask there is indifference. That is what all the faces of evil have in common: indifference."[5]

The one radiant exception to this indifference of Christians in Sighet was a young Christian woman named Maria, who had served as a housekeeper for the family and had grown very close to them. When the family was enclosed within the ghetto, Maria found a way through the barricades and brought them extra food. On the Sunday night after the Nazis arrived, she tried to convince the family to escape with her to a secluded cabin in the mountains. The family refused because they believed that they needed to stay with their fellow Jews. In his memoirs, Wiesel holds up Maria as a heroic exception to the failure of their neighbors:

> I think of Maria often with affection and gratitude. And with wonder as well. This simple, uneducated woman stood taller than the city's intellectuals, dignitaries and clergy. My father had many acquaintances and even friends in the Christian community, but not one of them showed the strength of character of this peasant woman. Of what value was their faith, their education, their social position, if it aroused neither conscience nor compassion? It was a simple and devout Christian woman who saved her town's honor.[6]

Wiesel's father, mother, and younger sister died in the concentration camps. His sisters Hilda and Bea survived and were reunited with Elie after the war. Wiesel himself was freed from Buchenwald (to which he and his father had been forcibly transferred near the end of the war) when the American armed forces liberated the camp on April 11, 1945. The American Army found twenty thousand emaciated prisoners when they seized the camp, hundreds of them children. After narrowly escaping death from food poisoning, Wiesel was taken with other Jewish youths to France and placed in a home sponsored by a Jewish children's aid group. As harsh as existence was in the camps, Wiesel's life during the years after his release continued to be a struggle for survival. He had lost his parents, had no money, and was a stateless person. Intent on pursuing his education, he obtained enough money from a refugee organization to enroll at the Sorbonne, where he studied literature, philosophy, and psychology. He took a special interest in the writings of Albert Camus and Franz Kafka. In order to survive he taught Hebrew to the children of French families, tutored students in the Talmud, and worked at summer children's camps.

Telling His Story

After his release from Buchenwald, Wiesel made a private vow not to speak or write about his experience in the concentration camps for ten years. In *A Jew Today* he explains, "So heavy was my anguish that I made a vow: not to speak, not to touch upon the essential for at least ten years. Long enough to see clearly. Long enough to learn to listen to the voices crying inside my own. Long enough to regain possession of my memory. Long enough to unite the language of man with the silence of the dead."[7] Near the end of that period he had an encounter that would lead him to share his story. Employed as a journalist for an Israeli newspaper, Wiesel had the opportunity to interview the distinguished French Catholic author François Mauriac. Mauriac was highly respected by the Jewish people for his participation in the French resistance to the Vichy government established by the Nazis. In the course of their conversation Mauriac spoke about his love for Jesus and his saving death on the cross. Wiesel, who had a strong sense of professionalism in his work as a journalist, reacted to Mauriac's musings in an uncharacteristic manner. He explains what happened in these words:

> Giving in to an angry impulse, I closed my notebook and rose. "Sir," I said, "you speak of Christ. Christians love to speak of him. The passion of Christ, the agony of Christ, the death of Christ. In your religion, that is all you speak of. Well, I want you to know that ten years ago, not very far

from here, I knew Jewish children every one of whom suffered a thousand times more, six million times more, than
Christ on the cross. And we don't speak about them. Can
you understand that, sir? We don't speak about them."[8]

Embarrassed by his outburst, Wiesel quickly concluded the interview and exited Mauriac's apartment, heading for the elevator. But
Mauriac rushed after him and convinced him to return. And then
Mauriac questioned him about his experience of the camps, urging
Wiesel to tell him everything. Wiesel informed the distinguished
author about the vow of silence he had taken. Reduced to tears,
Mauriac told Wiesel, "I think that you are wrong. Wrong not to
speak....Listen to the old man that I am: one must speak out—one
must also speak out."[9] It was during the following year that Wiesel
wrote his signature work *Night* and sent the manuscript to Mauriac.
Mauriac penned an influential foreword to the book and arranged for
its publication in France. In his foreword Mauriac describes the impact
that his meeting with Wiesel made on him: "I believe that on that day
I touched for the first time upon the mystery of iniquity whose revelation was to mark the end of one era and the beginning of another."[10]

Night is a grim but spellbinding account of Wiesel's experience as
a prisoner under the Nazis. Wiesel is starkly honest about his own
inner journey throughout this ordeal, including his struggles to believe
in God and his frustrations with God. Later, as he reflected on the book
he admitted that it is filled with paradox and appears to manifest
despair. So he kept on writing, drawing on the biblical and rabbinic
traditions to reflect on humanity's relationship with God. At the same
time, he said that he stood by everything that he had written in *Night*
and asserted that it is his most important work.[11]

One of the prevailing questions raised in *Night* is that of the *why*
and the *how* of praying in the midst of the dehumanizing experience
that Wiesel and his father were enduring. Near the beginning of the
book, as he and his fellow Jews are on a forced march into the camp,
Wiesel recalls coming upon the horrifying sight of a ditch into which
small children were being thrown and burned to death. Around him
someone began to recite the Kaddish, the traditional Jewish prayer for

the dead that includes the praise of God: "May God's name be blessed and magnified." Wiesel recalls his own inner thoughts and feelings at that moment: "For the first time I felt revolt rise up in me. Why should I bless his name? The eternal, Lord of the universe, the all-powerful and terrible, was silent. What had I to thank him for?"[12] In these arresting words we hear Wiesel articulate two aspects of the experience of people in the midst of innocent suffering: (1) revolt or protest; (2) the feeling that God is silent. Wiesel will continue to reflect on these two themes in his writings after *Night*. Nevertheless, he says that as he walked on past that terrible sight he found himself whispering the words of the Kaddish in spite of himself.

As life progresses in the camp Wiesel admits his struggles with faith and prayer, even though many of his fellow prisoners continued to speak about God. In his later memoirs he says that he did continue to pray, especially to practice the morning ritual prayers with his father.[13] But he was struggling mightily to make sense of what was happening. He recalls that some of the Jews in the camp spoke about God testing his people through this experience. We have seen that the theme of test or trial is a recurring one in the Hebrew and Christian scriptures and theological tradition. Wiesel writes of his inner response to this testing motif in these words: "How I sympathized with Job! I did not deny God's existence, but I doubted God's absolute justice."[14] Wiesel objects to the appeal to test or trial as a way of finding meaning in the experience of the Shoah, and like Job he grapples with the mystery of divine justice. In sympathy with the experience of Job, he sometimes speaks of his desire to bring God to court and charge God with injustice for the innocent suffering he sees all around him.[15]

Wiesel offers a moving description of the assembly of Jews in the camp on the eve of Rosh Hashanah, the Jewish New Year. There was a particularly heightened sense of anticipation about the last day of the Jewish year, an eschatological tension that filled the air: "The word 'last' rang very strangely. What if it were indeed the last day?"[16] Listening to the prayers recited by the assembly, Wiesel finds it difficult to pray. He is wrestling with the intense anger he feels inside: "'What are You, my God,' I thought angrily, 'compared to this afflicted crowd, proclaiming to You their faith, their anger, their revolt? What does Your greatness mean, Lord of the universe, in the face of all this weakness, this decomposition, and this decay? Why do You still trouble their sick minds, their crippled bodies?"[17] Here in rather disturbing terms Wiesel articulates the question of what kind of God the suffering person is to believe in: "What are You, my God?" How should people undergoing radical suffering conceive of God and of God's relation to the world?

Surely the most frequently quoted passage from *Night* is Wiesel's account of the prisoners being forced to watch the hanging of two men and a young boy. It is a text that is cited by virtually every theologian who reflects on God and the mystery of human suffering. The three condemned prisoners had been implicated in the bombing of an electric power station and sentenced to death. The other prisoners watched as the two men died quickly, but they saw the young boy hold on because he was so light—literally hanging between life and death for a half-hour. As they observed this grotesque spectacle, Wiesel recalls that he heard someone behind him ask, "Where is God? Where is He?" A few minutes later the same man posed the question again, "Where is God now?" Wiesel then writes, "And I heard a voice within me answer him: 'Where is He? Here He is—He is hanging here on this gallows....'"[18]

Wiesel does not explain the meaning of the response to the man's question that he heard inside himself. His words have been the object of diverse interpretations. Wiesel himself says that some have understood him to mean that God is dead—God has been exterminated like the young boy hanging on the gallows. In his memoirs Wiesel disputes this interpretation in a passage that is revelatory of his own approach to the mystery of God:

> Theorists of the idea that "God is dead" have used my words unfairly as justification of their rejection of faith. But if Nietzsche could cry out to the old man in the forest that God is dead, the Jew in me cannot. I have never questioned my faith in God. I have risen against His justice, protested His silence and sometimes His absence, but my anger rises up within faith and not outside it. I admit that this is hardly

an original position. But in these matters I have never sought originality. On the contrary, I have always aspired to follow in the footsteps of my father and those who went before him. Moreover, the texts cite many occasions when prophets and sages rebelled against the lack of divine interference in human affairs during times of persecution. Abraham and Moses, Jeremiah and Rebbe Levi-Yitzhak of Berdichev teach us that it is permissible for man to accuse God, provided that it be done in the name of faith in God.[19]

A significant theme that runs throughout *Night* and is also found in Wiesel's later writings is that of his relationship with his father. He cherishes the presence of his father in the camp, and their relationship achieves a new depth through their partnership in this ordeal. After the conclusion of the prayers recited by the prisoners on the eve of Rosh Hashanah, Wiesel recalls greeting his father simply by kissing his hand. He writes, "A tear fell upon it. Whose was that tear? Mine? His? I said nothing. Nor did he. We had never understood each other so clearly."[20] In his memoirs he comments about the days they shared in the camps: "I finally had my father to myself."[21] His father's presence was his motivation to live: "In the camps we were close, closer than ever, perhaps because we might be the last survivors of our family.... Because of him, I had to live; because of me, he tried not to die."[22] On a day in which he is sent out to work after it looks as if his father will not pass the process of "selection" (and thus be sent to the gas chamber), Wiesel is desperate to find out what happens. When he returns to the barracks and discovers that his father has not been sent to the chambers, it seems like a miracle to Wiesel. Afflicted with dysentery, his father dies in the bunk below him (January 28, 1945). Wiesel awakens the next morning to find that his father's body was removed before dawn, and he is not even sure whether he had stopped breathing when they took him to the crematory. This was an experience of loss that seared the soul of Wiesel with a depth that he has continued to express in the years since the war. He writes in his memoirs, "To this day I am mourning for my father, perhaps because I didn't mourn the day I became an orphan."[23]

While his father's presence inspired Wiesel to hold on, he also speaks of his struggles to remain faithful to him, especially when his father became weak and needed assistance. He had to fight the temptation to see his father as a burden. Recounting the brutal forced march of the prisoners to Buchenwald, Wiesel remembers the visit of a Polish rabbi who was revered by everyone in the camp. About Rabbi Eliahou Wiesel says, "He was like one of the old prophets, always in the midst of his people to comfort them. And, strangely, his words of comfort never provoked rebellion; they really brought peace."[24] Rabbi Eliahou comes to ask Wiesel if he has seen his son, from whom he has become separated during the long march. Wiesel replies that he has not seen him, but then he remembers something that frightens him. He recalls seeing the rabbi's son run ahead of his limping, staggering father, leaving him behind. Though the rabbi's son had stayed close to his father for three years in the camp, at the end he left his father behind because he had become a burden. Wiesel recalls his inner thoughts at that moment: "And, in spite of myself, a prayer rose in my heart, to the God in whom I no longer believed. My God, Lord of the Universe, give me strength never to do what Rabbi Eliahou's son has done."[25] Not long after this encounter, Wiesel visits his sick father in the infirmary; there he discovers that his father has not been fed, so he gives him some of his soup. Wiesel chastises himself, however, because he feels that he did not share his soup in a spirit of generosity but "with a heavy heart." He confesses, "No better than Rabbi Eliahou's son had I withstood the test."[26] The reader receives the impression that Wiesel's struggle to remain faithful to his father throughout this terrible ordeal was his way of staying faithful to himself and, perhaps, to God.

The Figure of Job and the Place of Protest

The protest against innocent suffering that is evident in *Night* is found throughout Wiesel's writings. He holds up Job as a biblical character who exemplifies this stance of protest from within faith. In a collection of essays on biblical figures Wiesel includes a reflection with the revealing title, "Job Our Contemporary."[27] Like the other essays in the book his exposition of the message of Job is articulated in the style of the midrashic commentary of the rabbis. It is illustrative of a number of themes in Wiesel's writings on suffering. Wiesel introduces his commentary by affirming the relevance of Job: "In times of stress it is to his words that we turn to express our anger, revolt or resignation. He belongs to our most intimate landscape, the most vulnerable part of our past."[28] Wiesel observes that whenever rabbinic commentary on the scriptures runs short of examples it quotes Job, no matter what the topic. He points out that the Midrash sometimes tries to discover reasons for Job's suffering, for example, that he was an advisor at Pharaoh's court who remained neutral on the question of whether to let the Israelites leave Egypt. Because of Job's neutrality on this all-important question he was later afflicted with suffering. Wiesel notes that such legends were invented to justify Job's subsequent ordeals: "Just as there is no crime without punishment, ideally there is no punishment without crime."[29] Wiesel argues that such explanations, which reflect a theology of retribution, are flawed. He accentuates Job's justice and innocence, and he comments on Job's cursing the day of his birth in this way: "And then, in desperation, he asked the eternal question of the persecuted: Why? Why me? Why now? What is the meaning of punishment inflicted on a Just Man? What is God doing, and where is His justice?"[30]

Wiesel also adduces rabbinic commentaries that liken Job's testing to that of Abraham. Some of these commentaries criticize Job for failing to recognize that he is not the only just person who has suffered. Wiesel objects to this strategy of consolation through comparison. "Job could have said that while the tragedy of one man may well be linked to that of another, or many others, that fact explains nothing and justifies nothing."[31] Wiesel continues, "No, tragedies do not cancel each other out as they succeed one another. On the contrary, they multiply and accumulate, becoming more unjust with every blow....The fact that Job's torments had a precedent does not imply that they have meaning."[32] Wiesel believes that when suffering people begin to empathize with others who are also suffering, this outreach does not make suffering any easier to accept or understand; it simply compounds the suffering. His response is similar when people attempt to link the sufferings of the Jews during the Shoah with other instances of tragic suffering in history.[33]

For Wiesel, Job is an exemplary character because of his courage in arguing with his three friends and with God. His friends had to choose between defending Job and taking a stand for God. They chose to defend God, a decision that Wiesel calls "the wrong choice."[34] They talked about God to one who was suffering, constructing theories derived from a system of theology that presumed to make sense of Job's experience. "These three self-righteous strangers from afar exaggerated when they tried to explain to Job events whose tragic weight rested only on his shoulders. *He* suffered, and *they* made speeches on suffering. *He* was crushed by sorrow, and *they* built theories and systems on the subjects of grief, suffering and persecution."[35] For Wiesel, the behavior of Job's three friends exemplifies precisely what a believer should *not* do in the face of innocent suffering.

In *Night* Wiesel speaks of the power and strength of his fellow prisoners, even as they are driven on a death march through the winter. While the German soldiers rotated their duty because of fatigue and cold, the prisoners plodded on through the snow. Wiesel reflects, "We were masters of nature, masters of the world. We had forgotten everything—death, fatigue, our natural needs. Stronger than cold or hunger, stronger than the shots and the desire to die, condemned and wandering, mere numbers, we were the only men on earth."[36] He makes a similar observation about the figure of Job. Job exhibited strength of character by refusing to submit to the arguments of his friends and continuing to question the justice of God. This was the only means of exercising power that he still had, and he used it.

> He rejected all easy solutions, all debasing compromises. He discovered within himself unequaled power and he reversed the roles. Though accused, condemned and repudiated, he defied the system that kept him imprisoned. He launched an inquiry and suddenly God was the defendant. Job spoke his outrage, his grief; he told God what He should have known for a long time, perhaps since always, that something was amiss in His universe."[37]

Though he had lost almost everything Job retained his ability to question, and this was an expression of his personal power.

Wiesel's admiration for Job's courageous protest leads him to express his disapproval of the ending of the book, especially Job's repentance in dust and ashes. The two speeches of God at the end offer no real explanations for Job's suffering or answers to his questions. Wiesel thinks that the monologues of God out of the storm should have aroused further indignation in Job. Job should have continued to argue his case with honesty and strength. Wiesel's commentary on this section of the book is emblematic of his approach to the mystery of innocent suffering: "Much as I admired Job's passionate rebellion, I am deeply troubled by his hasty abdication. He appeared to me more human when he was cursed and grief-stricken, more dignified than after he rebuilt his lavish residences under the sign of his newly found faith in divine glory and mercy."[38] In the imaginative style of rabbinic biblical commentary, Wiesel speculates that the true ending of the book was lost. Job really died without repenting: "He succumbed to his grief an uncompromising and whole man."[39] Or—and here Wiesel imagines another possibility—perhaps Job only pretended to abdicate before God; he actually continued to interrogate God.

Wiesel concludes his essay on Job on an autobiographical note. He says that in the years after the war he "was preoccupied with Job."[40] The figure of Job could be found everywhere in his world. "In those days he could be seen on every road of Europe."[41] Job is the biblical character who "personified man's eternal quest for justice and truth."[42] In an intriguing comment, Wiesel writes about Job: "Thus he did not suffer in vain; thanks to him, we know that it is given to man to transform divine injustice into human justice and compassion."[43] For Wiesel the question of the justice of God is the mystery with which human beings continue to grapple throughout history.

The preference for the stance of protest from within faith that is evident in Wiesel's essay on Job is found in other writings as well. Job's desire to initiate a lawsuit against God is reprised in Wiesel's play, *The Trial of God*. This drama is set in the town of Shamrogod in 1649, where a brutal pogrom has resulted in the murder of every Jewish family except for Berish the innkeeper and his daughter Hanna, who has been traumatized by rape. The experience of the pogrom has drained Berish of his vitality and his trust in God. On the feast of Purim Berish is visited by three Jewish men from another town. In the course of the evening's festivities, Berish proposes staging a trial in which God is the defendant. He assumes the role of prosecutor. After debating about who will serve as God's defense attorney, the group settles on a mysterious stranger named Sam. Berish pummels Sam with questions about divine justice—accusing God of hostility, cruelty, and injustice toward the chosen people.[44] Sam responds with calm, reasoned answers, questioning human wisdom about cosmic affairs and defending God's justice at every turn. The other characters admire Sam's respect for God and take him to be a holy man, a *tzaddik*. But in a chilling twist at the end the characters take out their Purim masks, and it is revealed that Sam is really Satan. It is Satan who has been providing a careful, reasoned defense for God in the face of the accusations of innocent victims.

In a lengthy interview published in 1999, Wiesel discussed his stance of protest from within the realm of faith.[45] Citing the work of Kafka, he expresses his belief that we can talk only *to* God, not *about* God. Wiesel said, "What I try to do is to speak to God. Even when I speak against God, I speak to God. And even if I am angry with God, I try to show God my anger. But even that is a profession, not a denial of God."[46] Wiesel asserts that despite the disillusionment caused by his experience of the Shoah he has never abandoned God. At times, however, he has needed to interrogate God: "I had tremendous problems with God, and I still do. Therefore I protest against God. Sometimes I bring God before the bench. Nevertheless, everything I do is done from within faith and not from outside."[47] Wiesel emphasizes that for Jews God is a friend, and one can argue fiercely with a friend without rejecting the friendship. Perhaps more than any other figure in the theological conversation since the Shoah, Elie Wiesel embodies the biblical teaching about the power of lamentation and the validity of protest from within a covenant relationship with God.

The Suffering of God

In his later reflections on God and suffering, Wiesel speaks of divine suffering. He draws on the concept of the Shekinah—the indwelling presence of God—that is found in the Jewish rabbinic and mystical traditions. When the people of God are afflicted by suffering, God is intimately close to them and deeply affected by their plight: "God accompanies his children into exile."[48] Even when the suffering of the people is a result of God's punishment for their infidelity, God continues to dwell with them and to experience the pain of this punishment. "Though imposed by God, the punishment goes beyond those upon whom it falls, encompassing the Judge himself. And it is God who wills it so. The Father may reveal Himself through His wrath; He may even sharpen His severity, but He will never be absent....God is everywhere, even in suffering and in the very heart of punishment."[49] Wiesel likes to recall a story from the Midrash that claims that when God sees the suffering of God's people among the nations God sheds two tears that fall into the ocean. These tears make a noise that is so loud it is heard around the world.[50]

According to Wiesel, however, the suffering of God with God's people offers no solution to the mystery of suffering, nor does it provide real consolation for suffering people. Indeed, he thinks that divine suffering compounds the experience of suffering—it does not alleviate human suffering. He maintains that "we can say that the suffering of the one does not cancel out the other; rather, the two are added together. In this sense, divine suffering is not consolation but additional punishment."[51] Neither does the suffering of God diminish the utterly mysterious character of the history of human suffering. Wiesel eschews all theological statements that bear any resemblance to theodicy. "How did God manage to bear His suffering added to our own? Are we to imagine the one as justification for the other? Nothing justifies Auschwitz. Were the Lord Himself to offer me a justification, I think I would reject it. Treblinka erases all justifications and answers."[52] In an interview he puts it succinctly: "God and the death camps. I will never understand that."[53]

In this same interview Wiesel's interlocutor asked him a question about the power of God. Making reference to a famous statement by Bonhoeffer about God's weakness, the interviewer asked whether it is "a weaker God, one who suffers, who can help us."[54] In his reply Wiesel emphasizes that he does not wish to speak of a weak God in addressing the mystery of suffering: "I am not convinced of that, since it contradicts the Jewish tradition. We do not believe in a weak God. God is the king of the universe, God is strong and omnipotent. God could do whatever God wants. But God does not."[55] He continues by declaring that God could bring the course of history to an end if God wanted to do so. "God could take away the murderer's strength and the victim's weakness. God does not do this, since God has God's reasons. We do not know. We have to live with the question of why God does not do it."[56]

If one can speak of an "approach" or a "strategy" that Wiesel adopts toward the mystery of suffering it would seem to entail living with the unanswered questions and addressing these questions honestly to God, all the while trusting in God's closeness to and identification with suffering people.

Dietrich Bonhoeffer

A Life of Resistance and Surrender

Dietrich Bonhoeffer was born in 1906 into a cultured, affluent family. His father was a well-known psychiatrist who taught at the University of Berlin. His mother was the granddaughter of a famous professor of church history (Karl August von Hase) and the daughter of a pastor and theologian.[57] During his university career Bonhoeffer decided to pursue the study of theology as a profession. At the time, he made this decision for academic reasons rather than as an expression of personal faith. He studied at the universities of Tübingen and Berlin, earning his licentiate at Berlin at the age of twenty-one. The topic of his licentiate was the doctrine of the communion of saints. One of his teachers was the famous historian of dogma Adolf von

Harnack. Though Bonhoeffer never studied with Karl Barth, Barth's thought also had a significant impact on him.

In his mid-twenties Bonhoeffer experienced a deepening of his theological vocation—a kind of personal conversion—in which the practice of his Lutheran faith became vitally important to him. He committed himself to personal prayer and to meditation on the Bible; he found special inspiration in the psalms and the Sermon on the Mount. Writing later about this personal transformation to his friend and confidante Eberhard Bethge, he described it as "a great libera-tion."[58] After a period of pastoral ministry in Barcelona, Bonhoeffer spent a year of study (1930–31) at Union Theological Seminary in New York. While in New York he became involved in the Abyssinian Baptist Church in Harlem, making many friends in the African American community. His experience of poverty in Harlem and racism in the United States influenced his later opposition to the racism of the Nazi regime.[59]

Bonhoeffer lectured periodically at the University of Berlin until the Nazis expelled him from the university in 1936. After Hitler came to power in 1933, however, Bonhoeffer lost interest in pursuing an aca-demic career, recognizing immediately that National Socialism was godless and disastrous. For Bonhoeffer "it became increasingly clear that academic discussion must give way to action" and that "it was imperative to relinquish the shelter and privilege of the academic ros-trum."[60] He became known for a famous radio address on the concept of the Führer given in February 1933, shortly after Hitler became chan-cellor of Germany. In a play on words, he warned his listeners that "the image of the 'leader' (Führer) will gradually become the image of the 'misleader' (Verführer)."[61]

Bonhoeffer spent time in England between 1933 and 1935, where he met the Anglican bishop George Bell, who became a significant contact in his later work for the resistance movement. In 1936 the Confessing Church (the branch of the Lutheran Church in Germany that opposed Hitler) called him to lead an emergency seminary for young ministers. He directed and taught in the seminary until the police closed it in September 1937. During this time he wrote his well-known work *The Cost of Discipleship*, a polemic against "cheap grace." Reflecting on his experience of the vibrant communal life that had been created at the seminary, he wrote *Life Together* in 1938.

On a lecture tour in the United States when war broke out in 1939, Bonhoeffer decided that he had an obligation to return to Germany. Writing to Reinhold Niebuhr he explained, "I will have no right to participate in the reconstruction of Christian life after the war if I do not share the trials of this time with my people."[62] Bonhoeffer then made the momentous decision to become more directly involved in the resistance movement. Attracted to pacifism before this (he had great admiration for Gandhi), he concluded that the evils of the Nazi regime made a more active form of resistance imperative. Through his brother-in-law, Hans von Dohnanyi, he became a civilian employee of the *Abwehr*, the German military intelligence. This agency, led by Admiral Wilhelm Canaris and General Hans Oster, was paradoxically a center of the resistance movement against Hitler. Bonhoeffer's work as a courier for the *Abwehr* enabled him to make contacts for the resistance abroad, including a meeting with Bishop Bell in Sweden. With his choice to work as a double agent in the military intelligence, Bonhoeffer had made the difficult decision to move out of the realm of the ecclesiastical into the political sphere, a move that isolated him from some of his ecclesial colleagues. This was a position in which "the church offered no protection and no prior justification for something that fell outside all normal contingencies."[63]

The resistance was behind two assassination attempts against Hitler in March 1943, neither of which was successful. It was also involved in the famous attempt carried out by Colonel von Stauffenberg on July 20, 1944. Bonhoeffer was arrested on April 5, 1943, along with his sister and brother-in-law. He spent the first eighteen months of confinement in the Tegel prison in Berlin. He was eventually allowed to have regular visitors in this prison. He became popular with and respected by many of the prison guards, some of whom helped to smuggle his writings out of prison. Because this prison was located near a locomotive factory, it became a frequent target of Allied bombing raids. Bonhoeffer's courageous and peaceful demeanor became a source of strength for his fellow prisoners and the guards during these attacks. Most of his letters and papers are addressed to Bethge, his friend and former student who was stationed as a soldier in Italy and was also involved in the resistance movement. With the failed attempt on Hitler's life in July 1944, and after the discovery by the Gestapo of incriminating evidence against members of the *Abwehr*, Bonhoeffer was moved to a more secure Gestapo jail. Eventually he was transferred to the concentration camps at Buchenwald and Flossenbürg and was hanged on April 9, 1945, together with Canaris, Oster, and others. His brother Klaus Bonhoeffer and his brother-in-law von Dohnanyi were also executed by the Nazis.

Of all of Bonhoeffer's work, his letters and papers from prison have made the greatest impact the postwar conversation about God and the mystery of suffering.[64] These writings are occasional and fragmentary, the reflections of a theologian imprisoned in a Nazi jail that was the target of Allied bombers and writing on scraps of paper to be secretly smuggled out of prison. Life in the Tegel prison and later in a Gestapo jail prevented him from achieving a systematic formulation of his thought. Scholars differ in their estimation of the relationship between the ideas of Bonhoeffer articulated in his final days and those expressed in earlier works such as *The Cost of Discipleship* and his *Ethics* (a work that is based on reflections written prior to his imprisonment, left unfinished but arranged and published posthumously in 1949).[65] Geffrey Kelly points out lines of continuity between Bonhoeffer's prison reflections and his earlier writings.[66] Bethge also takes note of this continuity, but he argues that "Bonhoeffer in 1944 was not merely saying the same thing as he had said in 1932."[67] I focus here on his prison writings while making occasional reference to his earlier works, especially *The Cost of Discipleship*.

Critique of Religion

The prison writings reveal Bonhoeffer's distrust of what he calls "religion" or the "religious." Referring to Karl Barth's critique of religion, Bonhoeffer asks, "How can Christ become the Lord even of those with no religion? If religion is no more than a garment of Christianity—and even that garment has had very different aspects at different times—then what is a religionless Christianity?"[68] He speaks of "the non-religious interpretation of theological concepts."[69] Sitting alone in his prison cell, within a Germany overtaken by Nazis and now under siege by the Allies, a world plunged into modern warfare and the age of technology, Bonhoeffer is convinced that the world has "come of age."[70] He asserts that humankind is "proceeding towards a time of no religion at all; men as they are now simply cannot be religious any more."[71] In his commentary on Paul's Letter to the Romans, Barth had contrasted religion, which consists of humanly invented approaches to God, with Christianity, which results from God's free self-revelation. Barth thought that religion diminished the utter transcendence of God and softened God's word of judgment.[72] Bonhoeffer builds on Barth's ideas in his prison writings, though he develops them further and applies them to the new situation in which he is writing.

What is Bonhoeffer getting at when he speaks of a religionless Christianity? While he provides no systematic explanation of this notion, it is instructive to situate it against the background of his own experience. Bonhoeffer was disillusioned by the indifference and even complicity of many Christians and ecclesial communities in Nazi Germany. He became convinced that true Christianity was not clothed in the safe, status quo practice of religion. He thought that such religious practice had lost the prophetic edge of the gospel and had become an expression of "cheap grace." In *The Cost of Discipleship* he had described cheap grace as "grace without discipleship, grace without the cross, grace without Jesus Christ, living and incarnate."[73] His involvement in the resistance had convinced him that some of the nonreligious people he knew—like his brother Klaus—were acting in a more "Christian" manner in the face of Nazi oppression than were Christian believers who regularly went to church but had become captive to Hitler's ideology.[74] He used the phrase "unconscious Christianity" to refer to a way of living that was not religious but that reflected the true meaning of the gospel.[75] Bonhoeffer emphasizes that authentic faith requires one to stake one's whole life on what he or she believes.[76]

In his biography of Bonhoeffer, Bethge argues that his critique of religion includes a number of dimensions.[77] Bonhoeffer asserted that to interpret Christianity in a religious sense meant to interpret it "metaphysically" and "individualistically." While Bonhoeffer offers no explanation here, by a "metaphysical" interpretation of Christianity he seems to mean the encapsulation of the message of the gospel within a Western metaphysical framework, which he thinks obscures the true gospel. With regard to the individualistic interpretation of Christianity, Bethge points out that Bonhoeffer had expounded a social vision of the gospel since the time of his thesis on the communion of saints.[78] He opposed any expression of Christianity fixated on interiority and lacking in social concern. This conviction became stronger in the last years of his life, when he risked everything in a conspiracy the aim of which was the building of a new Germany. By a "religious" sense of Christianity, Bonhoeffer also refers to a view that compartmentalizes faith, confining it to a single sphere of life rather than inspiring the commitment of one's whole being. He says that the religious act is always something "partial," while a genuine act of faith involves the whole of one's life.[79] An authentic response to the gospel demands a commitment to Christ that shapes all of the dimensions of one's life.

Finding God at the Center of Life

For Bonhoeffer, the act of Christian faith leads us to perceive and respond to the real concerns of the world. He says that God "must be found at the center of life: in life, and not only in suffering; in activity, and not only in sin."[80] Christians do not believe in a "God of the gaps"—a divine being to whom they appeal when science or some other form of human reasoning reaches a dead end. After reading a book on physics in prison, he writes to Bethge that this book "has brought home to me how wrong it is to use God as a stop-gap for the incompleteness of our knowledge. For the frontiers of our knowledge are being pushed back further and further...."[81] The God of the gaps becomes more and more irrelevant as human knowledge increases. And Bonhoeffer is convinced that believers must move away from a conception of God as the *deus ex machina*, the God to whom they cry out in extreme situations of life to intervene from above and save them. He argues, "Christ is the center of life, and in no sense did he come to answer our unsolved problems."[82]

In these prison writings Bonhoeffer expresses his conviction that we must find God and serve God right in the midst of the world, even a world that has become increasingly secular. He says, "God is the 'beyond' in the midst of our life. The Church stands not where human powers give out, on the borders, but in the center of the village."[83] Such a view of Christianity entails a stance that faces and responds to the concerns of the world, particularly the concerns of justice. The church must discover God's presence in the midst of the sweat, toil, and projects of everyday life. Bonhoeffer argues that this conviction is rooted in Christian belief in the resurrection: "The difference between the Christian hope of resurrection and a mythological hope is that the Christian hope sends a man back to his life on earth in a wholly new way which is even more sharply defined than it is in the Old Testament."[84] Christ takes us by the shoulders and turns us around to face the world; he does not want us to flee from the world.

A Suffering God

When Christians do enter fully into the world they discover a world scarred by intense suffering. Bonhoeffer felt the suffering of the world in a very personal way as he languished in a Nazi prison. He comes to the conclusion that the God who is encountered in the midst of the world—the God who is the beyond in the midst of life—is the God who suffers with the world. In his prison writings Bonhoeffer includes a provocative series of statements about divine suffering. He is clearly influenced by Martin Luther's theology of the cross, which teaches that God is revealed most fully in the weakness and suffering of the crucified Jesus. God is disclosed in what appears to be the most ungodly event. Reflecting on Jesus' cry of abandonment (Mark 15:34), Bonhoeffer comments, "God allows himself to be edged out of the world and on to the cross. God is weak and powerless in the world, and that is exactly the way, the only way, in which he can be with us and help us."[85] He argues that the New Testament "makes it crystal clear that it is not by his omnipotence that Christ helps us, but by his weakness and suffering."[86] For Bonhoeffer, the Bible, which he studied diligently while in prison, directs the disciple to the weakness, powerlessness, and suffering of God. As Bonhoeffer gazes out from his prison cell at the oppressive darkness enveloping his world, he thinks of God as deeply affected by evil and suffering and as grieving over it. God is present and active in the world not so much through divine power but in and through divine weakness. It is here that Bonhoeffer makes one of his most famous statements: "Only a suffering God can help."[87]

Christians are those who participate in the sufferings of God in the world. The gospel imperative to watch with Jesus in Gethsemane means that "man is challenged to participate in the sufferings of God at the hands of a godless world."[88] This demands that we be fully engaged in the affairs of the world. Returning to his critique of a religious version of Christianity, Bonhoeffer says, "It is not some religious act which makes a Christian what he is, but participation in the suffering of God in the life of the world."[89] He contrasts these two versions of Christianity in the first two verses of "Christians and Pagans," a poem that he wrote in July 1944:

> All people go to God in need,
> For help and calm and food they plead.
> That sickness, guilt and death may cease,
> All, Christians and Pagans, pray for peace.
>
> But some turn to God in God's need and dread,
> A God poor, despised, without roof or bread.
> By sin's harm weakened and by death distressed,
> Christians stand steadfast by their God oppressed.[90]

The first verse describes the "religious" approach to God; the second depicts the authentically Christian way. For Bonhoeffer the true Christian is the person who is engaged in service to others in the world and who in so doing "stands steadfast" by an oppressed God—a God who suffers with suffering women and men. Just as the sole concern of Jesus was the well-being of others, so Christians serve God "through a new life for others, through participation in the Being of God."[91] Kelly and Nelson comment on this poem in their exposition of Bonhoeffer's spirituality:

> Embedded in these middle lines is the theology of the cross. It conveys the message that God suffers in and with God's people....The poem's message leaps over the boundaries of religious propriety in affirming God in order to celebrate this fact of faith: For all, whether Christian or pagan, God needs our support even as God extends love in constant, ever present forbearance and forgiveness of our sins.[92]

Suffering for the Gospel

Bonhoeffer clearly affirms, then, that Christian discipleship demands a willingness to suffer with Christ, to identify with the suffering God revealed in the crucified Christ. He had expressed this conviction in writings authored before his imprisonment, especially in *The Cost of Discipleship*. There he wrote, "Just as Christ is Christ only in virtue of his suffering and rejection, so the disciple is a disciple only in so far as he shares his Lord's suffering and rejection and crucifixion."[93] He distinguishes between the suffering that is a result of our finitude and "the suffering which is the fruit of an exclusive allegiance to Jesus Christ."[94] Christians do not look for suffering, but "they simply bear the suffering which comes their way as they try to follow Jesus Christ and bear it for *his* sake."[95]

Bonhoeffer's reflection on the role of suffering in the life of discipleship intensified during his time in prison. On July 21, 1944—the day after the failed attempt to assassinate Hitler—he composed his "Stations on the Road to Freedom." The four "stations" that he delineates are discipline, action, suffering, and death. A person of remarkable self-discipline, Bonhoeffer says, "If you would find freedom, learn above all to discipline your senses and your soul."[96] As one who made the fateful decision to become actively involved in the German resistance, he asserts that true freedom demands action: "Never to hesitate over what is within your power, but boldly to grasp what lies before you."[97] Suffering is the third station on this path to freedom, and Bonhoeffer's meditation on it has an autobiographical ring: "O wondrous change! Those hands, once so strong and active, have now been bound. Helpless and forlorn, you see the end of your deed. Yet with a sigh of relief you resign your cause to a stronger hand, and are content to do so."[98] Death is the final stop on this road, and for Bonhoeffer it is the passageway into the pure freedom of the presence of God: "O freedom, long have we sought thee in discipline and in action and in suffering. Dying, we behold thee now, and see thee in the face of God."[99] A week later Bonhoeffer writes that "suffering is the extension of action and the perfection of freedom."[100] He finds this truth to be "very important and very comforting."[101]

Divine Providence

Even though Bonhoeffer speaks of God as weak and powerless in the world, his prison writings reveal an unfailing belief in the faithful presence and providential care of God. First of all, he expresses his confidence in the rightness of decisions he has made that have led him to where he is. Writing to Bethge, he says that he has not for a moment regretted returning to Germany in 1939 and that he considers his imprisonment as his own part in the fate of Germany.[102] Echoing the same sentiments four months later, he says that his life "has followed a straight and even course," and he claims, "If I should end my days here like this, that would have a meaning I could understand."[103] In one of the last preserved letters he tells Bethge, "You must never doubt that I am traveling my appointed road with gratitude and cheerfulness. My past life is replete with God's goodness, and my sins are covered by the forgiving love of Christ crucified."[104] This is a man who, though honest about his own personal struggles, appears to be at peace with his conscience.

Second, his prison writings indicate that he held on to a firm belief in divine providence. In a reflection written not long after his arrest and confinement at Tegel he says, "I believe that God both can and will bring good out of evil….I believe that even our errors and mistakes are turned to good account."[105] A year later, in April 1944, he pens these words in a letter to Bethge: "I can't help feeling that everything has taken its natural course; it has all been inevitable, straightforward, directed by a higher providence."[106] In August 1944, when the net is closing in upon him, Bonhoeffer eloquently expresses his trust in the presence of God. He counsels Bethge to "persevere in quiet meditation on the life, sayings, deeds, sufferings and death of Jesus in order to learn what God promises and what he fulfills." And then he adds, "One thing is certain: we must always live close to the presence of God, for that is newness of life: and then nothing is impossible for all things are possible with God; no earthly power can touch us without his will, and danger can only drive us closer to him."[107] Taking Bonhoeffer's prison writings as a whole, one can see that while he can speak of God as weak and powerless in the world, he clings to his belief that God has the final word when it comes to evil and suffering, and this word is a word of life. Indeed his fellow prisoner Payne Best reported that the final words Bonhoeffer spoke to him prior to his execution were, "This is the end—for me the beginning of life."[108]

Conclusion

Two eloquent—and at times disturbing—voices from the Shoah. The theologians whose thought we consider in subsequent chapters will converse with the witness of Wiesel and Bonhoeffer, as well as with other voices from the Shoah, in their discussion of God and suffering. Wiesel's chronicle of his own experience as he endured the brutality of the camps testifies to the power of evil in the world and the crisis of faith that often ensues when one suffers its onslaught. The questions he raises about what kind of God we believe in, how to pray in the midst of intense suffering, and the apparent silence of God are queries that later authors have been compelled to confront. His appeal to the legitimacy and the power of protest from within a stance of faith—deeply rooted in the Jewish tradition as it is—has captivated many contemporary thinkers. Wiesel's famous account of the hanging of the young boy and the question he heard inside himself—"Where is God?"—has provoked sustained reflection about the way in which one speaks of the presence of God in situations of intense suffering.

Bonhoeffer's efforts to rethink his understanding of God and of Christian discipleship while confined in a Nazi prison have also engaged the imagination of later theologians. We will see that Moltmann, for example, appeals to Bonhoeffer's axiom, "Only a suffering God can help," as he formulates his portrayal of God rooted in the story of Calvary. Not all theologians agree with Bonhoeffer's use of words like *weakness* and *powerlessness* to describe God, but they are forced to wrestle with the provocative ideas that he articulated in his prison writings. Moreover, the impact of Bonhoeffer's thought has been strengthened by the witness of his life, which he sacrificed in the effort to oppose the regime that perpetrated the Shoah.

Discussion Questions: www.paulistpress.com, Online Resources.

7

Jürgen Moltmann:
Theology from the Pit

Having listened to the voices of Elie Wiesel and Dietrich Bonhoeffer, we turn now to another figure whose life was shaped by the tragedy of World War II and the murder of Jews by the Nazis. This theologian, however, experienced the horror of these events from the "other side." Jürgen Moltmann is a German Protestant theologian who has attempted to construct a Christian systematic theology that keeps the harsh reality of human suffering front and center. His book *The Crucified God*, published in Germany in 1973, has become a point of reference in the contemporary theological conversation about God and suffering.[1] Moltmann is committed to a Christianity that faces suffering in the world both in its theologizing and in its practice of the faith. His theology has received criticism from a variety of perspectives, and we examine major critiques of Moltmann's thought on God and suffering. But Moltmann's keen awareness of the importance of the church attending to the reality of suffering in its preaching, teaching, pastoral care, and social action has resulted in writings that Christian theologians take seriously. Moltmann's ideas have led other thinkers—including those who disagree with him—to think more deeply about the Christian conception of God and God's relation to suffering.

Moltmann's Experience of World War II

Moltmann writes about his own experience of the war and postwar years in several of his works.[2] Drafted into the military by the Nazi government at age sixteen, he served at the front as an Air Force auxiliary. He was at his post in an anti-aircraft battery during the bombing of Hamburg by the British Royal Air Force in July 1943, an attack that killed more than forty thousand people, including a friend who was standing right next to him at the battery. About that experience he writes, "That night I cried out to God for the first time: 'My God, where are you?' And the question, 'Why am I not dead too?' has haunted me ever since. Why are you alive? What gives your life meaning?"[3] Moltmann grew up in a secular family of teachers who did not practice any religious faith. His energies and dreams were focused on mathematics and physics. He found his spiritual sustenance in the writings of Johann Wolfgang von Goethe and Friedrich Nietzsche. His traumatic experiences during the war, especially the bombing of Hamburg, catalyzed his personal search for God. Moltmann says, "Whenever I call up that catastrophe and descend into the dark pit of remembrance, I am overwhelmed again by fear and trembling."[4]

When the war ended in 1945, Moltmann was placed in a mass prisoner of war (POW) camp at Ostend in Belgium. Eventually he was transferred to camps for younger prisoners in Scotland and England. Moltmann's time in these camps was especially important for the growth of his faith and his decision to study theology. His initial months as a prisoner of war were a period of intense darkness and near-despair. In September 1945 he and his fellow prisoners in the camp in Scotland were confronted with photographs of the Nazi extermination camps at Belsen and Auschwitz. Though the young prisoners were tempted to deny the reality of what they saw in these pictures, this denial could not last: "But slowly and inexorably the truth filtered into our awareness, and we saw ourselves mirrored in the eyes of the Nazi victims. Was this what we had fought for? Had my generation, as the last, been driven to our deaths so that the concentration camp murderers could go on killing, and Hitler could live a few months longer?"[5] Moltmann graphically depicts the hopelessness that he felt as a young man confined to a prisoner of war camp and compelled to grapple with the shame caused by the Nazi war crimes.

In the midst of this darkness, an Army chaplain gave Moltmann a Bible, and Moltmann began to read it. He confesses that he did not understand much of what he read at first, but when he came upon the psalms of lament he felt a deep resonance with the sentiments expressed in these plaintive prayers. He was struck by Psalm 39:

> I was silent and still;
> I held my peace to no avail;
> my distress grew worse,
> my heart became hot within me. (Ps 39:2–3)

The words of this psalm, says Moltmann, "were the words of my own heart and they called my soul to God."[6] Then he read the account of the passion of Jesus and was captivated by Jesus' cry of abandonment from the cross (Mark 15:34). Moltmann describes the impact this Gospel text made on him:

> [W]hen I read Jesus' death cry, "My God, why have you forsaken me?", I knew with certainty: this is someone who understands you. I began to understand the assailed Christ because I felt that he understood me: this was the divine brother in distress, who takes the prisoners with him on his way to resurrection. I began to summon up the courage to live again, seized by a great hope. I was even calm when other men were "repatriated" and I was not. This early fellowship with Jesus, the brother in suffering and the redeemer from guilt, has never left me since. I never "decided for Christ" as is often demanded of us, but I am sure that then and there, in the dark pit of my soul, he found me. Christ's God-forsakenness showed me *where* God is, *where* he had been with me in my life, and where he would be in the future.[7]

Moltmann intensified his study of the Bible and theology in the POW camp, up to the time of his release in 1948. He read Bonhoeffer's *The Cost of Discipleship* as well as *The Nature and Destiny of Man* by Reinhold Niebuhr. He and his fellow prisoners were also deeply influenced by the kindness and acceptance they experienced from their Scottish and English neighbors, which contributed to Moltmann's later writing about reconciliation. He recalls that this acceptance "made it possible for us to live with the guilt of our own people, the catastrophes we had brought about and the long shadows of Auschwitz, without repressing them and without becoming callous."[8] In a talk given in 1995 Moltmann reflected on these experiences, referring to the biblical story of Jacob wrestling with God (Gen 32:25–32). He speaks of his own grappling with God at that critical time in his life, from which he emerged limping but blessed: "We were given what we did not deserve, and received of the fullness of Christ 'grace upon grace.'"[9] Moltmann's theological reflection on God and suffering can only be understood in light of this intense, deeply personal experience he had as a young man. From the hopelessness of the "pit" he had a profound experience of grace mediated by his identification with the crucified Christ.

When Bonhoeffer's prison writings were first published in 1951, Moltmann read them with great interest and was particularly inspired by Bonhoeffer's assertion that "only a suffering God can help."[10] The notion of a God who suffers with suffering human beings gave him comfort and profoundly influenced the portrait of God that he would develop in his theology. In 1961 he visited the extermination camp at Maidanek, an unforgettable experience about which he says, "I would have rather sunk to the ground than gone on."[11] The memory of the victims of the Shoah haunted him. Throughout his theological career Moltmann has continued to wrestle with the reality of the Shoah; it remains the backdrop of all of his theologizing. Reflecting on his book *The Crucified God* thirty years after its initial publication, he described it as "an attempt to speak to God and to speak about God in the shadows of Auschwitz and in view of the victims of my people."[12]

The Cross as Center and Criterion of Christian Theology

Moltmann has sought to dialogue with those who question the existence of a good God because of the scandal of innocent suffering in the world. This position, often labeled as "protest atheism," is represented in the works of the French philosopher Albert Camus among others. Moltmann points out that suffering is "the rock of atheism."[13] The experience of innocent suffering radically calls into question belief in an omnipotent, just God: "For a God who lets the innocent suffer and who permits senseless death is not worthy to be called God at all."[14]

Moltmann maintains that the classical arguments for the existence of God prove to be inadequate in the face of innocent suffering. Such arguments, as found, for example, in the famous "five ways" of Aquinas (*Summa Theologiae* I, 2, 3), begin with the experience of contingency and infer that there must be a first cause that is necessary and infinite. Using the principle of analogy, this way of thinking appeals particularly to the experience of the good, of excellence, for its speech about the divine. The creaturely excellences experienced in this world give us some limited insight into the perfection found in God, who is the transcendent source of every contingent good. Moltmann argues that atheists also begin with their experience of the world, but they focus on the "unjust and absurd world of triumphant evil and suffering."[15] This experience of negativity leads them to infer not a good and righteous God but "a capricious demon, a blind destiny, a damning law or an annihilating nothingness."[16] Moltmann concludes that "if one argues back from the state of the world and the fact of its existence to cause, ground, and principle, one can just as well speak of 'God' as the devil, of being as of nothingness, of the meaning of the world as of its absurdity."[17]

Moltmann takes aim especially at the principles of divine impassibility and omnipotence as espoused in classical theism. He thinks that the notion of an impassible God collapses in the face of the criticisms of protest atheism. He equates divine impassibility with indifference: a lack of concern for and engagement with suffering creatures. The God of classical theism, he thinks, does not in any way identify with or draw close to suffering human beings. This is the divine being rejected by Camus and other protest atheists. "For a God who is incapable of suffering is a being who cannot be involved. Suffering and injustice do not affect him. And because he is so completely insensitive, he cannot be affected or shaken by anything. He cannot weep, for he has no tears. But the one who cannot suffer cannot love either. So he is also a loveless being."[18] Moltmann also reasons that the God of classical theism is "only almighty" and thus is incapable of experiencing helplessness and powerlessness. Such a being is less perfect than human beings, who do have these experiences.[19] Protest atheism, he thinks, must be taken seriously by Christians and, if it is, it will force us to question the principles of classical theism, especially divine impassibility and a conception of divine omnipotence that excludes weakness and vulnerability.

Where should believers go to respond to the criticisms of protest atheism? Moltmann is convinced that the challenges of protest atheism must be met by a radical theology of the cross. Like Bonhoeffer, his thinking about this question has been significantly influenced by Martin Luther, who contrasted the theology of the cross with a theology of glory. For Luther, a theology of glory "looks upon the invisible things of God as though they were clearly perceptible in those things that have actually happened," while a theologian of the cross is one "who comprehends the visible and manifest things of God seen through suffering and the cross."[20] Luther concluded that God reveals Godself most fully in suffering and the cross. Moltmann builds on Luther, arguing that Christian discourse about God should commence not with rational reflection on creation but with the revelation of God in Christ. In particular, Christian theology must focus on the God who is present in the crucified Christ and, therefore, is personally involved in human sorrow and suffering. "The only way past protest atheism is through a theology of the cross which understands God as the suffering God in the suffering of Christ and which cries out with the godforsaken God, 'My God, why have you forsaken me?'"[21] The God revealed in the crucified Christ is the God to whom suffering people can relate and in whom they can rediscover their dignity.

Moltmann's theology is characterized by dialectical rather than analogical thinking.[22] Analogical discourse searches for points of contact between human experience and God. Analogy is the language of ordered relationships articulating similarity within difference. The primary Christian symbol for the analogical imagination is usually the incarnation. As David Tracy points out, the experience of the grace of

God in Christ prompts the analogical imagination to perceive and articulate "some fundamental trust in reality itself as constituting an order in spite of all absurdity and chaos."[23] Dialectical discourse accentuates the infinite qualitative difference between God and the world: God's ways are not our ways. Its watchword is "Let God be God."[24] It focuses on rupture at the heart of human pretension, guilt, and sin. Negation is the fundamental way of glimpsing truth about God and the ways of God. For dialectical thinking the primary Christian symbol is the cross. "The cross, as cross, exposes the contradictions in the present, the nonidentity of the present with God's word, the need for a theological negative dialectics."[25]

Though he does not reject all analogical discourse in theology, Moltmann accents knowledge of God through what is unlike God, through the ungodly: "Applied to Christian theology, this means that God is only revealed as 'God' in his opposite: godlessness and abandonment by God."[26] Authentic knowledge of God "is achieved not by the guiding threads of analogies from earth to heaven, but on the contrary, through contradiction, sorrow and suffering."[27] This expression of Christian faith, Moltmann thinks, is not vulnerable to atheistic critiques of belief like those found in Ludwig Feuerbach, Karl Marx, Sigmund Freud, and Nietzsche. These philosophers criticized belief in God as merely a projection of human wishes for security and consolation. Moltmann insists that the God revealed in the crucified Christ is far from such a projection of human desires. Faith in this God, rather, confounds all human reasoning about the divine. Such belief is "a crucifying form of knowledge, because it shatters everything to which a man can hold and on which he can build, both his works and his knowledge of reality, and precisely in so doing sets him free."[28] The dialectical mode of thinking that characterizes Moltmann's theology leads him to feature paradox in his discourse about God. In the face of the mystery of suffering, he thinks that God-talk rooted in Christian revelation must be characterized by paradox, and sometimes he pushes paradox to the limits of intelligibility. Moltmann thinks that such paradoxical statements are necessary to express the wisdom of the cross.

Telling the Story of Calvary

Moltmann engages in theology through dramatic narrative. He tells the story of God's revelation in Jesus as the drama of God's immersion in human history. This method gives his theology a lively quality that is lacking in some expressions of theology. It also sometimes poses the challenge of systematic consistency. When one retells a story, one's version of the narrative can change; it can undergo shifts that result in a message that is less than systematic.

Moltmann addresses the entire story of Jesus, including his birth and public ministry, in certain works, for example, *The Way of Jesus Christ*. But his main focus, especially in his earlier writings, is the drama of Jesus' death and resurrection. Moltmann is convinced that the story of Jesus' suffering and death should be understood not simply as an event that took place between Jesus and his enemies—those who crucified him. Consistent with his stress that the God in whom Christians believe is the triune God, Moltmann conceives of Jesus' death and resurrection as an event within the Trinity. He believes that the theological meaning of Good Friday and Easter is disclosed only through a reflection on what was happening among the Father, Son, and Holy Spirit. "The theology of the cross must be the doctrine of the Trinity and the doctrine of the Trinity must be the theology of the cross, because otherwise the human, crucified God cannot be fully perceived."[29] As he puts it, the cross is an event between God and God.[30]

For Moltmann the key to grasping the meaning of the cross is found in Jesus' cry of abandonment, as expressed in Mark 15:34 and Matthew 27:46 (though Moltmann usually refers to Mark's version). While he is aware that later Christian reflection has shaped the passion narratives, he argues that this cry—"My God, my God, why have you forsaken me?"—accurately portrays the experience of Jesus on Calvary. If there were not a core of historical truth in this scandalous passage, he thinks, the Christian church would never have preserved it. Moltmann argues that the later accounts of Jesus' death in Luke and John softened the stark portrayal given by Mark. "The idea that Jesus' last words to the God whom he had called upon as Abba, dear Father, could have been 'You have abandoned me', could surely never have taken root in Christian belief unless these terrible words had really been uttered, or unless they had at least been heard in Jesus' death cry."[31]

Moltmann also seizes upon the term *paradidonai* (to hand over, deliver up) that is found in some New Testament passages, for example, in Paul's panegyric to the love of God in Romans: "He who did not withhold his own Son, but gave him up for all of us, will he not with him give us everything else?" (Rom 8:32). He argues that this notion of handing over has "an unambiguously negative significance."[32] The Father delivers over the Son to death on the cross. Moltmann employs dramatic language to depict this action of the Father. He says that the Gospel accounts of Jesus' prayer in Gethsemane tell us that the Father rejects this prayer. The Father "withdraws from the Son, leaving him alone."[33] Moltmann asserts that "the Father forsook him and delivered him up to the fear of hell. The One who knew himself to be the Son is forsaken, rejected and cursed."[34] Moltmann appeals to the statement of Paul in Galatians about Christ becoming a curse for us as a biblical warrant for this interpretation (Gal 3:13). "When Jesus is forsaken by God on the cross, it means that he has been cast off by God."[35] This abandonment of the Son by the Father is the cause of Jesus' most acute suffering in his passion. Because of this abandonment, Jesus suffers the pains of hell. The cry of Jesus from the cross is a "cry of despair."[36] In this interpretation of the cross, Moltmann is influenced by Luther and Calvin, who thought that the crucified Jesus had endured hell and the wrath of God in our stead.[37]

The suffering of Jesus on the cross, then, is reflective of the suffering of the Trinity in this event. Moltmann claims that all three persons of the Trinity suffer, though each suffers in a distinct way. The Son suffers because of his abandonment by the Father. The Son is separated from the Father with whom he had been united in love from eternity. He dies a Godless death; he experiences what the Jews called the "hiding of God's face" (*hester panim*). The Father suffers the death of the Son in the infinite grief of love. The Father loses the Son. While these are two different kinds of suffering, there is a unity of will between the

Father and the Son. Each surrenders himself out of love. In typically dialectical language, Moltmann claims that at Calvary the Father and Son are separated yet also one. He also speaks of the sufferings of the Spirit in this event, asserting that "the sufferings of Christ are also the sufferings of the Spirit, for the surrender of Christ also manifested the self-emptying of the Spirit."[38] Moltmann proposes the image of a division, or bifurcation, that takes place in God because of the death of Jesus. God undergoes a split within Godself. The suffering of Christ at Calvary affects the innermost life of the Trinity. In Moltmann's words, "What happens on Golgotha reaches into the very depths of the Godhead and therefore puts its impress on the trinitarian life of God in eternity."[39]

Because at Calvary the Father and Son surrender themselves in love, the Spirit, who is the bond of mutual love between them, is poured out on all creation. This Spirit is the source of new life for the world. From the death that takes place within God the new life of the Spirit is given. It is through the life-giving Spirit that the Father raises Jesus from the dead. It is the Spirit who justifies sinners and fills the forsaken with the love of God. "Through the force of his surrender of himself to death on the cross, Christ sends the Spirit of life. That is the revelation of love in the pain of God, which makes new life for sinners and the dying possible....For the Holy Spirit is the 'source of life' and brings life into the world—whole life, full life, unhindered, indestructible, *everlasting* life."[40]

For Moltmann, God can and does suffer. He integrates into his theological portrait of God the axiom of Bonhoeffer that he found so consoling as a teenage prisoner of war: only a suffering God can help. He is convinced that only faith in a suffering God can help the modern person who is struggling to believe while living in a world scarred by the suffering of the innocent. And it is just such a God who is revealed in Jesus. If "God was in Christ," as Paul says in his Second Letter to the Corinthians (2 Cor 5:19), then Jesus' suffering was the suffering of God.[41] Moltmann argues that the core of truth in the classical teaching about divine impassibility is that God does not suffer as creatures do. God does not suffer from any deficiency of being, nor does

God suffer out of any necessity or compulsion. But there is such a thing as active suffering—suffering-with-another that one freely undergoes out of love. Here Moltmann speaks of compassion in the literal sense of the term—a "suffering-with" out of love. God suffers not out of any deficiency in the divine being but out of the abundance of God's love. God's compassion is an expression of divine perfection. In this context, Moltmann articulates a fundamental principle that shapes his argument: "Were God incapable of suffering in any respect, and therefore in an absolute sense, then he would also be incapable of love."[42] He is convinced that love, in its human and divine expressions, contains within itself the possibility of actively sharing in the suffering of one's beloved. He asserts, "The *Deus impassibilis* is a God without heart and without compassion, a cold heavenly power."[43] Among the Christian texts to which Moltmann appeals to ground this claim of divine passibility is the passage from Origen's *Homilies on Ezekiel* that we examined in chapter 3.[44]

Moltmann envisions God overcoming the evil and suffering that plague God's good creation by taking them up within Godself. "Only if all disaster, forsakenness by God, absolute death, the infinite curse of damnation and sinking into nothingness is in God himself, is community with this God eternal salvation, infinite joy, indestructible election and divine life. The 'bifurcation' in God must contain the whole uproar of history within itself."[45] Even the horrors of the Shoah are taken up into the life of the Trinity in order that God may overcome them: "Like the cross of Christ, even Auschwitz is in God himself. Even Auschwitz is taken up into the grief of the Father, the surrender of the Son and the power of the Spirit."[46] While this view is in no way a theological justification for what happened in the Shoah, it does offer a vision of hope: "God in Auschwitz and Auschwitz in the crucified God—that is the basis for a real hope which both embraces and overcomes the world, and the ground for a love which is stronger than death and can sustain death."[47]

Moltmann cites Wiesel's description of the hanging of the young boy and the question that haunted both Wiesel and him in the wake of the Shoah: "Where is God?" He notes the ambiguity in the "answer" Wiesel gives in *Night* ("He is hanging here on this gallows"), but he interprets this passage to signal God's presence in and with the suffering one. Like Wiesel, he appeals to the Jewish tradition of the Shekinah—God's indwelling presence with God's people. According to this tradition, "God went into exile with those who were deported, and shared Israel's sufferings in exile as the God who is homeless in this godless world."[48] Moltmann, then, interprets the passage from Wiesel in this way:

> Where that child hangs on the gallows God hangs on the gallows too. Where that child suffers torment, God himself is tormented. Where that child dies, God himself suffers the child's death....even in the hell of Auschwitz God was there—but not as the Lord of history: as the victim among millions of victims.[49]

In this context Moltmann appeals to Psalm 139 and its meditation on the omnipresence of God. Because Jesus the Son suffered death in abandonment on Calvary, no one else need suffer alone. God is with them in their suffering; indeed, God is suffering with them.

God and Creation

Moltmann's theology of the cross makes it evident that he conceives of God and the world in the closest possible relationship. He envisions this relationship as a reciprocal one in which not only is the world affected by the divine presence and activity, but the triune God is also affected by what takes place in the world. In his view of the relationship of God to creation, Moltmann takes positions distinct from those of classical theism.

Classical theism, especially in its Catholic versions, highlights the gratuity of creation and of grace. As we saw in our discussion of Aquinas, this theology maintains that the triune God did not have to create the world in order to satisfy a divine need for completion. There is nothing lacking in God. Hypothetically, God could have remained blissful in Godself without creation. Creation is a pure gift given for the benefit of creatures, not of God. Moreover, having created the world, God could have remained the distant divine artisan who did not enter into a covenant relationship with the human family. There was no necessity for God to share God's own life with us, to invite us into friendship. Christians believe, however, that this hypothetical state of a creation devoid of the offer of grace (this possibility is called "pure nature") never existed. Based on the witness of the Bible, we believe that from the beginning of human existence God called men and women into a covenant relationship marked by trust, obedience, and fidelity.[50]

Moltmann disagrees with the way in which the classical tradition accentuated the gratuity of creation and grace. He argues that talking about what God "could have done" is misleading, since it obscures the true nature of divine freedom.[51] God's freedom should not be understood as absolute freedom of choice. Rather, divine freedom is God's freedom to be who God is, that is, self-communicating love. God's freedom lies in doing the good that God is, which means communicating Godself. Moltmann asserts that "in loving the world he [God] is entirely free because he is entirely himself."[52] God's freedom is found in the friendship that God offers to men and women. Reflecting his account of Calvary, Moltmann says about God, "His freedom is his vulnerable love, his openness, the encountering kindness through which he suffers with the human beings he loves and becomes their advocate, thereby throwing open their future to them."[53]

In his theology of the Trinity, Moltmann envisions the love within the Trinity as the love of like for like. The eternal love of Father, Son, and Holy Spirit for one another does not, however, satisfy what Moltmann describes as "God's longing for 'his Other' and for that Other's free response to the divine love."[54] This divine desire for the other can only be fulfilled through God's relationship with created beings. There would be something lacking, or unfulfilled, in God if there were no creation. Therefore, Moltmann can say, "For it is impossible to conceive of a God who is not a creative God. A non-creative God would be imperfect compared with the God who is eternally creative. And if God's eternal being is love, then the divine love is also more blessed in giving than in receiving."[55] Moltmann eschews an image of divine perfection as having no needs; rather, God's longing for the "other" of creatures is an expression of divine perfection, though a perfection conceived differently from the classical tradition. In his words, "God is *not perfect* if this means that he did not in the craving of his love want his creation to be necessary to his perfection."[56]

For Moltmann, God's self-emptying begins not with the incarnation or the cross but with creation itself. God's act of creating is an act of kenosis. He borrows the concept of *zimsum* from Jewish mystical theology.[57] Because God is infinite, all in all, God must "contract" in order that creation may exist. God creates by withdrawing himself, making a space for creation to be. Moltmann envisions creation, then, as "a self-humiliation on God's part, a lowering of himself into his own impotence."[58] Creation, in some sense, is something that God suffers and endures. Thus creation exists within God, not outside of God, since there is no "outside" of God. This is a panentheistic view of God and the world: God in the world and the world in God. This vision is a feminine image of the relationship between God and the world: "God creates the world by letting his world become and be in *himself*: Let it be!"[59]

This means that human history also exists within God. And for Moltmann human history makes a real difference to the being of God, to each of the persons of the Trinity in their relationships with one another. On this point, the influence of the thought of G.W.F. Hegel on Moltmann is evident.[60] Moltmann conceives of a "bifurcation" taking place within God at the death of the Son at Calvary: a split within the divine being that lets all of the suffering of human history into God. "All human history, however much it may be determined by guilt and death, is taken up into this 'history of God', i.e., into the Trinity, and integrated into the future of the 'history of God.'"[61] Rather than being a "closed circle of perfect being in heaven," the Trinity is "eschatologically open history."[62] The life of the Trinity is a story inextricably interwoven with the human story:

> The Trinity therefore also means the history of God, which in human terms is the history of love and liberation. The Trinity, understood as an event for history, therefore presses towards eschatological consummation, so that the "Trinity

may be all in all," or put more simply, so that "love may be all in all," so that life may triumph over death and righteousness over the hells of the negative and of all force.[63]

Moltmann even claims that "the creation of the world and human beings for freedom and fellowship is always bound up with the process of God's deliverance from the sufferings of his love."[64] He sometimes relates this openness of the Trinity to the sending of the Spirit at Pentecost, but in other places it seems that human history has impinged upon God from the beginning of creation.[65] Moltmann thinks of the inauguration and fulfillment of the kingdom of God as a history that has an effect on the Trinity as well as upon creation.[66] The fulfillment of the Trinity, like the fulfillment of human history, lies in the future.

The New Creation

This focus on the future has been characteristic of Moltmann's writings since his first major work, *Theology of Hope* (1964). His approach to God and the mystery of suffering can only be understood within the perspective of his conception of the future fulfillment of creation in God. Moltmann was influenced by the philosophy of Ernst Bloch, especially Bloch's great work *The Principle of Hope*. Though not writing as a Christian thinker, Bloch thought that the Bible awakened an eschatological awareness in human consciousness.[67] Moltmann argues that the experience of reality as a history open to the future is in fact universal. Christians should conceive of God as "the coming God"—the God who comes to us out of God's future with whole new possibilities for the present. "So God comes to meet men and women out of his future, and in their history reveals to them new, open horizons, which entice them to set forth into the unknown and invite them to the beginning of the new."[68] Christians should be people who pray "messianically, with eyes wide open for God's future in the world."[69]

From this vantage point, Moltmann highlights the Christian doctrine of the parousia. Rather than treating the parousia as an afterthought in Christology, as has often been done in Christian theology, he thinks of it as the keystone in the Christian understanding of the person and saving work of Jesus. Moltmann says that he wants to grasp Christ dynamically, "in the forward movement of God's history with the world."[70] Though Jesus inaugurated the kingdom of God through his ministry, death, and resurrection, he is still the Messiah who is "on the way" to establishing the fullness of the reign of God. Moltmann emphasizes that Jesus' person and mission will be seen in their complete truth and significance only when the new creation is established. He conceives of the appearances of the risen Jesus to the apostles as experiences in which his followers saw him as he will be in the future, in the coming glory of God. The future is already present in the risen Christ.[71] Paradoxically, Moltmann also asserts that Christ is still at work in history, still completing his mission as Messiah. He is still the suffering servant who heals through his wounds and endures the birth pangs of the new creation. Moltmann even suggests that Jesus "grows into" his messiahship, "since he is molded by the events of the messianic time which he experiences."[72] The risen Christ "is not yet the Christ of the parousia who comes in the glory of God and redeems the world, so that it becomes the kingdom."[73] Christians must keep in mind that, while the love of God has become manifest in Jesus, "the glory of God has not yet broken forth out of its hiddenness."[74] Moltmann envisions the parousia of Christ as the completion of the way of Jesus: "'Christ on the way' arrives at his goal. His saving work is completed."[75] Christian praxis in the present should consist of action inspired by the vision of the kingdom given by Jesus; it must be shaped by the coming reign of God, which invites us to new possibilities in the present.

Moltmann's writings about death, judgment, and eternal life are marked by an abiding conviction about salvation for all people. Because Jesus suffered abandonment on the cross and descended into hell he became the brother of the dead and their redeeming ancestor. Thus he has opened the world of the dead for the future of resurrection and eternal life.[76] The judgment of Christ does not consist of punishment and reward but of making the saving righteousness of God prevail for all people. Moltmann maintains that the judgment that Christ will bring is God's creative justice.[77] Divine justice heals and saves both the victims and the perpetrators of oppression. It brings justice to the victims and enables the perpetrators to die to their evil actions and the burden of their guilt and to discover new life together with their victims.[78] Moltmann says of Christ's judgment, "The purpose of his judgment is not reward or punishment, but the victory of the divine creative righteousness and justice, and this victory does not lead to heaven or hell but to God's great day of reconciliation on this earth."[79] In the meantime, all of the dead are kept sheltered in God, awaiting the day of resurrection.

God's revelation in Jesus points us to the new creation that God will establish, in which the glory of God will be revealed to all. Having spoken of God's act of creating as a withdrawal of the divine self—making a space within Godself for creation to be—Moltmann conceives of final fulfillment as the ending of God's self-restriction. "God de-restricts himself and manifests his glory so that in the transfigured glory he may be 'all in all.'…Heaven and earth find their final, transfigured form in God's unrestricted omnipresence itself."[80] This new creation, Moltmann argues, does not refer to a heavenly realm but to a new creation of the earth. It will entail "the rebirth of the cosmos to its enduring form."[81] It will redeem not only the horrific suffering that human beings have inflicted on one another but also the suffering and death that is intrinsic to the process of evolution. Because evolution proceeds by way of selection, many creatures have perished in the process. But God's new creation will entail "the bringing back of all things out of their past."[82] Everything that was lost in evolution will be gathered into God's kingdom. Moltmann speaks of this new creation as the reconciliation of all things, and he often appeals to the biblical motif of the sabbath in his reflection on it. The goal of creation is the sabbath in which God will arrive at his rest.[83]

Moltmann says that when he was sitting behind the barbed wire in a prisoner of war camp as a teenager he learned what it meant to hope. The call to be people of hope permeates his theology. In one of his meditative writings he reflects on "the command to hope." He says, "We learn to hope in the experiences life brings us. We come to know its truth if we are forced to stand our ground against despair. We come to know its power when we realize that it keeps us alive in the midst of death."[84] His grappling with the mystery of suffering is suffused with the hope for God's new creation that is anticipated in the resurrection of Christ. He likes to cite the observation of John Chrysostom: "It is not so much sin which plunges us into disaster; it is rather our despair."[85] Acknowledging that our future in God is enveloped in the darkness of mystery, Moltmann says that though we do not know *what* awaits us we do know *who* awaits us. He asks, "Why shouldn't we trust the one we have trusted throughout our life once our lifetime ends?"[86]

Theodicy and the Mystery of Suffering

The theodicy question—the justification of a good, all-powerful God in the face of innocent suffering—receives ambiguous treatment in Moltmann. In one place he says that this theoretical question "presupposes an apathetic, untouchable God in heaven...."[87] This is precisely the image of God that Moltmann wants to deconstruct in his theology. Instead of asking the theoretical question in the midst of his own traumatic experiences as a teenager, Moltmann says that he asked the more existential question: "Where is God?" In other places, however, Moltmann says that the theodicy question is an important query that believers must live with until the fulfillment of history in the new creation. He writes, "If the question of theodicy can be understood as a question of the righteousness of God in the history of the suffering of the world, then all understanding and presentation of world history must be seen within the question of theodicy."[88] Drawing on the double meaning of the German word *Prozess* (the term can mean "trial" or "process"), he argues that all of human history after the death and resurrection of Christ is a theodicy process and trial.[89] "With God's raising of the Christ murdered on the cross, a universal theodicy trial begins which can only be completed eschatologically with the resurrection of all the dead and the annihilation of death's power—which is to say the new creation of all things."[90] In a sense, God is on trial throughout the course of human history.

Moltmann usually suggests, then, that the question of the *why* of innocent suffering in a creation loved by God is the salient issue of human history. On the one hand, this question cannot be answered in this life. At the same time, it is a question that should never be dismissed. We have to live with this open question, which exists like an open wound in this world.[91] The task of faith and theology is to make it possible for us to survive with this open wound—to continue living in hope. Moltmann insists that Christian faith does not make suffering a less significant question for believers; in fact, he argues, those who believe in the God of Jesus Christ find suffering to be a particularly urgent question: "The more a person believes, the more deeply he experiences pain over the suffering in the world, and the more passionately he asks about God and the new creation."[92] He argues that people who are justified by faith in Christ "weep over this world which Albert Camus describes as the place 'where children suffer and die.'"[93] Believers protest against evil and suffering in the world and live in longing for God's new creation.

Moltmann clearly does not pretend to resolve the theodicy question in his theology. He knows that he has not answered the question about the reason for the existence of evil and suffering, especially innocent suffering, in the world. He thinks that the Christian doctrine of original sin is limited in its capacity to address this mystery. Though there is certainly a connection between sin and suffering, "experience of suffering goes far beyond the experience of guilt and the experience of grace."[94] Suffering, he suggests, "has its roots in the limitations of created reality itself."[95] Moltmann does think, however, that the conception of God that he develops in his works helps believers cling to hope in the face of this dark mystery. Rooted in his account of Calvary, this view of God illumines God's solidarity with suffering human beings and God's vulnerability to the scourge of suffering within creation. Moltmann's God is deeply affected by the suffering of creation, and God is struggling to bring life out of suffering. Indeed, for Moltmann the future of God's very self is inextricably linked with the redemption of a world wounded by suffering.

Critical Responses to Moltmann

Moltmann's contribution to the theological conversation about God and the mystery of suffering has aroused a number of critical reactions. Among the many topics addressed by theologians who dialogue with Moltmann, three themes are of particular relevance to our discussion: his account of what took place at Calvary; his assertion of the passibility of God; and his treatment of divine freedom. Because these critical reactions to Moltmann have become such an integral part of the theological conversation it is important to pause here and offer a brief summary of them.

First, some theologians have argued that the way in which Moltmann tells the story of Calvary results in a strange or even sadistic conception of God. German theologian Dorothee Sölle, who also addressed the mystery of suffering in her writings, gave the most notable version of this critique not long after Moltmann wrote *The Crucified God*,[96] concluding that Moltmann's portrayal of the Father handing over the Son to death and abandoning the Son represents an attempt "to develop a 'theology of the cross' from the perspective of the one who originates and causes suffering."[97] Sölle observes, "The author is fascinated by God's brutality."[98] She also criticizes Moltmann's interpretation of Gethsemane, in which Jesus supposedly saw himself as cast out by a God who had become inaccessible to him. Sölle interprets the experience of Jesus at Gethsemane as an experience of assent, in which the cup of suffering becomes the cup of strengthening. Sölle appreciates Moltmann's intention to construct a theological portrait of God that accentuates God's involvement in human suffering and God's compassion for suffering people, but she thinks that the way in which he tells the story of Calvary contradicts that intention. The Father who abandons the Son is not a compassionate God. Marc Steen sympathizes with Sölle's critique and concludes, "The conception that the Father really abandons and rejects His Son implies an extremely strange conception of God, which cannot simply be deduced from the Crucified."[99]

Moltmann has attempted to respond to Sölle's criticisms.[100] He claims that she misunderstood him to mean that in Jesus' death the

Father is the active subject and the Son is the passive object. Moltmann emphasizes that the Father is always on the side of the Son and that both suffer, though in different ways. Both are surrendering themselves in love. And in the resurrection God turns the cross into something good for humanity. These rejoinders of Moltmann, however, do not really address the difficulties inherent in some of his statements about the Father who actively delivers up the Son to death on the cross.[101] In the very work in which he responds to Sölle's criticism, Moltmann says, "When Jesus is forsaken by God on the cross, it means that he has been cast off by God."[102] At times Moltmann's language is so strong and lacking in nuance that one could easily get the impression that the Father is cruel in the way he relates to the Son.

Second, a number of theologians criticize Moltmann's attempt to integrate suffering into the divine being. Karl Rahner addresses the thought of Moltmann as well as that of Hans Urs von Balthasar when he says, "To put it crudely, it does not help me to escape from my mess and mix-up and despair if God is in the same predicament."[103] Rahner adds, "From the beginning I am locked into its [history's] horribleness while God—if this word continues to have any meaning at all—is in a true and authentic and consoling sense the God who does not suffer, the immutable God, and so on."[104] Rahner also wonders where Moltmann gets his knowledge about the suffering of the Trinity: "What do we know so precisely about God?"[105] J. B. Metz argues that it is not theologically legitimate to speak of a suffering God or suffering in God. He thinks that such an idea would lead to an eternalization of suffering.[106] Like Rahner, Metz also questions the source of Moltmann's knowledge about the inner life of the Trinity, suggesting that his speculations border on Gnosticism.

The discussion of contemporary Thomists in chapter 4 made it clear that these authors also object to the idea of suffering in God. William Hill admits the originality of Moltmann's theological ideas but thinks that they ultimately result in a trimming of the transcendence of God: "Moltmann's view that God suffers in himself is, in effect, to have God will to be something less than God."[107] Michael Dodds, in dialogue with Moltmann, argues that a suffering God is "an ontologically imperfect being" who "will inevitably seek his own perfection and try to overcome his own deficiency."[108] For Thomas Weinandy, while a suffering God may appear to be a good idea, it would demand that God and creation exist on the same ontological order. Thus, God would exist on the same level of being in which evil exists. Such a view "has disastrous philosophical and theological consequences."[109] Weinandy also contends that Moltmann's account of the death of Jesus as an event that took place within the Trinity "reduces the passion and death of Jesus to a myth whereby what would be taking place in history is but a mythical expression of what is actually taking place on a divine transcendent level."[110] The death of Jesus must be kept as an event that happened within human history. These Thomists also object to Moltmann's equating of divine impassibility with indifference. They argue that the conception of God developed by Aquinas entails God's intimate presence to and involvement with the world.

Third, theologians also question Moltmann's account of divine freedom. Some argue that by denying freedom of choice on the part of God with respect to creation and the offer of grace Moltmann has compromised divine transcendence. Hill attributes this problem to the influence of Hegel on Moltmann, which leads to a constraining of God's freedom.[111] Steen says, "From the standpoint of Christian theology, one can propose that God's transcendence is only guaranteed if His relationship to man and the world is conceived in terms of freedom and grace."[112] He concludes that Moltmann "mortgages the idea of divine freedom."[113] Steen argues, "The idea of a God who needs His creatures in order to reach completion and who is in a sense ontologically dependent on world history, enfeebles the conviction that God is really free."[114] These theologians conclude that by his attenuation of divine freedom Moltmann portrays a God who creates us and relates to us not simply to communicate God's goodness but to complete God's own life. They contend that such a view of God is not faithful to the biblical and theological tradition of Christianity.

This is a brief and incomplete account of the theological conversation that has been generated by Moltmann's treatment of God and suffering. I have not included the comments of theologians who are more sympathetic to Moltmann. The abundance of response to his thought is indicative of the impact that his ideas have made on the ongoing dialogue about the mystery of suffering. Whatever one thinks of Moltmann's theology, he remains an intriguing thinker. He has been consistent in his commitment to make the reality of suffering a central concern of all Christian theology, and in so doing he has forced other theologians to address this mystery. Helen Bergin observes that "Moltmann's insistence on God's identification with human suffering offers a God who is immersed in the pain of the world."[115] Moltmann's theological portrait of a suffering God has compelled theologians of a more traditional bent to reexamine the theological tradition and to explore the ways in which this tradition, even in its classical expressions, has endeavored to illumine the closeness of God to human suffering.

Discussion Questions: www.paulistpress.com, Online Resources.

8

Edward Schillebeeckx:
Holding on to the
Hand of God

Our exploration of the theology of Jürgen Moltmann surfaced a number of themes that are also addressed in the work of the Dominican theologian Edward Schillebeeckx. In many ways, Schillebeeckx makes an intriguing dialogue partner for Moltmann. They are both concerned to address the stark reality of evil and human suffering in the world, though the ways in which they construct a Christian response to these realities diverge.[1]

Schillebeeckx was born in Antwerp, Belgium, in 1914, the sixth of fourteen children. He died in December 2009 at the age of ninety-five. Though he attended a Jesuit high school as a teenager, he decided to enter the Flemish province of Dominicans in 1934 and was ordained a priest in 1941. During his studies in philosophy he was influenced by Dominican professor and spiritual director Dominic De Petter, who integrated the insights of phenomenology (developed by thinkers like Edmund Husserl and Martin Heidegger) with Thomistic philosophical principles. Schillebeeckx says that DePetter always connected philosophy with the concerns of humanity, making the effort to relate philosophical concepts to human experience.[2] Although Schillebeeckx later moved away from the method and some of the philosophical convictions of his former teacher, the centrality of *experience* for the doing of theology remained an abiding feature of his thought.[3]

Schillebeeckx pursued his doctoral studies in theology at Le Saulchoir, the Dominican house of studies in Paris. His thinking was particularly influenced by two Dominican professors who later became pivotal figures at Vatican II: Yves Congar and Marie-Dominique Chenu. Congar's study of tradition would influence Schillebeeckx's writings on experience and tradition.[4] The scholarship of Chenu, Schillebeeckx's dissertation director, blended extensive historical research with a vital concern for contemporary social issues. Schillebeeckx says about Chenu, "For me he was the embodiment of the Dominican ideal as I wanted to experience it."[5] Chenu introduced the phrase the "signs of the times" into theology. Schillebeeckx cites him as a mentor who taught him to listen to people's experience in doing theology. After completing his doctoral dissertation on the sacraments, Schillebeeckx taught dogmatic theology at the Dominican house of studies in Louvain. He then moved to Nijmegen University in 1958, where he served as professor of dogmatic and historical theology until 1983.

Schillebeeckx's theology was also shaped by his experience of the Second Vatican Council and his service to the church in the Netherlands in the years following the council. He was an advisor to the Dutch bishops at Vatican II, where he also lectured to bishops from other countries and commented on the proposed conciliar schemas. He was involved in the Dutch Pastoral Council in 1966 and later in the development of critical communities of Catholics that arose in the Netherlands. These innovative faith communities were critical of injustice in society and of what they perceived to be unjust structures in the church.[6] As William Portier puts it, Schillebeeckx "served as a kind of theological midwife for a new way of experiencing the church in the Netherlands."[7] This pastoral experience influenced his later writings on ecclesiology, especially his theological reflections on ministry and authority in the church.[8]

Schillebeeckx's thought underwent development during his lengthy career as a theologian. His Dominican heritage gave him a fundamentally Thomistic orientation that we will recognize as we explore his approach to God and the mystery of human suffering. But his was a critical Thomism that integrated the insights of modern streams of thought like phenomenology, hermeneutics, and critical theory.

Phenomonology, which is grounded in sustained reflection upon human existence in the world, contributed the category of "encounter" as the fundamental mode of existing.[9] This theme is evident in his early book *Christ the Sacrament of the Encounter with God*, and it is also found in his later christological works, which emphasize the importance of the encounter between Jesus and others. Schillebeeckx begins the introduction to his lengthy work *Christ: The Experience of Jesus as Lord* in this way: "It began with an encounter."[10] He emphasizes that the Christian understanding of grace and salvation is rooted in and must always be related to personal encounter with Jesus.

His study of hermeneutics—the science of interpretation—led Schillebeeckx to devote attention to the relationship of experience to interpretation and of theory to praxis. His discussion of the connections between experience and interpretation in the first chapter of *Christ: The Experience of Jesus as Lord*, and his insistence that "experience is always interpreted experience,"[11] reflect his immersion in the study of hermeneutics. This hermeneutical turn affected his extensive study of Christology and soteriology, in which he explored the question of how to make the biblical testimony about Jesus relevant to contemporary Christian life.

Like Moltmann, Schillebeeckx was also influenced by the critical theory of the Frankfurt School, represented by thinkers like Theodor Adorno, Max Horkheimer, and Jürgen Habermas. This critical theory, inspired in part by Marxist thought, assumes that "the interpretation of any tradition likely involves systematic distortions of communication in the interests of those who have power and privilege."[12] It insists on the remembrance of those who have lived on the "underside" of history, many of whom have experienced needless suffering and death. Critical theory demands that claims to definitive political and social solutions for the human predicament be relativized, since such totalizing solutions tend themselves to become oppressive. This line of thinking influenced the development of a number of themes in Schillebeeckx's theology, including the experience of negative contrast, the ministry of Jesus to the marginalized, the essential importance of orthopraxis, and the Christian vocation to solidarity with the poor.

The Problem of Evil and the Search for Human Liberation

Schillebeeckx addresses themes in the Christian tradition against the backdrop of a world that he views as scarred by oppressive evil and massive human suffering. He reflects upon the tradition from a global perspective that recognizes that millions of people live in miserable conditions with little hope of relief and no one to listen to their concerns. Robert Schreiter observes that "concern with the massiveness of human suffering has become a pervasive theme in all of Schillebeeckx's work since the late 1960's."[13] In an essay on Schillebeeckx's Christology, John Galvin points out that

> his quest for a suitable starting point common to all human life, and therefore accessible to all leads him to concentrate on the universal experience of evil, the bitter awareness that the history of the human race is a history of suffering. Without disparaging the significance of other concerns, Schillebeeckx remains convinced that the problem of evil, concretized most disturbingly in the suffering of the innocent, is both the primary issue that has preoccupied religions and philosophies of the past and present and the most urgent challenge faced by Christianity today.[14]

Schillebeeckx acknowledges that suffering is a fact of life that often has positive effects. We will see that he also perceives in the experience of suffering the possibility of new insight. He notes that a "school of suffering" can be transformative and lead to spiritual maturity.[15] For one thing, the experience of suffering often leaves people with deeper sensitivity to the pain of others. There is also self-sacrificial suffering for a good cause. Fidelity to any worthwhile commitment must include the willingness to suffer for it. Thus, sometimes meaning can be derived from the experience of suffering. Nevertheless, Schillebeeckx insists that in human history there is in fact "a barbarous excess" of suffering and evil, much of which cannot be described as meaningful. In an oft-quoted passage, he reflects on this disturbing abundance of suffering and evil:

218

> Furthermore, this suffering is the alpha and the omega of the whole history of mankind; it is the thread by which this historical fragment is recognizable as human history: history is an "ecumene of suffering." Because of their historical extent and their historical density, evil and suffering are the dark fleck in our history, a fleck which no one can remove by an explanation or interpretation which is able to give it an understandable place in a rational and meaningful whole.[16]

This statement may appear to represent a negative, pessimistic view of reality. Schillebeeckx, however, is not at all negative or pessimistic in his theological perspective, though he maintains that Christian theology must take account of the concrete reality of the world. He states that one of the tasks of theology is to safeguard belief in and hope for a liberating, saving power that loves men and women and will overcome evil: "Theology therefore opposes any kind of doom thinking, though theologians, like everyone else, are at the same time convinced that we live in a bewildering mixture of meaning and meaninglessness."[17] For Schillebeeckx the word of the gospel is a message of resounding hope, though a hope that must be cultivated and clung to amidst a human history that is darkened by suffering.

Schillebeeckx maintains that it is impossible to construct a rational explanation for the presence of suffering in the world. Suffering is not a problem; it is a mystery, the total meaning of which defies human reasoning. Evil and suffering cannot be situated within a larger matrix that captures the ultimate meaning of creation and human history. At the same time, Schillebeeckx argues that the experience of suffering opens up possibilities for new insight into reality, especially new insight into *what should be*. "Suffering for Schillebeeckx emerges as the privileged locus of revelation both of what lies beyond us and what makes us be who we actually are. The experience of suffering leads to a prophetic stance toward reality, to the ongoing proclamation that 'reality ought to be different,' to the calling into question reality as it is and how it is justified."[18]

Schillebeeckx elucidates this possibility of new insight through his discussion of negative contrast experiences. He thinks that all human beings have such experiences, whether or not they reflect upon them or name them as such. They entail our natural human reaction to evil and suffering in the world, to things that we instinctively know should not be. When we hear of evils like child abuse or ethnic cleansing, normal people instinctively feel revulsion and protest. We immediately realize that "there is something wrong with this picture." Schillebeeckx states that such contrast experiences

> form a basic human experience which as such I regard as being a pre-religious experience accessible to all human beings, namely that of a "no" to the world as it is....What we experience as reality, what we see and hear of this reality daily through television and other mass media, is evidently not "in order"; there is something fundamentally wrong. This reality is full of contradictions. So the human experience of suffering and evil, of oppression and unhappiness, is the basis and source of a fundamental "no" that men and women say to their actual situation of being-in-this-world.[19]

Schillebeeckx does not stop there, with the negativity of contrast experiences. He argues that our reaction to evil and suffering also includes, at least implicitly, a positive moment. It awakens insight into something better; it occasions an intuition into goodness and value that should be realized. Robert Schreiter observes, "The contrast opens up not just the opposite of the previously experienced reality, but often new, unexpected worlds as well."[20] For Schillebeeckx there is an element of longing, even of transcendence, in every contrast experience—a movement toward the good. He considers the insight given in contrast experiences as a form of knowledge that is identical neither with contemplation nor technical rationality. He calls it "a critical epistemological force which leads to new action, which anticipates a better future and seeks to put it into practice."[21] This kind of knowledge provides a link between contemplative and technical approaches to reality. Schillebeeckx writes:

> Nevertheless, a positive element in this fundamental experience of contrast, the second element in this basic experi-

ence, is this human indignation, which cannot be made light of. There are ethics here, and perhaps even more. (I myself see here what in the Catholic tradition of faith has been called "natural theology," although that was set in a rather different context.) This human inability to give in to the situation offers an illuminating perspective. It discloses an openness to another situation which has the right to our affirmative "yes."[22]

Schillebeeckx believes that Christian theology must address this "openness to another situation" that is intrinsic to human experience. What Christians say about God and Christ should be related to the human quest for meaning and liberation in a world where there is a surplus of suffering. The experience of salvation from God in Christ must always be connected with human flourishing, which entails the overcoming of evil and suffering. For Schillebeeckx, "salvation history is a happening which liberates men and women."[23] "Only in a secular history in which men and women are liberated for true humanity can God reveal his own being."[24] Stridently opposing any dualistic separation of the temporal and eternal, the spiritual and the material, Schillebeeckx holds that Christian proclamation of salvation from God in Christ must be enfleshed in a praxis that promotes the well-being of all people, especially the poor and oppressed. When Schillebeeckx was asked in an interview about the meaning of conversion, he responded, "You are converted inwardly when you choose in favor of solidarity with others. That is quite clear from the gospel—you are called on to liberate others, to set others free first."[25]

This perspective has led Schillebeeckx, especially in his later writings on Christology, to accent "the primacy of the soteriological."[26] He wants to articulate, in categories comprehensible to the contemporary person, the meaning of salvation and the way in which God offers salvation to the human family. "In an important way, his whole christological project is about discovering a new soteriology for a postmodern world."[27] This is clear especially in *Christ: The Experience of Jesus as Lord*, in which he engages in a detailed exploration of the constitutive elements of New Testament understandings of grace. After this discussion of the

New Testament data, he endeavors to construct a Christian understanding of salvation for today.[28] Schillebeeckx says that "the question of salvation is the great driving force in our present history, not only in a religious and theological context but also thematically."[29]

The Option for Narrative

Confronted with the reality of evil and massive suffering in the world, Schillebeeckx opts for narrative over theory in his theological method. He assigns evil and the suffering that results from it to the realm of mystery: "Thus, suffering and evil can provoke scandal; however, they are not a *problem*, but an unfathomable, theoretically incomprehensible *mystery*."[30] Explanations and theories are more suited to problems than to mystery. In commenting on Schillebeeckx, John Galvin points out that theories about evil and suffering "can easily prove counterproductive, as they may suggest that evil is inevitable, ineradicably rooted in the order of things, and thus promote an attitude of resignation and passivity."[31] Schillebeeckx is convinced that resignation before the reality of evil is contrary to the Christian message. For him evil and suffering should be opposed, not explained. He thinks that "the only adequate response is via a practical exercise of resistance to evil, not a theory about it."[32]

Such resistance, however, demands some kind of support, some form of grounding. Schillebeeckx turns to narrative for this grounding; he is convinced that human experience has a narrative structure.[33] The primary way in which we share our experiences with one another is through word, especially by the telling of stories. Schillebeeckx asserts that when faced with the mystery of evil and suffering "people do not argue against suffering, but tell a story."[34] Stories are capable of integrating the experience of contrast in ways that theories and explanations cannot. The telling of stories allows our experience, especially the experience of suffering, to be expressed with a range of meaning that transcends conceptual articulation.[35] Galvin summarizes the thought of Schillebeeckx on this topic:

222

> Unlike theories, which tend to domesticate problems and thus to perpetuate them, the telling and retelling of stories preserves dangerous memories, awakens liberating hopes, and provides a framework for expressing the specific anticipation of a better future in parables and symbols—the only suitable vehicles of communication in a world where evil still abounds.[36]

For Christians, the story that is remembered and retold is that of Jesus of Nazareth. Schillebeeckx insists that we must tell the whole story of Jesus, not just his death and resurrection but also his public life and ministry. His lengthy works on Christology focus not on christological formulas, even that of Chalcedon. Nor does he develop a soteriological theory, like the famous theory of satisfaction formulated by Anselm of Canterbury in the eleventh century. Schillebeeckx narrates the story of Jesus as the story of God. He envisions Jesus as the parable of God and attempts to describe the way in which people experienced salvation from God in their encounters with Jesus. His methodology is similar to Moltmann's insofar as both resort to narrative in addressing the mystery of suffering and articulating a Christian notion of salvation. Schillebeeckx, however, does not attempt to describe the inner life of the Trinity in its relation to the history of Jesus. Using critical exegesis, he chronicles the story of the earthly Jesus and the ways in which the experience of salvation from God in Jesus was lived and articulated in the early Christian communities.

Telling the Story of Jesus

Proclamation of the Kingdom

In discussing Jesus' saving work, Schillebeeckx is convinced that one should devote considerable attention to his public life and ministry. Christian soteriology has often focused exclusively on Jesus' death and resurrection, he believes, and minimized the salvific significance of Jesus' proclamation of the kingdom of God. "Schillebeeckx presents Jesus' public life as a sustained and varied offer of definitive salvation from God in a context marked by intense suffering and correspondingly heightened longings."[37]

When asked by an interviewer about the "key word" in the story of Jesus, Schillebeeckx answered "kingdom."[38] Jesus, he says, offers no precise definition of the kingdom of God. The character and content of this kingdom are illumined in his parables and lifestyle, especially his encounters with the various people he meets. The message of the kingdom of God that Jesus preached and embodied in his behavior reflects a God whose concern is the concern of humankind, whose coming rule means life and wholeness for people. "God's rule is God's state of being God and our recognition of the rule or kingdom of God brings about our salvation, our state of being human."[39] The proclamation of God's rule leads Jesus to show particular concern for those who are most vulnerable in society. Schillebeeckx offers this summary of the notion of the kingdom:

> The kingdom of God is the saving presence of God, active and encouraging, as it is affirmed or welcomed among men and women. It is a saving presence offered by God and freely accepted by men and women which takes concrete form above all in justice and peaceful relationships among individuals and peoples, in the disappearance of sickness, injustice and oppression, in the restoration to life of all that was dead and dying. The kingdom of God is a changed new relationship of men and women to God, the tangible and visible side of which is a new type of liberating relationship among men and women within a reconciling society in a peaceful natural environment.[40]

One way in which Jesus proclaimed the kingdom was through his ministry of healing and exorcism. These mighty deeds were interpreted to be the actions of the eschatological prophet promised in Deuteronomy 18:15–18. Indeed, Schillebeeckx argues that the identification of Jesus as the eschatological prophet represents the primary Christian designation of Jesus, which formed the foundation for the confessions of Jesus as Messiah and Son of God. Schillebeeckx contends that, though the miracle tradition was expanded in Christian reflection on the life of Jesus, there is a historically firm basis for affirming that Jesus acted as both a healer and an exorcist. His dealings with people afflicted by illness and the demonic were one way in which people experienced salvation from God in and through him.

Jesus also disclosed the meaning of God's reign in and through his fellowship at table with all kinds of people, including those who were considered disreputable by the religious and civil leaders of his day. "To a great extent Jesus' action consisted in establishing social communication and opening up communication above all where excommunication or expulsion was officially in force...."[41] Influenced by critical theory and by the thought of Emmanuel Lévinas, Schillebeeckx considers the category of "communication" important for a Christian understanding of salvation.[42] For those who had been officially or unofficially excluded from the community, Jesus restored communication with God and other people. The conduct of Jesus at table showed that he was the eschatological messenger of God's openness toward sinners.[43]

Jesus' Experience of God

In what was Jesus' proclamation of the kingdom of God rooted? Schillebeeckx says that the impulse and guiding force behind this proclamation, as well as the courage to be faithful to it amid the experience of rejection, arose from Jesus' experience of God as "Abba." He underlines the importance and uniqueness of this Abba experience of Jesus as it plays out in his life and continues on the cross. It was more foundational and pervasive than is indicated by the three New Testament passages in which the Aramaic word *Abba* appears (Mark 14:36; Rom 8:15; Gal 4:6). Schillebeeckx argues that "apart from the reality of this very original *Abba* experience his message is an illusion, a vacuous myth."[44] He calls it "the source and secret of his being, message and manner of life."[45] This experience entailed "an immediate awareness of God as a power cherishing people and making them free."[46] Jesus' address of God connoted simplicity, closeness, and confidence on the one hand, and reverence and obedience on the other. It was intimate, but not casual, language. Indeed, the only Gospel reference to the word *Abba* appears in Mark's account of Jesus' prayer in Gethsemane, where Jesus is depicted as submitting to the will of the Father at a moment of wrenching struggle and enveloping darkness.

Jesus' Abba experience was, Schillebeeckx claims, a contrast experience. While this statement may at first be perplexing, what Schillebeeckx means is easy to discern. The Gospels give us solid evidence that Jesus had firsthand knowledge of the pain of this world. He came face to face with the power of evil and its destructive effects in the lives of people. His gut-wrenching reaction to the leper who knelt before him, begging for relief from that dreaded disease, is but one example of Jesus' direct encounter with human suffering (see Mark 1:40–45). Much of Jesus' ministry was an engagement in a kind of mortal combat with the powers that drained people of life. But in and through those encounters, underneath all that Jesus said and did, was a profound experience of God as the loving opponent of evil. Schillebeeckx likes to speak of the God of Jesus as "pure positivity."[47] This designation represents his gloss on Aquinas's notion of God as "pure activity." Schillebeeckx emphasizes that this understanding of God is the result, not simply of philosophical reflection, but of a thoughtful reading of the Gospels. The God proclaimed by Jesus is purely the source and ground of life, of the good. Neither death nor negativity finds its origin in God in any way.

The Death of Jesus

Schillebeeckx insists that the crucifixion of Jesus "was the intrinsic historical consequence of the radicalism of both his message and his lifestyle, which showed that all 'master-servant' relationships were incompatible with the lifestyle of the kingdom of God."[48] He is critical of theological reflections on Jesus' death that overlook the circumstances of Jesus' death and consider it apart from Jesus' public ministry. Such reflections, he believes, lead to distortion in our understanding of Jesus and our image of God. Christian interpretation of the death of Jesus must be connected to his life, especially his public ministry. The proclamation of the kingdom that Jesus made in word and deed proved to be a threat to those in religious and political authority: "his message and conduct must have caused a deep offense to at least conventional Jewish belief and practice."[49] He argues that the New Testament evidence leads us to place the rupture in the life of Jesus, not in the crucifixion itself, but in the earlier rejection of his message and praxis. This experience of rejection began even in his ministry in Galilee, though Jesus continued to move toward Jerusalem in order to make a final offer of salvation. "Even before Good Friday Jesus is the 'rejected one' and also feels himself to be so on the basis of the historically short 'record' of his public career."[50]

Schillebeeckx offers a nuanced interpretation of the biblical material dealing with Jesus' approach to his death. He suggests that Jesus did not, from the beginning, expect that his life and mission would inevitably end in historical failure and violent death.[51] Nevertheless, even though the Gospel passion predictions evince later reflection by the Christian community, it is clear that Jesus became increasingly aware of the conflict for which he was headed. Schillebeeckx's study of the Synoptic Gospels leads him to conclude that "from a particular moment in his career he must have rationally come to terms with the possibility, in the longer term probability and in the end actual certainty of a fatal outcome."[52] This gradually increasing certainty of a violent death would have been bolstered by Jesus' knowledge of the fate of John the Baptist.

Schillebeeckx describes with some complexity the way in which Jesus integrated this increasing awareness of impending death into his life and mission. He is concerned not to place what he considers to be later Christian affirmation of the salvific import of Jesus' death onto the lips of Jesus, though he also wants to take account of the New Testament evidence indicating that Jesus did not approach his death as an event devoid of meaning. Schillebeeckx argues that Jesus did integrate his death into his self-surrender—his surrender to God in and through his loving service to humanity. Still, he does not want to assert that Jesus explicitly spoke of his imminent death as having salvific significance, and he thinks that one must uphold the dual reality of the negativity of Jesus' violent death and the fact of his integration of it into his service to God and others: "On the basis of a critically justified exegesis, it is essential to affirm Jesus' integration of his violent death into his surrender of himself to God and his offer of salvation to men....Despite this, however, it is impossible to deny the negativity of that death as rejection."[53]

Schillebeeckx appeals to the Last Supper narratives for indications of Jesus' approach to his own death. Even though these narratives are overlaid with elements of later Christian interpretation influenced by the celebration of the Eucharist, we must accept the historical probability that Jesus' words and/or actions at this meal manifested a meaningful awareness of what was about to happen to him and communicated hope to his disciples. Schillebeeckx focuses on the tradition of the offering of the cup found in Mark 14:25 as a sign of Jesus' trust that his fellowship with the disciples was stronger than death.[54] He considers Jesus' passing of the cup to his disciples to be an interpretative sign of his entire life as a concrete offer of salvation from God. This symbolic action shows that "Jesus felt his death to be in some way or other part and parcel of the salvation-offered-by-God, as a historical consequence of his caring and loving service of and solidarity with people."[55] This does not mean that Jesus explicitly proclaimed his death to be a saving event. "One is bound to say that in fact no certain logion of Jesus is to be found in which Jesus himself might be thought to ascribe a salvific import to his death."[56] Nevertheless, as one final act of fidelity to God and service to others, this death takes on a meaning it would not otherwise have. Later Christian interpretation of the redemptive significance of Jesus' death built upon his integration of his death into his life and mission.

In his treatment of the crucifixion and resurrection, Schillebeeckx underscores the dialectical tension between the negativity of a brutal, unjust execution and the positive meaning given to this death by Jesus' self-surrender and by God's acceptance of it in the resurrection. First, he insists that the cross, in and of itself, must be soberly viewed in all its stark negativity. Christian glorification of the cross obscures the fact of what really happened there: Jesus was crucified by human injustice. Schillebeeckx describes the cross as "the index of the anti-divine in human history"—the radical expression of sin.[57] Thus he rejects Moltmann's trinitarian interpretation of the cross as "an event between God and God,"[58] contending that the way Moltmann tells the story of

Calvary projects onto God what was, in fact, caused by human injustice. Historically considered, it is not accurate to speak of God the Father "handing over" the Son to death. Rather, Jesus was crucified by people who were threatened by his words and deeds, and this crucifixion represented human rejection of the salvation from God offered in Jesus:

> God, who according to Leviticus "abominates human sacrifices" (Lev. 18:21–30; 20:1–5), did not put Jesus on the cross. Human beings did that. Although God always comes in power, divine power knows no use of force, not even against people who are crucifying his Christ. But the kingdom of God still comes, despite human misuse of power and human rejection of the kingdom of God.[59]

From an examination of the New Testament evidence, Schillebeeckx concludes that for Jesus the cross is an Abba experience, though it is an experience undergone in darkness and silence: "Jesus did not die, after all, in the certain knowledge that he would rise again after his suffering and death. He was not able to situate suffering and death either."[60] Despite this darkness and the pain of uncertainty, however, Jesus continues to hold God's hand in radical trust. Of all of the words from the cross found in the Gospels, Schillebeeckx argues, only the loud cry of Jesus can be historically warranted.[61] Though the content of this cry cannot be definitively ascertained, the citation of Psalm 22 implies a cry of trust, though trust expressed in the midst of severe pain. Thus, the cross is the ultimate contrast experience: the terrible suffering of a violent death, but also an experience that is filled with and gives rise to hope in the God of salvation to whom Jesus entrusted his life. His suffering and dying constitute "a breaking of the life which he entrusts to his God, in grief, but with all his heart."[62] In a statement that does grant salvific significance to the cross, Schillebeeckx says that "this belonging to God in an 'anti-godly' situation seems to effect our salvation."[63] Ultimately, it is communion with God that saves.

According to Schillebeeckx's interpretation of the crucifixion, God does not intervene to save Jesus or to remove the starkness of death, but neither does God abandon Jesus. Jesus did not receive any favored treatment from the God with whom he enjoyed a unique relationship. In its negativity, the cross remains a mystery, even for Jesus. However, God is silently present to Jesus at this moment, just as God is silently present to all those who suffer. Schillebeeckx does not accept Moltmann's interpretation of Jesus' death as including abandonment by the Father; rather, "on exegetical grounds we must resolutely reject the possibility that Jesus himself had been abandoned by God."[64] The citation of the first line of Psalm 22 in the passion narratives of Matthew and Mark adduces the entirety of the psalm. Read as a whole, this psalm is indeed a prayer of anguish, but it is also a confession of trust in God. It concludes with an expression of praise and thanksgiving for deliverance by God. For Schillebeeckx, God's silent presence to Jesus at Calvary is an experience of the divine that is mediated by negativity. It does not annul the feelings of failure and alienation that are evident in this terrible death. Still, we must say that for Jesus and for all those who suffer, "*God nevertheless remains near at hand* and that salvation consists in the fact that man still holds fast to God's invisible hand *in* this dark night of faith."[65]

God's silent presence at Calvary is confirmed and validated in the resurrection. In the resurrection the faithful presence and power of God erupt from within. In Christian theology the resurrection can be interpreted in two related but distinct ways. First, it can be viewed as the completion of Jesus' life and death. Here resurrection is seen as the other side of death, and Jesus' death is interpreted as a death into resurrection. This viewpoint is reminiscent of the depiction of Jesus' death in the Gospel of John, and it is articulated in a compelling way in the theology of Karl Rahner.[66] Second, resurrection can be envisioned as a new creative act of God, a corrective to what happened to Jesus in his death. Resurrection is God's "Yes" to Jesus, spoken definitively in the face of the deafening "No" to Jesus shouted by all who rejected him.

In his interpretation of the resurrection Schillebeeckx strives to affirm the truth that is present in both of these perspectives. He incorporates the notion that the resurrection confirms and completes all that Jesus' life and ministry were about. It is God's endorsement of Jesus' life, and it is anticipated by the unique communion with God that Jesus experienced throughout his life. He says that the resurrection is "the divine recognition of the permanent validity of Jesus' living and dying."[67] Nevertheless, Schillebeeckx places greater emphasis on the resurrection as a new creative act of God that corrects what was done to Jesus, fearing that if one views it simply as the reverse side of Jesus' death, such an interpretation will minimize the negativity of this death. In raising Jesus from the dead, God breaks through humanity's rejection of definitive salvation offered by Jesus. "In the risen Jesus God shows himself to be the power of anti-evil, of unconditional goodness that in sovereign fashion refuses to recognize, and breaks, the overweening power of evil."[68] Schillebeeckx attempts to hold together the two traditional perspectives on resurrection in dialectical tension: "Insofar as the resurrection of Jesus is God's yes to the person and life of Jesus, God approves of Jesus' fulfillment in his death of love for God and man. Insofar as the resurrection is God's corrective to the negative of death, God gives Jesus a renewed and exalted life."[69]

How should we interpret those expressions of the Christian tradition that attribute saving efficacy to the death of Jesus? On this question the reader of Schillebeeckx encounters some of the most complex, highly nuanced, and dialectical passages in his writings. One must recognize that underneath these passages lies Schillebeeckx's protest against the Christian tendency to glorify human suffering and idealize the cross. Schillebeeckx takes the thesis that negativity cannot arise from God and applies it to the death of Jesus. If this thesis is correct (if God is pure positivity), he argues, then it is impossible to find a divine reason for the death of Jesus: "Therefore, first of all, we have to say that we are not redeemed *thanks* to the death of Jesus but *despite* it."[70] Some commentators stop here and conclude that this statement contains, in a nutshell, Schillebeeckx's understanding of death in general and of the death of Jesus in particular. Schillebeeckx says, however, that in the resurrection of Jesus, God has so overcome the negativity of this death that in faith we can profess that even the negative aspects of our history have an indirect role in God's plan of salvation. God's overcoming of this terrible experience of suffering fills the experience with meaning, though without stripping it of its negativity. Referring to the Markan motif of the necessity of Jesus' death, Schillebeeckx asserts that "we shall never be able to give a reason...for the significance for salvation history of this improper expression 'the divine must.' On the one hand it contains the insight that man is redeemed by Jesus *despite* the death of Jesus." On the other hand, God so transcends this *despite* because "through the resurrection of Jesus from the dead he conquers suffering and evil and undoes them that the expression 'despite the death' in fact does not say enough. However, the terms in which we could fill this unfathomable, 'does not say enough' in a positive way, with finite, meaningful categories, escape us."[71]

From this vantage point, Schillebeeckx speaks of the need to express salvation from God "in the non-identity of the history of Jesus' suffering and death."[72] Schillebeeckx is saying that the suffering of Jesus and the evil that caused it remain outside of God: "Jesus did not contaminate God himself by his own suffering."[73] On this point, too, Schillebeeckx differs from Moltmann, who claims that God takes up the negativity of human suffering within Godself. Schillebeeckx rejects any theoretical reconciliation between the nondivine negativity of Jesus' suffering and death and the salvation effected by God in and through the overcoming of this death. This salvation through God's non-identity with and overcoming of human suffering is what grounds Christian hope:

> So faith in Jesus makes it possible to affirm together the two theoretically irreconcilable aspects in our human history: evil-and-suffering and salvation or a final good, enabling, allowing, and obliging us none the less, in a way that is grounded in Jesus, to give the last word to well-being and goodness, because the Father is greater than all our suffering and grief and greater than our inability to experience the deepest reality as in the end a trustworthy gift.[74]

What the Story of Jesus Tells Us about God and Suffering

Schillebeeckx's interpretation of the ministry, death, and resurrection of Jesus becomes the guiding light for his understanding of the

232

way in which Christians should think and speak about God in the face of human suffering. He stresses that Christians should not try to explain suffering. We should not construct theories about the reasons for the presence of suffering in the world, systematic explanations that seek to reconcile innocent suffering with belief in an all-good, all-powerful God. He is not enamored of traditional theodicies, since he is convinced that the pervasive presence of senseless suffering in the world falls outside the bounds of every rational system.

Schillebeeckx also has difficulty with the language of "permission" and "allowance" that has traditionally been part of Christian theology and spirituality. Classical theology proposes that, though God does not actively will evil and suffering, God does permit it in view of a greater good. Usually that "greater good" is related to the gift of human freedom. Schillebeeckx understands the point of such language, but he thinks that talk about God's permitting evil and suffering can be misleading. On this point, Schillebeeckx is complex. He does affirm a kind of blanket permission of God in creating the world, especially a world in which human beings have freedom. As he puts it, seen from God's side creation entails a sort of "divine yielding": a making room for the other. Here Schillebeeckx seems close to Moltmann's notion of God's self-emptying in the act of creation: God gives creative space to human beings and, in so doing, makes Godself vulnerable. History becomes an adventure full of risks. Schillebeeckx even employs the metaphor of signing a blank check: "The creation of human beings is a blank cheque which God alone guarantees. By creating human beings with their own finite and free will, God voluntarily renounces power. That makes God to a high degree 'dependent' on human beings and thus vulnerable."[75]

Schillebeeckx is willing, then, to admit a kind of blanket permission granted by God in the act of creating finite beings and bestowing the gift of human freedom. Nevertheless, he apparently finds "permission" language problematic when it is applied to particular instances of human suffering, for example, God's "allowing" this woman to contract breast cancer or "permitting" that innocent person to be murdered by a soldier or a terrorist. Such God-talk can easily evoke the idea of God as a neutral bystander who stands back and watches people suffer without doing anything about it. For Schillebeeckx, we should never speak of God actively willing or causing evil and suffering, nor should we speak of God permitting or allowing it. We should simply say that God is busy about the work of overcoming evil and suffering, as exemplified in God's raising Jesus from the dead. Believers should envision and speak about a God who is on the move in overcoming—conquering—the evil and suffering that plague the human family. In the heading of one chapter of his book *Christ: The Experience of Jesus as Lord*, Schillebeeckx succinctly expresses his understanding of the way in which the God of Jesus Christ relates to human suffering: "God does not want mankind to suffer."[76] His in-depth study of the New Testament leads him to conclude that the God revealed in Jesus does not want humankind to suffer and acts to overcome suffering.

What, then, does Schillebeeckx see as the origin of evil? He appeals to the Thomistic category of the "initiative of finitude" to account for the origin of evil and suffering in the world. In this context, Schillebeeckx's main focus is on moral rather than physical evil: "As soon as there are *creatures*, there is the *possibility* (not the necessity) of a negative and original *initiative of finitude*, if I can put it that way."[77] Evil and suffering do not necessarily follow from finitude, but they draw their possibility from there. Drawing on Aquinas again, he emphasizes that while God is the first (primary) cause of creation, the human being is the first cause of a defect of the will. A choice for evil *"begins exclusively from the finite without any contribution on God's side,"* though it does not "checkmate God."[78] God remains pure positivity, from whom no form of evil originates.

Schillebeeckx does address physical evil when he discusses the reality of human death. In an early essay, he says that for the human person who is bound up with his or her bodiliness in the world, death is "unintelligible and absurd."[79] Death is not the creation of the good God; rather, it is the result of sin—"the own manufacture of sinful humanity."[80] Death is the "gift" of sinful humanity to God; it was the only thing that God did not possess.[81] In *Christ the Sacrament of the Encounter with God*, Schillebeeckx calls death "the utmost effort of Satan and sinful man to stamp out everything godly in the world."[82] In his later book *Christ: The Experience of Jesus as Lord*, he addresses the reality of death in the context of formulating seven "anthropological constants" that characterize human existence. Under the constant of "the conditioning of people and culture by time and space," he discusses the dialectical tension that exists between nature and history.[83] Death represents the extreme exponent in this dialectic. The inescapability of dying is a reminder to us that some forms of suffering persist and that attempts at salvation based merely on human effort and planning will always be incomplete. Further along in this same work, he says about death: "What ought to signify integration, unity, and wholeness as the conclusion of human life is in reality the dissolution of a particular man in history."[84] Even for the Christian death remains impenetrable, though "through the death of Jesus, seen in the light of his resurrection, the Christian has the assurance that suffering and death cannot separate him from God."[85] Throughout his writings, then, Schillebeeckx views physical death in a negative light. It does not come from the hands of the God who is pure positivity. For Schillebeeckx, while the death and resurrection of Jesus give believers hope for enduring communion with God beyond death, death itself has a negative valence. It is not part of God's design for creation.

This approach to evil and human suffering seems to imply that in some sense God has a struggle on God's hands—that God's power is a power to respond to us in and through all of the turmoil of human history. This is the way in which Schillebeeckx sees it. He refuses to adopt Bonhoeffer's language of a God who is "weak and powerless" in the world. Schillebeeckx thinks that describing God as powerless would leave the final word to evil and suffering rather than to the God of life.[86] At the same time, he expresses caution about speaking of God as "omnipotent." He argues that the omnipotence of God is not a central theme in the Bible. For example, his reading of the Hebrew scriptures leads him to conclude that "the history of God with Israel is to a large degree the history of one who constantly sees his plans failing and has constantly to react afresh, tactically and strategically."[87] The bottom line of Christian faith is that God will be victorious over evil and suffering, as exhibited and effected in the death and resurrection of Jesus. But, Schillebeeckx argues, God never breaks in from the outside to effect salvation. Rather, God works faithfully, patiently from within. God's power to save is inwardly present, just as it was for Jesus on Calvary. It is a power of love that challenges, giving life and freedom to human beings. God does not retaliate against those who refuse God's offer. Appealing to Revelation 3:20, Schillebeeckx says, "Out of respect for our freedom God refuses to force the door of our heart and our free will. But God continues to be present in redemption and forgiveness: God does not go away and continues to knock." Moreover, "God is also present to save beyond this limit, if necessary as the final judge."[88]

Consequences for Christian Life

For Schillebeeckx, this conception of God and God's relation to human suffering has practical consequences for Christian life. It means that Christians are called to be people of narrative and praxis—people of memory and reflective action. First, believers must keep the memory of human suffering—the remembrance of the ongoing passion of humanity. Christians are called to live in solidarity with suffering people and to enable suppressed stories of suffering to be told, whether they be stories of individuals or narratives about peoples who are the victims of systematic oppression. Christians also keep the memory of another story: the story of Jesus' life, death, and resurrection. This story, remembered and lived out in discipleship, speaks to us about the God of the kingdom, the God of pure positivity who overcame the death of Jesus in the resurrection and who is on the move to overcome all evil and suffering. The story of Jesus assures us that entering into communion with suffering people and acting from within to bring life out of death is characteristic of God. This memory is not the same as an explanation, for suffering remains a mystery. As Schillebeeckx puts it, "It is just not possible to speak meaningfully about Auschwitz and, however hard you try, you can't situate it anywhere in God's plan."[89] The only appropriate response of the believer is the "nevertheless" of faith in the God revealed by Jesus. Suffering is a scourge, a terrible reality that is intractable to rational explanation. Nevertheless, we believe in the God of Jesus, the God who is present to and in communion with all suffering persons and who is on the move to overcome their suffering.

This memory should lead to action, to praxis. It moves believers to thoughtful, reflective action that seeks to alleviate human suffering and fights against the causes of suffering. This praxis has both mystical and political dimensions; it entails "the harmonizing of a contemplative approach with a concern for liberation."[90] Believers are summoned to offer resistance to evil, to refuse to allow evil the right to exist. In the face of evil and suffering, then, Christians are people who remember and who act. And they engage in that memory and praxis in the light of faith in a God who is pure positivity.

In the course of this remembrance and praxis, believers experience fragments of salvation. We have seen that for Schillebeeckx Jesus' entire career is the embodiment of salvation from God. In his life and ministry Jesus emphasizes the gratuitousness of our redemption and liberation. He refuses to heal human violence through divine force. In the cross of Jesus we learn that God is also present in life where he may appear to be absent. Jesus shows us that salvation can also be found in suffering, even in an unjust execution. In his death Jesus participated in the brokenness of the world. "This means that God determines in absolute freedom, down the ages, who and how he wills to be in his deepest being, namely a God of men and women, an ally in our suffering and our absurdity, and also an ally in the good that we do. In his own being he is a God for us."[91] Schillebeeckx summarizes what Christians mean by salvation: "We Christians learn…to express the content of what God is and the content of what men and women can be, in other words the content of human salvation, from the career of Jesus. We are liberated to new, authentically human possibilities of life." Jesus' redemption liberates us

> to accept that despite sin and guilt we are accepted by God;…to live in this world without ultimate despair about our existence;…to look death in the face as not having the last word;…to commit ourselves disinterestedly for others in the confidence that such dedication is ultimately of deci-

sive significance (Matt 25);...to accept experiences of peace, joy and communication and to understand them as manifestations of God's saving presence;...to...struggle for economic, social and political justice;...to be free from one-self in order to...be free to do good to others.

Thus do Christians experience "faith in the God who discloses himself in Jesus Christ as the sacred mystery of all-embracing love: experiences of salvation from God."[92]

When Schillebeeckx writes about divine judgment and eternal life, he arrives at a different conclusion from that of Moltmann, who speaks about the judgment of Christ as a creative justice that heals and saves both the victims and the perpetrators of oppression. Schillebeeckx observes that heaven and hell are asymmetrical affirmations of faith.[93] Christian belief in eternal life with God is based on the experience of living communion with God in grace. This gift of grace is made possible by God's overcoming death in the resurrection of the crucified Jesus. Christian belief in heaven has a definitive quality about it that is not true of the teaching about the possibility of eternal loss. Schillebeeckx rejects the notion of hell as a state of eternal torment, existing alongside heaven. Such a view is based on vengeance. Never-theless, he argues, the seriousness of the human drama should not be trivialized by a cheap view of divine mercy. Schillebeeckx proposes that those who do evil—the oppressors in human history—may punish themselves eternally. It may be that such evildoers simply no longer exist at death. They cease to exist and will not be remembered in heaven. There is no ground for their eternal existence because they have failed to love: "The evil do not have eternal life; their death is in fact the end of everything: they have excluded themselves from God and the community of the good, nor does any new heaven await them on earth."[94] This exclusion is not the result of a punitive act of God; rather it is something that people who definitively choose evil do to themselves. As Schillebeeckx puts it, "God does not take vengeance; he leaves evil to its own, limited logic!"[95]

Conclusion

Schillebeeckx would have been the first to admit that his discussion of God and human suffering is inadequate to the mystery. He acknowledged that "the picture of God which we produce is constantly broken."[96] His theological arguments invite critical comment. John Galvin has suggested that Schillebeeckx's emphasis on the passivity and negativity of Jesus' death may not do justice to the complete reality of the crucifixion.[97] Galvin thinks that his treatment of Jesus' approach to his own death may be too minimal, particularly in his assertion that Jesus did not speak of his impending death as having salvific significance. Galvin proposes that "the possibility of finding a broader direct basis in Jesus' life for the interpretation of his death deserves further exploration."[98]

It seems clear, too, that Schillebeeckx needed to offer a more coherent account of his position on God's "permission" of evil and suffering. As we have seen, he explicitly rejects the use of language about God allowing or permitting suffering. At the same time, he suggests a kind of "blanket permission" by God in creating the world and giving freedom to human beings, an act that he thinks entails a "divine yielding" and for which he uses the metaphor of signing a blank check. Schillebeeckx thinks that permission language used for God and suffering simply represents the dead end of human thinking about this mystery. But there does seem to be some ambiguity in his thought on this theme, and one wonders if he takes seriously enough the valid theological concerns that traditional permission language was trying to address.

Schillebeeckx formulated his Christology in a way that is grounded in the New Testament confessions about Jesus and that seeks to make Christian faith in Jesus comprehensible to modern people. While he explicitly affirms the christological doctrine of Chalcedon and of other church councils, he does not focus on this conciliar teaching, and he thinks that it represents a narrowing of the rich, pluriform New Testament confession of Jesus. His Christology begins with an analysis of the public ministry of Jesus and the encounters that a variety of people had with him. As we have seen, he argues that the primary identification of Jesus by early Christians was that of eschatological prophet—an identification that forms the basis for other expressions of the identity of Jesus. It must be asked, however, whether Schillebeeckx's avoidance of the conciliar teaching does not lead to a minimizing of the doctrine of the incarnation. In our treatment of theology in the early church and the thought of Aquinas, we have seen how important Christian confession of the incarnation has been for addressing the questions surrounding God's relation to human suffering. Belief in the incarnation provides theological grounds for speaking of God's closeness to the experience of human suffering. This attention to the theology of the incarnation seems to be a missing link in Schillebeeckx's Christology, particularly in his later works.

Even with these critical comments, however, it is clear that Schillebeeckx's treatment of the questions we are exploring is both theologically fruitful and pastorally helpful. His way of narrating the story of Jesus' public ministry elucidates the character of the God whose drawing near means life for people. His account of Jesus' death and resurrection illumines the communion between God and Jesus that endured at the nadir of the crucifixion, and it discloses the way in which the power of God was present and at work from within. Schillebeeckx's sober presentation of the negativity of suffering, even of Jesus' suffering on the cross, and his testimony about a God who opposes this suffering and acts to overcome it, can provide hope and guidance for those who battle to the end against forms of suffering they must endure. When a person is confronted with inexplicable suffering and the question of the "why" of this suffering will not go away, perhaps Schillebeeckx's advice about prayer in this situation is as helpful as anything that can be said:

> It [prayer] shouldn't continue with your saying: God must have an intention here, but rather with your saying: we are still in God's hands, even in grim situations like this one. This terrible event isn't the last word. And you have to say that with all the strength that is in your being.[99]

Discussion Questions: www.paulistpress.com, Online Resources.

9

Gustavo Gutiérrez:
The Suffering of the Poor

Gustavo Gutiérrez traveled to Chicago in the fall of 2008 to lecture at an academic conference celebrating the fortieth anniversary of the gathering of Latin American bishops at Medellín, Colombia. While I was driving him to and from the conference sessions, he shared freely about his personal life, his work with the poor, and his career as a theologian. I asked him about the years of his adolescence, most of which were spent bedridden with osteomyelitis, a condition that has left him with a noticeable limp. He spoke about his struggles with the painful and debilitating effects of that affliction, especially during the times of two difficult surgeries he had to undergo in his youth. But he also reflected on the benefits of those years, including the experience of the loving care of his family and the spiritual lessons he learned from his ordeal. In listening to Gutiérrez, I was reminded of remarks he made in an interview with Daniel Hartnett published in *America* magazine in 2003. He said that he had learned much about hope during the years when he was confined to bed as a young person: "There certainly were reasons for discouragement, but also very present was the gift of hope that came to me through prayer, reading, family and friends."[1] This early experience of personal suffering, along with the hope that Gutiérrez learned to cultivate from within that experience, was a preparation for his work as a theologian who is committed to giving voice to the suffering of the poor. It also left him with a deep sensitivity to the pain of others.

The Life and Thought of Gutiérrez

Gutiérrez grew up in a close-knit Peruvian family that knew the struggles of the poor. His father was a city worker and his mother was unschooled. He is part Amerindian, a Quechuan.[2] An avid reader and promising student, Gutiérrez attended the University of San Marcos in Lima, engaging in medical studies with the hope of becoming a psychiatrist. Gutiérrez eventually decided that he wanted to become a priest rather than a physician. He entered the seminary in Santiago, Chile, but was soon sent to Europe to pursue studies in philosophy, psychology, and theology. He studied in Belgium, France, and Rome, earning a master's degree in theology at Lyons and being ordained to the priesthood in 1959. He would return to Lyons in 1985 for a doctoral defense, for which he presented his corpus of theological works as his doctoral "thesis."[3]

When Gutiérrez returned to Peru as a priest, he taught theology at the Pontifical Catholic University in Lima and served as an advisor to the National Union of Catholic Students.[4] He also immersed himself in pastoral ministry in an impoverished section of Lima. James Nickoloff points out that during these early years of priestly ministry Gutiérrez "encouraged his listeners to examine the meaning of human existence and the place of God in the world in which they lived,"[5] a world characterized by the grinding poverty that afflicted the majority of Peruvians in the 1960s and still scars the lives of many Latin Americans today. Gutiérrez was closely attentive to the events of Vatican II, and he attended the fourth session of the council as a theological assistant to Bishop Manuel Larrain of Chile. He also became very interested in popular movements in Latin America in the church and among the poor in general. What he would later call "the irruption of the poor" became for Gutiérrez a critical sign of the times that the church and theology needed to take into account. The poor were making their voices heard and were asking about liberation. One important ecclesial dimension of this phenomenon was the growth of "base ecclesial communities" throughout Latin America—small communities of Christians who met regularly to reflect together on the word of God and on their own lives of faith. Some of these communities also engaged in analysis of the social situation in which they lived, leading them to explore paths of liberation from oppression through social and political action.

Gutiérrez soon became convinced that the theological method in which he had been trained in Europe was not adequate for theologizing in the Latin American context. He notes that "as a result of a Latin American cultural tradition imposed by colonization, theology as practiced among us simply echoed the theology developed in Europe."[6] Latin American theologians drew on European theology without attention to their own context, resulting in excessively abstract presentations of the faith. This changed when these theologians began to pay attention to the movements that were taking place in society and the church in the 1960s. Gutiérrez observes that "the urgency and rich resources of the commitment that many Christians were beginning to make to the process of popular liberation during the 1960s raised new questions based on Latin American reality, and they pointed to new and fruitful ways for theological discourse."[7] He soon became convinced that theology must be engaged with and expressive of the historical situation in which it is immersed. And he would become the leading Latin American thinker in the development of a new theological methodology.

Gutiérrez was closely involved in the meeting of the Latin American bishops at Medellín. He served as an official theologian at the conference, made contributions to the documents on peace, justice, and the poverty of the church, and drafted two major speeches for Cardinal Juan Landazuri Ricketts, archbishop of Lima.[8] Gutiérrez's repeated references to and quotations from the documents of Medellín in his later writings reveal the significance of this ecclesial event for him. The bishops began by assessing the overall situation of Latin America, especially the widespread poverty that afflicted the people. They denounced "institutionalized violence"—the violence embedded in oppressive social, economic, and political structures—and they called on Christians to become involved in the transformation of society. They spoke about base ecclesial communities and employed the term *libera-*

tion. The bishops envisioned the redemptive work of Christ as having liberating effects on all aspects of human existence. Gutiérrez likes to quote a passage from the Medellín document on justice that articulates this conviction: "It is the same God who, in the fullness of time, sends his Son in the flesh, so that he might liberate all men from the slavery to which sin has subjected them: hunger, misery, oppression and igno-rance, in a word, that injustice and hatred which have their origin in human selfishness."[9] He considers the Medellín conference to mark a critical moment in the maturing of the Latin American church—its coming of age. The church was beginning to face the problems of soci-ety, especially the suffering caused by massive poverty.[10]

Gutiérrez formulated his theological methodology in *A Theology of Liberation*, first published in 1971. He speaks about his work as "a theo-logical reflection born of the experience of shared efforts to abolish the current situation and to build a different society, freer and more human."[11] After discussing various understandings of theology in the Christian tradition, Gutiérrez defines it as critical reflection on praxis in the light of faith.[12] Theology is a second step; it does not produce pastoral activity but reflects on it and helps to orient it. In later writ-ings, Gutiérrez says that the "first step" consists of both "contemplation and practice."[13] In *A Theology of Liberation*, he argues that the starting point for theology must be the facts and questions derived from the world and from history. The theologian "will be someone personally and vitally engaged in historical realities with specific times and places. He [she] will be engaged where nations, social classes, people struggle to free themselves from domination and oppression by other nations, classes and people."[14] Gutiérrez envisions the purpose of liberation the-ology as both explicative and transformative. Theology "does not stop with reflecting on the world, but rather tries to be part of the process through which the world is transformed."[15] In this effort the theologian does not assume a neutral, or purely objective, viewpoint but identifies with the poor and other marginalized people of the world who live in oppressive circumstances.

Gutiérrez's thought has developed during the forty years since the publication of *A Theology of Liberation*. Along the way, his work was investigated by the Congregation for the Doctrine of the Faith (CDF) and the Peruvian bishops, who found nothing unorthodox in his writings. Instructions from the CDF in 1984 and 1986 expressed concerns about the methodology and content of liberation theology, concerns that Gutiérrez has attempted to address in subsequent writings.[16] Partly in response to critiques of liberation theology as overly materialistic in its vision, Gutiérrez has made a significant contribution to the development of a liberation spirituality through works such as *We Drink from Our Own Wells* (1983), *On Job* (1986), and *The God of Life* (1989). He has also reflected critically on his own use of the tools of social analysis, particularly ideas drawn from Marxist theory like class struggle.[17] Nevertheless, he has maintained his commitment to a theology that is formulated from the vantage point of the poor and marginalized of the world.

The liberation theology developed by Gutiérrez, then, is rooted in the experience of human suffering. In this regard, his theology bears similarities to that of Schillebeeckx, with whose thought Gutiérrez came into contact when he studied at Lyons. In a 1995 address to the Peruvian Academy of the Spanish Language, Gutiérrez reflected on theology as a discipline: "If we don't go down or rather up into the world of everyday suffering, of consuming anguish, of ever-burning hope, the theological task has no substance."[18] He speaks of this entry into the world of suffering as a conversion that is necessary for authentic theologizing.[19] Gutiérrez and other liberation theologians understand poverty to be the most pervasive cause of suffering in the world. While they recognize forms of suffering that cut across all socioeconomic strata, these theologians envision poverty to be the most fundamental instantiation of human suffering. In the introduction to *On Job*, Gutiérrez includes a quotation from Archbishop Desmond Tutu that grounds liberation theology in the experience of human suffering:

> Liberation theology more than any other kind of theology issues out of the crucible of human suffering and anguish. It happens because people cry out, "Oh God, how long?" "Oh God, but why?..." All liberation theology stems from trying to make sense of human suffering when those who suffer are

the victims of organized oppression and exploitation, when they are emasculated and treated as less than what they are: human persons created in the image of the Triune God, redeemed by the one Savior Jesus Christ and sanctified by the Holy Paraclete.[20]

The World of the Poor

Gutiérrez first formulated his conception of three theological meanings of poverty in a course that he taught in Montreal in 1967. James Nickoloff suggests that this threefold framework was generally adopted by the Latin American bishops during their conferences at Medellín and Puebla[21] and reprised in the introduction to the revised edition of *A Theology of Liberation*.[22] The first meaning of poverty is the economic, or material, poverty that afflicts the majority of people in the world. Gutiérrez insists that theologians and believers must begin here, lest they fall prey to an idealization of poverty. This form of poverty "is something that God does not want."[23] It stands in contrast to the reign of God proclaimed by Jesus. The second form of poverty is spiritual poverty, that is, openness to the will of God in one's life. This is the kind of poverty that is praised in the scriptures.[24] Gutiérrez identifies the third form of poverty as solidarity with the poor, which includes protest against the conditions under which they suffer. In *The Power of the Poor in History*, he highlights the significance of this third expression of poverty for the life of the Latin American church: "To proclaim the gospel from a situation of identification with the poor is to convene a church in solidarity with the popular masses in Latin America, in solidarity with their aspirations, with their struggles to have a place in their own history."[25] Though Gutiérrez reflects on the meaning of spiritual poverty in some places in his writings, he focuses most explicitly on the first and third meanings of poverty.

With regard to economic poverty, Gutiérrez strives to depict for his readers the contours of the world in which the poor live. He repeatedly points out that the poor have often been idealized by people who are economically advantaged. They have been caricatured as simple people who are content with "their lot" and "close to God." Such ide-alization represents a distancing from the real world in which the poor live and an avoidance of the challenges that poverty poses to the eco-nomically advantaged. Gutiérrez also cautions against speaking abstractly about "the poor" as a social class in a way that does not attend to the concrete concerns and hopes of real people. In his later writings, he emphasizes the need to build friendships with people who live in poverty, and he takes every opportunity to describe in detail the real world of impoverished people whom he knows, always emphasiz-ing that material poverty leads to unjust and premature death. A pas-sage from *We Drink from Our Own Wells* displays Gutiérrez's profound sensitivity to the world of the poor:

> It is a frightening and deeply saddening experience to come in contact, through conversations and through pastoral work among the people, with the miseries that descend upon the poor in an endless procession. There are countless small things: wants of every kind, the abuse and contempt that the poor endure, lives tormented by the search for employment, incredible ways of earning a living or—more accurately—earning a crust of bread, mean bickering, sepa-ration of family members, sicknesses not found at other lev-els of society, infant undernourishment and death, unjust prices for products and commodities, total confusion about what is necessary for themselves and their families, delin-quency springing from abandonment and despair, the loss of one's own cultural values.[26]

In his *America* interview, Gutiérrez points out that poverty has a visibility today that it did not have in the past. Because of modern means of communication, it is impossible to ignore the glaring dispar-ity between the rich and the poor of the world. He says, "The faces of the poor must now be confronted."[27] Moreover, we have a better under-standing of the causes of poverty today than in the past: "There was a time when poverty was considered to be an unavoidable fate, but such a view is no longer possible or responsible. Now we know that poverty is not simply a misfortune; it is an injustice." He adds, "Christians cannot forgo their responsibility to say a prophetic word about unjust economic conditions."[28]

This conviction that poverty is ultimately a result of injustice correlates with the prominent role that sin plays in Gutiérrez's theology. He rejects the doctrine of temporal retribution, which was discussed in our exploration of the Hebrew scriptures. In his extended reflection on the Book of Job, he argues that this teaching is "a convenient and soothing doctrine for those who have great worldly possessions, and it promotes resignation and a sense of guilt in those who lack possessions."[29] It claims that the poor themselves are to blame for their situation. Throughout the history of the church this teaching has been revived in various forms that denigrate the poor. Gutiérrez holds that the profound human suffering caused by massive poverty in the world is indeed a sinful situation but is one for which those in power have responsibility. In *A Theology of Liberation*, he asserts that sin, which he conceives of as a breach of communion with God and one's fellow human beings, is the ultimate cause of poverty, injustice, and oppression. While the structural reasons for poverty must be analyzed and remedied, "behind an unjust structure there is a personal or collective will responsible—a willingness to reject God and neighbor."[30]

Gutiérrez was questioned about the role of sin in his theology during his 1985 doctoral defense at Lyons. He pointed out that theological currents prevalent in the 1960s seemed to downplay the significance of sin and to be "overoptimistic with regard to history."[31] Gutiérrez even suggests that the introduction to Vatican II's Pastoral Constitution on the Church in the Modern World (*Gaudium et Spes*) was "tinged by that optimism."[32] In a country like his own, he says, the negative aspects of the modern world are blatantly obvious. Such a context demands a straightforward acknowledgment of the reality and effects of sin. "It is impossible, therefore, that we should not be aware of the effects that this situation of poverty and death is having in today's world. Therefore, too, sin has an important place in the theology of liberation."[33] Though considerable emphasis was placed on social sin when liberation theology first arose, a greater sense of balance between personal and social sin was struck in subsequent works of liberation theology. Gutiérrez believes, then, the suffering caused by poverty is in fact caused by sin—not the sin of the poor themselves but the sin of those responsible for the conditions in which the poor are forced to live.

Gutiérrez's emphasis on the sinful situation of poverty in the modern world comes into play when he dialogues with the writings of Bonhoeffer. It is clear that he has great respect for Bonhoeffer's courageous witness in opposing the Nazi regime, and he finds Bonhoeffer's prison writings to be compelling. In a reflection on Bonhoeffer's prison letter of June 8, 1944, Gutiérrez maintains that Bonhoeffer clearly perceived the challenges that the modern world—the "world come of age"—put before the church. He commends Bonhoeffer for wanting to "face squarely the fact of a humanity come of age, to accept this new world without reserve, to come to grips with its questions right in the middle of the field of battle, instead of heading rabbitlike for the bushes or the shadow of a massive old wall, to reason upon the faith without any nostalgia for what is no more...."[34] At the same time, Gutiérrez thinks that Bonhoeffer did not pay adequate attention to the situation of "the writhing mass of the poor and the despoiled" in the modern world.[35] He was not sensitive enough to the injustice upon which modern society has been built; he was too accepting of the modern world. Gutiérrez does, however, take note of a passage in an earlier letter in which Bonhoeffer speaks of the "incomparable value" of learning "to see the great events of the history of the world from beneath: from the viewpoint of the useless, the suspect, the abused, the powerless, the oppressed, the despised—in a word, from the viewpoint of those who suffer."[36] Gutiérrez proposes that Bonhoeffer's insight into the significance of seeing the world "from beneath" represents an advance in his thinking. Though this idea is not fully developed in his theology, it is reflected in some later writings in which he "became more sensitive to the concrete, material things of human life: health, good fortune, and so on—the very things often missing from or denied to the fringes of modern society."[37]

In his dialogue with Bonhoeffer, as well as his interaction with European political theology represented by J. B. Metz and Jürgen

Moltmann, Gutiérrez argues that Latin American theologians have a different starting point from European theologians.[38] He acknowledges that the dialogue that has taken place between European political theology and Latin American liberation theology has been fruitful in some respects. But he thinks that the central concern of political and most forms of European theology has been dialogue with the nonbeliever who lives in an increasingly secularized world. The starting point of liberation theology is not the nonbeliever but the "nonperson"—the poor, marginalized person whose dignity is not respected: "Our question is how to tell the nonperson, the nonhuman, that God is love, and that this love makes us all brothers and sisters."[39]

Gutiérrez's reflections on the third theological meaning of poverty—solidarity with the poor—are extensive and profound. The person whom he holds up as a model of solidarity with the poor is Bartolomé de Las Casas, the sixteenth-century Dominican friar and bishop who stridently opposed the treatment of indigenous peoples in the Americas by the Spanish conquistadors.[40] The conquest and enslavement of indigenous peoples was justified by a theology that claimed that they were an inferior race of people and by the missionary mandate to convert them to the gospel. Las Casas refuted this theology, affirming the human dignity of the native peoples and teaching that the missionary endeavor required the promotion of social justice. Moreover, Las Casas claimed that the salvation of the Christian conquerors was jeopardized by their mistreatment of the indigenous peoples.[41] He perceived the face of the suffering Christ in these oppressed people, speaking of "Jesus Christ, our God, scourged and afflicted and crucified, not once, but millions of times."[42] Gutiérrez argues that Las Casas was able to arrive at such insights because his theology was rooted in concrete practice, in real commitment to the struggles of the native peoples. "Bartolomé de Las Casas was a man of action. His theological work is but an element of this action of his—part of his commitment to and involvement with the Indians."[43] In defiance of those in power, Las Casas practiced solidarity with the poor and oppressed of his day. He claimed that "God has a very fresh and living memory of the smallest and most forgotten."[44]

Gutiérrez insists that every Christian is called to practice this third form of poverty—solidarity with the poor. This dimension of the Christian vocation has now attained official status in the church's teaching about the preferential option for the poor. This doctrine, present in germ in the documents of Medellín, formulated explicitly at Puebla in 1979,[45] and repeated often in talks given by Pope John Paul II, is for Gutiérrez the greatest contribution of Latin America to the world church.[46] He contends that the term *poverty* refers to the materially poor—the person "who is treated as a nonperson, someone who is considered insignificant from an economic, political and cultural point of view."[47] The term *preferential* is employed because the love of God has two dimensions, the universal and the particular. God loves every person without exception; no one exists outside the realm of the Creator's love. At the same time, "God demonstrates a special predilection toward those who have been excluded from the banquet of life."[48] Their suffering elicits the particular concern of the Creator. Gutiérrez notes that the term *option* has a weaker sense in English than it does in Spanish, in which it denotes commitment: "The option for the poor is not optional, but is incumbent upon every Christian."[49] This option for the poor entails standing in solidarity with the poor and working against the causes of poverty.

In a more recent essay, Gutiérrez reflects on the reaffirmation of the teaching about the preferential option for the poor at the 2008 CELAM meeting in Aparecida, Brazil.[50] In an address to the bishops at the conference, Pope Benedict XVI said, "The preferential option for the poor is implicit in the Christological faith in the God who became poor for us, so as to enrich us with his poverty (2 Cor 8:9)."[51] Gutiérrez argues that the preferential option for the poor is deployed in three areas: the following of Jesus, theological work, and the proclamation of the gospel. First, commitment to the poor is an essential component of discipleship rooted in belief in the God of life. Gutiérrez quotes from a homily given by Archbishop Oscar Romero in 1978: "There is a criterion for knowing whether God is close to us or far away: all those who worry about the hungry, the naked, the poor, the disappeared, the tortured, the imprisoned—about any suffering human being—are close to God."[52] Second, the preferential option for the poor is significant for theological work because it roots theology in the concrete realities of history: "theology is a reflection that tries to accompany a people in their sufferings and joys, their commitments, frustrations, and hopes, both in becoming aware of the social universe in which they live and in their determination to understand better their own cultural tradition."[53] Third, the preferential option for the poor is essential for the proclamation of the gospel because there is a connection between justice and God's gratuitous love. Repeating a theme that he develops in other writings,[54] Gutiérrez argues that the kingdom of God proclaimed by Jesus is both gift and demand. The reign of God's love must be accepted as a free gift, but it also makes demands upon believers, especially "the recognition of the full human dignity of the poor and their situation as daughters and sons of God."[55] For Gutiérrez the primary Christian response to the suffering of the poor is clearly an active solidarity that includes accompaniment of the people and struggle against the causes of suffering.

Jesus Reveals the God of Life

For Gutiérrez the foundation of the Christian call to solidarity with the poor is belief in Jesus as the Christ and the Word made flesh:[56] "The great hermeneutical principle of the faith, and hence the basis and foundation for all theological reasoning, is Jesus Christ. In Jesus we encounter God. In the human Word we read the word of the Lord."[57] Close attention to the person and saving work of Jesus permeates all of Gutiérrez's writings, particularly those in which he treats the mystery of suffering.

Though most liberation Christologies take as their starting point the ministry of Jesus of Nazareth (they are "christologies from below"),[58] Gutiérrez combines reflection on the mystery of the incarnation with meditation on the historical Jesus: "Jesus Christ is precisely *God become poor*."[59] Jesus was born into lowliness, born of Mary among a people who at the time were dominated by the greatest empire of the age. In a striking passage, Gutiérrez describes the incarnation as "an incarnation into littleness and service in the midst of the overbearing power exercised by the mighty of this world; an irruption that smells of the stable."[60] The lowliness of the incarnation is further demonstrated in the fact that Jesus lived in Galilee—a region in Israel far from the center of religious and political power. "Thus Jesus, a Galilean (Nazareth was in Galilee), proclaims his message in a place that was unimportant and marginal. It is from among the poor and despised that the message comes of the universal love that the God of Jesus Christ has for humankind."[61]

Gutiérrez's exposition of the ministry of Jesus bears similarities to that of Schillebeeckx. He emphasizes Jesus' identification with the least members of society and his disclosure to them of "the God of life." Because for the people of Israel life meant communion, one way in which Jesus bestowed life was by bringing men and women—especially marginalized men and women—into communion with God and with one another. This is evident particularly in his table fellowship with those considered undesirable. Jesus' message and his manner of life turn the reigning order upside down.[62] Gutiérrez likes to speak of this reversal as the "messianic inversion," summarized in Jesus' teaching that the last shall be first.[63] In his ministry Jesus manifests a new understanding of power as service rather than domination. Disciples are called to imitate Jesus by using their creativity and initiative for service to the least of the world, rather than for domination over others.

Gutiérrez's treatment of Jesus' proclamation of the kingdom of God is nuanced, reflecting careful consideration in light of a variety of critiques of liberation theology. Arguing against an exclusively interiorized view of the kingdom, Gutiérrez describes it as "something planned by God that occurs at the heart of a history in which human beings live and die and welcome or reject the grace that changes them from within."[64] It is a reign of love and justice that is God's plan for human history. As we have seen, Gutiérrez proffers a dialectical understanding of the kingdom as entailing gift and demand, universality and preference. The kingdom that Jesus preaches is pure gift because it is the result of God's unmerited love for all human beings. At the same time, Jesus' proclamation of the kingdom includes a call to repentance, which means accepting the demands of the reign of God. Gutiérrez emphasizes that nothing makes more demands upon us than the experience of gracious, lavish love. This is precisely what happens in the lives of those who encounter God in Jesus. "Only when the gratuitousness of this love has been grasped is it possible to understand the imperious demands for works in behalf of the neighbor."[65] Acceptance of the kingdom requires believers to pay special attention to the suffering of the poor. It means "refusing to accept a world that instigates or tolerates the premature and unjust deaths of the poor."[66]

Gutiérrez is convinced that the dual dimensions of universality and preference must also be held in tension if we are to grasp the meaning of Jesus' proclamation of the kingdom of God. The kingdom of God is universal; no one is excluded from either the gift or the demand of the kingdom. Paul was the preeminent messenger of the universality of God's reign, grounding his proclamation of the gospel to all nations in the resurrection of Christ. The resurrection is "an affirmation and promise of life for all human beings without exception."[67] At the same time, Jesus' proclamation of the reign of God is characterized by preference for the least of the world. Gutiérrez adduces a host of Gospel texts and themes in making this argument, including Luke's account of Jesus' inaugural proclamation in the Nazareth synagogue, the stories of Jesus' encounters with tax collectors and prostitutes, the beatitudes in Matthew and Luke, and the Magnificat in Luke's Gospel. He thinks that the Gospel accounts of Jesus' ministry make it clear that the despised of this world are those whom God prefers. This preference is not dependent upon the moral character of the poor; it is simply the result of God's gratuitous love for men and women who are most in need. Gutiérrez often quotes a statement from Puebla that pertains to this preferential option: "The poor merit preferential attention, whatever may be the moral or personal situation in which they find themselves."[68]

Gutiérrez agrees with Schillebeeckx's contention that the cross of Jesus should never be isolated and considered apart from his public ministry. Jesus' death, he maintains, is the result of his fidelity to his mission of proclaiming the life-giving reign of God. "Jesus' death is the consequence of his struggle for justice, his proclamation of the kingdom, and his identification with the poor."[69] In *The God of Life*, he adduces the Johannine account of the meeting of the Sanhedrin after the raising of Lazarus (John 11:45–53). This Gospel story shows that "the powerful men among his people are alarmed by the success of Jesus' preaching; they see it challenging their interests, which they have grown accustomed (we know of similar cases today!) to identifying with the interests of the people as a whole."[70] The words of Caiaphas—"It is better for you to have one man die for the people than to have the whole nation destroyed"—demonstrate that Jesus' death "will permit the situation to continue as before; the powerful will again be able to breathe easy."[71] Those in power fear that Jesus' message and ministry will disturb the order of their world and jeopardize the privileges they enjoy, so they conspire to be rid of him.

Gutiérrez addresses Jesus' cry from the cross at the very end of his book *On Job*.[72] He relates the prayer of Jesus in his passion to Job's laments. In this brief but complex discussion, he argues that the attribution of the opening line of Psalm 22 to the dying Jesus suggests an experience that included both abandonment and communion. These words "speak of the suffering and loneliness of one who feels abandoned by the hand of God."[73] By making the psalm his own, Jesus "offered to the Father the suffering and abandonment of all humankind."[74] His communion with the suffering of human beings "brought him down to the deepest level of history at the very moment when his life was ending."[75] This was truly an experience of sinking into the depths. At the same time, Gutiérrez proposes, the psalm taken as a whole also reflects Jesus' abiding communion with the Father: "He who has been 'abandoned' abandons himself in turn into the hands of the Father."[76] The message of the cross is one of "communion in suffering and in hope, in the abandonment of loneliness and in trusting self-surrender in death as in life."[77] Gutiérrez also argues that the cry of Jesus from the cross should awaken Christians to the suffering of all innocent people. "To adopt a comparison that Bonhoeffer uses in another context, the cry of Jesus is the *cantus firmus*, the leading voice to which all the voices of those who suffer unjustly are joined."[78] For Gutiérrez, then, in his suffering on the cross Jesus is in the most profound solidarity with all the poor of history and, in that moment, he entrusts his life and mission to the Father.

The Father's raising of Jesus from the dead is the signature act of the God of life. In Gutiérrez's doctoral defense at Lyons, one of the examiners expressed his opinion that the "point of reference" in Gutiérrez's theology had moved from the exodus (a salient theme in liberation theology) to Easter, and that "the main axis" of his thought had become the victory of life over death.[79] Gutiérrez replied in fundamental agreement with his interlocutor, noting that the question of life and death had become increasingly significant for all liberation theologians. As he put it, the theology of liberation "is, in a sense, a theology of life confronted with a reality full of death: physical and cultural death, but also death in the Pauline sense, since sin is also death."[80] Gutiérrez suggested that there had been an evolution in liberation theology that was making it "increasingly a theology of life, of resurrection."[81]

The resurrection of Jesus is both confirmation and correction in the theology of Gutiérrez. It is the confirmation of Jesus' mission: through it the Father confirms the gift of life that was offered in Jesus' life and ministry, especially in his proclamation of the kingdom of God. It is also correction because it is "the death of death."[82] The resurrection of Jesus is the sign of God's liberation breaking into this world; it reveals that the God of life is more powerful than the forces of sin and injustice. Gutiérrez emphasizes that Christians are called to bear witness to the resurrection through their commitment to their sisters and brothers, particularly by their preferential option for the poor: "The God in whom we believe is the God of life. Belief in the resurrection entails defending the life of the weakest members of society. Looking for the Lord among the living [see Luke 24:5] leads to commitment to those who see their right to life constantly violated. To assert the resurrection of the Lord is to assert life in the face of death."[83]

Gutiérrez's account of the saving work of Christ centers on the theme of *liberation*. His view of liberation was deeply influenced by the concept of "integral liberation" articulated by Pope Paul VI in his encyclical *Populorum Progressio*.[84] In *A Theology of Liberation*, Gutiérrez formulated a three-level framework of liberation that he has consistently applied in his theology and that also influenced the statements of the Latin American bishops.[85] These three levels must always be held together, though they are distinct in nature. First, Gutiérrez proposes the level of social and political liberation: the creation of a just socio-economic and political order. This dimension of liberation has to do with freeing the poor from oppression. Second, he speaks of what might be called the "psychosocial" level of liberation, described by Gutiérrez as the human person assuming conscious responsibility for his or her own destiny. For those who selfishly promote their own interests, this aspect of liberation means a movement away from excessive self-concern to concern for others. For people who have been crushed by oppressive conditions, it entails liberation from the lack of a sense of self to self-possession and creative initiative.[86] Third, Gutiérrez delineates the level of liberation from sin. This is the most profound dimension of liberation: "Christ the Savior liberates man from sin, which is the ultimate root of all disruption of friendship and of all injustice and oppression."[87] Liberation on this level includes profound communion with Christ. Gutiérrez argues that the three levels of liberation that he has sketched entail "a single, complex process, which finds its deepest sense and its full realization in the saving work of Christ."[88]

In this liberation framework, soteriology relates closely to eschatology. This has been a sensitive topic for liberation theology, one to which Gutiérrez has tried to be attentive. He does not want his view of the liberating work of Christ to be understood as a temporal or a political messianism, but neither does he wish to espouse a spiritual-ized notion of salvation that limits it to an interior state of being or the gift of eternal life. He insists that salvation history and human history are not two separate spheres of history. "Rather, there is only one human destiny, irreversibly assumed by Christ, the Lord of history."[89] Appealing to the Gospel testimony about the ways in which Jesus made the kingdom of God present in his ministry, Gutiérrez argues that to work to transform the world is a salvific work. To struggle against misery and exploitation and to work to build a more just society is already part of the salvific work of Christ that is moving toward its complete fulfillment. While the liberating work of Christ transcends

anything that human beings can accomplish, actions on behalf of justice are integral to this liberation. He articulates his position on soteriology and eschatology in a nuanced way in a passage that talks about
"the growth of the kingdom":

> The growth of the kingdom is a process which occurs histor-
> ically in liberation, insofar as liberation means a greater ful-
> fillment of man. Liberation is a precondition for the new
> society, but this is not all it is. While liberation is imple-
> mented in liberating historical events, it also denounces their
> limitations and ambiguities, proclaims their fulfillment, and
> impels them effectively towards total communion. This is
> not an identification. Without liberating historical events,
> there would be no growth of the kingdom. But the process
> of liberation will not have conquered the very roots of
> oppression and the exploitation of man by man without the
> coming of the kingdom, which is above all a gift. Moreover,
> we can say that the historical, political liberating event *is* the
> growth of the kingdom and *is* a salvific event; but it is not *the*
> coming of the kingdom, not *all* of salvation.[90]

Gutiérrez's Interpretation of the Book of Job

In his introduction to the theology of Gutiérrez, James Nickoloff
comments on the significance of the Book of Job for his theology: "No
book of the Bible has received more attention from Gutiérrez as he has
wrestled with the agonizing problem of how to affirm the gratuitous
love of God at the origin of all things, the central theme of biblical revelation, in the face of the suffering of the innocent."[91] Readers of
Gutiérrez's works discover references to Job scattered throughout his
writings. In his *America* interview, Gutiérrez reflects on what he learned
about the virtue of hope from the parishioners to whom he ministered
in a poor section of Lima. It was the experience of discovering an
enduring sense of hope among the poor, he said, that led him to write
a book about Job.[92]

The full title of Gutiérrez's thought-provoking reflection on Job is *On Job: God-Talk and the Suffering of the Innocent*. The subtitle bears particular significance. He thinks that the central focus of this biblical story is not simply suffering in itself; it is the question of how one should talk about God in the face of innocent suffering in the world. This biblical book is all about "God-talk."[93] What kind of language should suffering people use in talking to God and about God? Gutiérrez argues that if people in situations of suffering are able to enter into an authentic relationship with God and find a correct way of speaking about God, then it will be possible for others who are not in such a predicament to do the same.[94]

In our selective survey of interpretations of Job in chapter 1 of this book, we saw that Susan Mathews highlighted the question posed by the satan to God: "Does Job fear God for nothing (*hinnam*)?" (Job 1:9). Mathews suggests that the salient issue in the book is whether or not Job clings to God with a faith founded on serving God, not out of self-interest but "for nothing." Gutiérrez also features this question in his interpretation of the book, asserting that the wager between God and the satan pertains to the disinterestedness of Job's service of God. He articulates the central question of the story as "the role that reward or disinterestedness plays in faith in God and in its consistent implementation."[95] Can there be a faith in God that is not self-serving, that believes in and serves God without expectation of a reward? Gutiérrez interprets the story as affirming that Job eventually matures into such a faith through the experience of his suffering and, especially, through his personal encounter with God.

A hermeneutical principle is at work in Gutiérrez's interpretation of Job. Gutiérrez perceives development in Job's outlook and understanding as the story proceeds: "A progress and maturation is observable in the book as a whole."[96] The book is not a compilation of cycles of speeches that are simply repetitious. "On the contrary there are important advances and changes of tone in the several rounds of speeches and as the various personages of the story make their appearance."[97] Deepening insight into the mystery of God and of suffering can be discerned, particularly on the part of the figure of Job.

After the introductory section, Gutiérrez explores what he calls the "language of prophecy." This is one of the two essential languages that he believes must be integrated for appropriate discourse about God in the face of innocent suffering. The category of prophecy is, of course, central to Gutiérrez's theology and to liberation theology as a whole. Liberation theology usually understands itself as an heir to the legacy of the biblical prophets and in its Christology it often highlights the theme of Jesus as the rejected prophet. And the prophetic vocation of denunciation and annunciation—denouncing injustice and announcing the reign of God—is at the heart of its understanding of the mission of the church.

For Gutiérrez one dimension of the language of prophecy is lament—the forthright crying out to God engaged in by the person who is suffering. He interprets the Book of Job as a witness to the importance of lament, even of protest, as a form of prayer. This biblical book confirms the truth that we saw in our exploration of the psalms of lament as well as in the personal witness of Elie Wiesel. Gutiérrez emphasizes that Job's cries of complaint, even his cursing of the day he was born, do not represent a rejection of God. Rather, they manifest, even if in an unconventional form, a profound act of self-surrender and hope in God.[98] The poor of this world can resonate with the searing laments of Job, as they attempt to speak to and about God in the midst of misery and oppression. Gutiérrez accentuates the fact that God never accuses Job of blasphemy for his utterance of such heartfelt and bold complaints.

The contrast between Job's arguments and the exhortations of his friends based on the logic of temporal retribution reveals two distinct types of theological reasoning. Job's friends begin with a set of doctrinal principles that they then apply to Job's case. Job, on the other hand, begins with his experience—the experience of profound suffering that for him is inexplicable. Gutiérrez argues that the theology of Job's friends lacks a sense of the mystery of God.[99] "The self-sufficient talk of these men is the real blasphemy: their words veil and disfigure the face of a God who loves freely and gratuitously. The friends believe in their theology rather than in the God of their theology."[100] The lamentation of Job is grounded in his personal experience and is, according to Gutiérrez, an appropriate way of speaking in the face of innocent suffering. It is one dimension of the language of prophecy.

Gutiérrez then introduces another aspect of prophetic discourse: Job's identification with the situation of the poor. This is where he believes that Job makes an initial advance in insight about God and suffering. Job begins to realize that he is not the only person who is suffering. "The poor of this world are in the same boat as he: instead of living, they die by the roadside, deprived of the land that was meant to support them."[101] Gutiérrez cites Job 24:2–14 as a classic text that expresses Job's new vantage point and eloquently depicts the oppression experienced by the poor. This passage ends with the chilling statement, "The murderer rises at dusk / to kill the poor and needy, / and in the night is like a thief" (Job 24:14). Gutiérrez asserts that the broadening of Job's perspective to include the sufferings and injustices experienced by the poor helps Job to develop the rudiments of a new way of talking about God.[102] From this point on in the story Job focuses less on his own individual suffering and more on the suffering that afflicts a multitude of people, especially the poor. "Now that he is sharing the lot of the poor in his own flesh, his talk of God becomes more profound and truthful. The point is that commitment to the poor provides firm ground for prophetic talk of God."[103] Here Gutiérrez adopts a position somewhat different from that of Elie Wiesel. In his essay on Job, Wiesel claimed that a person's awareness that he or she is not the only one who is suffering does nothing to alleviate the pain; rather, it only compounds the suffering. Gutiérrez maintains that, while Job's identification with the poor does not remove his own suffering, it does enable him to acquire deepened insight into mystery and it frees him from excessive self-preoccupation.

Thus, the first form of discourse about God that is needed in the face of suffering is the language of prophecy, which for Gutiérrez embraces lament and protest as well as solidarity with the poor and crying out for justice. But the language of prophecy is not sufficient in and of itself. Contemplative discourse is also necessary, and he claims that Job is schooled in that language in the course of his wrestling with the experience of suffering. Gutiérrez chronicles a movement within Job from a desire for an arbiter (9:33), to the affirmation of the presence of a witness (16:19), and finally to the hope for a redeemer (19:25). In chapter 9, Job wants to initiate a lawsuit against God, though he realizes the futility of such an action because there is no arbiter who would make it possible for him to speak to God. Gutiérrez concludes, "It becomes increasingly clear as the debate progresses that this arbiter can only be God."[104] God is the one who will resolve the crisis in his life. After further complaints about his plight, Job moves from the desire for an arbiter to the need of a witness. Despite his intense suffering and sustained protest, Job says, "Even now, in fact, my witness is in heaven, / and he that vouches for me is on high" (16:19). Gutiérrez interprets this profession of Job as "an expression of confidence in a mysterious mediator, someone who will defend him in the suit he is carrying on with God...."[105] Though Job does not identify this witness, he affirms that there will be someone to testify to his innocence.

From his trust in the presence of a witness, Job continues to utter protest against his suffering but is also inspired to affirm the presence of a redeemer (go'el): "For I know that my Redeemer lives, and that at the last he will stand upon the earth; and after my skin has been thus destroyed, then in my flesh I shall see God, whom I shall see on my side, and my eyes shall behold and not another" (19:25–27). Gutiérrez describes this famous passage as "an act of faith that seems to lack any human basis"[106] and argues that when Job affirms the existence of a go'el, he is referring to God, not to an intermediary distinct from God.[107] He suggests that in this confession of faith Job adopts a dialectical approach that posits God as both judge and defender, enemy and friend. "He has just now accused God of persecuting him, but at the same time he knows that God is just and does not want human beings to suffer."[108]

From Gutiérrez's point of view, this progression from the desire for an arbiter, to affirmation of a witness, to confession of a redeemer represents a movement into deeper contemplation of God. He argues that these passages bespeak Job's growing realization that God's mercy is greater than God's justice or "that God's justice is to be understood only in the context of prior and gratuitous love."[109] This deepening insight into God includes an affirmation of God as the source of life. "The God who ('at the end') will not allow him to be destroyed in the world of injustice and loneliness is a living God. God's will that human beings should live is stronger than anything else and represents God's final word."[110]

Job's schooling in contemplative discourse reaches its high point in his encounter with God out of the whirlwind. Gutiérrez insists that it is not enough simply to point to the fact that Job is allowed to encounter God. One must also pay attention to the content of the divine speeches.[111] He proposes that the first speech (38:1—40:2) emphasizes the plan of God, while the second (40:7—41:34) discloses God's just government of the world. The salient insight that Job receives is that "God's plan has its origin in the gratuitousness of creative love."[112] God's revelation to Job of the creative divine power shows that the doctrine of retribution is not the key to understanding the universe. Rather, the reason for believing "for nothing" is the free and unmerited initiative of divine love. This is "the very hinge on which the world turns."[113] The pleasure and joy that God takes in creation reveals the gratuitousness of God's actions. Rain falls even on deserts, for no reason that is apparent to human beings (38:25–27). God's speeches are a vigorous rejection of a purely anthropocentric view of creation; not everything that exists was made to be directly useful to human beings. The world of nature expresses the freedom and delight of God in creating. Gutiérrez takes this insight a step further by proposing that the author of Job wants readers to conclude that what holds for the world of nature holds with all the greater reason for the world of history. He asks, "Must all that happens in history, including God's action, necessarily fit hand in glove with the theological categories that reason has developed?"[114] This means that, contrary to the theology of retribution espoused by the friends of Job, it is not possible to discover in detail the reasons for God's action. The divine speeches are a forceful reminder to Job of the incomprehensible character of God, which entails God's freedom and gratuitousness.

Gutiérrez's interpretation of Job 40:9–14 is intriguing, and it relates to references to the thought of Bonhoeffer that he makes in other writings. In this passage, God dares Job to "look on all who are proud, and bring them low" and to "tread down the wicked where they stand" (40:12). Gutiérrez interprets these statements to suggest that God is challenging Job to do something that even God cannot accomplish. God's power is limited by human freedom; not even God can bring low the proud and tread down the wicked, at least during the course of human history. In *The Power of the Poor in History*, Gutiérrez cited Bonhoeffer's assertion that the God of Jesus Christ is the weak God who saves us not through his domination but through his weakness. Gutiérrez seems to approve of Bonhoeffer's idea, calling it "a concept charged with force and power.[115]...God in Christ is a God of suffering, and to share in his weakness is to believe in him. This is what it means to be a Christian."[116] His interpretation of Job 40:9–14 reflects his earlier engagement with Bonhoeffer and is worth quoting in full:

> That the words [of this passage] are ironic is clear. But this time there is no mention of God's power or of God's delight in creation or of God's sense of humor. Rather the Lord is explaining, tenderly and, as it were, shyly, that the wicked cannot simply be destroyed with a glance. God wants justice indeed, and desires that divine judgment (*mishpat*) reign in the world; but God cannot impose it, for the nature of created beings must be respected. God's power is limited by human freedom; for without freedom God's justice would not be present within history. Furthermore, precisely because human beings are free, they have the power to change their course and be converted. The destruction of the wicked would put an end to that possibility. In other words, the all-powerful God is also a "weak" God. The mystery of divine freedom leads to the mystery of human freedom and to respect for it.[117]

Gutiérrez also proffers an evocative interpretation of the surrender of Job to God (42:1–6). He refers to Wiesel's imaginative suggestion that perhaps Job only pretended to surrender while maintaining his personal integrity by continuing to protest to God. Gutiérrez says, "I disagree with his interpretation but I find it very captivating."[118]

Gutiérrez perceives three dimensions to Job's final surrender: an acknowledgment that God has plans and that these are being carried out; a discovery of previously unrecognized aspects of reality; a joyous encounter with the Lord.[119] These insights impel Job to abandon his attitude of complaint and sadness. In arguing this last point, Gutiérrez is dependent on a translation of 42:6 (Job's repentance) by Dale Patrick.[120] The NRSV version reads, "Therefore I despise myself / and repent in dust and ashes." Patrick's translation, however, interprets the word for "repent" (*niham* used with the preposition *'al*) to mean "to change one's mind." Thus, Gutiérrez argues that the text actually has Job saying, "I repudiate and abandon (change my mind about) dust and ashes."[121] He contends that Job's final reply expresses not contrition but *"a renunciation of his lamentation and dejected outlook."*[122] Gutiérrez thinks that this response represents a high point in contemplative speech about God. Job is surrendering to God with a renewed sense of trust and joy; he is putting aside his sackcloth and ashes. This surrender reveals that Job now believes in God in a disinterested way.

For Gutiérrez, the author of the Book of Job wanted to find an appropriate language about God that would do justice to the situation of suffering. This biblical writer did not intend to provide a rational explanation for suffering but a way of talking about God that takes the reality of innocent suffering into account. The story of Job reveals the necessity for an integration of prophetic and contemplative discourse if one is to speak correctly about God in the face of innocent suffering. Justice alone is not the final word on how we are to talk about God; it must be situated within the framework of God's gracious love. Gutiérrez finds a link between these two forms of discourse, since God's special love for the poor and oppressed is grounded in God's gratuitous love. It is not dependent upon the moral or religious virtue of the poor. "Prophetic language makes it possible to draw near to a God who has a predilection for the poor precisely because divine love refuses to be confined by the categories of human justice."[123]

Gutiérrez emphasizes that each form of discourse that he has identified is incomplete without the other. "Mystical [contemplative] language expresses the gratuitousness of God's love; prophetic language expresses the demands this love makes....Both languages are necessary and therefore inseparable; they also feed and correct each other."[124] Gutiérrez's personal experience of commitment to justice on behalf of the poor seems to have convinced him that without the contemplative dimension of the Christian life such commitment tends to lose its way and to suffer exhaustion.[125] In reading the works of Gutiérrez, one discovers that he accentuates this conviction with greater force as the years go on. In the introduction to *On Job*, he likens encounter with the Lord to the experience of human love. At times this encounter reaches ineffable depths: "When words do not suffice, when they are incapable of communicating what is experienced at the affective level, then we are fully engaged in loving."[126] Gutiérrez argues that the twofold language of the prophetic and the contemplative was the language of Jesus, even on the cross. His crying out to God from the depths of suffering was emblematic of prophetic discourse; his surrender of his life to the Father in enduring trust was the ultimate expression of contemplative language. Followers of Jesus are also invited to integrate these two languages into their lives of discipleship, particularly as they grapple with the mystery of suffering.

Conclusion

As articulated so eloquently by Desmond Tutu, the liberation theology that Gutiérrez was instrumental in initiating has its starting point in suffering: the misery of the economically poor and other marginalized peoples. Gutiérrez's sensitivity to the plight of the poor is extraordinary, and his articulation of the ways in which poverty and oppression drain the life out of people is compelling. Few theologians have succeeded in awakening the consciousness of believers and theologians to the suffering of the "nonpersons" of the world in the way that Gutiérrez has. He has put a face on the mystery of suffering and invited his readers to gaze on that face.

A careful reading of the works of Gutiérrez reveals development in his thought. His earlier works are replete with concepts and terminology drawn from Marxist theory. Sometimes these ideas and terms seem to be employed uncritically. For example, at times he seems to divide the human race into the oppressors and the oppressed. Such rhetoric is understandable given the dehumanizing deprivation he saw all around him, though it can strike the reader as simplistic. In his later writings, while he remains firmly committed to exposing the injustice of poverty, he more readily acknowledges its complexity.[127] He continues to consider the poverty endured by so many people in the world to be a sinful situation, though he is more careful about specifying blame for that situation.

Gutiérrez's creative and thought-provoking interpretation of the Book of Job reflects the insights of someone who has thought deeply about the meaning of this biblical work and the mystery of suffering that it addresses. As with every interpretation of Job, some aspects of Gutiérrez's reading of the story leave the reader with questions. For example, his elucidation of Job's deepening insight into the freedom and gratuitousness of God in history and the fact that God's actions do not fit into our theological categories certainly reflects an important truth. There is, however, a very fine line between affirming the freedom and gratuitousness of God's actions and leaving open the possibility that God is capricious in God's dealings with us. The reader of the Book of Job is bound to wonder how the inexplicable misery suffered by Job is related to the free and gracious action of God in his life. Gutiérrez begins to address this question, I believe, when he says that "God's will that human beings should live is stronger than anything else and represents God's final word."[128] But it seems that he needs to say more about the characteristic activity of the God of Jesus Christ, while still recognizing that all of our God-talk is inadequate to the mystery. He addresses these issues at greater length in his later book, *The God of Life*. In this work he makes it clear that the free and gracious action of God in history is always directed toward the promotion and preservation of life.

These critical comments notwithstanding, Gutiérrez's proposal of the necessity of two "languages"—the prophetic and the contemplative—for our talk about God in the face of innocent suffering represents a distinctive contribution to Christian theology and spirituality. This idea reveals his own attentive listening to the experience of the poor whom he has served in Latin America. It is well grounded in scripture and the church's theological tradition, and it resonates with pastoral experience. The back-and-forth movement between prophetic and contemplative discourse—crying out and gazing in silent reverence—seems to mark the experience of many people of faith who wrestle with their own suffering or the suffering of those they love. Gutiérrez's emphasis on the need to integrate these two forms of discourse rings true to experience. I return to this proposal in my discussion in the final chapter of this book.

Discussion Questions: www.paulistpress.com, Online Resources.

10
Elizabeth Johnson: Suffering and Hope from a Feminist Perspective

Elizabeth Johnson is the foremost Catholic feminist theologian in the United States. Her reputation spread widely after the publication in 1992 of *She Who Is: The Mystery of God in Feminist Theological Discourse.*[1] In this book Johnson constructed a systematic theology of God grounded in the Judeo-Christian tradition but articulated in feminine symbolism. She discusses the mystery of God and suffering in an important chapter of this foundational work. She also addresses this theme in her subsequent books on Mary and the saints and in a later work that surveys a variety of approaches to the theology of God.[2]

Johnson has listened carefully to the theological conversation about God and suffering that we have explored in this study.[3] She incorporates insights from a number of perspectives in an attempt to offer an intelligible approach from a feminist viewpoint. Johnson has paid close attention to chronicles of suffering and protest from the Shoah, like those of Elie Wiesel and Dietrich Bonhoeffer. She would agree that this cataclysmic event represents a kind of watershed in the history of theology: "Taking the measure of the Shoah, one simply could not go on as before crafting interpretations that would allow this magnitude of suffering to make some kind of sense in God's plan for the world."[4] Adopting a basically Thomistic orientation in her theology, she builds on key principles from the theology of Aquinas, as well as insights from modern Thomists like William Hill and W. Norris Clarke. She draws on the thought of Edward Schillebeeckx, particularly his description of the public ministry of Jesus and the way in which he tells the story of Calvary. She reads the work of Jürgen Moltmann critically, but she also finds elements of his theology of the crucified God to be compelling. She has been inspired by Gustavo Gutiérrez's reflections on the Book of Job as well as by the writings of other liberation theologians who lift up the suffering of the poor throughout the world and theologize from the "underside" of history. And Johnson has been schooled by the contribution of a rich variety of feminist theologians from diverse social locations, including Dorothee Sölle, Rosemary Radford Ruether, and Wendy Farley.[5] Johnson's theology integrates the best insights of these and other thinkers into an illuminating way of speaking about the mystery of God in a world that is deeply scarred by suffering.

Constructing a Catholic Feminist Theology

While Johnson is concerned about the suffering of all human beings—indeed the suffering of all creatures—she explores in a particular way the suffering of women past and present. She is convinced that the sexism that pervades human history and the contemporary world has had pernicious effects on the well-being of women. This sexism expresses itself in personal attitudes and social structures. *Androcentrism* names the attitude that men are inherently superior to women and so act as a norm for society in ways that women do not. *Patriarchy* refers to the system of social structures that is both the result of this androcentric perspective and a factor in perpetuating it. These structures are envisioned as permeating society and church in ways that are so deeply established and ingrained that most do people not even recognize their existence or effects. In the view of Johnson and other feminist thinkers, the feeling that there is something natural about men being in positions of authority is an expression of the pervasive character of both androcentrism and patriarchy. All of this generates a diminished respect for the full humanity of women, their dignity as children of God. Like the liberationist theology of Gutiérrez, Johnson's feminist theology is theology with an interest. It is at the service of the freeing of women from systemic oppression and helping them to recognize their full dignity as women in society and the church.

Johnson portrays the deep and multifaceted suffering of women in history in a number of places in her works. In her chapter on the mystery of suffering in *She Who Is*, she mentions the trial and execution of women accused of witchcraft by the Inquisition:[6] "For reasons that had much to do with the threatened patriarchal dominance of spiritual and healing power, hundreds of thousands, perhaps more than a million women were annihilated in the name of God."[7] Johnson also connects the plight of women past and present with the sufferings and hopes associated with Mary in the scriptures. She observes that many impoverished women in Latin America understand Mary as a poor woman like them: "a villager who lived her trust in God in the midst of hard daily labor, she knows their struggle and their pain."[8] In her discussion of the awkward and dangerous situation in which Mary was put because of her conception of Jesus by the Holy Spirit, Johnson asserts that this Gospel story "places Mary in solidarity with women who suffer violence or the threat of violence from patriarchal authority, affirming against all social consensus that God is with them."[9] And in her reflection on the Johannine scene of Mary at the foot of the cross (John 19:25–27), she maintains that "this scene conjures up all the anguish and desolation a woman could experience who had given birth to a child, loved that child, raised and taught that child, even tried to protect that child, only to have him executed in the worst imaginable way by the power of the state."[10] Johnson's theology does not simply treat the mystery of suffering as one topic among many that theologians must address. To a large extent, it emerges from the living memory of the suffering experienced by women throughout history, and it is committed to exposing and counteracting the causes of this suffering.

Johnson is convinced that one of the ways in which the theologian must confront sexism is to examine language used for the divine. Referring to God exclusively in male images and terminology, she argues, has at least three "pernicious effects."[11] First, because there are no alternatives, this language is taken literally. Johnson insists that no language about God provides a direct transcript of the divine. Thus, when masculine language about God is viewed as literally descriptive of the divine, it leads to a form of idolatry. Second, "the exclusive use of patriarchal language for God also has powerful social effects."[12] It legitimizes male dominance in society and the church. Third, such constricted naming of the divine implies that women are less like God than are men. Though Christianity affirms that both men and women are created in the image and likeness of God, Johnson is convinced that the exclusive use of masculine terms and images for God subtly promotes the idea that God is reflected more luminously by men than by women.

Johnson argues, then, that masculine and feminine terms and images for the divine are of equal legitimacy, even though both are inadequate to the mystery of God, who is neither male nor female. Given that there has been an almost exclusive use of male terminology in Christian teaching and practice, she finds it essential to rectify this situation by developing language for God drawn from the experience of women. Rather than simply referring to feminine "traits" in God or to a feminine "dimension" of the divine (usually associated with the Holy Spirit), Johnson asserts that feminine images can refer to the whole of the divine mystery in ways that are just as adequate (and inadequate) as masculine images.[13] Such naming of God from the experience of women is, in her view, an act of empowerment for women and a source of healing from the effects of oppression. It also yields enriched insight into the mystery of God.

Johnson engages in feminist theology as one standing within the Catholic Christian tradition. While some feminist theologians reach outside of the Christian tradition to find building blocks for their theologies, Johnson remains rooted in this tradition, striving to give voice to what she feels is most liberating within it. Though she is convinced that the patriarchal bias of the Christian heritage must be deconstructed, her primary aim is constructive rather than deconstructive. She searches the tradition to retrieve insights and themes that are life giving for both women and men—elements that have often been suppressed in classical presentations of Christian theology. As she puts it, "The hope is to discover dormant theological themes and neglected history that will contribute to a future of full personhood for women."[14] Her approach "newly envisions Christian symbols and practices that would do justice to the full humanity of women as a key to a new whole."[15] Johnson's work is deeply rooted in the Christian tradition and reflective of Catholic sensibilities, and nowhere is this more evident than in her treatment of the mystery of God and the experience of human suffering.

Speech about the God Who Is Mystery

In our investigation of the thought of Aquinas on suffering, we explored his understanding of analogy. Aquinas thought that we can make true predications about God because of the relationship that creatures have to God, who is the source of their existence. The dynamic of analogy entails a threefold movement, or play of the mind: an attribution of a perfection to God that is drawn from creaturely experience; a negative movement whereby one negates the creaturely limitations inherent in our experience and understanding of this perfection; and a movement of transcendence in which we affirm that this perfection exists in God in an eminent manner, a way that exceeds our human comprehension. Despite all of the predications about God that Aquinas makes in his theology, his thought is imbued with a deep and enduring sense of the incomprehensibility of God. Even with the benefit of revelation, all of our knowledge of the divine is a knowing of the Unknown.

Johnson has studied the tradition of analogy in detail, and her familiarity with it profoundly influences her theology, especially when talking about God and the mystery of suffering. Early in her career, she explored the critique of analogy given by Wolfhart Pannenberg, the influential German Lutheran theologian.[16] While his thought on analogy has undergone development during the course of his theological career, in his early writings Pannenberg concluded that the way in which analogy was employed in theology resulted in an obscuring of the infinite qualitative difference between God and creatures. It also diminished the wonder of the incarnation, in which God who is nothing like us became like us in Jesus Christ. Pannenberg thought that both the transcendence of God and the freedom of God in revealing Godself to creatures were compromised by the dynamic of analogy, which is founded on the assumption of a common likeness between Creator and creature. In Johnson's words, Pannenberg believes that because of the way in which analogical predication about God operates, "we end up presiding over the reality of God in our concepts."[17] We lose a sense of the mystery of God and forget that God's ways are not our ways.

Johnson does not entirely agree with Pannenberg's critique of analogy. She believes that there are safeguards in this tradition that preserve an abiding awareness of divine transcendence and freedom, as found, for example, in the thought of Aquinas. She acknowledges, however, that critiques like that of Pannenberg have a salutary, chastening effect on Christian theology and spirituality. They caution us against thinking that we ever have God "figured out." Johnson often underlines the teaching about God's incomprehensibility in her writings. She says, for example, "No human concept, word, or image, all of which originate in experiences of created reality, can circumscribe the divine reality, nor can any human construct express with any measure of adequacy the mystery of God, who is ineffable."[18] She appeals to a well-known essay of Karl Rahner in which Rahner argues that for the contemporary person this teaching about divine incomprehensibility is more than an idea; it reflects the way in which many people actually experience God today:[19] "The indifference of secular culture coupled with the ambiguity of history creates an ambience in which even for believers the experience of divine absence is often characteristic of faith itself."[20] And Johnson remarks that the experience of suffering "adds a sharper edge to this doctrine of divine hiddenness."[21] Amidst the scourge of suffering that continues to afflict human history, "only lament and the courage of hope against hope enable the community to continue walking by divine light, inextricably darkened by the power of evil."[22] As with the thought of Aquinas, it is important to take note of Johnson's emphasis on the incomprehensibility of God when exploring her treatment of human suffering.

How, then, does Johnson understand analogical predications about the divine? Building on Aquinas, she affirms that our knowledge and speech about God are grounded in the reality of creaturely participation in the being of God—what she likes to call the "awesome concept of participation."[23] Creatures have being (*esse*) insofar as they participate in the being of God, who is being-itself—the very wellspring of being. "The mystery of God is the livingness of being who freely shares being while creatures participate."[24] This participation in being is a gift from the Creator, an abiding gift that entails an enduring presence of God to every creature but also implies a certain autonomy for the creature. Johnson appreciates the metaphor of fire that is often employed by Aquinas: fire is the cause of everything that is on fire. God is like the fire of being who "lights up" creation with the gift of being. She affirms that "the whole world exists by being lit with the fire of being itself, which people call God."[25] Because of this gift of being there is a connection between creatures and God that enables us to know and relate to God.

In her treatment of analogy, Johnson underlines the significance of the negative moment in the dynamic of speaking about God. Even when attributing the most sublime perfections to God (for example, love), we must acknowledge the limited manner in which we experience, know, and name these perfections. She speaks of a "movement through negation toward mystery, and consequently the nonliteral although still meaningful character of [its] speech about God."[26] She sides with that part of the Thomistic tradition that focuses on the judgment, rather than the concept, in analogical predication about God. God is not contained in any concept. Rather, the knowledge of God attained through analogy is accomplished "in a judgment of the human spirit that affirms God to be inconceivable while at the same time intuiting that the perspective opened up by the intelligible contents of a concept gives a view of God that is trustworthy."[27] In this process, "God is darkly surmised while remaining in essence conceptually inapprehensible."[28] Johnson's reading of the tradition of analogy accentuates the humility that should characterize all discourse about God. She believes that the modesty with which we should approach our naming of God is all the more necessary when we are dealing with the mystery of suffering.

Because God is infinitely greater than even our richest concept or name, we need to use many names to speak of God. We have already seen that Johnson insists that the inclusion of language about God drawn from women's experience is one antidote to what she considers to be the impoverishment and even idolatry that results from the exclusive use of masculine language for God. One of the theologically under-employed names for the divine found in the Bible is that of Wisdom, *Sophia* in Greek. Prominent especially in the wisdom literature of the Hebrew scriptures, Sophia is a feminine image for the divine (for example, Wis 7:22—8:1). In an early essay, Johnson argues that the figure of Wisdom in the Hebrew scriptures represents a personification of God's own self in creative and saving involvement with the world. "The wisdom literature celebrates God's gracious goodness in creating the world and in electing and saving Israel, and does so in imagery which presents the divine presence in the woman's *Gestalt* of divine Sophia."[29] Christians tapped into this wisdom tradition in order to speak of Jesus' ontological relationship with God, as expressed in New Testament hymns like John 1:1–18 and Colossians 1:15–20. This leads Johnson to speak of the God-Jesus relationship in terms of Sophia-God and her child, and of Jesus as Sophia-incarnate. Her reference to God as Holy Wisdom represents an attempt to expand the names for God and to do so from the experience of women, all the while emphasizing that every name is limited in what it discloses about the divine.

Jesus and the Character of Divine Love

Theology of the Incarnation

Feminist Christology, like other forms of liberationist Christology, usually begins with concentration on the public ministry of Jesus. It starts "from below." The Christology of Elizabeth Johnson, however, like that of Gustavo Gutiérrez, integrates careful consideration of belief in the incarnation with attention to the ministry, death, and resurrection of Jesus. In Jesus, Holy Wisdom has become flesh, has self-emptied to participate in the beauty and the tragedy of human history. The incarnation discloses the salvific solidarity of God with all human beings, particularly with those who suffer the most. It entails "God's plunging into human history and transforming it from within."[30] Christian belief in the incarnation assumes that the transcendent God is "capable of personal union with what is not God, the flesh and spirit of humanity."[31] Divine transcendence and divine immanence are not contraries but correlatives, and divine immanence is expressed with greatest intensity when Holy Wisdom becomes flesh in Jesus.

Johnson emphasizes that the incarnation involves God's entering into union with *humanity* in order to offer life and effect salvation. While there is no dispute about the historical maleness of Jesus, she and other feminist theologians contend that the gender of Jesus has in itself no salvific significance. She makes this point to counter tendencies in the history of Christianity that infer a special normativity for men because of the maleness of Jesus or that suggest that the maleness of Jesus implies a male God. She cites the famous axiom of Gregory Nazianzen, adduced in the early church by those who fought to uphold the complete humanity of Jesus: "What is not assumed is not redeemed, but what is assumed is saved by union with God."[32] It is God's assumption of human nature, not the male gender, that makes possible the healing of a wounded humanity. She argues that the teaching of the christological councils of the early church makes it clear "that it is not Jesus' maleness that is doctrinally important but his humanity in solidarity with the whole suffering human race."[33] This principle of God's solidarity with a wounded, suffering humanity is central to Johnson's Christology and to her portrayal of the God who is disclosed in Jesus Christ.

In more recent writings, Johnson has connected the incarnation with ecological concerns, employing a phrase coined by Niels Gregersen, "deep incarnation."[34] She points out that the famous statement found in the prologue to the Gospel of John says that "the Word became flesh" (1:14). She argues that *sarx* (flesh) in this text "signifies what is material, perishable, fragile—in a word, finite, the opposite of divinity clothed with majesty."[35] In this critical statement the Gospel of John "affirms that the Word was uttered into earthiness, entered into the sphere of the material and mortal to shed light on all from within."[36] Therefore, Christian belief in the incarnation implies that in Jesus God became inextricably connected with the entire material creation. God's salvific intentions extend to the whole cosmos, not just to the human family. All of creation will share in the redemption accomplished by Christ. Those who believe in Christ, then, are summoned to active concern for the well-being of all creation.

The Public Ministry of Jesus

Johnson's account of the public ministry of Jesus bears affinities to the descriptions of Gutiérrez and Schillebeeckx, though she does not engage in detailed discussion of the Gospel narratives in the way that Schillebeeckx does. In a programmatic statement she depicts Jesus as "the prophet and child of Sophia sent to announce that God is the God of all-inclusive love who wills the wholeness and humanity of everyone, especially the poor and heavy-burdened. He is sent to gather all the outcast under the wings of their gracious Sophia-God and bring them to shalom."[37] The symbol of the reign of God, which was the focal point of Jesus' preaching, points to that state of affairs in which God's will is done on earth as it is in heaven. And the will of God "is nothing less than redemption, the end of sin and suffering and death, the flourishing of all creatures."[38] God's passion for the wholeness of creatures is evident in Jesus' healings and exorcisms, which lead not simply to spiritual healing but to the relief of bodily suffering. The "shalom" that Jesus offers means life for the whole person.

Johnson highlights the inclusivity of Jesus' table fellowship, whereby he reached out to bring those considered distant from God into communion with himself and with the God whom he addressed as "Abba." His table companions included women, who became Jesus' followers, faithful supporters, and first proclaimers of the resurrection. "Through his ministry Jesus unleashes a hope, a vision, and a present experience of liberating relationships that women, the lowest of the low in any class, as well as men, savor as the antithesis of patriarchy."[39]

Intrinsic to the salvation that Jesus offers, then, are new possibilities for relationship characterized not by domination but by friendship and mutuality. His way of relating was particularly life giving for women who, though traditionally marginalized, "interact with Jesus in mutual respect, support, comfort and challenge, themselves being empowered to acts of compassion, thanksgiving, and boldness by Spirit-Sophia who draws near in him."[40] His manner of relating to the powerful and the marginalized of his day is one reason that Jesus became a threat to the religious and civil leaders.

The Death of Jesus

Like others in the tradition of liberationist theology, Johnson interprets the death of Jesus as the result of his fidelity to the mission given to him by God. Despite intensifying opposition and increasing certainty of a violent death, Jesus remained faithful to this mission, even to embracing a death that included everything that makes death terrifying. "The friendship and inclusive care of Sophia are rejected as Jesus is violently executed, preeminent in the long line of Sophia's murdered prophets."[41] Johnson emphasizes this perspective on Jesus' death in contrast to soteriologies that envision it as payment for sin. Such transactional scenarios inevitably portray Jesus as a passive victim and, even worse, depict God as an exacting ruler who demands blood-payment for human wrongdoing. While these soteriologies are not devoid of meaning, they are "inseparable from an underlying image of God as an angry, bloodthirsty, violent and sadistic father, reflecting the very worst kind of male behavior."[42] She contends that the rejection and crucifixion of Jesus are contrary to the will of God. Like Schillebeeckx, Johnson argues that God did not put Jesus on the cross; human beings did that.

Johnson speaks of Jesus' death as including the experience of abandonment by God.[43] Like Moltmann, she comments on his cry of dereliction from the cross (Mark 15:34), describing it as "that unforgettable, anguished cry" that bespeaks the "spiritual agony" that Jesus endured.[44] Johnson wants to underline the fullness of Jesus' descent into the darkness and pain of death. At the same time, she asserts, the resurrection discloses that "the crucified one is not, in the end, abandoned."[45] Though Johnson is influenced by Moltmann's depiction of the depths of Jesus' suffering, she does not envision the crucifixion as the result of the Father handing over the Son to death and abandoning him on the cross. Such a portrayal might easily convey the image of a sadistic God.[46] In her interpretation of the saving death of Jesus, "soteriology shifts from the model of God as the perpetrator of the disaster of the cross to the model of God as participant in the pain of the world."[47] The crucified Jesus is not the victim whom God sacrifices on the cross but the very presence of God descending into the depths of human pain and suffering.

Jesus' death on the cross signifies and effects God's solidarity with suffering people of all times; indeed, it discloses God's solidarity with the entirety of creation, which groans in agony (see Rom 8:18–25). Johnson says, "The cross signifies that God, who is love, whose will stands in contrast to such misery, nevertheless freely plunges into the midst of the pain and tastes its bitterness to the bitter end in order to save."[48] The cross is a "parable" that effects this divine solidarity with suffering creatures: "The cross in all its dimensions, violence, suffering, love, is the parable that enacts Sophia-God's participation in the suffering of the world."[49] She maintains that divine solidarity is a powerful force; it engenders hope and empowers people to resist the forces of evil. The story of the cross is, in her words, a story of "heartbreaking empowerment."[50]

Resurrection

Like the Christology of Schillebeeckx and to some extent that of Gutiérrez, Johnson's account of the person and saving work of Jesus can be described as resurrection centered. The resurrection of Jesus is the supreme disclosure of the meaning of Jesus' life and death; the way that God acts in the world; the future of creation. She emphasizes that the resurrection of Jesus involves a transformation of his entire person that is unique and unimaginable from our vantage point. It is an action of Sophia-God through the power of the Spirit. "Her pure, beneficent, people-loving Spirit seals him in new unimaginable life as pledge of a future for all the violated and the dead."[51] This transformation in the

Spirit releases the presence of Jesus throughout the world.[52] Jesus' entire historical existence is redeemed and validated by the God in whom he trusted and to whom he was faithful to the end. The resurrection is, thus, the divine confirmation of Jesus' life, though it is also correction, since it reverses the judgment of Jesus' accusers. It shows that, despite the historical rejection of his ministry, "Jesus' compassionate, liberating words and deeds are the living sacrament of God reestablishing the right order of creation, according to the priority of saving divine compassion for everyone and especially for the last, the heavy-burdened, and those of no account."[53] In other words, God's raising of Jesus reveals that in his ministry Jesus did, in fact, authentically disclose the character of the living God, the true form of divine love. The resurrection also reveals that Jesus' death on the cross was "neither passive, useless, nor divinely ordained, but is linked to the ways of Sophia forging justice and peace in an antagonistic world."[54] God did not ordain Jesus' death; his crucifixion was contrary to God's intentions. But his death is not useless because he is active within it; his death is the supreme expression of his fidelity to his Abba-God and his resurrection is an act of God bringing life out of death.

The resurrection also reveals something of what God is like and how God acts in creation and human history. The raising of Jesus evinces God's fidelity to Jesus at his darkest hour; though he plunged into the depths of human suffering Jesus was not in fact abandoned by God. It also manifests God's deepest intentions vis-à-vis human suffering and death: "Thus is disclosed God at God's most typical: *hesed* and *emeth*, loving kindness and fidelity that says an ultimate 'yes' to life and 'no' to suffering, sin, and death."[55] And the raising of Jesus gives us clues into the ways in which God's *power* works in the world. The theme of divine power—important to feminist theologians, who criticize patriarchal construals of God's power—is a recurring topic in Johnson's writings. In an oft-quoted sentence, she says about the resurrection, "The victory of shalom is won not by the sword of the warrior god but by the awesome power of compassionate love, in and through solidarity with those who suffer."[56] God works from within to give life, particularly through God's compassionate solidarity with suffering people.

This divine solidarity is powerful enough to heal and set free, even to raise Jesus from the dead and establish him in an entirely new, transformed existence.

Like Christian belief in the incarnation, affirmation of Jesus' resurrection also unleashes hope for the future not just of the human race, but of the entire cosmos. On this point Johnson's theology bears similarities to that of Moltmann, who argues that God's new creation will extend to the entire natural world, including those creatures that have perished in the evolutionary process. Johnson likes to quote a statement of Karl Rahner on the resurrection in which Rahner said that in the risen Jesus "a piece of this world, real to the core" is now with God in glory.[57] She also cites Ambrose of Milan's reflection on Jesus' resurrection: "In Christ's resurrection the earth itself arose."[58] The resurrection of Jesus entails the transformation and eternal validity of his whole person, including his body. This signature divine act discloses, then, that the material—the earthly—is also the object of God's concern and participates in the saving, renewing action of God. "Far from being left behind or rejected, the evolving world in its endless permutations will be transfigured by the life-giving action of the Creator-Spirit."[59] Once again, a foundational Christian doctrine implies a summons to human beings to care for the earth.

God and the Mystery of Suffering

The Inadequacy of Theodicy

Johnson's reading of authors like Wiesel, Bonhoeffer, Schillebeeckx, and a variety of feminist theologians leads her to the conviction, articulated repeatedly in her writings, that rational attempts to reconcile suffering with belief in a good, all-powerful God are ineffective. They fail to convince and often result in the domestication of evil and suffering. She would affirm that certain forms of suffering stimulate moral and spiritual growth in our lives. But when discussing the Shoah and other egregious manifestations of evil that have inflicted massive suffering on innocent people, she employs the term *surd*: such evil "is an irrational force that cannot be made to fit meaningfully into a divine plan for the world."[60] She argues that attempts to rationalize such evil "drown out the voices of the victims."[61] Johnson draws on the work of Wendy Farley, particularly Farley's notion of "radical suffering." According to Farley, radical suffering is suffering that does not lead to a greater good but represents an attack on one's personhood as such. It cripples the soul, diminishing the ability of the person to exercise personal freedom as well as to hope in and love God. In experiences of radical suffering, "the destruction of the human being is so complete that even the shred of dignity that might demand vindication is extinguished."[62] Radical suffering cannot be rationally reconciled with an overarching divine purpose for the well-being of the world. Johnson forcefully expresses her view about the failure of theodicies in this passage:

> The most astute theodicies pale before the depth of torment in the history of the world. Evil is indeed the surd which shatters every rational system of thought. Anyone who works out a rational way to integrate evil and radical suffering in an ordered fashion into a total intellectual system of which God is a part thereby justifies it. Such efforts, in my judgment, are doomed to fail.[63]

Influenced by Schillebeeckx and J. B. Metz, Johnson proposes that what is needed in place of theodicy is remembrance and narrative or, as she puts it, "narrative memory in solidarity."[64] She develops this idea in the context of her discussion of the communion of saints in *Friends of God and Prophets*. The memory of suffering, so often suppressed by individuals and groups of people, must be awakened in order to preserve personal and corporate identity and to elicit resistance against the causes of suffering. This is a "dangerous memory," since it empowers victims to take action against the causes of suffering. As an example, Johnson cites the women who faithfully protested at Argentina's Plaza de Mayo on behalf of those kidnapped and murdered by an oppressive military regime. From a Christian perspective, the memory of the passion of Jesus is a dangerous memory that "summons up in a special way the concrete crosses of so many historical victims vanquished by injustice, persons defined by dominant voices as unimportant, while hope in the resurrection anticipates a liberating future precisely for them."[65]

Like Schillebeeckx, Johnson preferences narrative over theory in discourse about the mystery of suffering. Story is self-involving; it enables suppressed questions to be brought to the surface and empowers suffering people to endure and resist. The telling of stories is transformative in a way that theories are not. Johnson cites the stories of the martyrs of El Salvador in the 1980s, told by a struggling, oppressed people and related to the accounts of the martyrs of the early church in ways that instilled courage and hope.[66] Narrative also enables people to recognize and affirm the experiences of grace and meaning that occur even in the midst of suffering. It can name the grace without pretending to impose a framework of intelligibility on the experience of suffering.

Memory and narrative lead to solidarity with other people who are suffering. Johnson is convinced that solidarity is a powerful, indeed an empowering, force. This includes solidarity with both the living and the dead, especially the deceased who have been victims of oppression. She describes the doctrine of the communion of saints as "a symbol of this solidarity that transcends time in a graced connection of witness and care."[67] Inspired by Latina and African American theologians, Johnson insists that this should not be a "cheap solidarity" that remains at the level of the notional or that ignores the real differences between people and cultures. Authentic solidarity leads to conversion of heart, to alliance with those who are suffering and oppressed. And it moves us to acknowledge and appreciate the differences among people, even among those who experience similar forms of suffering.

God of Sheer Aliveness

When Johnson does engage in discourse about divine mystery in the face of the scourge of suffering, she is inspired by the Thomistic understanding of God. We saw that she grounds the possibility of analogical predication about God in creaturely participation in the being (esse) of God. In her rendering of this notion of participation, Johnson highlights Aquinas's portrayal of the dynamism of God: God is pure to-be in whose act of existence all creatures are given a share. This conception of God is a theological rendering of the God of life revealed in the person and ministry of Jesus. Johnson asserts that "to say that the very essence of holy mystery is 'to be' is to credit God with pure liveliness, with a superabundance of actuality that transcends imagination."[68] Such insight into the reality of God arises from both positive and negative experiences. Wonder at the fact that anything at all exists leads one to surmise God as "the unoriginate welling up of the fullness of life in which the whole universe participates."[69] Protest and struggle against evil and suffering move one to affirm God "as the power of resistance, healing and liberation."[70] God who is pure liveliness, then, is the source not just of the existence but also of the flourishing of creatures in the face of the forces of suffering and death. Johnson asserts that Sophia-God is "sheer, exuberant, relational aliveness in the midst of the history of suffering, inexhaustible source of new being in situations of death and destruction, ground of hope for the whole created universe...."[71] In this respect, Johnson's reflection on the Christian doctrine of God bears similarities to Schillebeeckx's notion of God as "pure positivity."

While Johnson builds on the Thomistic idea of God as pure to-be, pure activity, she fills out this conception in a different way. She changes the root metaphor of this God-talk from an impersonal one of motion (*motus*) to a personal one of relation. Johnson has great difficulty with the Thomistic assertion that God has no real relation to the world. She respects Aquinas's intention to preserve the transcendent freedom of God, but she argues that such language obscures the God of Christian belief especially for women, for whom connectedness and mutuality are prized as excellences. The picture of God presented in much of classical theology, she thinks, has been that of the powerful, all-sufficient ego, totally in charge of every event and entirely independent of the need for others. Johnson argues that such a view of God is anthropomorphic, drawn from the ideal of "the solitary, dominant male."[72] From the perspective of most women, experiences of affiliation, mutuality, and connection are seen as reflections of divine perfection. From this viewpoint, the God who is pure activity, sheer aliveness, should be viewed as a mystery of personal connectedness.

Christian belief in the Trinity affirms that God is a mystery of relatedness, a vibrant communion of life and love. Johnson emphasizes that "being related is at the very heart of divine being."[73] She envisions creation and the offer of grace as the outpouring of the triune God's inner relational life to the world. Johnson affirms the traditional teaching about the freedom of creation: God does not create the world out of any necessity. Both creation and God's self-communication in grace are gifts freely given. Still, the God of the Bible is in fact the God who is fundamentally related to the world. Johnson strives to protect divine transcendence and freedom by emphasizing that the relation between God and the world is asymmetrical: the world is dependent upon God in a way that God is not dependent upon the world.[74] But she also asserts that the relation between God and the world entails mutuality. The world makes a difference to God; what happens to creatures makes an impact on God.

Like Moltmann, but in a way that more carefully affirms divine freedom and transcendence, Johnson envisions a panentheistic relation between God and the world. She describes this as a relationship "whereby everything abides *in* God, who in turn encompasses everything, being *above all and through all and in all'* (Eph. 4:6)."[75] Whereas classical theism accented divine transcendence over divine immanence, and pantheism weights immanence over transcendence, panentheism "attempts to hold onto both in full strength."[76] This perspective envisions God in the world and the world in God, in a model of reciprocal relation. Though God is radically distinct from the world, and the world does not exhaust the being of God, creation is permeated with the presence of God, the One in whom and through whom it exists.

Divine Self-Limitation

Johnson maintains that a Christian panentheism presupposes some form of divine self-limitation. We saw that in their views of the relationship between God and creation, Jürgen Moltmann posited a divine self-emptying, and Edward Schillebeeckx spoke of a divine yielding. In both perspectives, by fashioning creation and giving freedom to human beings, the infinite God makes a space for creatures to be and becomes vulnerable to the response of free creatures. Johnson takes up these ideas in her discussion of God and creation. Like Moltmann, she appeals to the Jewish mystical notion of *zimsum*, God's self-limitation in creation.[77] God makes a space within Godself for the world to dwell. The self-emptying that is affirmed of Christ in the New Testament (Phil 2:6–11) is characteristic of God from the beginning of creation. This kenosis "is the pattern of Sophia-God's love always and everywhere operative."[78] Johnson cites a comment of her former teacher, William Hill, who said that the idea that in creating God empties himself out kenotically, making room within Godself for the non-divine to be, is consonant with Aquinas's conception of the relation between God and creation.[79] Johnson points out that the best (though still inadequate) metaphor for this Creator-creation relationship is taken not from the experience of men but from the event of a woman's conceiving and giving birth to a child.

As Johnson puts it, "God makes room for creation by constricting divine presence and power."[80] When we examined Johnson's reflections on the resurrection of Jesus, we saw that she reimagines the power of God as love that works from within to bring life. It is an empowering rather than a domineering presence and agency. Christians, she maintains, have traditionally likened the power of God to the controlling might of an absolute monarch:

> Modeled on the all-determining power of a patriarchal ruler, divine power is traditionally interpreted to mean that God is ultimately in control of whatever happens so that nothing occurs apart from the divine will. This ruler may well be benevolent but "his" exercise of power is unilateral and brooks no opposition except what "he" allows."[81]

Johnson's positing of divine self-limitation in creation entails a challenge to such a view of divine power. Like Schillebeeckx, she says that in the actual order of creation there are limits to God's power, though the power of God to effect salvation for a beloved creation will not be defeated in the end. Within the course of history, however, events take place that should not be connected with the will of God. God's respect for human freedom, and his respect for the natural laws and the randomness that are at work in an evolving universe, preclude a unilateral understanding of divine power.[82] She speaks of divine power as real and effective, but she describes it as "the liberating power of connectedness that is effective in compassionate love."[83] God empowers people through God's faithful presence to and solidarity with them. The experience of women, Johnson thinks, leads to a conception of divine power as power-with rather than power-over. The power of God is a "sovereign love which empowers."[84]

A Compassionate God

Johnson's emphasis on solidarity and her understanding of the power of God make it clear that compassion is a central category in her theology. Adopting a position different from that of Aquinas, she speaks of divine compassion as God's real suffering-with God's beloved creatures. Here the influence of Moltmann and many feminist theologians who espouse divine suffering is evident. She argues that the notion of an immutable, impassible God is not meaningful to women. Commenting on the traditional principle of divine impassibility Johnson says, "From a feminist perspective, the idea that God might permit great suffering while at the same time remaining unaffected by the distress of beloved creatures is not seriously imaginable."[85] She argues that the ability to enter into compassionate solidarity with another—freely to suffer with another—represents an excellence, not an imperfection, in God.

In chapter 4, we explored the reasoning behind Aquinas's affirmation of divine immutability and impassibility, though we also noted that these attributes are primarily negative, denying to God all creaturely forms of change and suffering. We examined the argument made by the twentieth-century Thomist William Hill concerning Aquinas's understanding of God's compassion. God, who has no needs and cannot suffer in Godself, loves in a totally other-centered manner. God's love for creatures means God's willing good to them. God's love is omnipotent—capable of overcoming any evil—and God enlists Godself on the side of suffering creatures in order to dispel evil and suffering. In that respect God is truly compassionate. But God is not compassionate in the literal sense of suffering with suffering creatures. Compassion in that sense is an expression of finite, not infinite, love. Johnson learned much from Hill and, as we have seen, has a Thomistic orientation in her theology. Nevertheless, she argues that the conception of love articulated by Aquinas (and Hill) "prescinds from the reciprocity entailed in mature relations."[86] Mature human love—our best source for analogical predication about the love of God—means more than willing the good of the beloved. It also entails "an openness to the ones loved, a vulnerability to their experience, a solidarity with their well-being, so that one rejoices with their joys and grieves with their sorrows."[87] This deeper form of love, which is expressed in compassion, is reflective of God's love. Johnson hastens to add that the suffering of God should be conceived as a free, active suffering on God's part. It is not a suffering that God necessarily endures, which is forced on God from outside or is due to some intrinsic deficiency in divine being. It is a chosen suffering-with out of solidarity with the people whom God loves so deeply. Whatever God's suffering entails, we must uphold the infinite, qualitative difference between God's suffering and the suffering of creatures. But for Johnson, God's free suffering with others, God's "compassion" in the real sense of that term, represents an excellence, not a deficiency or limitation. It is a perfection that, in her view, should be ascribed to God.

In an attempt to speak more descriptively about the suffering and compassionate love of God, Johnson adduces four metaphors drawn from women's experience, three of which are also reflective of the experience of some men.[88] First, she points to the pain of childbirth, of bringing new life into the world. She cites the well-known passage from Deutero-Isaiah in which the prophet likens God to a woman crying out in labor (Isa 42:14). She thinks that the experience of the travail of childbirth can enrich our image of God by evoking a God who is in labor struggling to bring forth justice in the world. Human beings are called to become partners with God in this process of birthing justice in the world. Second, she describes the passion of women throughout history who have fought against injustice. This passion includes righteous anger against all that inflicts harm on innocent people. It is legitimate, she believes, to speak of a suffering God who is passionately concerned about the oppressed and who gets angry when there is injustice. Third, Johnson reflects on the grief of women who lose loved ones. She believes that this deeply painful experience can tell us something about the God who grieves over the evil done to and in creation. We can rightfully speak about a God who grieves. Finally, Johnson points to the countless experiences of degradation suffered by women around the world—the horrors of physical, sexual, and emotional abuse. She proposes that the cross of Jesus reveals that, in Christ, God has known something of this abuse, this degradation. All four of these examples are limited in their application to God, as is every human experience. The attribution of any of these experiences of pain and sorrow to the divine falls under the rule of analogical predication about God, in which there is similarity but ever greater dissimilarity. But Johnson argues that these experiences of women can shed light on what God is like, on how God actively, freely suffers with people. She is convinced that God-talk in the face of innocent suffering should include discourse about the God who suffers with us.

In more recent lectures and publications Johnson applies this idea of a suffering God to the pain and travail of all of creation, not simply to human suffering. In an essay on Christology and ecology she appeals to Paul's words about the groaning of creation (Rom 8:22), proposing that an ecological Christology interprets the cross of Jesus "as a sign that divine compassion encompasses the natural world, bearing the cross of new life throughout the endless millennia of dying entailed by evolution."[89] Such a view of divine compassion represents a challenge to human beings to enter into solidarity with the earth and all suffering creatures.

Does this talk about a suffering God really help us as we grapple with the suffering of humankind and of "otherkind"? From Johnson's perspective, such discourse does not help if we are looking for a solution to the mystery of suffering. As we have seen, she is convinced that the strategies of theodicy inevitably fail. She notes that in the wake of the Shoah the appropriate question is not *why* God permits such things to happen or *how* they can be reconciled with God's governance of the world. The critical question, articulated so poignantly by Wiesel, is, *Where* is God to be found in the midst of suffering?[90] Johnson argues that belief in a God who can and does freely suffer with us facilitates the praxis of hope.[91] It leads to the conviction that God is to be found right in the midst of experiences of pain, faithfully present in compassionate solidarity with those who suffer. This belief provides hope amidst inexplicable suffering and engenders the strength to continue on in trust, to fight against the causes of suffering when that is possible and not to despair when there is nothing more humanly that can be done. It provides hope, too, because it is a conviction grounded in the experience of the death and resurrection of Jesus. This event manifests a God whose compassionate solidarity opens up a future through even the most negative experiences.

Conclusion

Johnson's work is a cogent and impressive articulation of feminist theology written from a Catholic perspective. She is very conscious of the limitations of her own background and social location as a white, educated woman living in an affluent nation. Thus, she rejects the notion that in her theology she speaks for "women" in general; she recognizes, for example, the critical importance of listening to differing viewpoints offered by theologians of African, Asian, and Hispanic descent. Still, she offers an eloquent expression of the insights, concerns, hopes, and sufferings of many women of faith. Her focus on the importance of relationship, connection, and mutuality in the lives of women represents a significant contribution to theology and the life of the church. Though she is unyielding in her criticism of the silencing of women's voices in society and the church, her central aim is constructive. She endeavors to draw from the rich store of sources in the Christian tradition to construct a systematic theology that does justice to the concerns and hopes of women of faith and, in so doing, enriches the whole church.

Johnson's writings on a variety of theological themes reveal a basic coherence and consistency in her thought. In her later works she builds upon insights gained in earlier study, for example, her research into the tradition of analogy and her exploration of the theme of Wisdom in the scriptures and the Christian tradition. This coherence is evident in her discussion of God and suffering. She denies the possibility of constructing an overarching theological system that would rationally integrate the reality of evil and the horrors of human suffering. Nevertheless, the positions that she articulates on a panentheistic relation between God and the world, the centrality of divine solidarity in the work of redemption, divine power as empowering love, and the reality of divine compassion do fit together in a meaningful way. Some of the themes developed by Johnson are reminiscent of the mystical thought of Julian of Norwich, especially solidarity, compassion, and mutuality. It could be argued that Johnson gives compelling, systematic expression to many of the ideas that Julian intuited through her mystical experience.

Like many feminist theologians, Johnson often contrasts her own theological positions with those of theologies constructed from a patriarchal perspective. She identifies patriarchy as the source of innumerable oppressive attitudes and structures throughout history in the church and society. Many of her allusions to the deleterious effects of patriarchy are convincing. And there is certainly no shortage of patriarchal thinking and structures in the contemporary church and world. But I wonder if Johnson and other feminist theologians do justice to the complexity of human relationships and behavior by seemingly deriving all that is wrong with the world from patriarchy. It can seem that "patriarchy" becomes an artificial construct that encompasses all distortions in relationships and social structures, which then is understood to be the source of all evil. In a sense, patriarchy becomes the primary effect of what in the Christian tradition has been known as original sin. It seems to me that the tradition as a whole contains resources for recognizing that, while patriarchy is a real factor in human history that has had enormously destructive effects, evil and the suffering that results from it are so complex and far-reaching that they cannot be derived from any one system or attitude.

In the conclusion to chapter 6, we explored the views of a number of theologians who criticize Jürgen Moltmann for integrating suffering into the divine being and who argue that Moltmann's position leads to a number of theological problems, including a trimming of divine transcendence. Do such critiques also apply to the positions taken by Johnson? These theologians would not agree with her position that divine love, not just human love, entails suffering because of the mutuality and vulnerability that characterize God's relationship to creatures. At the same time, Johnson is quite careful to preserve the freedom and transcendence of God in terms that are consistent with the tradition. She emphasizes that divine compassion entails a free, active suffering with beloved creatures; she views it as an expression of the fullness of divine love. Attentive to the dynamics of analogical language, she also acknowledges that when we talk about divine suffering we do so under all the limitations that pertain to discourse about the divine. Though she thinks that it is legitimate and theologically important to speak of God's suffering with suffering people (and other suffering creatures), she is well aware that the dynamics of this divine suffering are shrouded in the incomprehensible mystery of God. In the end, while a theologian may or may not agree with Johnson's position on divine suffering, he or she would have to acknowledge Johnson's efforts to preserve the fundamental concerns of the tradition, particularly with regard to divine transcendence and freedom.

Discussion Questions: www.paulistpress.com, Online Resources.

11
Toward a Theology
of God and Suffering

In the introduction to this volume, I suggested that all believers—even those who have never formally studied theology—have at least an implicit theology of God and suffering. This theology is expressed in statements we make about suffering and words we address to people who are experiencing suffering. It is also evident in our personal and communal prayer. I encouraged readers to become more attuned to the ways in which they think about God and suffering and to enter into a conversation with the expressions of the Judeo-Christian tradition that we have explored in these chapters. Having engaged in that same dialogue myself, I conclude this book by offering my own reflections on this critically important theme. I have titled this chapter "Toward a Theology of God and Suffering," because I do not presume to present a comprehensive theological synthesis here. Rather, I suggest elements of a theological approach to the mystery of suffering that are convincing to me. I do so while keeping in mind the observation I made in the introduction: theology is not only faith seeking understanding, it is also prayer seeking understanding. Thus, an appropriate theological approach to the mystery of suffering should facilitate healthy, vital prayer for people who are experiencing suffering.

The *Memoria Passionis*

Theologians such as Jürgen Moltmann, J. B. Metz, and Gustavo Gutiérrez highlight the responsibility of Christians to preserve the memory of the passion: the remembrance of the sufferings of Jesus of

Nazareth and the memory of the sufferings of countless others throughout the course of history. In so doing, these theologians align their thinking with important spiritual writers in the Christian tradition like Paul of the Cross (1694–1775), who became famous for professing a special vow focused on the *memoria passionis*. For mystics like Julian of Norwich and Paul of the Cross, the memory of the passion was the mediation of their most profound experience of God. Our exploration of Julian in chapter 5 showed that this remembrance led to deepened insight into the depths of God's love. The memory of the passion became a window into a love that was costly, even for God.

The *memoria passionis* also entails remembrance of and compassionate solidarity with suffering people. This solidarity extends to victims of oppression whose voices are often ignored by the privileged of this world. The memory of the contemporary passion is, as Metz has often pointed out, a dangerous memory because it gives recognition to people whose lives have been consigned to forgetfulness by those who are in power. Christians, then, should be people who face the stark reality of suffering and listen attentively to the cries of suffering people. While Christianity is not a "cult of suffering," it does proclaim a Messiah who was crucified and who, as the risen One, is present in solidarity with the crucified of every age. Followers of Jesus, then, are called to be present to the often inexplicable suffering of the world, refusing to become anesthetized to the tragic dimensions of human existence. And they are challenged to be sensitive to people who struggle with their faith because of their experience of suffering. Christians are people who never cease to be scandalized by what Schillebeeckx called the "barbarous excess of suffering" in human history.[1]

Jesus and the Character of God

Through the centuries, believers who adhere to the Judeo-Christian tradition have grappled with their understanding of the God revealed in the Hebrew and Christian scriptures. This wrestling is evident in the diverse interpretations of the meaning of suffering found in the Hebrew scriptures, which we examined in chapter 1. The author of the Book of Job presented a direct challenge to the doctrine of retribution that had been so influential for the faith of ancient Israel. While the image of God presented in Job is imbued with mystery, the biblical book clearly challenges a narrow view of the divine as confined in a straitjacket of reward and punishment. In the writings of Elie Wiesel, including his reflections on Job, we witnessed in chapter 6 a contemporary Jew whose life has been marked by a fierce struggle with the question of how to speak about the God of the covenant in the light of his own experience of the horrors of the Shoah.

Christians, too, continue to develop their perception of the God of Jesus Christ through a living dialogue with the tradition in light of historical experience. In its Dogmatic Constitution on Divine Revelation (*Dei Verbum; DV*), the Second Vatican Council speaks of the contemplation of the tradition by the whole people of God, and it affirms that the tradition that comes from the apostles makes progress in the church with the help of the Holy Spirit (*DV* 8). This development should not be understood as a linear progression toward ever more luminous insight into the divine. It is, rather, a jagged journey punctuated by critical moments that include the tragic events of history. The Shoah is one such tragedy that has led to intense dialogue with the tradition about the God of the Bible. This horrific event has compelled many believers to reflect anew about their image of God.

Christians are impelled to turn to the story of Jesus in their grappling with the character of God. This story includes his ministry as well as his death and resurrection. Schillebeeckx is correct in his insistence that an authentic description of the salvation-from-God found in Jesus must attend to his ministry of proclaiming the reign of God in word and deed. In our exploration of Jesus' proclamation of the kingdom, we saw that when the rule of God became present in him people found life. They experienced the *shalom* (wholeness; peace) to which Elizabeth Johnson refers in her summary of Jesus' kingdom ministry. In Jesus' powerful words and deeds, creation was being restored to the condition intended by God. This restoration affected the bodily as well as the spiritual dimensions of life. The Markan accounts of the cleansing of the leper and the cure of the man with the withered hand are emblematic of this dynamic. Jesus' visceral reaction to the sight of the leper who kneels before him leads to a healing mediated by his touch of this man with a dreaded disease (Mark 1:41–45). His frustration with synagogue opponents who resist the healing of the man with the withered hand reflects his communion with the God of the sabbath, the God who acts to save life (3:1–6). In his ministry, Jesus engages in sustained combat with forces of evil that drain the life out of people. In so doing he reveals the God whom Gutiérrez rightly names "the God of life."

The Gospels recount that Jesus' life-giving ministry quickly provoked the hostility of some people, especially certain religious leaders. In order to interpret the meaning of his death, it is necessary to view it in the context of his public ministry. In the face of mounting opposition, Jesus remained faithful to his mission, courageously journeying to Jerusalem with his proclamation of God's salvific rule. I am convinced that the crucifixion of Jesus should be envisioned as the outcome of his fidelity to the mission he received from the God he called "Abba." I argue that it was not the Father who put the Son on the cross. Jesus was executed because people rejected the salvation that he proclaimed and found him to be a threat that needed to be eliminated. Though in the light of the resurrection the New Testament authors affirm a divine necessity to Jesus' unjust death, this necessity can be understood as a confession that Jesus' death was, in a mysterious way, encompassed within the saving designs of God. From this vantage point, I have difficulty with certain aspects of Moltmann's intra-trinitarian account of Calvary.

Should we say that Jesus was really abandoned on the cross? Was he forsaken by God—or, in classical terms, did the Father forsake the Son? It is clear that the Gospels (especially Mark and Matthew) present a Jesus who entered into the darkest regions of human suffering. He truly tasted the bitterness of a death that was agonizing in every respect. Though we have no direct access to the psychology of Jesus, it may well be that he *felt* abandoned by the God he had addressed so intimately as "Abba." But, as many scholars point out, the quotation of the first line of Psalm 22 by Mark and Matthew evokes the entire psalm, which as a whole is a prayer of trust in a faithful God and of hope for vindication.

And in light of the experience of the resurrection, I do not think we should assert that Jesus was abandoned by his Abba-God. The notion that Jesus underwent death as one forsaken by God in order that his followers would never have to experience such abandonment does not convince. It suggests a view of redemption as substitution, in which God (or, the first person of the Trinity) inflicts on Jesus what should have been inflicted on sinful human beings. This conjures up the image of a vindictive God. Moreover, if Jesus is the exemplar for his followers in life and in death, the idea that he was abandoned by God inevitably raises the specter of God's abandonment of all suffering people. A believer might rightly ask, "If even Jesus experienced abandonment in his suffering, why shouldn't I experience it as well?"

No, the experience of the resurrection discloses that Jesus' death at Calvary was an experience of *communion* in the midst of darkness and unspeakable suffering. Schillebeeckx's image of Jesus holding on to the hand of the God who was silently present to him at this moment of suffering is, I believe, an illuminating one. Schillebeeckx is right in affirming that it is communion with God that saves, and that is what happened at Calvary. The Easter experience discloses that the Father was faithfully present to the Son in his suffering, silently at work from within to overcome the powers of death. The God who is revealed in Jesus' death and resurrection is the God whose character comes to be known as *tenacious fidelity* and *enduring communion*. Indeed, this God could be named the One-Who-Never-Abandons-Beloved-Sons-and-Daughters —especially when they are suffering.

The reflections of Gerald O'Collins on the revelatory significance of the resurrection shed light on the character of God disclosed in the Jesus-event. The raising of Jesus reveals that his death as an act of loving service—an act that culminated a life of loving service—was accepted by his Abba-God. It also discloses that God is definitively revealed in Jesus. And, as O'Collins eloquently argues, the resurrection of Jesus shows that God can be found in the suffering one. O'Collins' words are worth repeating here: "But with the resurrection the disclosive power of the cross comes into play, and shows that the weak, the despised, and suffering—those who become fools for God's sake—can serve as special mediators of revelation (and salvation)."[2] Thus, a Christian can read Wiesel's account of the hanging of the young boy and interpret his statement that God "is hanging here on this gallows" as an affirmation that, at such a terrible moment of apparent godlessness, God is to be found in the suffering one. Finally, the raising of Jesus from the dead reveals that the God whom Jesus proclaimed in his kingdom ministry is the God who brings life out of death. This pivotal event is the grammar of God's activity in the world. What happened to Jesus is happening wherever God is present (thus, everywhere): God is on the move, acting from within, to bring new life out of all the wretched manifestations of death that oppress people. This is God's characteristic act.

In what way should we speak of Jesus' life, death, and resurrection as "saving"? There have been a number of soteriological theories in the history of the Christian tradition, none of which has been defined as dogma by the church. Anselm's theory of satisfaction is the most famous account of the saving work of God in Jesus. A careful reading of Anselm's work shows that his was not a soteriology of appeasement, though this was the way his theory was sometimes presented in popular preaching. Anselm's understanding of the dynamics of satisfaction is predicated on God's will to restore the order of creation and offer salvation to humanity. His argument is replete with subtle nuances that require careful distinctions. Even with these distinctions, however, his theory of satisfaction can still evoke the image of a "payment" scenario—Jesus' death as payment for sin. Elizabeth Johnson and many other feminists demonstrate the liabilities of such a scenario, particularly with respect to the image of God that is conveyed.

One soteriological framework that I find illuminating was proffered by Karl Rahner.[3] In his account of the saving work of God in Jesus, Rahner employs the logic of sacramental causality. He wants to counteract any notion of Jesus' death as placating an angry God. Rather, Rahner emphasizes, the entire story of Jesus originates in the merciful love of God. Appealing to the principle that sacraments cause grace because and insofar as they signify grace, Rahner argues that we can speak of Jesus' ministry, death, and resurrection as the sacrament—

the efficacious sign—of God's salvific grace. Jesus signifies and enacts the victory of God's saving self-communication to the world. An analogy drawn from ordinary life may help here. When a mother embraces her troubled child, her action is motivated by her love for that child. The embrace does not cause the love; it is because she loves her child that she embraces her. At the same time, the embrace is essential because through it the mother's love is effectively communicated—made present—to the child. In an analogous way, the person and career of Jesus originate in the unfathomable love of God for all people. The entire Jesus-event is the result of God's faithful love for a wounded humanity and a fractured world. His kingdom ministry, his total gift of self in his death, and his resurrection efficaciously communicate—make irreversibly present—this saving self-communication of God. This soteriological perspective highlights the merciful, life-giving love of God as the source and end of the Jesus-event. It reminds us that Jesus' life, death, and resurrection constitute the decisive manifestation of the character of God's love. This is the truth that captivated Julian of Norwich as she reflected on her experience of Christ.

The experience of God's self-disclosure in Jesus and through the Holy Spirit led Christians to conceive of God in trinitarian terms. They began to profess and to formulate theologically a trinitarian monotheism. Christians envision the God of Jesus Christ as a communion of life and love in God's very self. The mystery of mutual relationship lies at the very heart of God. Employing the classical names for the divine persons, Father, Son, and Spirit exist as an eternal bond of giving and receiving. In Johnson's words, God is not a single monolith but "a living fecundity of relational life."[4] It is this trinitarian God whom Thomas Aquinas designated as "Pure Activity" (*Actus Purus*), pointing to the eternal dynamism, the undiminished vitality that characterizes the divine being.

There is a completeness to this inner life of God that precludes the necessity of creation. Yet believers can envision creation as the free, gracious outpouring of this divine life that brings the non-divine into existence and continually sustains it. The God who *is* loving relationship in God's very being freely enters into a loving relationship

300

with every creature. With Karl Rahner we can envision the gift of creation in light of God's intention to offer grace, to communicate Godself to men and women. As Rahner puts it, "God wishes to communicate himself, to pour forth the love which he himself is. That is the first and last of his real plans and hence of his real world too."[5] If someone asked a Christian, "What is life all about, anyway? What does it all mean?," the Christian answer might well be stated in this way: "There is a God and God wanted to give of self in love." This is the deepest meaning of reality; it is the "logic" at the heart of the universe.

If human beings are created in the image and likeness of the triune God, this means that we are "hardwired" for relationship. We exist as relational beings, and we flourish only through a life with others marked by mutual giving and receiving. Walter Kasper suggests that the ontological primacy of relationality, rooted in the Trinity, implies that "the meaning of being is the selflessness of love."[6] From this perspective, the narcissism that pervades much of the Western world actually represents an obfuscation of the depths of reality. Self-absorption alienates us from our true identity as creatures made in the image of a relational God. The centrality of mutual relationship connects with the *memoria passionis*. It suggests that we grow and mature as human persons when we enter into bonds of reciprocity with suffering people. Ignoring or avoiding people in pain makes us less than truly human; such negligence diminishes everyone.

God and the World

It seems theologically appropriate to adopt a panentheistic view of the relation between God and the world: the world exists within God and is permeated by the divine presence, though God remains distinct from the world and creation does not exhaust the being of God. This model conceives of the finite as encompassed by the infinite. If creation is depicted as in some fashion "outside" of God, one encounters the theological problem of conceiving of the infinite God as part of a larger whole. The panentheistic model bespeaks a reciprocal relationship between God and the world. It also reflects the classical principle, articulated masterfully by Aquinas, that the transcendence and immanence of God exist in direct proportion. We can recall the statement of Aquinas in the eighth question of the *Summa Theologiae* (*ST*): "During the whole period of a thing's existence, therefore, God must be present to it, and present to it in a way in keeping with the way in which the thing possesses its existence" (*ST* I, 8, 1). Julian's mysticism also reflects this relationship between divine transcendence and immanence, for example, when she speaks of Christ as "our clothing, who wraps and enfolds us for love, embraces us and shelters us."[7] Julian's imagery illumines the indescribable nearness of God to the world and the world to God. The transcendent God is indeed closer to us than we are to ourselves.

Moltmann, Johnson, and others have appealed to Jewish mystical thought in conceiving of self-limitation by God in the act of creation. God "withdraws," making a space within Godself for creation to exist. The ecological theologian Denis Edwards, attentive to the evolutionary processes within creation, articulates this idea in trinitarian terms: "The universe can be understood as unfolding 'within' the Trinitarian relations of mutual love....The shared divine life is the ambience in which the universe is brought to life and enabled to unfold."[8] This is a kenotic understanding of creation that envisions the self-emptying of God in the Christ-event (Phil 2: 6–11) as emblematic of the way in which God acted in bringing the world into existence. We saw that William Hill maintained that this notion of God making room within Godself for the nondivine to exist is consistent with Aquinas's understanding of the relation between God and creation. The idea that the infinite God limits Godself in order that the finite may exist and flourish is, I believe, a compelling one. It envisions creation as a free act of selfless love on the part of God, who so deeply desires to share the divine life with creatures that God is willing to undergo self-limitation. Such language is, of course, analogical; it is spatial language referring to a God who is pure spirit and is not spatially delimited. Like all statements about the divine, it is an inadequate depiction of the mystery of God and God's relation to the world. It does, however, point to a truth that is worthy of reflection.

As Johnson pointed out, a panentheistic conception of God and the world suggests a relationship of mutuality between God and creation. We saw that classical theology denied a bond of mutuality or reciprocity between God and the world. It feared that such language would make God dependent upon the world; in fact, it thought that characterizing the God-world relationship as mutual would reduce the Creator to the ontological level of the creature. This is one reason Aquinas asserted that God has no "real relation" to the world. God is transcendent to creation and has nothing to gain from the world. God relates to the world but does so purely for the benefit of creatures, not for any benefit to Godself. As Brian Davies puts it, for Aquinas God remains unchangeably God even though there are creatures that are created and sustained by God.[9]

With Aquinas and classical theism we must affirm the transcendence and freedom of God with respect to the world. God did not create this vast and ancient universe in order to fulfill some need in the divine. Having created, God relates to creatures, including human beings, as God and not as a finite being. Nevertheless, it seems theologically counterintuitive to deny any sense of mutuality between God and the world. It is counterintuitive particularly for a theology grounded in the Bible, in which the theme of covenant is central to both Testaments. Moreover, if in a trinitarian ontology relationship has a primary significance, predicating mutuality between God and human beings seems appropriate. One can affirm God's transcendence and freedom with respect to creation and still maintain that God graciously enters into a relationship with us that is marked by reciprocity. As Johnson and others argue, the relationship between God and the world remains asymmetrical: the world is dependent upon God in a way that God is not dependent upon the world. Nevertheless, inspired by the covenantal theology of the Hebrew and Christian scriptures, we can affirm that the world makes a real difference to God and that God is in some manner (in a way that is beyond our ken) affected by what happens in the world—especially by what happens to human beings. When Julian says that we are God's "bliss" and that God "will never have his full joy in us until we have our full joy in him," this is more than mystical hyperbole.[10] It reflects the profound truth that God has freely entered into a relationship with human beings that has mutual effects. While human beings cannot in any way diminish the fullness of God's being, it seems right to maintain that the God who has chosen to call us into a covenant relationship has made Godself vulnerable to our response. Irenaeus of Lyons famously said that the glory of God is the human being fully alive; in so doing, he at least implied that God's happiness and human flourishing are connected, even if we are unable to arrive at a complete understanding of the dynamics of this relationship. God has a stake in human happiness and in the fulfillment of all of creation.

Divine Power

The self-limitation of God in creating the universe raises the question of God's power. If the God revealed in Jesus Christ is the God who brings life out of death, the God who is on the move against the powers of evil, why is evil so potent and suffering so pervasive in our world? In our survey of the thought of modern theologians we have witnessed a movement to reconceive the notion of the power of God. In different ways, and to varying degrees, some thinkers have suggested a qualification of God's omnipotence by which God lets creation be and gives space for the freedom of human beings. Bonhoeffer spoke of God as weak and powerless in the world, though we saw that in the end he did express confidence in divine providence and in God's power over evil and death. Moltmann conceives of God's self-emptying in creation, and Schillebeeckx employs the image of God signing a blank check in granting freedom to human beings. Johnson gives the most explicit attention to the topic of divine power, criticizing patriarchal conceptions and arguing that in the actual order of creation there are limits to God's power, though God's intention to accomplish salvation will not be thwarted in the end. From a feminist perspective she suggests that God's power within creation should be understood as power-with rather than as power-over.

The Christian tradition has always taken into account the power that God has granted to human beings in bestowing the gift of freedom. There have been countless debates about how exactly to conceive of the relationship between God's gracious, providential action in history and free human response to that divine action. These controversies have not settled much, though the teaching about the primacy of grace in salvation is a firm Catholic (and not just Protestant) doctrine. Nevertheless, the tradition of Christian theology and spirituality has maintained that human beings have the capacity to reject the loving designs of God for the world. Augustine's disputes with the Pelagians and his wrestling with the question of the suffering of baptized babies led him to formulate a robust doctrine of original sin. He envisioned the "first sin" as a heinous crime that severely wounded human nature and scarred human history. It left people with a propensity toward evil. Aquinas attributed primary causality to human beings with respect to the introduction of moral evil into God's good creation. Moral evil arises completely from our side, with no contribution from God's "side." Julian's experience of the crucified Christ led her to conclude that sin is the cause of all of the pain in human history. Schillebeeckx spoke of a negative and original initiative of finitude on the part of human beings, as a way to account for the origin of evil and suffering in the world. These and other representatives of the tradition have suggested that the divine power to save and bestow life must reckon with the human capacity to contravene God's intentions for beloved creatures.

Gutiérrez suggests that contemporary Christian theology needs to take sin more seriously in dealing with the mystery of suffering. Theologizing from the vantage point of the poor, who so often are victims of injustice, Gutiérrez challenges us to acknowledge the destructive effects of sin in history. It may be that overreaction to a heavy emphasis on sin in Catholic theology and spirituality has resulted in the unwarranted optimism about history that Gutiérrez criticizes. It would seem that the memory of the horrendous evils of the Shoah, as well as of Cambodia, Bosnia, Rwanda, Darfur, and countless other atrocities of recent history, should convince us of the power of people to inflict terrible suffering on one another and deep scars on human history. We must always resist the temptation to attribute the suffering of individuals or of groups directly to their personal or corporate sins.

We have seen that the biblical theology of retribution, while containing a grain of truth, is severely limited in its ability to explain the reasons for human suffering. At the same time, in dealing with human suffering, Christian theology must give due attention to what Benedict XVI calls "the mass of sin which has accumulated over the course of history, and continues to grow unabated today."[11]

How should theology deal with suffering that is the result of what has traditionally been designated as "physical" or "natural" evil? Should we appeal to the doctrine of original sin when facing the deaths of a hundred thousand people in the 2004 South Asia tsunami, or the loss of more than two hundred thousand people in the 2010 earthquake in Haiti, or the condition of mental illness, which makes life so difficult for many people? Are such phenomena symptoms of a cosmic reflex to the introduction of evil into creation by human beings? Is nonhuman nature "fallen" because of original sin? It seems to me that we run up against the limits of theological reasoning in dealing with events and conditions like those mentioned. Denis Edwards wisely observes that "in any authentically *theological* approach to natural evil, we must stand with the Book of Job (38—42) before the mystery of God and God's creation, and acknowledge that there is a great deal we do not know."[12]

In his encyclical *Spe Salvi*, Benedict XVI says that the suffering that is a part of human existence "stems partly from our finitude and partly from the mass of sin that has accumulated over the course of history."[13] The pope does not specify which forms of suffering are caused by our finitude; he simply proffers this distinction. He does suggest, however, that the reality of sin is not the theological explanation for all human suffering. Some contemporary theologians stress that in creating an evolving world God establishes the interplay of natural forces that act as secondary causes within creation. These forces lead to developments that can be categorized under scientific law, as well as to random mutations that are essential for the appearance of novelty in the universe. This development results in loss on different levels, such as the disappearance of certain species through the processes of natural selection, the deaths of animals through predation, and the loss of human life as a result of earthquakes and tsunamis. Just as God limits

Godself in granting freedom to human beings, God also limits Godself in allowing the cosmos to develop with its own relative autonomy. Denis Edwards cites the views of the theologian and scientist John Polkinghorne, who envisions God "as the great *allower* and *respecter* of freedom, including the freedom of physical processes."[14] Polkinghorne argues that "God is committed not just to respect human freedom but to respect the integrity of the created universe, along with its laws and processes."[15] Edwards, who rejects a view of nonhuman nature as "fallen," paints a picture of a God who is engaged with creation, respecting the processes inherent within it, and who suffers with and delights in the unfolding of creation.

In my view, the Christian theologian encounters a dark mystery in attempting to deal with questions about natural evil. Edwards's observation that in such matters we confront a great deal that we do not know is a salutary reminder for theologians and believers. I do not think that the doctrine of original sin can be used as a theological explanation for all human suffering that is caused by natural forces. But neither do I wish to label such suffering as merely the "natural byproduct" of physical processes in the cosmos. Currently, there is a strong theological reaction against an anthropocentric understanding of the cosmos, inspired by an awareness of the devastation wrought in creation by the senseless and destructive actions of human beings. The human person is envisioned as part of a web of life that includes the entire cosmos; we are not the "lords" of the universe for whose benefit everything else was created. This critique of anthropocentrism has a certain merit, but it may also obscure other truths that are essential to Judeo-Christian belief. When we witness the human suffering caused by the 2010 earthquake in Haiti, there is something instinctive in us that reacts against the position that this toll of suffering is the "byproduct" of the evolutionary development of the universe. (This is true even though we also recognize that, had the people of Haiti not suffered such impoverished conditions, the loss of life there would have been much less.) The massive loss of human life caused by this earthquake makes it something more than just a "geological event." When someone whom we know contracts HIV, there is something instinctive in us that reacts against a view that the existence of this microorganism is intrinsic to the evolutionary development of the earth and that it is merely flourishing as it lives in different host organisms, whether animal or human. It is just "doing what viruses do."

Jesus gave us insight into the character of God when he reached out to touch the leper and free him from that dreaded disease. He did not simply tell the man that his affliction was part of the conditions of finitude. While he did not heal everyone, he did reveal the God who was acting to restore creation to what God intended, which included the defeat of those forces that drain the life out of people. Thus, though it may go against the grain of contemporary theology, I suggest that theologians need to avoid the kind of "de-centering" of the human person that relativizes the significance of the human suffering caused by forces in nature. I offer no theological answer for the suffering caused by earthquakes, tsunamis, mental illness, HIV, and the like. But I suggest that the biblical witness, particularly the Gospel accounts of the ministry of Jesus, reflects a focus on the human that is not necessarily detrimental to the environment. It is a view that situates natural forces within the larger horizon of God's intentions to bestow life on God's beloved daughters and sons. It suggests that God is on the move against all the forces—whether generated by nature or by human beings—that deprive people of life.

The Compassion of God

Great thinkers within the Christian tradition have strained and struggled to preserve the transcendence and freedom of God while also acknowledging God's intimate presence to suffering people. The tradition has never been content with a God whose transcendent perfection would preclude closeness to the pain and tragedy that permeate human history. It wants to extend divine compassion as far as possible. This tension is evident within patristic and medieval theology, even when the majority of theologians clearly affirm the impassibility of God. The classical way in which this tension was handled was through the principle of the communication of idioms: because of the unity of the person of Christ one can affirm that in the passion the Son of God truly suffered, though in his human nature, not in his divine nature. We saw that the principle of the communication of idioms was particularly important for the Christologies of Cyril of Alexandria and Thomas Aquinas. Cyril could stretch the limits of language and speak of the "impassible suffering of the Son."[16] Aquinas could affirm that in the crucifixion of Jesus "the impassible God suffers and dies."[17] Benedict XVI apparently makes a similar move in *Spe Salvi*, though his approach is not entirely clear. The pope says that God "desired to suffer for us and with us." He quotes an expression from Bernard of Clairvaux: *"Impassibilis est Deus, sed non incompassibilis."* Benedict translates this phrase to mean "God cannot suffer, but he can *suffer with*." He then makes reference to the incarnation and the passion of Jesus, as he affirms that God "became man in order to *suffer with* man in an utterly real way."[18] The pope appears to be drawing on the christological principle of the communication of idioms in this section of his letter, though it is possible that he wants to affirm that the divine nature itself is impinged upon by the suffering of human beings.

The warnings by theologians within the Thomistic tradition about trimming God's transcendence in the interest of making suffering human beings feel better are worthy of serious consideration. Jean-Pierre Torrell asserts that making God share our sufferings would turn God into an idol. As he puts it, "That god would not be God."[19] In a similar vein, Thomas O'Meara argues that "a suffering god is a momentarily consoling myth for the sick but not a credible cause of the universe."[20] Michael Dodds claims that a suffering God "will inevitably seek his own perfection and try to overcome his own deficiency."[21] And he appeals to the incarnation to argue that affirming of God a human suffering in Jesus makes more theological sense than predicating of God "some hypothetical sort of 'divine suffering,' itself alien to our experience."[22] These theologians and others are convinced that the move within theology to introduce suffering into the divine nature ultimately reduces God to the level of a creature. Moreover, they rightly argue that the accounts of classical theism given by some modern theologians have been distorted. When Moltmann claims that the impassible God "is a God without heart and without compassion, a cold heavenly power," he is not accurately representing the God of Augustine and Aquinas.[23] And references to the "static God" of classical theism, which students of theology sometimes encounter, clearly misrepresent the God whom Aquinas describes as "Pure Activity," full of life and dynamism.

These arguments notwithstanding, I suggest that the affirmation that God can and does freely suffer with beloved creatures out of the fullness of divine love is a credible theological position. In response to Dodds, it is possible to maintain that, if Jesus is the definitive revelation of God in human history, his human suffering discloses the God who (even in the divine nature) shares in our suffering. I believe that Johnson is right in arguing that the best (though still inadequate) source of analogical predication for divine love is mature human love. She is also correct in her assertion that such love entails reciprocity—an openness to others and a vulnerability to their experiences. The willingness to be present to others in compassionate solidarity and to be affected by their pain constitutes an excellence within our experience. It is, I believe, an attribute that Christians should affirm of God, even as they recognize the inherent limitations of such an affirmation. Theologians who espouse the classical tradition argue that discourse about a God who suffers-with is anthropomorphic. But feminist theologians are correct, I believe, in pointing out that the portrait of the impassible God painted in classical theism is also anthropomorphic. So much depends upon how one envisions perfection.

The affirmation of God's capacity to suffer with suffering people does not necessarily reduce God to the level of the creaturely. We cannot know precisely what divine suffering entails; it is a dimension of the mystery of God. It is possible, however, to affirm that God can freely enter into this suffering, allowing the divine self to be affected by the pain of human history, and still remain God. God does so as God, not as a creature, and thus as the One who promises to bring life out of death and to put an end to all suffering. God offers compassionate solidarity with suffering people not out of any compulsion but in freedom, out of the fullness of divine love. While classical theism suggests that God's suffering with beloved creatures would detract from the pure altruism of divine love, an argument can be made that such compassionate solidarity manifests the depth of God's love. It does not render God helpless to save; God remains the savior who brings life out of death and who will ultimately overcome the forces of evil that induce suffering. But this saving God is also a God whose love for sons and daughters (and for all of creation) is so profound that God opens the divine self to be impinged upon by our sorrows.

Perhaps this debate is analogous to the historic dispute between the Jesuits and Dominicans about grace and free will. It may simply be irresolvable. Pastorally, there is no great impasse between the two positions. Even theologians who reject the notion of suffering in God affirm that the human suffering of Jesus was truly the suffering of the Son of God. And they acknowledge that through the incarnation God has in a certain way united Godself with every human being and with people who are suffering.[24] A pastoral minister from either theological perspective can confidently assure a person who is suffering that God knows his or her experience from the inside. Nevertheless, I believe that Johnson is correct when she argues that affirming God's compassionate solidarity with the suffering of this world facilitates the praxis of hope. There are some situations in which the best answer to the question of God's presence and activity is to say that God is grieving with God's suffering people. That is not a solution to the mystery of suffering, nor does it mean that God's power to act in a salvific way has been checkmated. It does mean, however, that God is affected by the harm done to and in God's beloved creation, particularly the harm suffered by people. This affirmation is, I believe, a source of hope for people who are enduring suffering.

The Varieties of Faith

The Judeo-Christian tradition demonstrates that faith is "a many-splendored thing." Through the centuries faith in the God of Abraham and Sarah, and of Jesus Christ, has encompassed a rich variety of expressions. It has included the arguing of Job, the loud lamentation of the psalmists, and the protest of an Elie Wiesel laboring under the haunting shadow of Auschwitz and seeing his father's wracked body in the night watches. This faith has also been expressed in and through the sometimes baffling trust and docility of holy men and women, including many of the mystics. We see it in Julian who, though she questions God about evil and suffering, identifies wholeheartedly with the suffering Christ and counsels meekness and trust in God. This same trust is evident in many so-called simple believers—people who endure chronic suffering yet do so with profound trust in God. Sometimes the faith of such believers is viewed as unenlightened, but in many cases it exhibits a depth and tenacity that surpasses that of the theologically sophisticated.

Just think for a minute about the different ways in which the Gospels portray the death of Jesus. Mark and Matthew retain their own unique perspectives in their narratives of Jesus' passion, but each represents Jesus as uttering the opening verse of Psalm 22: "My God, my God, why have you forsaken me?" (Mark 15:34; Matt 27:46). Mark adds that Jesus dies with "a loud cry" (15:37). In both portraits, Jesus experiences the fierce assault of death and cries out in agony. Luke's account is somewhat different. Jesus still suffers on the cross, of course, and he is mercilessly mocked by passersby for not saving himself. But Luke presents Jesus as praying the words of Psalm 31 at his dying moment: "Father, into your hands I commend my spirit" (Luke 23:46; Ps 31:5). The noble Lukan Jesus commends his spirit to the Father, just as he had placed his entire life at the service of the mission given to him by the Father. He makes this commendation with a sense of serenity. The account in the Gospel of John depicts the crucifixion as the hour of glory in which Jesus reigns from the cross. Jesus' last words are, "It is finished" (John 19:30). The Greek term (*tetelestai*) has the connotation of "completed" or "accomplished." Jesus has fulfilled his mission and, as Donald Senior puts it, dies with "majestic assurance."[25] All four evangelists are telling the story of the one death of the person whom Christians profess as savior and Lord, but they present distinct perspectives on this death.

Why is this important? Among other reasons, it is significant because people die differently. Even people of strong faith die differently. Pastoral ministers experience this diversity as they accompany people through the process of death. Some people struggle to the very end against the power of death, straining against its incursion into their lives. They feel the fierce assault of death and experience the depths of darkness, as did the Jesus of Mark and Matthew. Others are able to arrive at an acceptance of their impending death and exhibit a sense of peace, even amidst the throes of death. They are similar to the Lukan Jesus. Still others, perhaps fewer in number, resemble the Johannine Jesus. They are convinced that they have accomplished in their lives what God put them on earth to do, and they see their death as a victorious homecoming to God. Distinct manners of dying among people of faith. But the diversity among the passion narratives suggests to us that each way can be a *dying with Christ*. Each can be an expression of trust, of grasping on to the hand of God. The Christian tradition suggests that there is more than one way that people of faith may respond to the experience of suffering.

The scriptures, the martyrdom tradition, and the testimony of holy women and men through the centuries suggest that closer union with God entails movement through suffering and darkness toward life-giving communion. The path is that of configuration to the crucified and risen Jesus. This is true however one wants to name the causes and the meaning of that suffering. This testimony tells us that certain forms of suffering can be productive and enriching in one's life of faith. Christians are invited to identify with the suffering Christ in order to grow in friendship with God. Moreover, the New Testament reminds us that authentic discipleship entails the willingness to suffer for the gospel in a world where people continue to reject the saving love of God. The willingness to suffer for and with Christ can become a powerful witness to the truth of the gospel.

Having said this, however, Christianity is not a cult of suffering, and believers are not compelled to hold that every form of suffering is productive for the life of faith. Johnson's appeal to the notion of "radical suffering" articulated by Wendy Farley alerts us to certain forms of suffering that crush the soul. Nor does the Christian tradition require us to maintain that God wants us to suffer. I am in fundamental agreement with the chapter heading in Schillebeeckx's book *Christ* of which we took note: "God does not want mankind to suffer."[26] The God revealed in Jesus Christ is the God who does not want people to suffer and who is faithfully at work to heal and overcome the suffering that plagues the human family and the rest of creation.

Two Languages

Gutiérrez thinks that the author of the Book of Job was searching for an appropriate language about God that would do justice to the situation of the suffering of the innocent. He argues that this biblical book illumines the need for two forms of discourse when people are plunged into the depths of suffering: the prophetic and the contemplative. Gutiérrez is convinced that it is the integration of these two modes of discourse that facilitates appropriate language about God and vital communication with God in the midst of experiences of suffering.

Prophetic discourse includes courageously speaking out against the injustice that is the cause of so much suffering in this world. It also entails the bold crying out to God that is characteristic of the lament tradition. For Walter Brueggemann the lament psalms embody the conviction that there is nothing "out of bounds" in our dialogue with God: "Everything belongs to this conversation of the heart."[27] And he suggests that these laments, even in their stark honesty, reflect the confidence that God accompanies people through the "deathly places" in life.[28] Suffering people can learn from the rich tradition of the lament, which reminds us that God was so real for the Jewish people—so closely involved in their lives—that they felt that everything needed to be brought to God in prayer.

At the same time, his own experience of engagement with prophetic discourse has convinced Gutiérrez that this way of talking is not enough if one is to be sustained in faith. Contemplative discourse is also necessary. This is the language of interpersonal love that goes deeper than words. The passage from Gutiérrez quoted in chapter 9 is telling: "When words do not suffice, when they are incapable of communicating what is experienced at the affective level, then we are fully engaged in loving."[29] Thomas Merton describes contemplation as "spontaneous awe at the sacredness of life, of being. It is gratitude for life, for being. It is a vivid realization of the fact that life and being in us proceed from an invisible, transcendent and infinitely abundant source."[30] This gratitude for life seems to characterize the attitude of believers who exhibit a remarkable capacity to endure suffering with steadfast trust in God. Merton proceeds to say that "contemplation is also the response to a call: a call from Him who has no voice, and yet who speaks in everything that is, and who, most of all, speaks in the depths of our being: for we ourselves are words of His."[31] For the Christian, contemplation involves the deepened awareness that we are in Christ and that Christ lives in us, or, as Paul articulated it so memorably, "It is no longer I who live, but it is Christ who lives in me" (Gal 2:20). The language of contemplation emerges from a stance of loving reverence before the gracious mystery of God.

Usually in the lives of people of faith there is a back-and-forth movement between these two forms of discourse. There is clearly the need for honest crying out to God. At the same time, God's grace at work in the lives of suffering people can lead them to a profound awareness of God's loving presence to them and of God's intense desire to offer life. Very few people attain a steady state of perfectly peaceful equilibrium in the face of serious suffering. At times even the most contemplative person needs to rail against suffering and cry out in lament to God. But through the power of God's grace, people can move toward a strengthened friendship with God grounded in the trust that God is deeply involved in their lives and will be faithful to them.

Theology and Mystery

I began this book with a story about the couple who attended a presentation that I gave on prayer and suffering in a church hall. Mary wanted to know how she and her husband should talk about God when, after her husband survived a serious automobile accident without injury, the teenage daughter of some close friends was tragically killed in a crash. How could they continue to talk about the "miracle" of her husband's escape from injury when their friends were mourning the loss of their daughter? At the time, I responded to Mary in the best way I could, though my response was filled with hesitation and stammering. I suggested that they found themselves immersed in the realm of mystery in their dilemma and that there were no satisfying theological explanations that could be given. I added that the invitation for Christians is to continue to believe that God was present in each of those "deathly" situations, faithfully at work from within to bring new life out of death.

I suspect that my answer sounded hollow to Mary and John, though it was the only thing I knew to say. Mary was asking the question of *why*—Why did her husband survive without injury while her friends' daughter lost her life, and at such a young age? We have seen in this study that the *why* question is the topic of theodicy, and we have noted the radical limitations of theodicy. The questions that most theologians think are more important today are the *where* and the *how* questions. Where can I find God in the midst of this experience? How do I conceive of God present and active in this situation? Still, the *why* question never leaves us. I believe that Moltmann is right when he claims that this is the salient question of human history. We have to live with this open question, which exists like an open wound in this world.[32] The task of faith and of theology is to help us to survive with this open wound—to continue living in hope.

In his Letter to the Romans, Paul addressed the mystery of suffering that he confronted in his own life and that he perceived as permeating creation itself. After speaking about the groaning of creation, he reminds the Christians at Rome of their experience of the love of God in Christ:

> Who will separate us from the love of Christ? Will hardship, or distress, or persecution, or famine, or nakedness, or peril, or sword?...No, in all these things we are more than conquerors through him who loved us. For I am convinced that neither death, nor life, nor angels, nor rulers, nor things present, nor things to come, nor powers, nor height, nor depth, nor anything else in all creation, will be able to sep-

arate us from the love of God in Christ Jesus our Lord. (Rom 8:35,37–39)

This is the language of contemplation. Paul provides no solution to the mystery of suffering. But he does speak a word of hope in the God who is tenaciously faithful to us, the God who brought life out of death for Jesus. This bringing life out of death is God's signature activity. If the expression is not improper, we might say that this is what God does for a living. We cannot always see how God is doing that; we are not able to trace the lines of God's activity with precision. But, inspired by the faithful presence of the risen Christ, we cling to the hope that this is what God is doing on our behalf all of the time.

Discussion Questions: www.paulistpress.com, Online Resources.

Notes

Introduction: Facing the Mystery

1. I have been inspired by the extended reflection of Gustavo Gutiérrez on the biblical character of Job. The English title of his book is *On Job: God-Talk and the Suffering of the Innocent* (Maryknoll, NY: Orbis, 1987). Gutiérrez considers the question of the most appropriate discourse about God in the face of innocent suffering, symbolized in the figure of Job.

2. Clemens Sedmak, *Doing Local Theology* (Maryknoll, NY: Orbis, 2002), 75.

3. See *The Analogical Imagination: Christian Theology and the Culture of Pluralism* (New York: Crossroad, 1981).

4. David Tracy, *Plurality and Ambiguity: Hermeneutics, Religion and Hope* (San Francisco: Harper & Row, 1987), 18–19.

5. Richard Hanson, "The Achievement of Orthodoxy in the Fourth Century AD," in *The Making of Orthodoxy: Essays in Honor of Henry Chadwick,* ed. Rowan Williams (Cambridge, UK: Cambridge University Press, 1989), 145. See also Hanson, *The Search for the Christian Doctrine of God* (Grand Rapids, MI: Baker Academic, 1988/2005), 109–16.

6. Elizabeth Schüssler-Fiorenza and David Tracy, "The Holocaust as Interruption and the Christian Return into History," in *The Holocaust as Interruption, Concilium,* vol. 175 (Edinburgh: T & T Clark, 1984), 83–86.

7. Arthur Cohen, *The Tremendum: A Theological Interpretation of the Holocaust* (New York: Crossroad, 1981).

8. Elie Wiesel, *Night* (New York: Hill & Wang, 1960; New York: Bantam Books, 1982), 62.

9. Quoted by John Hick in *Evil and the God of Love* (San Francisco: Harper & Row, 1977), 5.

10. John Thiel, *God, Evil and Innocent Suffering: A Theological Reflection* (New York: Crossroad, 2002), 37–38.

11. Hick, *Evil and the God of Love,* 256.

12. Thiel, *God, Evil and Innocent Suffering,* 42.

13. For a vigorous critique of the procedures of theodicy, see Terrence W. Tilley, *The Evils of Theodicy* (Washington, DC: Georgetown University Press, 1990).

14. John Thiel argues that theodicies, in all of their varieties, deny the reality of innocent human suffering. They "refuse to allow innocent suffering to stand before God." See *God, Evil and Innocent Suffering*, 52.

15. Harvey Egan describes the theology of Karl Rahner as "prayer seeking understanding" in *Karl Rahner: Mystic of Everyday Life* (New York: Crossroad, 1998), 81.

16. It is clear that Aquinas did not exclusively choose Aristotle as a philosophical dialogue partner; he also utilized insights from Plato and the Platonic tradition in his theology.

17. See his thought-provoking reflection on the God of the scriptures entitled *The God of Life*, trans. Matthew O'Connell (Maryknoll, NY: Orbis, 1991).

Chapter 1: The Hebrew Scriptures

1. Erhard Gerstenberger and Wolfgang Schrage, *Suffering*, trans. John E. Steely (Nashville: Abingdon, 1980), 69.

2. Daniel Simundson, *Faith under Fire: Biblical Interpretations of Suffering* (Minneapolis: Augsburg, 1980). See also Simundson, "Suffering," in *The Anchor Bible Dictionary*, vol. VI, ed. David Noel Freedman (New York: Doubleday, 1992), 219–25. Daniel Harrington, *Why Do We Suffer? A Scriptural Approach to the Human Condition* (Franklin, WI: Sheed & Ward, 2000).

3. This theme is elucidated by Gerstenberger and Schrage, *Suffering*, 98–102.

4. Harrington, *Why Do We Suffer?* 15.

5. Simundson, "Suffering," 220.

6. Harrington, *Why Do We Suffer?* 24.

7. Simundson, "Suffering," 220.

8. Harrington, *Why Do We Suffer?* 24.

9. Claus Westermann, *Creation*, trans. John Scullion (Philadelphia: Fortress, 1974), 89–90.

10. Simundson, "Suffering," 220.

11. Ibid., 221.

12. Ibid.

13. Bernhard Anderson, *Understanding the Old Testament*, 3rd ed. (Englewood Cliffs, NJ: Prentice-Hall, 1975), 411.

14. Harrington, *Why Do We Suffer?* 27–28.

15. Simundson, *Faith under Fire*, 31–34.

16. Harrington, *Why Do We Suffer?* 3.

17. Ibid.

18. Ibid., 4–5. See also Bernhard Anderson, *Out of the Depths: The Psalms Speak for Us Today* (Philadelphia: Westminster, 1970), 56–58. Anderson notes that between the petition and the concluding thanksgiving in some psalms are "words of assurance" that may have been spoken by a priest or prophet in a cultic setting.

19. Harrington, *Why Do We Suffer?* 5.

20. Anderson notes that "the laments are really expressions of praise— praise offered to God in the time of his absence." See *Out of the Depths*, 56.

21. Some biblical scholars think that Psalm 22 bears the marks of different stages of composition. For example, in his commentary on the psalms, Carroll Stuhlmueller (following Albert Gélin) argues that the second song of thanksgiving in the psalm (vv. 27–31) may be a later addition, either by the author or from the community through the use of the psalm in the liturgy. See Carroll Stuhlmueller, *Psalms 1*, Old Testament Message Series (Wilmington, DE: Michael Glazier, 1983), 147–50.

22. Gerstenberger and Schrage, *Suffering*, 133.

23. Walter Brueggemann, *Israel's Praise: Doxology Against Idolatry and Ideology* (Philadelphia: Fortress, 1988), 143.

24. Walter Brueggemann, *The Message of the Psalms* (Minneapolis: Augsburg, 1984), 51.

25. Ibid., 52.

26. Ibid.

27. Simundson, "Suffering," 222.

28. Harrington, *Why Do We Suffer?* 3.

29. The notion of suffering as sacrifice is discussed by Harrington, *Why Do We Suffer?* 53–68. See also Simundson, *Faith under Fire*, 63–69; Gerstenberger and Schrage, *Suffering*, 91–96.

30. Harrington, *Why Do We Suffer?* 55.

31. Harrington (ibid., 56) dates the prophecy of Second Isaiah to the years 539–37 BCE.

32. Ibid., 58.

33. Ibid. In his commentary on Second Isaiah, Christopher Seitz argues for an individualist interpretation. He thinks that the servant was given the difficult mission of proclaiming that God could use even affliction and death in making Israel a light to the nations. This servant was persecuted and afflicted and finally died. A new generation of followers of this prophetic servant "glimpsed into the mystery of his death and saw there not an end but a fulfillment and an inauguration." Their appreciation of the life and role of the servant is expressed in Second Isaiah. See "The Book of Isaiah 40–66," in *The New Interpreter's Bible*, vol. VI (Nashville: Abingdon, 2001), 320. Richard Clifford takes a mediating position on the question of the servant's identity. He argues

that the servant is the prophet in a dialectical relationship with the people. Like Moses and Jeremiah, the prophet stands between the people and God. These great figures experience in advance what will happen to the people. "The prophet is fulfilling the vocation of the people Israel, offering them an example and a warning. His songs evoke the great servant of the Lord, Moses, as well as Jeremiah and, of course, his great predecessor, Isaiah of Jerusalem." See "The Major Prophets, Baruch and Lamentations," in *The Catholic Study Bible*, 2nd ed., ed. Donald Senior and John J. Collins (Oxford, UK: Oxford University Press, 2006), 290–91.

34. Harrington, *Why Do We Suffer?* 59–60.

35. Clifford, "The Major Prophets, Baruch and Lamentations," 291.

36. Ibid.

37. John McKenzie, *The Two-Edged Sword: An Interpretation of the Old Testament* (New York: Doubleday, 1966), 256.

38. Harrington, *Why Do We Suffer?* 33.

39. Carol A. Newsom, "The Book of Job: Introduction, Commentary and Reflections," in *The New Interpreter's Bible*, vol. IV, 326.

40. Carol Newsom points out that it is possible that a single author wrote the entire book, employing divergent styles within it. See Newsom, "The Book of Job," 323.

41. Harrington, *Why Do We Suffer?* 32.

42. Dianne Bergant comments, "Verses 25–27 are some of the most difficult of the book. There is no single interpretation of the ideas expressed." *Job, Ecclesiastes*, Old Testament Message Series, vol. 18 (Wilmington, DE: Michael Glazier, 1982), 108.

43. Harrington, *Why Do We Suffer?* 40.

44. Newsom, "The Book of Job," 615.

45. Harrington, *Why Do We Suffer?* 47.

46. Newsom, "The Book of Job," 634.

47. Bergant, *Job, Ecclesiastes*, 213.

48. Newsom, "The Book of Job," 627.

49. Ibid., 629.

50. Ibid.

51. Ibid., 631.

52. Ibid., 632.

53. Susan Mathews, "All for Nought: My Servant Job," in *The Bible on Suffering: Social and Political Implications*, ed. Anthony J. Tambasco (New York/Mahwah, NJ: Paulist Press, 2001), 51–71.

54. Ibid., 53.

55. Ibid., 59.

56. Ibid., 68.

57. Harrington, *Why Do We Suffer?* 71.

58. John J. Collins, "Early Jewish Apocalypticism," in *The Anchor Bible Dictionary*, vol. I, 283.

59. Ibid. In making this comment, Collins cites the work of Adela Yarbro Collins, "Early Christian Apocalypticism," *Semeia* 36 (1986): 7.

60. Harrington, *Why Do We Suffer?* 73.

61. Scholars point out that the traditions found in the Book of Daniel antedate its composition. The book, consisting of tales of conflict and contest in chapters 1–6 and of apocalyptic visions in chapters 7–12, was edited by a final redactor. See Susan Mathews, "When We Remembered Zion: The Significance of the Exile for Understanding Daniel," in *The Bible on Suffering*, 95.

62. Harrington, *Why Do We Suffer?* 72.

63. Ibid., 82.

64. Ibid., 83.

65. Gerstenberger and Schrage, *Suffering*, 98–102; Terence Fretheim, *The Suffering of God* (Philadelphia: Fortress, 1984). For reference to the suffering of God, see also Brueggemann, *Israel's Praise*, 133.

66. Gerstenberger and Schrage, *Suffering*, 99.

67. Fretheim, *The Suffering of God*, 108.

68. Ibid., 111.

69. Ibid., 116.

70. Ibid., 123.

71. Ibid., 127.

72. Ibid., 128.

73. Ibid., 137.

74. Ibid., 140.

75. Ibid., 148.

76. For a helpful discussion of this distinction as it appears in classical theology, see Brian Davies, *The Thought of Thomas Aquinas* (Oxford, UK: Clarendon Press, 1992), 60–75.

Chapter 2: New Testament Perspectives on Suffering

1. Daniel Harrington, *Why Do We Suffer? A Scriptural Approach to the Human Condition* (Franklin, WI: Sheed & Ward, 2000), 89–144.

2. N. T. Wright, *Jesus and the Victory of God* (Minneapolis: Fortress, 1996), 199–203.

3. John P. Meier, *A Marginal Jew: Rethinking the Historical Jesus*, vol. 2: *Mentor, Message and Miracles* (New York: Doubleday, 1994), 240.

4. John Meier, "Jesus," in *The New Jerome Biblical Commentary* (Englewood Cliffs, NJ: Prentice Hall, 1990), 1320.

5. Meier, *A Marginal Jew*, 300.

6. Ibid., 349.

7. Ibid., 450.

8. Ibid.

9. Raymond Brown, *Introduction to New Testament Christology* (New York: Paulist Press, 1994), 66, n. 88.

10. Wright, *Jesus and the Victory of God*, 176.

11. Brown, *Introduction to New Testament Christology*, 66.

12. Wolfgang Schrage, in Erhard Gerstenberger and Wolfgang Schrage, *Suffering*, trans. John E. Steely (Nashville: Abingdon, 1980), 265.

13. Meier, *A Marginal Jew*, 726. Brown concurs: "The tradition that Jesus was one who performed cures and did other extraordinary actions is as old as the tradition of his words and must be taken seriously in any historical discussion" (*Introduction to New Testament Christology*, 62).

14. Brown, *Introduction to New Testament Christology*, 64. In similar fashion, Wright observes that Jesus never performed mighty works in order to impress. Rather, he saw these actions as part of the inauguration of the sovereign and healing rule of Israel's covenant God. See *Jesus and the Victory of God*, 191.

15. Brown, *Introduction to New Testament Christology*, 64–65.

16. Wright, *Jesus and the Victory of God*, 194.

17. Gerstenberger and Schrage, *Suffering*, 263–64.

18. Harrington, *Why Do We Suffer?* 103.

19. Gerstenberger and Schrage, *Suffering*, 139.

20. Ibid., 243.

21. Ibid., 164.

22. Meier, "Jesus," 1326.

23. Rudolf Bultmann is famous for his claim that Jesus did not speak of his death and thus that we cannot know anything about his approach to it. See Bultmann, *Jesus and the Word*, trans. Louise Pettibone Smith and Erminie Huntress Lantero (New York: Charles Scribner's Sons, 1934/1958), 213–14. Meier and others draw on the work of Heinz Schürmann in their argument that we can draw valid conclusions about Jesus' attitude toward his impending death. See Schürmann, *Begegnung mit dem Wort*, ed. J. Zmijewski (Bonn, 1980), 273–309.

24. Gerald O'Collins, *Christology: A Biblical, Historical and Systematic Study of Jesus* (Oxford, UK: Oxford University Press, 1995), 81. O'Collins's discussion of Jesus' human consciousness is notable for its fairness and balance.

25. Meier, "Jesus," 1326.

26. Ibid.

27. Brown, *Introduction to New Testament Christology*, 49.

28. O'Collins, *Christology*, 76.

29. Ibid.

30. Meier, "Jesus," 1326.

31. Ibid.

32. Brown, *Introduction to New Testament Christology*, 46–47.

33. Ibid., 47.

34. Meier, "Jesus," 1326.

35. John Meier, "The Eucharist at the Last Supper: Did It Happen?" *Theology Digest* 42 (1995): 335–51.

36. Ibid., 349.

37. Ibid.

38. Ibid., 350.

39. For a summary of the New Testament traditions about the resurrection of Jesus, see Raymond Brown, "The Resurrection of Jesus," in *The New Jerome Biblical Commentary*, 1373–77; O'Collins, *Christology*, 82–112; John Galvin, "Jesus Christ," in *Systematic Theology: Roman Catholic Perspectives*, vol. 1 (Minneapolis: Fortress, 1991), 297–301.

40. Brown, "The Resurrection of Jesus," 1375.

41. Ibid.

42. In addition to Brown, O'Collins, and Galvin, see Raymond Collins, *First Corinthians*, Sacra Pagina, vol. 7 (Collegeville, MN: Liturgical Press, 1999), 528–39; Hans Conzelmann, *1 Corinthians: A Commentary on the First Epistle to the Corinthians*, trans. James W. Leitch, Hermeneia Series (Philadelphia: Fortress, 1975), 248–63.

43. Galvin, *Systematic Theology*, 300; Collins, *First Corinthians*, 531. Conzelmann argues for a Hellenistic origin, while Collins says that "most scholars (e.g., Joachim Jeremias, John Kloppenborg) are convinced that it originated in a Palestinian context."

44. Conzelmann, *1 Corinthians*, 255.

45. Collins does not settle this question (530); Galvin suggests that recent authors think that the phrase refers to a moment of decisive divine action (300).

46. Collins, *First Corinthians*, 532.

47. Galvin's essay is helpful for its summary of the positions of Rudolf Bultmann, Willi Marxsen, Wolfhart Pannenberg, Karl Rahner, Edward Schillebeeckx, and Rudolf Pesch. See also Walter Kasper, *Jesus the Christ* (New York: Paulist Press, 1976), and the discussion by O'Collins in *Christology*, 82–112.

48. O'Collins, *Christology*, 99.

49. Kasper, *Jesus the Christ*, 139–40.

50. Galvin, *Systematic Theology*, 313.

51. O'Collins, *Christology*, 97–104.

52. Wolfhart Pannenberg, *Jesus: God and Man*, trans. Lewis Wilkins and Duane Priebe (Philadelphia: Westminster Press, 1968/1977), 69.

53. O'Collins, *Christology*, 98.

54. Ibid., 100.

55. Ibid., 101.

56. Ibid.

57. Ibid., 102.

58. Gerstenberger and Schrage, *Suffering*, 182.

59. Some New Testament scholars argue that Second Corinthians is actually a composite of two or more letters written by Paul to the Christian community at Corinth. Carolyn Osiek points out that "newer scholarship, with its emphasis on literary analysis, tends to try to look at the letter as a unified whole." See the Reading Guide, *The Catholic Study Bible*, ed. Donald Senior and John J. Collins, 2nd ed. (Oxford, UK: Oxford University Press, 2006), 459.

60. Jan Lambrecht, *Second Corinthians*, Sacra Pagina, vol. 8 (Collegeville, MN: Liturgical Press, 1999), 23.

61. Ibid., 78.

62. Harrington, *Why Do We Suffer?* 128. Harold Attridge offers a comprehensive survey of scholarly opinions regarding the authorship, date, and addressees of this letter. After assessing the evidence for various suggested authors (e.g., Apollos, Barnabas, Priscilla) he argues that the limits of historical knowledge preclude positive identification of the author. He concludes that a precise date of composition has not been proven, and he gives a range of dates of 60 to 100 CE. Attridge thinks that the most likely locus for the community that is addressed is Rome, particularly because of the attestation of Hebrews in the First Letter of Clement. See Harold Attridge, *The Epistle to the Hebrews*, Hermenia Series, ed. Helmut Koester (Philadelphia: Fortress, 1989), 1–13.

63. Harrington, *Why Do We Suffer?* 128.

64. Attridge, *The Epistle to the Hebrews*, 13. Attridge comments, "If one element serves to focus the overall paraenetic program of Hebrews it is the exhortation to be faithful" (23).

65. Harrington, *Why Do We Suffer?* 129.

66. Juliana Casey, *Hebrews*, New Testament Message Series, vol. 18 (Wilmington, DE: Michael Glazier, 1980), 11.

67. Attridge, *The Epistle to the Hebrews*, 87.

68. Harrington, *Why Do We Suffer?* 130.

69. Ibid. Harrington adduces Sirach 2:1 and 6:32 and 2 Maccabees 6:14,16 as texts that conceive of suffering in terms of God's disciplining activity

on behalf of his people. Attridge also makes note of the wisdom background for this idea. See *Epistle to the Hebrews*, 361.

70. Casey, *Hebrews*, 83.

71. Donald Senior, *1 & 2 Peter*, New Testament Message Series, vol. 20 (Wilmington, DE: Michael Glazier, 1980), 3. See also Senior's commentary on First Peter in *1 Peter, Jude and 2 Peter*, Sacra Pagina, vol. 15, ed. Daniel J. Harrington (Collegeville, MN: Liturgical Press, 2003).

72. Senior, *1 & 2 Peter*, 3.

73. Patricia McDonald, "The View of Suffering Held by the Author of 1 Peter," in *The Bible on Suffering*, 177.

74. Senior, *1 & 2 Peter*, 6.

75. John Donahue and Daniel Harrington argue that Rome is the setting of Mark's Gospel. See *The Gospel of Mark*, Sacra Pagina, vol. 2 (Collegeville, MN: Liturgical Press, 2002), 41–46.

76. Wilfrid Harrington, *Mark*, New Testament Message Series, vol. 4 (Wilmington, DE: Michael Glazier, 1979), xii. Harrington suggests that the setting for the Gospel is the Roman province of Syria, close to the tragic events of the Jewish-Roman conflict. He speculates that the Christian community there may have received Christian refugees from this war. Donahue and Harrington (45) note that Gerd Theissen argues for a provenance in southern Syria near the border of Palestine. Theissen thinks that Mark 13 reflects the evangelist's adaptation of apocalyptic material to his own situation after the destruction of the Jerusalem Temple in 70 CE. See Theissen, *The Gospels in Context* (Minneapolis: Fortress, 1991).

77. Frank Matera, *New Testament Christology* (Louisville: Westminster John Knox, 1999), 10.

78. Donahue and Harrington, *The Gospel of Mark*, 89. Donahue and Harrington (and other scholars) point out that some manuscripts of Mark replace this word with *orgistheis* ("being angered"). Some scholars prefer the latter reading because it is the more difficult reading; they argue that later copyists changed *anger* to *compassion* to make the passage more acceptable. Donahue and Harrington, however, assert that *splanchnistheis* is preferred because of the weight of the best manuscripts, the fact that copyists did not alter other passages that present Jesus as angry (3:5; 10:14), and the description of Jesus as compassionate in other healing narratives in the Gospel (6:34; 8:2).

79. Ibid., 91.

80. Harrington, *Mark*, 13.

81. Matera, *New Testament Christology*, 11.

82. Donald Senior, *The Passion of Jesus in the Gospel of Mark* (Wilmington, DE: Michael Glazier, 1984), 143.

83. Ibid., 15.

84. Matera, *New Testament Christology*, 18.

85. Senior, *The Passion of Jesus in the Gospel of Mark*, 72.

86. Ibid., 76.

87. Ibid., 77.

88. Ibid., 125–26.

89. Ibid., 123.

90. Ibid., 124. For a detailed study of the interpretation of the cry of Jesus from the cross, see Gerard Rossé, *The Cry of Jesus on the Cross: A Biblical and Theological Study*, trans. Stephen Wentworth Arndt (New York: Paulist Press, 1987). For a study of twentieth-century Catholic interpretations of Mark 15:34, see Paul Zilonka, CP, *Mark 15:34 in Catholic Exegesis and Theology: 1911–1965* (Rome: Pontifical Gregorian University, 1984).

91. Donahue and Harrington, *The Gospel of Mark*, 452.

92. Senior, *The Passion of Jesus in the Gospel of Mark*, 129.

93. Senior describes this verb as a technical term within the passion tradition that refers to the arrest of John and Jesus. It is found in 1:14; 3:19; 9:31; 10:33; 14:10, 11, 18, 21, 41, 42, 44; 15:1,10,15. It is also used to describe the sufferings of the disciples as they undertake their mission in 13:9, 11. *The Passion of Jesus in the Gospel of Mark*, 17, n. 4.

94. Daniel Harrington, "What and Why Did Jesus Suffer According to Mark," *Chicago Studies* 34 (1995): 32–41, at 38.

95. Ibid.

96. Senior, *The Passion of Jesus in the Gospel of Mark*, 64.

97. Gerstenberger and Schrage, *Suffering*, 236–37.

98. Senior, *The Passion of Jesus in the Gospel of Mark*, 47.

99. Ibid.

100. Harrington, "What and Why Did Jesus Suffer?" 37.

101. Donahue and Harrington, *The Gospel of Mark*, 32.

102. The Roman historian Tacitus describes these persecutions and betrayals, as does the Christian writer Clement of Rome. See Tacitus, *Annals*, 15.44, cited by Brown, *An Introduction to the New Testament*, 162. In his letter to the Christian community at Corinth, Clement says that "by reason of jealousy and envy the greatest and most righteous pillars of the church were persecuted and contended even unto death" (1 Clem 5:2).

103. Donahue and Harrington, *The Gospel of Mark*, 34.

Chapter 3: Early Christian Sources

1. Cyprian of Carthage, *The Lapsed*, nn. 5–7, trans. Maurice Bévenot, *St. Cyprian: The Lapsed and The Unity of the Catholic Church*, Ancient Christian Writers,

n. 25 (Westminster, MD: Newman Press, 1957), 16. This passage is cited in James Walsh, SJ, and P. G. Walsh, eds., *Divine Providence and Human Suffering*, Message of the Fathers of the Church, vol. 17 (Wilmington, DE: Michael Glazier, 1985), 36–38.

2. Henry Chadwick, *Augustine*, Past Masters (Oxford, UK: Oxford University Press, 1986), 97.

3. Ibid.

4. Athanasius of Alexandria, *Against the Pagans*, n. 6, trans. Robert W. Thomson, *Athanasius: Contra Gentes and De Incarnatione* (Oxford, UK: Clarendon Press, 1971), 17; Walsh and Walsh, *Divine Providence and Human Suffering*, 23.

5. Ibid.

6. Basil of Caesarea, *God Is Not the Author of Evils*, n. 5; Walsh and Walsh, *Divine Providence and Human Suffering*, 23. Like Athanasius, Basil identifies sin as the reason that evil was introduced into God's good creation.

7. Augustine, *Confessions*, trans. Henry Chadwick (Oxford, UK: Oxford University Press, 1992), VII, iii, 4.

8. Ibid., VII, xii, 18.

9. Augustine, *The Enchiridion on Faith, Hope and Love*, trans. Henry Paolucci (Washington, DC: Regnery Gateway, 1961), 11.

10. Ibid., 12.

11. Ibid., 11. See Thomas Aquinas, *Summa Theologiae* Ia., 2, 3, ad 1.

12. John Hick, *Evil and the God of Love* (San Francisco: Harper & Row, 1977), 56–58.

13. Plato, *Symposium*, 210E–211B, cited in Joseph M. Hallman, *The Descent of God: Divine Suffering in History and Theology* (Minneapolis: Fortress, 1991), 2.

14. Plato, *Republic*, 381b, trans. G.M.A. Grube (Indianapolis: Hackett, 1974), 51.

15. Thomas Weinandy, *Does God Suffer?* (Notre Dame, IN: University of Notre Dame Press, 2000), 71.

16. Aristotle, *Metaphysics* 1072b, trans. W. D. Ross, in *Introduction to Aristotle*, ed. Richard McKeon (New York: Random House, 1947), 284.

17. Weinandy, *Does God Suffer?* 71.

18. In *Metaphysics*, 1072b, Aristotle writes, "If then, God is always in that good state in which we sometimes are, this compels our wonder; and if in a better this compels it yet more. And God is in a better state. And life belongs to God; for the actuality of thought is life, and God is that actuality, and God's self-dependent actuality is life most good and eternal. We say, therefore, that God is a living being, eternal, most good, so that life and duration continuous and eternal belong to God; for this is God."

19. Weinandy, *Does God Suffer?* 71.

20. Aristotle, *Metaphysics*, 1073a.

21. Plotinus, *Enneads* 3, 6, cited in Hallman, *The Descent of God*, 16.

22. Hallman, *The Descent of God*, 16.

23. Justin Martyr, *Apology* 1, 20, cited in Hallman, *The Descent of God*, 31.

24. Aristides, *Apology*, 1, cited in Weinandy, *Does God Suffer?* 88.

25. Ibid., 7, cited in Weinandy, *Does God Suffer?* 88.

26. Irenaeus of Lyons, *Against Heresies*, 2.34.2, cited in Weinandy, *Does God Suffer?* 92.

27. Ibid., 2.13.3, cited in Weinandy, *Does God Suffer?* 92.

28. Hallman, *The Descent of God*, 110.

29. Augustine, *City of God*, trans. Marcus Dodds (New York: Random House, 1950), 21.15.

30. Augustine, *Exposition of Psalm 74.5*, trans. Maria Boulding, *Expositions of the Psalms 73–98*, *The Works of Saint Augustine: A Translation for the Twenty-First Century*, vol. 18 (Hyde Park, NY: New City Press, 2002), 43.

31. Augustine, *City of God*, 22.2.

32. Ibid.

33. See Hallman, *The Descent of God*, 112–23.

34. Augustine, *City of God*, 15.25.

35. Ibid.

36. Hallman, *The Descent of God*, 117.

37. Augustine, *De div. Quaest*, 2.2.3, cited in Hallman, *The Descent of God*, 121.

38. Ignatius of Antioch, *Romans*, 6.3, trans. Cyril Richardson, *Early Christian Fathers* (New York: Simon & Schuster, 1996), 105.

39. Origen, *Homilies on Ezekiel* 6:6, cited in Weinandy, *Does God Suffer?* 98–99.

40. Hallman, *The Descent of God*, 41, quoting Robert Grant, *The Early Christian Doctrine*, 31.

41. See Hallman, *The Descent of God*, 41; he cites *Selecta in Ezekiel* 16:8.

42. Hallman cites Origen's *Homily on Numbers* 23:2; *The Descent of God*, 41–42.

43. Origen, *Fragments on John*, 51; Hallman, *The Descent of God*, 43.

44. Origen, *On First Principles*, 4.15; Hallman, *The Descent of God*, 45.

45. Tertullian, *Against Marcion* 1, 25; Weinandy, *Does God Suffer?* 101.

46. Tertullian, *Against Marcion*, 2.16.7; Hallman, *The Descent of God*, 53.

47. Tertullian, *Treatise Against Hermogenes*, 12, 5; Hallman, *The Descent of God*, 60–61, citing *Corpus Christianorum, Series Latina* 1, 407.

48. Hallman, *The Descent of God*, 46–49. Hallman notes the divergent scholarly opinions about the authorship of this work on 46, n. 107.

49. Ibid., 93–94.

50. Ibid., 100.

51. Ibid., 66.

52. Weinandy, *Does God Suffer?* 112.

53. Ibid.

54. Ibid., 111.

55. Ibid.

56. Elizabeth Johnson raises this question in her dialogue with the Thomist William Hill, in *She Who Is: The Mystery of God in Feminist Theological Discourse* (New York: Crossroad, 1992), 265–66.

57. In addition to Weinandy and Hallman, see the following: Richard Hanson, *The Search for the Christian Doctrine of God: The Arian Controversy*, 318–381 (Grand Rapids, MI: Baker Academic, 1988/2005); Paul Gavrilyuk, *The Suffering of the Impassible God: The Dialectics of Patristic Thought* (Oxford, UK: Oxford University Press, 2004); John O'Keefe, "Impassible Suffering? Divine Passion and Fifth-Century Christology," *Theological Studies* 58 (1997): 39–60.

58. Gavrilyuk, *The Suffering of the Impassible God*, 75.

59. Ibid., 79.

60. Ibid., 75–79.

61. Ibid., 77.

62. Ibid., 80.

63. *Acts of John*, 98–99; quoted in Gavilyuk, *The Suffering of the Impassible God*, 82. See also Hans-Josef Klauck, "Community, History, and Text(s): A Response to Robert Kysar," in *Life in Abundance: Studies of John's Gospel in Tribute to Raymond Brown, SS*, ed. John R. Donahue (Collegeville, MN: Liturgical Press, 2005), 86–87. Klauck suggests that this work may have been composed as early as 150 CE in Asia Minor.

64. Ignatius of Antioch, *Letter to the Smyrnaeans*, 6, 3, in Richardson, ed., *Early Christian Fathers*, 114.

65. Ignatius of Antioch, *Letter to the Trallians*, 10; *Early Christian Fathers*, 100.

66. Gavrilyuk, *The Suffering of the Impassible God*, 71. The passage that is cited is from *The Passion of Perpetua*, 15.

67. Hanson, *The Search for the Christian Doctrine of God*, 103.

68. Hanson explains that Arians were convinced that the transcendent God could not come into contact with the created world. The Son was the kind of being who could be a mediator between God and the things created by God. See *The Search for the Christian Doctrine of God*, 101.

69. Ibid., 114.

70. *Opus Imperfectum in Matthaeum* XI; cited in Hanson, *The Search for the Christian Doctrine of God*, 114.

71. A mid-fourth-century Arian creedal statement attributed to Eudoxius, bishop of Antioch, articulates both of these central Arian principles: the subor-

dination of the Word (Son) and the Word's taking the place of a human soul in Christ. See Eudoxius, *Rule of Faith*; cited by Hanson in *The Search for the Christian Doctrine of God*, 112.

72. Hanson, *The Search for the Christian Doctrine of God*, 41. Gavrilyuk takes issue with this claim by Hanson. He argues that the opponents of the Arians did in fact confront the scandal of the cross, upholding the inseparability of the human and divine natures in Christ. He says that the orthodox "emphasized that in all the actions and experiences of the Logos the human and divine natures were inseparable. The Logos may be said to suffer in the flesh, advance in the flesh, and the like" (133).

73. Athanasius, *Orations against the Arians*, III, 27, in *The Christological Controversy*, ed. Richard Norris (Philadelphia: Fortress, 1980), 85.

74. Gavrilyuk, *The Suffering of the Impassible God*, 174.

75. Athanasius, *Orations against the Arians*, I, 16, in *The Trinitarian Controversy*, ed. William Rusch (Philadelphia: Fortress, 1980), 79.

76. J.N.D. Kelly, *Early Christian Doctrines* (San Francisco: Harper & Row, 1978), 286.

77. Athanasius, *Orations Against the Arians*, III, 29, in Norris, *The Christological Controversy*, 87.

78. Norris, *The Christological Controversy* (Philadelphia: Fortress, 1980), 20–21. See, for example, *Orations against the Arians*, III, 37; Norris, 96.

79. Gerald O'Collins, *Christology: A Biblical, Historical and Systematic Study of Jesus* (Oxford, UK: Oxford University Press, 1995), 168.

80. Later in the controversy, Nestorius was ready to accept the title of *Theotokos*, but it was too late by then. See O'Collins, *Christology*, 186–87.

81. Nestorius, "First Sermon against the *Theotokos*," in Norris, *The Christological Controversy*, 128.

82. O'Collins, *Christology*, 186.

83. Cyril of Alexandria, *Oratio ad Dominias*, 31; cited in Brian McDermott, *Word Become Flesh: Dimensions of Christology* (Collegeville, MN: Liturgical Press, 1993), 255.

84. Cyril, *Second Letter to Nestorius*, in Norris, *The Christological Controversy*, 133.

85. Ibid.

86. O'Keefe, "Impassible Suffering?" 48.

87. Nestorius, *Second Letter to Cyril*, in Norris, *The Christological Controversy*, 139.

88. Gavrilyuk, *The Suffering of the Impassible God*, 146.

89. Cyril of Alexandria, *Letter to Monks* (PG 77.36D), cited in O'Keefe, "Impassible Suffering?" 45.

90. O'Keefe, "Impassible Suffering?" 45. O'Keefe refers here to state-

ments Cyril makes in his *Scholia on the Incarnation* and *That Christ Is One*. In his study, Thomas Weinandy agrees with Joseph Hallman that the phrase "the Impassible suffered" (*apathos epathen*) is not found in Cyril's Greek, even though this phrase is often used to describe Cyril's position. But, Weinandy argues, the phrase does express Cyril's meaning—as is evident in other similar statements. Weinandy points out that Cyril states "that within the suffering body was the Impassible" (*Second Letter to Nestorius*, 5) and that "he [the Son] was in the crucified body claiming the sufferings of his flesh as his own impassibly" (*Third Letter to Nestorius*, 6). See Weinandy, *Does God Suffer?* 202–3, n. 58.

91. Cyril of Alexandria, *Third Letter to Nestorius*, Anathema 12; cited in Weinandy, *Does God Suffer?* 201.

92. Gavrilyuk, *The Suffering of the Impassible God*, 158. Gavilyuk here quotes Cyril from *That Christ Is One*, 760c.

93. O'Keefe, "Impassible Suffering?" 52.

94. Gavrilyuk, *The Suffering of the Impassible God*, 172.

95. Ibid.

96. Ibid., 173.

97. Cyprian, *The Lapsed*, n. 6; Walsh and Walsh, *Divine Providence and Human Suffering*, 37.

98. Augustine, *The City of God*, 1.1.

99. Ibid., 21.13.

100. Ibid., 22.22.

101. James Walsh, Introduction to *Divine Providence and Human Suffering*, 13.

102. Cyprian, *The Lapsed*, n. 5; Walsh and Walsh, *Divine Providence and Human Suffering*, 37.

103. Augustine, Sermon 256, in *The Works of Saint Augustine: A Translation for the Twenty-First Century, Sermons III/7*, trans. Edmund Hill (New Rochelle, NY: New City Press, 1993).

104. John Damascene, *The Orthodox Faith*, 2.29; Walsh and Walsh, *Divine Providence and Human Suffering*, 119, citing PG 94.964.

105. Titus of Bostra, *Against the Manicheans*, 2.14; Walsh and Walsh, *Divine Providence and Human Suffering*, 55, citing PG 18, 1160–61.

106. Augustine, *The City of God*, 1.1.

107. Basil, *God Is Not the Author of Evils*, 3; Walsh and Walsh, *Divine Providence and Human Suffering*, 39.

108. James Walsh and P. G. Walsh point out that some scholars doubt that Prosper is the author of this poem, since it supposedly reflects traces of Pelagianism. Prosper was a supporter of Augustine's theology of grace and an opponent of Pelagianism. Walsh and Walsh suggest that these scholarly doubts "may be too astringent, especially as Prosper in his later years is known

to have toned down his anti-Pelagian polemic." See *Divine Providence and Human Suffering*, 64.

109. *A Poem on Divine Providence*, 805; Walsh and Walsh, *Divine Providence and Human Suffering*, 88–89.

110. *A Poem on Divine Providence*, 884; Walsh and Walsh, *Divine Providence and Human Suffering*, 89.

111. Hick, *Evil and the God of Love*, 82–89.

112. Augustine, *Confessions*, VII, xiii, 19.

113. Hick, *Evil and the God of Love*, 87.

114. Augustine, *On Free Will*, III, xv, 44, in *Augustine: Earlier Writings*, The Library of Christian Classics, vol. VI, trans. John H. S. Burleigh (Philadelphia: Westminster, 1953).

115. Augustine, *The City of God*, 11, 18.

116. Ibid.

117. Ibid., 11, 23.

118. Augustine, *The Enchiridion on Faith, Hope and Love*, 27.

119. Cyprian, Letter 8; Walsh and Walsh, *Divine Providence and Human Suffering*, 127.

120. *A Poem on Divine Providence*, 805; Walsh and Walsh, *Divine Providence and Human Suffering*, 87.

121. Walsh and Walsh, *Divine Providence and Human Suffering*, 91.

122. John Chrysostom, *On Providence*, 12; Walsh and Walsh, *Divine Providence and Human Suffering*, 92, citing *Sources Chrétiennes*.

123. Augustine, *The City of God*, 20, 2.

124. William B. Palardy, unpublished lecture on Augustine and the Mystery of Suffering, given at Saint John's Seminary, Boston, MA, February 2001.

125. Elizabeth Clark, *The Origenist Controversy: The Cultural Construction of an Early Christian Debate* (Princeton, NJ: Princeton University Press, 1992), 227–44.

126. *Pelagius's Expositions of the Thirteen Epistles of St. Paul II: Text and Critical Apparatus*, ed. Alexander Souter (Cambridge, UK: Cambridge University Press, 1926), Romans 5:12, p. 45.

127. The Latin Vulgate translation of this verse included the phrase *in quo* ("in whom") as a translation of the Greek *eph hō*. This translation conveys the idea that all have sinned in Adam, that in a mysterious way everyone shares in the personal act of our ancestor Adam. Modern translations of the Greek, such as the New Revised Standard Version used here, translate *eph hō* as "because" or "inasmuch as" or "seeing that." These translations imply that all have sinned, that through their personal sins all share in the condition of subjection to the power of sin about which Paul speaks. Joseph Fitzmyer translates this Greek

phrase as "with the result that"—giving a stronger emphasis to the link between our personal sin and the sin of the first human beings. See Fitzmyer, "Romans: A New Translation with Introduction and Commentary," in *The Anchor Bible*, vol. 33 (New York: Doubleday, 1993), 405, 416–17. Concerning the interpretation of this verse, Fitzmyer says, "Thus Paul in v 12 is ascribing death to two causes, not unrelated: to Adam and to all human sinners. The fate of humanity ultimately rests on what its head, Adam, has done to it. The primary causality for its sinful and mortal condition is ascribed to Adam, no matter what meaning is assigned to *eph hō*, and a secondary causality to the sins of all human beings" (416).

128. Augustine, *The City of God*, 21, 14.

129. Clark, *The Origenist Controversy*, 242–43.

130. Bernard McGinn, *The Foundations of Mysticism: Origins to the Fifth Century*, vol. 1 of *The Presence of God: A History of Western Christian Mysticism* (New York: Crossroad, 1994), 249.

131. Ibid., 250. See also Gerald Bonner, "Augustine's Concept of Deification," *Journal of Theological Studies* 37 (1986): 369–86.

132. Augustine, *Exposition of Psalm 62*, 2, in *The Works of Saint Augustine: A Translation for the Twenty-First Century, Expositions of the Psalms III/20*, trans. Maria Boulding, OSB (Hyde Park, NY: New City Press, 2004).

133. Augustine, *Exposition of Psalm 85*, 1, in *The Works of Saint Augustine: A Translation for the Twenty-First Century, Expositions of the Psalms, III/18*, trans. Maria Boulding, OSB (Hyde Park, NY: New City Press, 2002).

134. Augustine, *Exposition of Psalm 62*, 2.

Chapter 4: Thomas Aquinas

1. I am indebted to Elizabeth Johnson (in class lectures at the Catholic University of America) for the articulation of these two foundational presuppositions.

2. Thomas O'Meara, *Thomas Aquinas: Theologian* (Notre Dame, IN, and London: University of Notre Dame Press, 1997), 91.

3. All quotations from the *Summa Theologiae* are taken from the translation in the Blackfriars series (New York: McGraw-Hill and London: Eyre and Spottiswoode, 1964).

4. All quotations from the *Summa Contra Gentiles* are taken from the University of Notre Dame Press edition, translated by Anton Pegis (1976).

5. Jean-Pierre Torrell, OP, *Saint Thomas Aquinas: Spiritual Master*, vol. 2, trans. Robert Royal (Washington, DC: Catholic University of America Press, 2003), 371–72.

6. Herbert McCabe, "The Involvement of God," *Blackfriars* 66 (1985): 465.

7. *Commentary on John* I, 18, lect. 11, n. 219. Cited by Torrell, *Saint Thomas Aquinas*, 51.

8. Torrell, *Saint Thomas Aquinas*, 33.

9. O'Meara, *Thomas Aquinas*, 92.

10. Ibid., 93.

11. In this section, I am indebted to the excellent classroom lectures of my former professor, Elizabeth Johnson.

12. Brian Davies, *The Thought of Thomas Aquinas* (Oxford, UK: Clarendon Press, 1992), 55.

13. David Burrell, *Knowing the Unknowable God: Ibn-Sina, Maimonides, Aquinas* (Notre Dame, IN: University of Notre Dame Press, 1986), 59–60.

14. William J. Hill, "The Historicity of God," *Theological Studies* 45 (1984): 331.

15. Burrell, *Knowing the Unknowable God*, 49.

16. O'Meara, *Thomas Aquinas*, 92.

17. Elizabeth Johnson, *She Who Is: The Mystery of God in Feminist Theological Discourse* (New York: Crossroad, 1992), 236.

18. McCabe, "The Involvement of God," 469.

19. O'Meara, *Thomas Aquinas*, 101.

20. William Hill, "Does Divine Love Entail Suffering in God?" *God and Temporality*, ed. Bowman Clarke and Eugene Long (New York: Paragon House, 1984), 65.

21. Torrell, *Saint Thomas Aquinas*, 77.

22. O'Meara, *Thomas Aquinas*, 94.

23. Herbert McCabe, Glossary to vol. 3 of the Blackfriars edition of the *Summa Theologiae*, "Knowing and Naming God," 109.

24. Torrell, *Saint Thomas Aquinas*, vol. 2, 77.

25. Fergus Kerr, "God in the *Summa Theologiae*: Entity or Event?" The Bradley Medieval Lecture, December 6, 2002, at Boston College. Cited with the permission of the author.

26. McCabe, "The Involvement of God," 470.

27. Torrell, *Saint Thomas Aquinas: Spiritual Master*, vol. 2, 75.

28. McCabe, "The Involvement of God," 470.

29. Michael Dodds compiles the passages from Aquinas, making particular note of *ST* II-II 30, 4 and I, 25, 3, ad 3. See "Thomas Aquinas: Human Suffering and the Unchanging God of Love," *Theological Studies* 52 (1991): 338. In his article, Dodds renders *misericordia* as "compassion." The Blackfriars translation of the *Summa Theologiae* translates it as "mercy."

30. Mark-Robin Hoogland distinguishes between *misericordia* and *compassio* in Aquinas, arguing that the latter simply means "to undergo/suffer with."

For Aquinas, while *compassio* can never be without *passio*, *misericordia* can be, although it never is in human beings. See *God, Passion and Power: Thomas Aquinas on Christ Crucified and the Almightiness of God* (Leuven: Peeters, 2003), 198.

31. Dodds, "Thomas Aquinas," 333.

32. Hill, "Does Divine Love Entail Suffering in God?" 64.

33. Thomas Gilby, Appendix 4 of vol. 8 of the Blackfriars edition of the *Summa Theologiae*, "Creation, Variety and Evil," 160.

34. Gilby translates *malum poenae* usually as "pain" and sometimes as "penalty." He renders *malum culpae* as "fault." In a note he explains, "*Poena*, pain or penalty, not pain as an affective condition (*tristitia*) though this may be involved, nor penalty as punishment for a breach of law, though this too may be involved, but a condition of lacking an appropriate good" (Blackfriars, vol. 8, 124, n. a). Davies translates these terms as "evil suffered" and "evil done" (*The Thought of Thomas Aquinas*, 92).

35. Davies, *The Thought of Thomas Aquinas*, 96.

36. Ibid., 95.

37. Ibid.

38. O'Meara, *Thomas Aquinas*, 118.

39. Anselm of Canterbury, *The Virgin Conception and Original Sin*, chaps. 1–7, 27, in *A Scholastic Miscellany: From Anselm to Ockham*, ed. Eugene R. Fairweather (Philadelphia: Westminster Press, 1956), 184–93, 199–200.

40. Davies, *The Thought of Thomas Aquinas*, 262.

41. In a footnote to *Summa Theologiae*, I-II, 113, 10, Cornelius Ernst comments on Aquinas's understanding of human nature. He says, "The human 'nature' about which St. Thomas is speaking here is not a pure Aristotelian nature, but a 'nature' created by God as part of a total divine plan for its final transfiguration into glory." See vol. 30 of the Blackfriars edition of the *Summa Theologiae*, "The Gospel of Grace," 199, n. a.

42. Davies, *The Thought of Thomas Aquinas*, 272–73.

43. Aquinas, *Expositio Super 1 ad Corinthios*, c. 15, lect. 1 (line 174 c). This passage is cited by Dodds, "Thomas Aquinas," 334, n. 18.

44. Dodds, "Thomas Aquinas," 334.

45. Ibid., 334–35.

46. Davies, *The Thought of Thomas Aquinas*, 313.

47. Aquinas, *Expositio Super ad Ephesios* 5, lect. 9 (line 105c). This passage is cited by Dodds, "Thomas Aquinas," 341.

48. Aquinas, *Expositio Super ad Colossenses* I, lect. 6 (line 56c). This passage is also cited by Dodds, "Thomas Aquinas," 341.

49. Dodds, "Thomas Aquinas," 341.

50. Mary Ann Fatula, *Thomas Aquinas: Preacher and Friend* (Collegeville, MN: Liturgical Press, 1993), 68.

51. Ibid., 73.

52. O'Meara, *Thomas Aquinas*, 135. Gerald O'Collins points out that in two places in the *Summa Theologiae* Aquinas alludes to the theme of Christ's death as an appeasement or placating of the Father (*ST* III, 48, 3 and 49, 4, ad 2). While this is not a principal idea in Aquinas's soteriology, O'Collins argues that its presence in the *Summa Theologiae* helped to open the door to the idea of Christ as the penal substitute propitiating the divine anger. See O'Collins, *Christology*, 206–7.

53. The ethicist Paul Wadell has written extensively and creatively on Aquinas's notion of charity as friendship with God. See, for example, his *Happiness and the Christian Moral Life: An Introduction to Christian Ethics* (Lanham, MD: Rowman & Littlefield, 2008), 23–44.

Chapter 5: Julian of Norwich

1. *Showings*, translated from the critical text with an introduction by Edmund Colledge, OSA, and James Walsh, SJ (New York: Paulist Press, 1978). References to the short text and the long text of this work are given by chapter and page numbers of this critical edition.

2. Introduction to *Showings*, 22.

3. Grace Jantzen, *Julian of Norwich: Mystic and Theologian* (New York: Paulist Press, 1988), 4. Jantzen notes that this name was used of her at the time.

4. Colledge and Walsh, Introduction to *Showings*, 18. See *The Book of Margery Kempe*, ed. W. Butler-Bowden (Oxford, UK: Oxford University Press, 1944), 54–56.

5. *Showings*, LT 2/177.

6. Jantzen, *Julian of Norwich*, 21.

7. Colledge and Walsh, Introduction to *Showings*, 19.

8. *Showings*, LT 51/270.

9. Jantzen, *Julian of Norwich*, 18–19.

10. This is the opinion of Colledge and Walsh, Introduction to *Showings*, 20. See also Joan M. Nuth, *Wisdom's Daughter: The Theology of Julian of Norwich* (New York: Crossroad, 1991), 10.

11. Colledge and Walsh refer to her comment in the final chapter, "This book is begun by God's gift and his grace, but it is not yet performed, as I see it" (LT, 86/342). They argue that the phrase "not yet performed" means that Julian had not yet retired from a monastic community to the more austere life of solitary enclosure (Introduction to *Showings*, 20–21).

12. Jantzen, *Julian of Norwich*, 25. Jantzen appeals to the depth of Julian's

life of prayer and her devotion to Christ. She argues that her phrase "not yet performed" refers to the wider dissemination of God's love (21).

13. Ibid., 6.

14. Jane F. Maynard, *Transfiguring Loss: Julian of Norwich as a Guide for Survivors of Traumatic Grief* (Cleveland: Pilgrim Press, 2006), 60–61.

15. Ibid., 62.

16. Jantzen, *Julian of Norwich*, 46.

17. *Showings*, ST 1/125–27; LT 2/177–78.

18. *Showings*, LT 2/178.

19. Ibid.

20. Ibid., LT 3/180.

21. Jantzen, *Julian of Norwich*, 55.

22. See Richard Rolle, *The English Writings*, ed. Rosamund S. Allen (New York: Paulist Press, 1988), 90–124.

23. Nuth, *Wisdom's Daughter*, 11.

24. *Showings*, LT 3/180.

25. Ibid., LT 18/210.

26. Jantzen, *Julian of Norwich*, 58.

27. *Showings*, LT 20/213.

28. Ibid., LT 20/214.

29. Jantzen, *Julian of Norwich*, 61. In his study of Julian's thought Christopher Abbott argues that Julian's perspective deepens and matures as she reflects on her experience. Abbott asserts that "in reconstructing her relation to the figure of Christ crucified Julian narrates her own movement from pious individualism to an inclusive compassion rooted in her developed understanding of Christ's identification with the Church." See *Julian of Norwich: Autobiography and Theology*, Studies in Medieval Mysticism, vol. 2 (Cambridge, UK: D. S. Brewer, 1999), at 77.

30. Jantzen, *Julian of Norwich*, 77–85; Nuth, *Wisdom's Daughter*, 12–16.

31. Nuth, *Wisdom's Daughter*, 15. Nuth cites the work on visionary mystics by Elizabeth Petroff, *Medieval Women's Visionary Literature* (New York and Oxford, UK: Oxford University Press, 1986).

32. *Showings*, LT 9/191.

33. Jantzen, *Julian of Norwich*, 80.

34. Ibid.

35. *Showings*, LT 20–22/214–18. See Nuth, *Wisdom's Daughter*, 138–41.

36. *Showings*, LT 20/214.

37. Ibid., LT 20/213.

38. Ibid., LT 23/218.

39. Ibid., LT 12/200.

40. Ibid., LT 24/220.

41. Jantzen, *Julian of Norwich*, 172.
42. *Showings*, LT 13/201.
43. Ibid., LT 68/315.
44. Ibid., LT 22/217.
45. Nuth, *Wisdom's Daughter*, 43.
46. LT 22/216.
47. Ibid., LT 22/217.
48. Ibid., LT 31/230.
49. Ibid., LT 31/230–31.
50. Ibid., LT 60/298.
51. Ibid.
52. Ibid., LT 60/298–99.
53. Colledge and Walsh, Introduction to *Showings*, 47.
54. Jantzen, *Julian of Norwich*, 90.
55. Ibid., 91.
56. Ibid., 91–92.
57. *Showings*, LT 27/225.
58. Ibid.
59. Ibid., LT 29/228.
60. Ibid., LT 39/244.
61. Ibid., LT 78/332.
62. Ibid., LT 27/224.
63. Ibid.
64. Ibid., LT 27/225.
65. Ibid., LT 37/241.
66. Ibid., LT 35/237.
67. Ibid., LT 61/300.
68. Nuth, *Wisdom's Daughter*, 121.
69. Ibid., 31–32.
70. *Showings*, LT 51/267.
71. Ibid., LT 51/269.
72. Ibid.
73. Ibid., LT 51/271.
74. Ibid., LT 51/274.
75. Ibid., LT 51/275.
76. Ibid., LT 51/276.
77. Ibid., LT 46/259.
78. Ibid., LT 49/264.
79. *Showings*, LT 29/228.
80. Ibid., LT 36/240.
81. Ibid., LT 82/338.

82. Ibid., LT 18/211.

83. Ibid., LT 28/226.

84. Ibid., LT 77/331.

85. Ibid., LT 47/261.

86. Ibid., LT 32/233.

87. Ibid., LT 33/234.

88. Ibid.

89. Ibid., LT 32/233.

90. Ibid., LT 32/232–33.

91. Ibid., LT 32/233.

92. Ibid., LT 48/263.

93. Ibid., LT 85/341.

94. Jantzen, *Julian of Norwich*, 186.

95. Ibid., 186–87.

96. *Showings*, LT 39/245.

97. Ibid., LT 38/242.

98. Jantzen, *Julian of Norwich*, 189.

99. Nuth, *Wisdom's Daughter*, 169.

100. *Showings*, LT 72/320.

101. Ibid., LT 4/181.

102. Ibid.

103. Ibid., LT 58/294.

104. Ibid.

105. Ibid., LT 52/279.

106. Ibid., LT 8/190.

107. Ibid., LT 5/183.

108. Ibid., LT 6/186.

109. Ibid., LT 23/218–19.

110. Ibid., LT 51/278.

111. Ibid., LT 72/320.

112. Jantzen, *Julian of Norwich*, 133.

113. *Showings*, LT 85/341.

114. Ibid., LT 86/342.

Chapter 6: Two Voices from the Shoah

1. Elie Wiesel, *Night*, trans. Stella Rodway (New York: Hill & Wang, 1960; New York: Bantam Books, 1982).

2. See *Messengers of God: Biblical Portraits and Legends*, trans. Marion Wiesel

(New York: Summit Books, 1976) and *Souls on Fire: Portraits and Legends of Hasidic Masters* (New York: Random House, 1972).

3. Elie Wiesel, *The Town beyond the Wall*, trans. Stephen Becker (New York: Holt, Rinehart and Winston, 1964), 150–64.

4. Ibid., 150.

5. Elie Wiesel in Carol Rittner, "An Interview with Elie Wiesel," *America* 159, no. 15 (1988): 400.

6. Elie Wiesel, *Memoirs: All Rivers Run to the Sea* (New York: Schocken, 1995), 70.

7. Elie Wiesel, *A Jew Today* (New York: Random House, 1978), 15.

8. Ibid., 18.

9. Ibid., 19.

10. François Mauriac, Foreword to *Night*, vii.

11. Wiesel in Rittner, "Interview with Elie Wiesel," 398.

12. Wiesel, *Night*, 31.

13. Wiesel, *Memoirs*, 81–82.

14. Wiesel, *Night*, 42.

15. See Elie Wiesel, *The Trial of God (As It Was Held on February 25, 1649, in Shamgorod): A Play in Three Acts*, trans. Marion Wiesel (New York: Random House, 1979). See also Ekkehard Schuster and Reinhold Boschert-Kimmig, *Hope against Hope: Johann Baptist Metz and Elie Wiesel Speak Out on the Holocaust*, trans. J. Matthew Ashley (New York: Paulist Press, 1999), 91.

16. Wiesel, *Night*, 63.

17. Ibid.

18. Ibid., 61–62.

19. Wiesel, *Memoirs*, 84.

20. Wiesel, *Night*, 65.

21. Wiesel, *Memoirs*, 80.

22. Ibid.

23. Ibid., 92.

24. Wiesel, *Night*, 86.

25. Ibid., 87.

26. Ibid., 102.

27. Wiesel, *Messengers of God*, 211–35.

28. Ibid., 211.

29. Ibid., 213–14.

30. Ibid., 218.

31. Ibid., 220.

32. Ibid., 221.

33. See Rittner, "Interview with Elie Wiesel," 399.

34. Wiesel, *Messengers of God*, 225.

35. Ibid.

36. Wiesel, *Night*, 83.

37. Wiesel, *Messengers of God*, 229.

38. Ibid., 233.

39. Ibid.

40. Ibid.

41. Ibid.

42. Ibid., 235.

43. Ibid.

44. Wiesel, *The Trial of God*, 125.

45. Schuster and Boschert-Kimmig, *Hope against Hope*, 91–95.

46. Ibid., 91.

47. Ibid.

48. Wiesel, *Memoirs*, 103.

49. Ibid.

50. Ibid., 105, and Schuster and Boschert-Kimmig, *Hope against Hope*, 97.

51. Wiesel, *Memoirs*, 104.

52. Ibid., 104–5.

53. Wiesel in Schuster and Boschert-Kimmig, *Hope against Hope*, 93.

54. Ibid., 97.

55. Ibid.

56. Ibid.

57. Eberhard Bethge, *Dietrich Bonhoeffer: A Biography*, rev. and ed. Victoria J. Barnett (Minneapolis: Fortress, 2000), 5–6.

58. Ibid., 205.

59. See Geffrey B. Kelly and F. Burton Nelson, *The Cost of Moral Leadership: The Spirituality of Dietrich Bonhoeffer* (Grand Rapids, MI: Eerdmans, 2003), 88–89.

60. Bethge, *Dietrich Bonhoeffer*, 258.

61. Ibid., 260. One meaning of the German word *Verführer* is "seducer."

62. Kelly and Nelson, *The Cost of Moral Leadership*, 27.

63. Bethge, *Dietrich Bonhoeffer*, 792.

64. Dietrich Bonhoeffer, *Letters and Papers from Prison*, ed. Eberhard Bethge, trans. Reginald H. Fuller (New York: Macmillan, 1953/1962).

65. Dietrich Bonhoeffer, *Ethics*, ed. Eberhard Bethge, trans. Neville Horton Smith (New York: Macmillan, 1955).

66. Geffrey Kelly, "'Unconscious Christianity' and the 'Anonymous Christian' in the Theology of Dietrich Bonhoeffer and Karl Rahner," paper delivered at the 1994 convention of the Catholic Theological Society of America, 2. For a summary of this paper, see *Proceedings of the Catholic Theological Society of America* 49 (1994): 206–7.

67. Bethge, *Dietrich Bonhoeffer*, 890.

68. Bonhoeffer, *Letters and Papers from Prison*, 163 (letter of April 30, 1944). See 198 for his remarks about Barth's criticisms of religion (letter of June 8, 1944).

69. Ibid., 198 (letter of June 8, 1944).

70. Ibid., 214 (letter of July 8, 1944).

71. Ibid., 162 (letter of April 30, 1944).

72. See Karl Barth, *The Epistle to the Romans*, trans. from the 6th ed. by Edwyn C. Hoskyns (London: Oxford University Press, 1933). For Barth's critique of religion, see among other passages 57 (commentary on Rom 2:1–2); 79 (Rom 3:2–3); 126–27 (Rom 4:6–9); 230–31 (Rom 7:1).

73. Dietrich Bonhoeffer, *The Cost of Discipleship*, rev. and unabr. ed., trans. Reginald H. Fuller (New York: Macmillan, 1963), 47.

74. Kelly, "'Unconscious Christianity,'" 1.

75. Bonhoeffer, *Letters and Papers from Prison*, 231 (letter of July 25, 1944).

76. Ibid., 238.

77. Bethge, *Dietrich Bonhoeffer*, 872–80.

78. Ibid., 874.

79. Bonhoeffer, *Letters and Papers from Prison*, 224 (letter of July 18, 1944).

80. Ibid., 191 (letter of May 25, 1944).

81. Ibid., 190 (letter of May 25, 1944).

82. Ibid., 191 (letter of May 25, 1944).

83. Ibid., 166 (letter of April 30, 1944).

84. Ibid., 205 (letter of June 27, 1944).

85. Ibid., 219–20 (letter of July 16, 1944).

86. Ibid., 220 (letter of July 16, 1944).

87. Ibid.

88. Ibid., 222 (letter of July 18, 1944).

89. Ibid., 223 (letter of July 18, 1944).

90. Ibid., 224–25. I have used the translation given in Kelly and Nelson, *The Cost of Moral Leadership*, 240.

91. Ibid., 238.

92. Kelly and Nelson, *The Cost of Moral Leadership*, 241.

93. Bonhoeffer, *The Cost of Discipleship*, 96.

94. Ibid., 98.

95. Ibid., 122; emphasis in the original.

96. Bonhoeffer, *Letters and Papers from Prison*, 228.

97. Ibid.

98. Ibid.

99. Ibid., 229.

100. Ibid., 232.

101. Ibid.
102. Ibid., 118–19 (letter of December 22, 1943).
103. Ibid., 158 (letter of April 11, 1944).
104. Ibid., 245 (letter of August 23, 1944).
105. Ibid., 27.
106. Ibid., 159 (letter of April 22, 1944).
107. Ibid., 243 (letter of August 21, 1944).
108. See Bethge, *Dietrich Bonhoeffer*, 927. Bethge cites Payne Best, *The Venlo Incident*, 200.

Chapter 7: Jürgen Moltmann

1. Jürgen Moltmann, *The Crucified God: The Cross of Christ as the Foundation and Criticism of Christian Theology*, trans. R. A. Wilson and John Bowden (New York: Harper & Row, 1974).
2. Among the passages in which Moltmann describes this experience are the following: *The Source of Life: The Holy Spirit and the Theology of Life*, trans. Margaret Kohl (Minneapolis: Fortress, 1997), 1–9; *How I Have Changed: Reflections on Thirty Years of Theology*, trans. John Bowden (Harrisburg, PA: Trinity Press International, 1997), 31–32; *God for a Secular Society: The Public Relevance of Theology*, trans. Margaret Kohl (Minneapolis: Fortress, 1999), 169–90; *Passion for God: Theology in Two Voices*, with Elisabeth Moltmann-Wendel (Louisville, KY: Westminster John Knox, 2003), 69–72; *In the End—The Beginning: The Life of Hope*, trans. Margaret Kohl (Minneapolis: Fortress, 2004), 33–35.
3. Moltmann, *The Source of Life*, 2.
4. Moltmann, *In the End—The Beginning*, 33.
5. Moltmann, *The Source of Life*, 4.
6. Ibid., 5.
7. Ibid.; emphasis in the original.
8. Moltmann, *In the End—The Beginning*, 35.
9. Moltmann, *The Source of Life*, 8.
10. Moltmann, *Passion for God*, 76.
11. Ibid., 70.
12. Ibid., 71.
13. Jürgen Moltmann, *The Trinity and the Kingdom: The Doctrine of God*, trans. Margaret Kohl (San Francisco: Harper & Row, 1981), 48.
14. Ibid., 47.
15. Moltmann, *The Crucified God*, 219.
16. Ibid., 220.

17. Ibid., 221.

18. Ibid., 222.

19. Ibid., 223.

20. Martin Luther, *Heidelberg Disputation*, 19–21, quoted in Jaroslav Pelikan, *The Christian Tradition: A History of the Development of Doctrine*, vol. 4, *Reformation of Church and Dogma (1300–1700)* (Chicago: University of Chicago Press, 1984), 155.

21. Moltmann, *The Crucified God*, 227.

22. See David Tracy, *The Analogical Imagination: Christian Theology and the Culture of Pluralism* (New York: Crossroad, 1981), 408. Tracy discusses Moltmann's use of the negative dialectics of Adorno and Horkheimer on 416. He notes that for Moltmann the cross "exposes the contradictions in the present, the nonidentity of the present with God's word, the need for a theological negative dialectics."

23. Ibid., 410.

24. Ibid., 415.

25. Ibid., 416.

26. Moltmann, *The Crucified God*, 27.

27. Ibid., 212.

28. Ibid.

29. Ibid., 241.

30. Ibid., 244.

31. Jürgen Moltmann, *The Way of Jesus Christ: Christology in Messianic Dimensions*, trans. Margaret Kohl (San Francisco: Harper & Row, 1990), 166.

32. Ibid., 172.

33. Moltmann, *The Trinity and the Kingdom*, 76.

34. Ibid., 78–79.

35. Moltmann, *The Way of Jesus Christ*, 172.

36. Moltmann, *The Trinity and the Kingdom*, 78.

37. Moltmann, *In the End—The Beginning*, 147.

38. Moltmann, *The Way of Jesus Christ*, 174.

39. Ibid., 173.

40. Moltmann, *The Source of Life*, 17, 19; emphasis in the original.

41. Moltmann, *The Way of Jesus Christ*, 177.

42. Moltmann, *The Crucified God*, 230.

43. Moltmann, *In the End—The Beginning*, 70.

44. Moltmann, *The Trinity and the Kingdom*, 23–25.

45. Moltmann, *The Crucified God*, 246.

46. Ibid., 278.

47. Ibid.

48. Moltmann, *God for a Secular Society*, 180.

49. Ibid.

50. Karl Rahner affirms this "double gratuity" but argues that Christians can envision the gift of creation in light of God's intention to offer grace, to communicate Godself to men and women. This self-communication of God attains its historical fulfillment in the incarnation of the Son of God. See "Concerning the Relationship between Nature and Grace," *Theological Investigations*, vol. 1, *God Christ, Mary and Grace*, trans. Cornelius Ernst, OP (Baltimore: Helicon, 1961), 310. Moltmann takes a similar position when he says that "in intention the incarnation precedes the creation of the world." See *The Trinity and the Kingdom*, 117.

51. Moltmann, *The Trinity and the Kingdom*, 53.

52. Ibid., 55.

53. Ibid., 56.

54. Ibid., 106.

55. Ibid.

56. Jürgen Moltmann, *The Church in the Power of the Spirit: A Contribution to Messianic Ecclesiology*, trans. Margaret Kohl (San Francisco: Harper & Row, 1977), 62; emphasis in the original. The reader might infer here that in speaking of what God "wanted" to do, Moltmann is suggesting some kind of divine decision with regard to creation and the offer of grace. Moltmann criticizes the language of "decision" as found, for example, in Karl Barth, though he uses it himself in *The Trinity and the Kingdom*, where he says, "By *deciding* to communicate himself, God *discloses* his own *being*" (58).

57. Moltmann, *The Trinity and the Kingdom*, 109. Moltmann appeals especially to the work of Isaac Luria for the concept of *zimsum*.

58. Ibid., 110.

59. Ibid., 109; emphasis in the original. We will see that Elizabeth Johnson also presents a panentheistic understanding of the God-world relation. She draws on the definition of *panentheism* given in *The Oxford Dictionary of the Christian Church*: "The belief that the Being of God includes and penetrates the whole universe, so that every part of it exists in Him, but (as against pantheism) that this Being is more than, and is not exhausted by, the universe." See Johnson, *She Who Is: The Mystery of God in Feminist Theological Discourse* (New York: Crossroad, 1992), 231.

60. Moltmann explicitly cites Hegel on 246 of *The Crucified God*. For a discussion of Hegel's influence on Moltmann, see Marc Steen, "Jürgen Moltmann's Critical Reception of K. Barth's Theopaschitism," *Ephemerides Theologicae Lovanienses* 67 (1991): 278–311, especially 294–97.

61. Moltmann, *The Crucified God*, 246.

62. Ibid., 255.

63. Ibid.

64. Moltmann, *The Trinity and the Kingdom*, 60.

65. Moltmann identifies Pentecost as the event in which the Trinity becomes open to human history on 89–90 of *The Trinity and the Kingdom*. On 4 of the same work he speaks about the entire history of the world as the history of God's suffering.

66. Ibid., 95.

67. Moltmann, *The Crucified God*, 99.

68. Moltmann, *In the End—The Beginning*, 87.

69. Ibid., 83.

70. Moltmann, *The Way of Jesus Christ*, xiii.

71. Moltmann, *The Church in the Power of the Spirit*, 58.

72. Moltmann, *The Way of Jesus Christ*, 139.

73. Ibid., 32.

74. Ibid.

75. Ibid., 314.

76. Ibid., 191.

77. Moltmann, *In the End—The Beginning*, 143.

78. Ibid.

79. Ibid.

80. Moltmann, *The Way of Jesus Christ*, 329.

81. Moltmann, *In the End—The Beginning*, 151.

82. Moltmann, *The Way of Jesus Christ*, 303.

83. Ibid., 302.

84. Jürgen Moltmann, *Experiences of God*, trans. Margaret Kohl (Philadelphia: Fortress, 1980), 19.

85. Ibid., 20. See also *In the End—The Beginning*, 93.

86. Moltmann, *In the End—The Beginning*, 139.

87. Moltmann, *Passion for God*, 70.

88. Moltmann, *The Crucified God*, 175.

89. Moltmann, *The Way of Jesus Christ*, 183.

90. Ibid.

91. Moltmann, *The Trinity and the Kingdom*, 49.

92. Ibid.

93. Moltmann, *The Way of Jesus Christ*, 187.

94. Moltmann, *The Trinity and the Kingdom*, 51.

95. Ibid.

96. Dorothee Sölle, *Suffering*, trans. Everett R. Kalin (Philadelphia: Fortress, 1975), 25–28. See also *Theology for Skeptics: Reflections on God*, trans. Joyce L. Irwin (Minneapolis: Fortress, 1995), 100.

97. Sölle, *Suffering*, 27.

98. Ibid.

99. Steen, "Jürgen Moltmann's Critical Reception of K. Barth's Theopaschitism," 303.

100. Moltmann, *The Way of Jesus Christ*, 175–77; *Passion for God*, 82–83.

101. Steen, "Jürgen Moltmann's Critical Reception of K. Barth's Theopaschitism," 303.

102. Moltmann, *The Way of Jesus Christ*, 172.

103. Karl Rahner, *Karl Rahner in Dialogue: Conversations and Interviews, 1965–1982*, ed. Paul Imhof and Hubert Biallowons, trans. Harvey Egan (New York: Crossroad, 1986), 126. Moltmann responds to Rahner's critique in *Passion for God*, 80–81, and in *History and the Triune God* (New York: Crossroad, 1992), 122–24.

104. Rahner, *Karl Rahner in Dialogue*, 127. In the course of his comments on Moltmann, Rahner appeals to the classical teaching of the communication of idioms: "I know of course and I have emphasized that the classical teaching on the Incarnation and the theology of the hypostatic union include and must include, even while avoiding Patripassianism (a suffering and dying God the Father), a meaningful and serious statement to the effect that *God died*" (126). Rahner deals with the themes of the immutability of God and the incarnation in *Foundations of Christian Faith*, trans. William Dych (New York: Crossroad, 1978), 212–28. Rahner is well known for saying about God, "He who is not subject to change in himself can *himself* be subject to change *in something else*" (220). He adds, "The mystery of the Incarnation must be in God himself, and precisely in the fact that, although he is immutable in and of himself, he *himself* can become something in another" (221).

105. Rahner, *Karl Rahner in Dialogue*, 127.

106. J. B. Metz, *A Passion for God: The Mystical-Political Dimensions of Christianity* (New York: Paulist Press, 1998), 70–71.

107. Hill, "Does Divine Love Entail Suffering in God?" 65.

108. Michael Dodds, "Thomas Aquinas: Human Suffering and the Unchanging God of Love," *Theological Studies* 52 (1991): 333.

109. Thomas Weinandy, *Does God Suffer?* (Notre Dame, IN: University of Notre Dame Press, 2000), 154.

110. Ibid., 226–27.

111. Hill, "Does Divine Love Entail Suffering in God?" 63.

112. Steen, "Jürgen Moltmann's Critical Reception of K. Barth's Theopaschitism," 304.

113. Ibid., 305–6.

114. Ibid., 306.

115. Helen Bergin, "The Death of Jesus and Its Impact on God—Jürgen Moltmann and Edward Schillebeeckx," *Irish Theological Quarterly* 52 (1986): 193–211, at 209.

Chapter 8: Edward Schillebeeckx

1. In this chapter I draw upon, though expand significantly, insights found in my article, "Holding on to the Hand of God: Edward Schillebeeckx on the Mystery of Suffering," *New Blackfriars* 89 (2008): 114–25.

2. Edward Schillebeeckx, in conversation with Huub Oosterhuis and Piet Hoogeveen, *God Is New Each Moment*, trans. David Smith (New York: Seabury, 1983), 13–14.

3. See Schillebeeckx's remarks in *Jesus: An Experiment in Christology*, trans. Hubert Hoskins (New York: Crossroad, 1979), 618–19. Maurice Merleau-Ponty was also a significant figure in phenomenology. In a personal conversation, Robert Schreiter has informed me that DePetter's later works were influenced by the thought of Merleau-Ponty, though this influence came after the time in which DePetter was teaching Schillebeeckx. Schillebeeckx met Merleau-Ponty in Paris and attended some of his lectures.

4. Mary Catherine Hilkert, "Discovery of the Living God: Revelation and Experience," in *The Praxis of Christian Experience: An Introduction to the Theology of Edward Schillebeeckx*, ed. Robert J. Schreiter and Mary Catherine Hilkert (San Francisco: Harper & Row, 1989), 45.

5. Schillebeeckx, *God Is New Each Moment*, 16.

6. Susan Ross, "Salvation in and for the World: Church and Sacraments," in *The Praxis of Christian Experience*, 108.

7. William Portier, "Interpretation and Method," in *The Praxis of Christian Experience*, 22.

8. See *Ministry: Leadership in the Community of Jesus Christ*, trans. John Bowden (New York: Crossroad, 1981); *The Church with a Human Face: A New and Expanded Theology of Ministry*, trans. John Bowden (New York: Crossroad, 1985); and *Church: The Human Story of God*, trans. John Bowden (New York: Crossroad, 1990), especially 187–228.

9. William Hill, "Human Happiness as God's Honor: Background to a Theology in Transition," in *The Praxis of Christian Experience*, 11.

10. Edward Schillebeeckx, *Christ: The Experience of Jesus as Lord*, trans. John Bowden (New York: Crossroad, 1983), 19.

11. Ibid., 31.

12. Portier, "Interpretation and Method," 26.

13. Robert Schreiter, "Edward Schillebeeckx: His Continuing Significance," in *The Praxis of Christian Experience*, 151.

14. John Galvin, "Retelling the Story of Jesus: Christology," in *The Praxis of Christian Experience*, 53–54.

15. Schillebeeckx, *Christ: The Experience of Jesus as Lord*, 724–25.

16. Ibid., 725.

17. Schillebeeckx, *Church*, 4.

18. Lucien Richard, *What Are They Saying about the Theology of Suffering?* (New York: Paulist Press, 1992), 29.

19. Schillebeeckx, *Church*, 5.

20. Schreiter, "Edward Schillebeeckx," 151.

21. Schillebeeckx, *Christ: The Experience of Jesus as Lord*, 818.

22. Schillebeeckx, *Church*, 5–6.

23. Ibid., 7.

24. Ibid.

25. Schillebeeckx, *God Is New Each Moment*, 99.

26. Schreiter, "Edward Schillebeeckx," 153.

27. Ibid.

28. See Schillebeeckx, *Christ: The Experience of Jesus as Lord*, 744–839.

29. Ibid., 791.

30. Ibid., 725.

31. Galvin, "Retelling the Story of Jesus," 54.

32. Schillebeeckx, *Jesus*, 620.

33. Hilkert, "Discovery of the Living God," 39.

34. Schillebeeckx, *Christ: The Experience of Jesus as Lord*, 698.

35. Schreiter, "Edward Schillebeeckx," 150.

36. Galvin, "Retelling the Story of Jesus," 54.

37. Ibid., 56.

38. Schillebeeckx, *God Is New Each Moment*, 22.

39. Edward Schillebeeckx, "The 'God of Jesus' and the 'Jesus of God,'" *Concilium*, vol. 93 (New York: Herder & Herder, 1974), 117.

40. Schillebeeckx, *Church*, 111–12.

41. Ibid., 116.

42. Schillebeeckx, *Jesus*, 613–14.

43. Ibid., 206.

44. Ibid., 635.

45. Ibid., 256.

46. Ibid., 268.

47. Schillebeeckx, *Christ: The Experience of Jesus as Lord*, 727.

48. Ibid., 794.

49. Schillebeeckx, *Jesus*, 97.

50. Ibid., 298.

51. Schillebeeckx, *Christ: The Experience of Jesus as Lord*, 828.

52. Schillebeeckx, *Jesus*, 301.

53. Schillebeeckx, "The 'God of Jesus' and the 'Jesus of God,'" 124.

54. Schillebeeckx, *Jesus*, 309–12. In his conversation with the Congregation for the Doctrine of the Faith (CDF), Schillebeeckx's treatment of this

Markan passage was addressed. In particular, his division of this verse into two parts was questioned. In his response to the CDF, Schillebeeckx admitted that in *Jesus* he gave the wrong impression that the second part of Mark 14:25 was secondary (not the authentic words of Jesus). He told the congregation that he considered both parts of the verse to be the words of Jesus. What is secondary is the combining of the two parts of the logion. See *The Schillebeeckx Case*, ed. Ted Schoof, trans. Matthew O'Connell (New York: Paulist Press, 1984), 129.

55. Schillebeeckx, *Jesus*, 310.

56. Ibid.

57. Schillebeeckx, "The 'God of Jesus' and the 'Jesus of God,'" 126.

58. Ibid.

59. Schillebeeckx, *Church*, 120–21.

60. Schillebeeckx, *God Is New Each Moment*, 108.

61 Schillebeeckx, *Jesus*, 317.

62. Schillebeeckx, *Christ: The Experience of Jesus as Lord*, 466.

63. Schillebeeckx, *Jesus*, 652.

64. Schillebeeckx, *Christ: The Experience of Jesus as Lord*, 824.

65. Ibid., 825; emphasis in the original.

66. See Karl Rahner, *Foundations of Christian Faith*, trans. William Dych (New York: Seabury, 1978), 264–85.

67. Schillebeeckx, *Christ: The Experience of Jesus as Lord*, 796.

68. Schillebeeckx, *Jesus*, 641.

69. Schillebeeckx, *Christ: The Experience of Jesus as Lord*, 799.

70. Ibid., 729.

71. Ibid., 729–30; emphasis in the original.

72. Schillebeeckx, "The 'God of Jesus' and the 'Jesus of God,'" 125; *Jesus*, 625.

73. Schillebeeckx, "The 'God of Jesus' and the 'Jesus of God,'" 125; see *Jesus*, 651.

74. Schillebeeckx, *Jesus*, 625.

75. Schillebeeckx, *Church*, 90.

76. Schillebeeckx, *Christ: The Experience of Jesus as Lord*, 724.

77. Ibid., 728; emphasis in the original.

78. Ibid., 729; emphasis in the original.

79. Edward Schillebeeckx, "The Death of the Christian," in *The Layman in the Church and Other Essays* (Staten Island, NY: Alba House, 1963), 38.

80. Ibid., 42.

81. Ibid., 45.

82. Edward Schillebeeckx, *Christ: The Sacrament of the Encounter with God,*

trans. Paul Barrett; English text rev. Mark Schoof and Laurence Bright (New York: Sheed & Ward, 1963), 22.

83. Schillebeeckx, *Christ: The Experience of Jesus as Lord*, 738–39.

84. Ibid., 793.

85. Ibid., 800.

86. Schillebeeckx, *Church*, 87.

87. Ibid., 88.

88. Ibid., 91.

89. Schillebeeckx, *God Is New Each Moment*, 107.

90. Schillebeeckx, *Christ: The Experience of Jesus as Lord*, 806.

91. Schillebeeckx, *Church*, 126.

92. Ibid., 132.

93. Ibid., 137.

94. Ibid.

95. Ibid., 138.

96. Ibid., 74.

97. John Galvin, "The Death of Jesus in the Theology of Edward Schillebeeckx," *Irish Theological Quarterly* 50 (1983/84): 176.

98. Ibid.

99. Schillebeeckx, *God Is New Each Moment*, 108.

Chapter 9: Gustavo Gutiérrez

1. Gustavo Gutiérrez, in Daniel Hartnett, "Remembering the Poor: An Interview with Gustavo Gutiérrez," *America* 188, no. 3 (February 3, 2003): 16.

2. Robert McAfee Brown, *Gustavo Gutiérrez: An Introduction to Liberation Theology* (Maryknoll, NY: Orbis, 1990), 23–24.

3. See Gustavo Gutiérrez, *The Truth Shall Make You Free: Confrontations*, trans. Matthew O'Connell (Maryknoll, NY: Orbis, 1990), 1–52.

4. James Nickoloff, Introduction to *Gustavo Gutiérrez: Essential Writings* (Maryknoll, NY: Orbis, 1996), 2.

5. Ibid.

6. Gustavo Gutiérrez, *A Theology of Liberation*, "Introduction to the Revised Edition: Expanding the View," trans. Sister Caridad Inda˚ and John Eagleson (Maryknoll, NY: Orbis, 1988), xxviii. Unless otherwise noted, references to *A Theology of Liberation* are taken from the original edition of the book (Spanish, 1971; English, 1973).

7. Ibid.

8. Nickoloff, Introduction to *Gustavo Gutiérrez*, 3–4.

9. *A Theology of Liberation*, 110. See Second General Conference of

Latin American Bishops, *The Church in the Present-Day Transformation of Latin America in the Light of the Council*, "Justice," n. 3 (Washington, DC: USCC—Division for Latin America, 1973), 41.

10. Gutiérrez offered this observation in a presentation entitled "Medellin, Aparecida, and the Future." This talk was given at DePaul University (Chicago) on October 30, 2008, and was part of the "Transformed by Hope" Conference, cosponsored by Catholic Theological Union and DePaul University. To my knowledge this talk has not been published. For an online link to the talk visit http://hope08conference.depaul.edu/.

11. Gutiérrez, *A Theology of Liberation*, ix.

12. Ibid., 11–12.

13. See, for example, *On Job: God-Talk and the Suffering of the Innocent*, trans. Matthew O'Connell (Maryknoll, NY: Orbis, 1987), xiii. Some would argue, perhaps, that "praxis"—correctly understood—integrates contemplation and practice/action. While that may be true, there does appear to be some development in Gutiérrez's thought on this matter, with a stronger emphasis on the contemplative or mystical dimension of faith evident in his later writings.

14. Gutiérrez, *A Theology of Liberation*, 13.

15. Ibid., 15.

16. See Congregation for the Doctrine of the Faith, "Instruction on Certain Aspects of the 'Theology of Liberation'" (*Libertatis Nuntius*), *Origins* 14, no. 13 (September 13, 1984): 193–204; and "Instruction on Christian Freedom and Liberation" (*Libertatis Conscientia*), *Origins* 15, no. 44 (April 17, 1986): 713–28.

17. For the fifteenth anniversary edition of *A Theology of Liberation*, Gutiérrez rewrote the section entitled "Christian Brotherhood and Class Struggle" (272–79 in the original edition) and entitled it "Faith and Social Conflict" (156–61 in the revised edition). In a note he explains, "I have rewritten the text in the light of new documents of the magisterium and by taking other aspects of the subject into account" (156). In his discussion of faith and social conflict, he says, "The universality of Christian love is, I repeat, incompatible with the exclusion of any persons, but it is not incompatible with a preferential option for the poorest and most oppressed. When I speak of taking into account social conflict, including the existence of the class struggle, I am not denying that God's love embraces all without exception. Nor is anyone excluded from our love, for the gospel requires that we love even our enemies; a situation that causes us to regard others as our adversaries does not excuse us from loving them. There are oppositions and social conflicts between diverse factions, classes, cultures, and racial groupings, but they do not exclude respect for persons, for as human beings they are loved by God and are constantly being called to conversion" (160).

18. Gustavo Gutiérrez, "Theological Language: Fullness of Silence," in *The Density of the Present: Selected Writings* (Maryknoll, NY: Orbis, 1999), 188.

19. Gutiérrez, *The Truth Shall Make You Free*, 5.

20. Gutiérrez, *On Job*, xiv–xv. See Desmond Tutu, "The Theology of Liberation in Africa," in *African Theology en Route: Papers from the Pan-African Conference of Third World Theologians, December 17–23, 1977, Accra, Ghana*, ed. Kofi Appiah-Kubi and Sergio Torres (Maryknoll, NY: Orbis, 1979), 163.

21. Nickoloff, Introduction to *Gustavo Gutiérrez*, 14.

22. Gutiérrez, *A Theology of Liberation*, "Introduction to the Revised Edition," xxv.

23. Ibid.

24. See *The God of Life*, trans. Matthew O'Connell (Maryknoll, NY: Orbis, 1991), 121.

25. Gustavo Gutiérrez, *The Power of the Poor in History: Selected Writings*, trans. Robert R. Barr (Maryknoll, NY: Orbis, 1983), 70.

26. Gustavo Gutiérrez, *We Drink from Our Own Wells: The Spiritual Journey of a People*, trans. Matthew O'Connell (Maryknoll, NY: Orbis, 1984), 114–15.

27. Gutiérrez, in Hartnett, "Remembering the Poor," 13.

28. Ibid.

29. Gutiérrez, *On Job*, 22.

30. Gutiérrez, *A Theology of Liberation*, 35.

31. Gutiérrez, *The Truth Shall Make You Free*, 30.

32. Ibid., 31.

33. Ibid.

34. Gutiérrez, *The Power of the Poor in History*, 228.

35. Ibid., 229.

36. Ibid., 231. Bonhoeffer's letter can be found in *Dietrich Bonoeffer: Gesammelte Schriften*, vol. 2, ed. Eberhard Bethge (Munich: Chr. Kaisere Verlag, 1965), 441.

37. Gutiérrez, *The Power of the Poor in History*, 232.

38. Ibid., 183–85.

39. Ibid., 193.

40. See Gutiérrez's study of Las Casas, *Las Casas: In Search of the Poor of Jesus Christ*, trans. Robert R. Barr (Maryknoll, NY: Orbis, 1993).

41. Gutiérrez, *The Power of the Poor in History*, 195.

42. Ibid., 197. Gutiérrez cites Las Casas, "Historia de las Indias," in *Obras Escogidas* (Madrid: BAE, 1958), 2: 356.

43. Gutiérrez, *The Power of the Poor in History*, 196.

44. Quoted by Gutiérrez in *Las Casas*, 194; see Las Casas, *Obras Escogidas*, 5:44b.

45. See III Conferencia General del Episcopado Latinoamericano, *La Evangelizacion en El Presente y en El Futuro de America Latina*, Puebla, nn. 1134, 1142.

46. Nickoloff, Introduction to *Gustavo Gutiérrez*, 12.

47. Gutiérrez, in Hartnett, "Remembering the Poor," 12.

48. Ibid.

49. Ibid.

50. Gustavo Gutiérrez, "The Option for the Poor Arises from Faith in Christ," *Theological Studies* 70 (2009): 317–26.

51. Pope Benedict XVI, "Brazil Visit: Address to CELAM," *Origins* 37, no. 2 (May 24, 2007): 20. The full statement is as follows: "The encounter with God is, in itself, and as such, an encounter with our brothers and sisters, an act of convocation, of unification, of responsibility toward the other and toward others. In this sense the preferential option for the poor is implicit in the Christological faith in the God who became poor for us so as to enrich us with his poverty (Cf. 2 Cor: 8:9)."

52. Quoted by Gutierrez in "The Option for the Poor Arises from Faith in Christ," 320. Gutiérrez cites Archbishop Oscar Romero, "La Iglesia cuya debilidad se apoya en Cristo: Quinto domingo del tiempo ordinario, 5 de febrero de 1978. Isaias 58:7–10, 1 Corintios 1:1–5, Mateo 5:13–16," *La palabra viva de Monseñor Romero*, http://servicioskoinonia.org/romero/homilias/A/780205.htm.

53. Gutiérrez, "The Option for the Poor Arises from Faith in Christ," 322.

54. See, for example, *The God of Life*, 118–20.

55. Gutiérrez, "The Option for the Poor Arises from Faith in Christ," 324.

56. See Nickoloff, Introduction to *Gustavo Gutiérrez*, 7.

57. Gutiérrez, *The Power of the Poor in History*, 61. See also *The Truth Shall Make You Free*, 3–4.

58. See Roger Haight, *An Alternative Vision: An Interpretation of Liberation Theology* (New York: Paulist Press, 1985), 106–8.

59. Gutiérrez, *The Power of the Poor in History*, 13; emphasis in the original.

60. Gutiérrez, *The God of Life*, 85.

61. Ibid., 99.

62. Ibid., 88.

63. Ibid.

64. Ibid., 101.

65. Ibid., 102.

66. Ibid.

67. Ibid., 109.

68. Puebla, n. 1142; *The God of Life*, 115.

69. Gutiérrez, *The Power of the Poor in History*, 15.

70. Gutiérrez, *The God of Life*, 25.

71. Ibid.

72. Gutiérrez, *On Job*, 97–101.

73. Ibid., 97.

74. Ibid., 99–100.

75. Ibid., 100.

76. Ibid.

77. Ibid.

78. Ibid., 101.

79. Gutiérrez, *The Truth Shall Make You Free*, 28. The examiner was Vincent Cosmao.

80. Ibid., 30.

81. Ibid.

82. Gutiérrez, *The God of Life*, 14.

83. Ibid.

84. Gutiérrez, *The Truth Shall Make You Free*, 119. See *Populorum Progressio*, n. 21.

85. Gutiérrez, *A Theology of Liberation*, 36–37.

86. Nickoloff, Introduction to *Gustavo Gutiérrez*, 10.

87. Gutiérrez, *A Theology of Liberation*, 37.

88. Ibid. See also *The Truth Shall Make You Free*, 121–22.

89. Gutiérrez, *A Theology of Liberation*, 153. See also *The Truth Shall Make You Free*, 22, where Gutiérrez acknowledges his dependence on the thought of Maurice Blondel, Henri de Lubac, and Karl Rahner on this point.

90. Gutiérrez, *A Theology of Liberation*, 177; emphasis in the original.

91. Nickoloff, Introduction to *Gustavo Gutiérrez*, 15.

92. Gutiérrez, in Hartnett, "Remembering the Poor," 16.

93. Gutiérrez, *On Job*, xvii.

94. Ibid., 15.

95. Ibid., 4.

96. Ibid., 16.

97. Ibid., 17.

98. Ibid., 10.

99. Ibid., 29.

100. Ibid.

101. Ibid., 31.

102. Ibid., 37.

103. Ibid., 48.

104. Ibid., 59.

105. Ibid., 62.

106. Ibid., 64.

107. Ibid., 65.

108. Ibid.

109. Ibid., 66.

110. Ibid.

111. Ibid., 69.

112. Ibid.

113. Ibid., 71.

114. Ibid., 75.

115. Gutiérrez, *The Power of the Poor in History*, 230.

116. Ibid.

117. Gutiérrez, *On Job*, 77–78.

118. Ibid., 124, n. 1.

119. Ibid., 83.

120. Ibid., 86–87. Gutiérrez cites Dale Patrick, "The Translation of Job XLII, 6," *Vetus Testamentum* 26 (1976): 369–71. He also cites an article by L. Kaplan in which Kaplan points out that Moses Maimonides translated the verse the same way in *Guide of the Perplexed*. See L. Kaplan, "Maimonides, Dale Patrick, and Job XLII, 6," *Vetus Testamentum* 28 (1978): 356–58.

121. Gutiérrez, *On Job*, 86.

122. Ibid., 87; emphasis in the original.

123. Ibid., 94.

124. Ibid., 95.

125. In a note, Gutiérrez takes issue with the interpretation of the Book of Job given by Jorge Pixley. Pixley stresses the limitation of God—the implications of God's historicity. God needs the help of Job in the historical task of establishing justice on earth. Gutiérrez agrees that "the task of establishing justice is indeed one to be carried out with God." But he thinks that the dimension of contemplation and gratuitousness is missing in Pixley's reading of Job: "And without this perspective, the commitment to justice loses its proper setting and scope. Historically, moreover, commitments lacking this perspective have quickly suffered exhaustion." See *On Job*, 127–28, n. 23. For Pixley's interpretation of the book, see Jorge Pixley, *El Libro de Job. Un commentario latinoamericano* (San José, Costa Rica, 1982).

126. Gutiérrez, *On Job*, xiv.

127. See, for example, *A Theology of Liberation*, "Introduction to the Revised Edition," xxi–xxv.

128. Gutiérrez, *On Job*, 66.

Chapter 10: Elizabeth Johnson

1. Elizabeth Johnson, *She Who Is: The Mystery of God in Feminist Theological Discourse* (New York: Crossroad, 1992).

2. Elizabeth Johnson, *Friends of God and Prophets: A Feminist Theological*

Reading of the Communion of Saints (New York: Continuum, 1998); *Truly Our Sister: A Theology of Mary in the Communion of Saints* (New York and London: Continuum, 2004); *Quest for the Living God: Mapping Frontiers in the Theology of God* (New York and London: Continuum, 2008).

3. As a doctoral student at the Catholic University of America, I was privileged to participate in a seminar on the topic of God and the mystery of human suffering led by Johnson.

4. Johnson, *Quest for the Living God*, 50.

5. In addition to the writings on suffering by Sölle (discussed in chapter 7), Johnson often cites Ruether, *Sexism and God-Talk: Toward a Feminist Theology* (Boston: Beacon, 1983); and Farley, *Tragic Vision and Divine Compassion: A Contemporary Theodicy* (Louisville, KY: Westminster/John Knox, 1990).

6. Johnson, *She Who Is*, 262–63.

7. Ibid., 262.

8. Johnson, *Truly Our Sister*, 13.

9. Ibid., 238.

10. Ibid., 293–94.

11. Johnson, *Quest for the Living God*, 98–99.

12. Ibid., 99.

13. See Elizabeth Johnson, "The Incomprehensibility of God and the Image of God Male and Female," *Theological Studies* 45 (1984): 441–65, at 454–60; *She Who Is*, 54–57.

14. Johnson, *She Who Is*, 29.

15. Ibid., 30.

16. See "The Right Way to Speak about God? Pannenberg on Analogy," *Theological Studies* 43 (1982): 673–92. In this essay, Johnson especially draws on Pannenberg's *Habilitationschrift, Analogie und Offenbarung: Eine kritische Untersuchung der Geschichte des Analogiebegriffs* (Heidelberg, 1955). See also, "Analogy and Doxology," *Basic Questions in Theology*, vol. 1 (Philadelphia: Fortress, 1970). For a later discussion of analogy by Pannenberg, see *Systematic Theology*, vol. 1, trans. Geoffrey W. Bromiley (Grand Rapids, MI: Eerdmans, 1991), 337–47, especially 344–45, n. 14.

17. Johnson, *She Who Is*, 116.

18. Elizabeth Johnson, ""The Incomprehensibility of God," 441.

19. Johnson, *She Who Is*, 110. See Karl Rahner, "Justifying Faith in an Agnostic World," *Theological Investigations*, vol. 21, trans. Hugh Riley (New York: Crossroad, 1988), 130–36.

20. Johnson, *She Who Is*, 110.

21. Ibid., 112.

22. Ibid.

23. Johnson, *Friends of God and Prophets*, 207.

24. Elizabeth Johnson, "Does God Play Dice? Divine Providence and Chance," *Theological Studies* 57 (1996): 3–18, at 11.

25. Johnson, *She Who Is*, 114.

26. Ibid., 116.

27. Ibid., 114.

28. Ibid.

29. Elizabeth Johnson, "Jesus the Wisdom of God: A Biblical Basis for a Non-Androcentric Christology," *Ephemerides Theologicae Lovanienses* 6 (1985): 261–94, at 274–75.

30. Johnson, *She Who Is*, 153.

31. Ibid., 168.

32. Ibid., 153. See Gregory of Nazianzus, *Epistola* 101.32; see also *Christology of the Later Fathers*, ed. Edward R. Hardy (Philadelphia: Westminster Press, 1954), 218.

33. Johnson, *She Who Is*, 165.

34. Elizabeth Johnson, "An Earthy Christology," *America* 200, no. 12 (April 13, 2009): 30. See Niels Gregersen, "The Cross of Christ in an Evolutionary World," *Dialog: A Journal of Theology* 40 (2001): 192–207, at 205. Johnson also addressed this theme in "Deep Incarnation," the Albertus Magnus Lecture, Siena Center, Dominican University, River Forest, IL, November 19, 2009. This lecture has been published by the university.

35. Johnson, "An Earthy Christology," 29.

36. Ibid.

37. Johnson, *She Who Is*, 157.

38. Johnson, "Deep Incarnation," 10.

39. Johnson, *She Who Is*, 157.

40. Ibid.

41. Ibid., 158.

42. Ibid.

43. Ibid.

44. Johnson, *Quest for the Living God*, 58.

45. Johnson, *She Who Is*, 159.

46. Johnson discusses critiques of Moltmann's theology of the cross in "Jesus and Salvation," *Proceedings of the Catholic Theological Society of America* 49 (1994): 1–18, at 14–15.

47. Ibid., 15.

48. Johnson, *Quest for the Living God*, 59.

49. Johnson, *She Who Is*, 159.

50. Ibid.

51. Ibid., 158.

52. Elizabeth Johnson, "And Their Eyes Were Opened: The Resurrection

as Resource for Transforming Leadership," lecture given to the Joint Assembly of the Conference of Major Superiors of Men and the Leadership Conference of Women Religious, Anaheim, CA, August 1995. To my knowledge, this lecture has not been published.

53. Ibid.

54. Johnson, *She Who Is*, 159.

55. Johnson, "And Their Eyes Were Opened."

56. Johnson, *She Who Is*, 159.

57. See Karl Rahner, "Dogmatic Questions on Easter," *Theological Investigations*, vol. 4, trans. Kevin Smyth (London: Darton, Longman and Todd, 1966), 128. Johnson quotes this text in her CMSM/LCWR lecture and in "Deep Incarnation," 14.

58. Johnson, "An Earthy Christology," 29. See Ambrose, *De excess fratris sui*, bk. 1, in *Patrologiae Latina* 16:1354.

59. Ibid.

60. Johnson, *Quest for the Living God*, 51.

61. Ibid.

62. Farley, *Tragic Vision and Divine Compassion*, 55; cited by Johnson in *She Who Is*, 249.

63. Johnson, *She Who Is*, 271.

64. Johnson, *Friends of God and Prophets*, 164.

65. Ibid., 168.

66. Ibid., 171.

67. Ibid., 177.

68. Johnson, *She Who Is*, 240.

69. Ibid.

70. Ibid.

71. Ibid., 243.

72. Ibid., 225.

73. Ibid., 228.

74. Johnson, *She Who Is*, 228.

75. Johnson, *Quest for the Living God*, 188.

76. Johnson, *She Who Is*, 231.

77. Ibid., 233.

78. Ibid., 234. See *Quest for Living God*, 196–97; "Does God Play Dice?" 16.

79. *She Who Is*, 234. William Hill, *The Three-Personed God: The Trinity as a Mystery of Salvation* (Washington, DC: Catholic University of America Press, 1982), 76, n. 53. Hill's words are: "Indeed, the deepest implication of St. Thomas's understanding of the reality of the finite order is that it exists only 'in' God; in the creative act God empties himself out kenotically, as it were, making room 'within' himself for the nondivine."

80. *She Who Is*, 233.

81. Ibid., 247.

82. See Johnson, "Does God Play Dice?" 3–18. In this essay, Johnson discusses the Christian doctrine of providence in the light of scientific theories about the role of chance and indeterminacy in evolution.

83. Johnson, *She Who Is*, 270.

84. Johnson, "Does God Play Dice?" 17.

85. Johnson, *She Who Is*, 253.

86. Ibid., 266.

87. Ibid.

88. Ibid., 254–64.

89. Johnson, "An Earthy Christology," 28.

90. Johnson, *Quest for the Living God*, 51.

91. Johnson, *She Who Is*, 266–69.

Chapter 11: Toward a Theology of God and Suffering

1. Edward Schillebeeckx, *Christ: The Experience of Jesus as Lord*, trans. John Bowden (New York: Crossroad, 1983), 725.

2. Gerald O'Collins, *Christology: A Biblical, Historical and Systematic Study of Jesus* (Oxford, UK: Oxford University Press, 1995), 101.

3. Karl Rahner, "The One Christ and the Universality of Salvation," *Theological Investigations*, vol. 16, trans. David Morland, OSB (New York: Seabury, 1979), 199–224. See also *Foundations of Christian Faith*, 283–84.

4. Elizabeth Johnson, *Quest for the Living God: Mapping Frontiers in the Theology of God* (New York and London: Continuum, 2008), 213.

5. Karl Rahner, "Concerning the Relationship between Nature and Grace," *Theological Investigations*, vol. 1, *God, Christ, Mary and Grace*, trans. Cornelius Ernst, OP (Baltimore: Helicon, 1961), 310.

6. Walter Kasper, *The God of Jesus Christ*, trans. Matthew J. O'Connell (New York: Crossroad, 1987), 310.

7. Julian of Norwich, *Showings*, translated from the critical text with an introduction by Edmund Colledge, OSA, and James Walsh, SJ (New York: Paulist Press, 1978), LT 5/183.

8. Denis Edwards, *The God of Evolution: A Trinitarian Theology* (New York: Paulist Press, 1999), 30–31.

9. Brian Davies, *The Thought of Thomas Aquinas* (Oxford, UK: Clarendon Press, 1992), 77.

10. *Showings*, LT 72, 320.

11. Benedict XVI, Encyclical Letter *Spe Salvi* ("Saved in Hope"), n. 36.

12. Edwards, *The God of Evolution*, 36.

13. Benedict XVI, *Spe Salvi*, n. 36.

14. Edwards, *The God of Evolution*, 44. Edwards cites Polkinghorne, *Reason and Reality* (London: SPCK, 1991), 84, and *Science and Providence* (London: SPCK, 1989), 66–67.

15. Ibid.

16. Cyril of Alexandria, cited by John O'Keefe in "Impassible Suffering? Divine Passion and Fifth-Century Christology," *Theological Studies* 58 (1997): 45. O'Keefe refers to statements Cyril makes in his *Scholia on the Incarnation 35*, in P. E. Pusey, ed., *S. Cyrilli Alexandriae epistolae tres oecumenicae* (Oxford, UK: Clarendon, 1987), 574, and *Quod unus sit Christus*, Sources Chrétiennes 97, 766–67.

17. Thomas Aquinas, *Expositio Super 1 ad Corinthios*, c. 15, lect. 1 (line 174c). Cited by Michael Dodds, "Thomas Aquinas: Human Suffering and the Unchanging God of Love," *Theological Studies* 52 (1991): 334, n. 18.

18. Benedict XVI, *Spe Salvi*, n. 39.

19. Jean-Pierre Torrell, *Saint Thomas Aquinas: Spiritual Master*, vol. 2, trans. Robert Royal (Washington, DC: Catholic University of America Press, 2003), 77.

20. Thomas O'Meara, *Thomas Aquinas: Theologian* (Notre Dame, IN, and London: University of Notre Dame Press, 1997), 94.

21. Dodds, "Thomas Aquinas," 333.

22. Ibid., 334–35.

23. Jürgen Moltmann, *In the End—The Beginning: The Life of Hope*, trans. Margaret Kohl (Minneapolis: Fortress, 2004), 70.

24. See Vatican Council II, *Gaudium et Spes* (Pastoral Constitution on the Church in the Modern World), n. 22.

25. Donald Senior, *The Passion of Jesus in the Gospel of John* (Collegeville, MN: Liturgical Press, 1991), 118.

26. Schillebeeckx, *Christ: The Experience of Jesus as Lord*, 724.

27. Walter Brueggemann, *The Message of the Psalms* (Minneapolis: Augsburg, 1984), 52.

28. Ibid.

29. Gustavo Gutiérrez, *On Job: God-Talk and the Suffering of the Innocent*, trans. Matthew O'Connell (Maryknoll, NY: Orbis, 1987), xiv.

30. Thomas Merton, *New Seeds of Contemplation* (New York: New Directions, 1961), 1.

31. Ibid., 3.

32. Jürgen Moltmann, *The Trinity and the Kingdom: The Doctrine of God*, trans. Margaret Kohl (San Francisco: Harper & Row, 1981), 49.

Index